STRENGTH TRAINING
FOR
LACROSSE

NSCA®
NATIONAL STRENGTH AND
CONDITIONING ASSOCIATION

Joel Raether, MAEd, CSCS, TSAC-F, RSCC*D

Matt Nein, MS, CSCS, RSCC*E

Editors

HUMAN KINETICS

Library of Congress Cataloging-in-Publication Data

Names: National Strength & Conditioning Association (U.S.), author. |
  Raether, Joel, editor. | Nein, Matt, editor.
Title: Strength training for lacrosse / National Strength and Conditioning
  Association ; Joel Raether, Matt Nein, editors.
Description: Champaign, IL : Human Kinetics, [2025] | Includes
  bibliographical references and index.
Identifiers: LCCN 2024017059 (print) | LCCN 2024017060 (ebook) | ISBN
  9781718216242 (paperback) | ISBN 9781718216259 (epub) | ISBN
  9781718216266 (pdf)
Subjects: LCSH: Lacrosse--Training. | Isometric exercise. | Muscle
  strength.
Classification: LCC GV989 .N38 2025 (print) | LCC GV989 (ebook) | DDC
  796.34/7--dc23/eng/20240513
LC record available at https://lccn.loc.gov/2024017059
LC ebook record available at https://lccn.loc.gov/2024017060

ISBN: 978-1-7182-1624-2 (print)

The web addresses cited in this text were current as of May 2024, unless otherwise noted.

Senior Acquisitions Editor: Roger W. Earle; **Managing Editor and Permissions Manager:** Hannah Werner; **Copyeditor:** Jenny MacKay; **Proofreader:** Karin Kipp; **Indexer:** Ferreira Indexing; **Graphic Designer:** Denise Lowry; **Cover Designer:** Keri Evans; **Cover Design Specialist:** Susan Rothermel Allen; **Photograph (cover):** Jack Dempsey; **Photographs (interior):** © Human Kinetics, unless otherwise noted; decorative photo on pages v, vii, ix, 1, 61, 163, 261, 267, 273, and 275 © Photodisc/Getty Images; **Photographer (interior):** Alberto E. Leopizzi; **Photo Asset Manager:** Laura Fitch; **Photo Production Specialist:** Amy M. Rose; **Photo Production Manager:** Jason Allen; **Senior Art Manager:** Kelly Hendren; **Illustrations:** © Human Kinetics, unless otherwise noted; **Printer:** Sheridan Books

We thank Matthew Sandstead, NSCA-CPT,*D, Scott Caulfield, MA, CSCS,*D, TSAC-F,*D, RSCC*E, and the National Strength and Conditioning Association (NSCA) in Colorado Springs, Colorado, for overseeing (Matthew and Scott) and hosting (NSCA) the photo shoot for this book. We also thank and recognize Alberto Leopizzi, owner and lead photographer of A Touch of Class Images, for taking the photos for this book.

Human Kinetics books are available at special discounts for bulk purchase. Special editions or book excerpts can also be created to specification. For details, contact the Special Sales Manager at Human Kinetics.

Printed in the United States of America   10 9 8 7 6 5 4 3 2 1

The paper in this book is certified under a sustainable forestry program.

Human Kinetics
1607 N. Market Street
Champaign, IL 61820
USA

United States and International
Website: **US.HumanKinetics.com**
Email: info@hkusa.com
Phone: 1-800-747-4457

Canada
Website: **Canada.HumanKinetics.com**
Email: info@hkcanada.com

STRENGTH TRAINING
FOR
LACROSSE

CONTENTS

Foreword by Dillon Ward   vi

Introduction by Matt Nein   viii

PART I: PRINCIPLES OF SPORT-SPECIFIC RESISTANCE TRAINING

1   Importance of Resistance Training   3

Karen Sutton and Brittany M. Ammerman

2   Analysis of the Sport and Sport Positions   11

John Cole and Justin Kilian

3   Testing Protocols and Athlete Assessment   27

Thomas Newman

4   Sport-Specific Program Design Guidelines   45

Nicole Shattuck and JL Holdsworth

PART II: EXERCISE TECHNIQUE

5   Total Body Exercise Technique   63

JL Holdsworth and Edward R. Smith, Jr.

6   Lower Body Exercise Technique   83

JL Holdsworth and Edward R. Smith, Jr.

7   Upper Body Exercise Technique   105

JL Holdsworth and Edward R. Smith, Jr.

8   Anatomical Core Exercise Technique   133

Andrew Sacks and Jessi Glauser

PART III: PROGRAM DESIGN GUIDELINES AND SAMPLE PROGRAMS

9   Off-Season Programming   **165**

Drazen Glisic (High School), Tracy Zimmer (College Women), David Eugenio Manning (College Men), and Joel Raether (Professional)

10   Preseason Programming   **203**

Drazen Glisic (High School), Tracy Zimmer (College Women), David Eugenio Manning (College Men), and Joel Raether (Professional)

11   In-Season Programming   **227**

Drazen Glisic (High School), Tracy Zimmer (College Women), David Eugenio Manning (College Men), and Joel Raether (Professional)

12   Postseason Programming   **247**

Drazen Glisic (High School), Tracy Zimmer (College Women), David Eugenio Manning (College Men), and Joel Raether (Professional)

References   260
Index   266
About the NSCA   272
About the Editors   273
About the Contributors   274
Earn Continuing Education Credits/Units   278

FOREWORD

DILLON WARD

The sport of lacrosse, especially for many professional players, has become a year-round occupation. Between the National Lacrosse League, Premier Lacrosse League, and Canadian National Team, I compete for 10 or more months nearly every year. How I spend my time off the floor directly affects my performance on the floor.

Growing up in a small town in Canada, I had no idea that I was about to step into a world where the importance of strength training was at the forefront of any athlete's success. When I first came up into the professional ranks, training outside of the game was barely on my radar. In my world, it was all lacrosse, all the time. My routine was simple: watch film, practice, and play. To me, that was the ultimate formula for success. I learned very quickly that what I was doing was no longer enough to perform at the highest level. My body needed more from me, and I was not giving it enough. It required weightlifting, footwork, reactionary drills, stretching, and, ultimately, recovery.

Playing lacrosse was all that I knew until I was drafted by the Colorado Mammoth of the National Lacrosse League. When I was introduced to the team's performance coach, Joel Raether, it all began to click for me. Coach Raether's background and experience have made him one of the most influential people that I have had the pleasure of working with throughout my career. I have witnessed and experienced the value of our team's training programs, preparation, and care throughout the year and of cultivating intricate plans to rehabilitate injured teammates, getting them back on the floor as quickly and effectively as possible. As a goalie, the emphasis on personal training encompasses a heavy focus on flexibility, footwork, and reactionary work, which has been a key to my success.

The attention to detail within my routine has had a direct correlation with progressing myself physically thus far in my career. There is no doubt that strength and conditioning have had a major part in my longevity.

Regardless of whether I am in-season or not, having a strength and conditioning professional work closely with me week in and week out to ensure that my body is where it needs to be is paramount. When I am out of season, I strive to focus on building strength to help me battle through the grind of not only the season but my year-round schedule. During the in-season, I focus more on explosiveness, reactionary work, and recovery, so that come game day, I am as close to 100% as possible. Due to the nature of my schedule and demands, I have developed and evolved in taking care of my body, maximizing my potential, and staying as healthy as possible through better strength and conditioning interventions.

Strength training in lacrosse has never been more pivotal to success than it is now. The game has evolved and athletes are bigger, faster, and stronger than they have ever been before. It is a blessing and a curse to compete at the highest level of lacrosse on an almost year-round basis. It is not lost on me how fortunate I am to do what I love for a living, year-round. Without having a sound training program and plan in place, it would not have been possible to strive for and achieve the success at the professional level that I have and continue to work toward. To take their game to the next level and achieve their goals, lacrosse athletes must take the work away from the game just as seriously as they do when they are on the floor. Their best assets will always be their ability and availability, which directly correlate to their training and recovery!

INTRODUCTION

MATT NEIN

Lacrosse is more than just a game; it is a sport that blends history, strategy, and athleticism into a captivating experience. Often referred to as the fastest game on two feet, lacrosse embodies a perfect and unique blend of aerobic endurance, speed, agility, power, strength, and finesse. The game consists of high-velocity sprints with precision passes and shots and of mental acuity combined with physical prowess. When these elements are put together, they create a dynamic and thrilling experience for everyone. Strength and conditioning has become the cornerstone of optimal lacrosse performance. This book will dive into the attributes that define a successful lacrosse athlete while providing insight on how these attributes can be developed through proper training.

Originating in the Indigenous cultures of North America, the historical elements of lacrosse have greatly contributed to physical abilities required to play in today's game. Lacrosse, also known as *tewaarathon*, was an activity often used to train for war, to develop and toughen up young warriors, and even to settle disputes. Games were played on fields described as hundreds of yards long to upward of miles apart with no boundaries (1). These elements required individuals playing the game to have the strength and stamina to handle intense conditions and battles in order to be victorious. Therefore, a warrior-like spirit formed and became a part of the sport. As lacrosse evolved and rules developed, the key elements of the sport were never lost. In today's game, whether it be field lacrosse or box lacrosse and whether the athletes are men or women, the warrior-like spirit still lives on.

Today, the game of lacrosse, for both men and women, requires athletes to have high levels of speed and agility, mobility and coordination, and strength and power. Resistance training contributes significantly to the development of these essential lacrosse skills, ultimately making an athlete more formidable on the field. Key lacrosse skills include the following:

- *Shooting power.* A powerful shot is a great weapon in lacrosse. Resistance training, particularly exercises that target the lower body and core, can significantly increase an athlete's ability to generate force when shooting, which translates to explosive shooting power.
- *Defensive dominance.* Defenders in lacrosse must possess strength to effectively push opponents off-balance, check the ball, and maintain their position. Upper body resistance training can help defenders gain an edge.
- *Offensive attacking precision.* Fine motor skills required for accurate stick handling, explosive speed and acceleration while cutting or changing direction, and handling body contact and checks can all be improved by resistance training. Strengthening exercises for the forearm and wrist can lead to more precise stick control and passing accuracy.

- *Ground ball control.* Physical strength plays a pivotal role in winning battles for ground balls, which are a vital part of lacrosse possession. A strong upper body and core provide the stability and power needed to scoop up ground balls, even in high-pressure situations.

With any physically demanding sport, there is a risk of injury. However, through appropriate assessments and developmentally appropriate progressions, resistance training can help reduce an athlete's risk of injuries, including the following:

- *Lower body injuries.* Lacrosse involves rapid changes in direction with coupling of deceleration and acceleration. Strong lower limb muscles and joints can better absorb the forces generated during these movements, reducing the risk of injuries such as sprains, strains, and anterior cruciate ligament tears.

- *Concussions.* While resistance training cannot directly prevent concussions, it can indirectly help by improving neck and shoulder strength. A strong neck and upper body can absorb some impact forces, potentially reducing the severity of head collisions.

- *Overuse injuries.* Imbalances in muscle strength can lead to overuse injuries and chronic pain. Resistance training programs can address these imbalances by targeting underused muscle groups and promoting structural integrity to minimize the risk of injuries.

Resistance training not only prevents injuries and enhances specific skills but also significantly improves overall performance on the lacrosse field by improving the following attributes:

- *Speed and agility.* Resistance training is not limited to just building muscle; it also enhances speed and agility. Plyometric exercises and resistance training can improve an athlete's ability to accelerate, change direction, and maintain a quick pace throughout a game.

- *Endurance.* Resistance training can be structured to improve endurance as well. By incorporating high-intensity interval training and circuit workouts, athletes can develop the cardiovascular fitness required for long, grueling lacrosse matches.

- *Mental toughness.* The discipline and dedication required for consistent resistance training can contribute to athletes' mental toughness. Knowing that they have put in the work in the gym can boost their confidence and mental resilience on the field.

To maximize the benefits of resistance training, lacrosse athletes should follow structured training programs designed by certified strength and conditioning professionals.

These programs should be tailored to the specific needs and positions of the athletes. This book will discuss the key elements to lacrosse programming within three different age categories (i.e., youth or high school, college, and professional) and also give examples of training programs during various times of the year, as follows:

- *Off-season training.* The off-season is the ideal time to focus on building strength and addressing any weaknesses. Athletes can engage in comprehensive resistance training regimens to prepare for the upcoming season.

- *Preseason training.* The preseason is the necessary bridge to bring athletes from the base training of the off-season to the sport-specific training that prepares them for the in-season.

- *In-season training.* During the season, athletes may shift their focus to maintenance and injury prevention. Reduced training volume but consistent strength and power work are essential to maintain gains without causing excessive fatigue.

- *Postseason training.* Recovery, injury care, and mental restoration are key goals for the postseason so that athletes are prepared for the rigors of the off-season.

- *Position-specific training.* Different positions in lacrosse require specific physical attributes. Attackers may prioritize speed and shooting power, while defenders need upper body strength and agility. Customized training programs address these position-specific needs.

In the world of lacrosse, resistance training is an essential pillar for success. By enhancing key skills, preventing injuries, and improving overall performance, resistance training can take a lacrosse athlete's game to the next level. With the right guidance and dedication, athletes can harness the power of resistance training to become formidable forces on the lacrosse field, contributing to their team's success and personal growth as athletes.

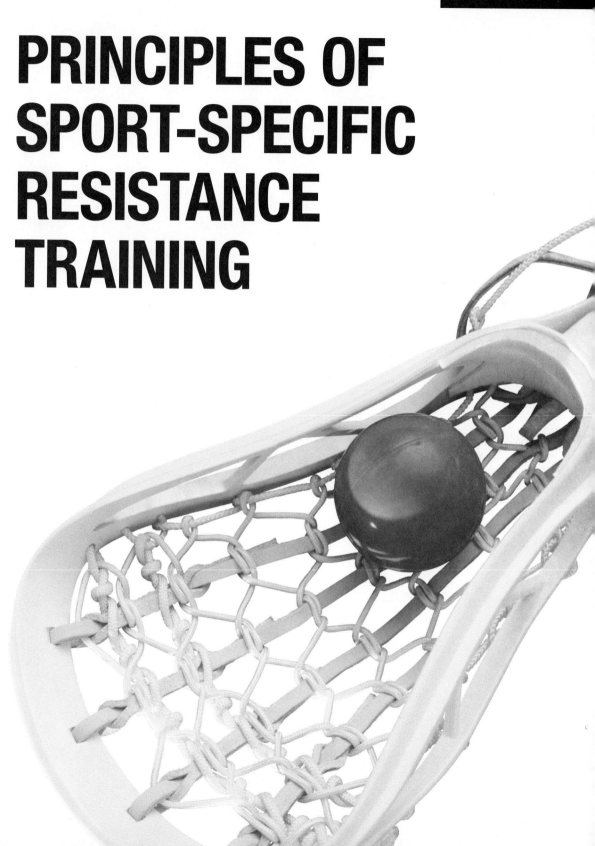

PART I

PRINCIPLES OF SPORT-SPECIFIC RESISTANCE TRAINING

1

IMPORTANCE OF RESISTANCE TRAINING

KAREN SUTTON AND BRITTANY M. AMMERMAN

Lacrosse has had a steady increase in participation at the youth, high school, and college levels for men and women and continues to be one of the fastest-growing sports. Lacrosse is a physically demanding sport that requires athletes to maximize their anaerobic capacity through repeated sprint intervals and explosive cutting movements, all with precise hand–eye coordination through manipulation of a ball and stick in the face of physical contact. Resistance training can increase strength, power, speed, agility, and overall in-game performance. Resistance training has also been shown to reduce the risk of injury. The primary focus of this chapter is to present the foundational benefits of resistance training for lacrosse athletes.

METABOLIC ADAPTATIONS

Anaerobic training is an activity that breaks down glucose for energy without using oxygen. Generally, anaerobic training activities are of short length with high intensity. With this definition in mind, it is logical to consider lacrosse to be a primarily anaerobic sport due to its high-intensity and short-duration intervals in the form of sprinting and cutting. Cells require adenosine triphosphate (ATP) to survive, and ATP can be created from three metabolic pathways: phosphagen, glycolytic, and oxidative. The first two (phosphagen and glycolytic) are relatively immediate pathways to make ATP, with the phosphagen pathway being almost immediate. Anaerobic training relies on these two pathways to create energy. The third pathway, oxidative, is largely used in aerobic training. In any case, resistance training has the potential to stress these pathways (1, 4-6, 9, 17, 27, 29). Altering the duration of rest intervals between sets or modifying intensity by increasing weight can affect which metabolic pathway will be used to create energy. In the sport of lacrosse, different metabolic pathways are used at different points within the game, and use of these pathways is also position-dependent.

Importantly, the demands of resistance training result in the release of hormones, such as testosterone, growth hormone, and cortisol (20, 22, 26). Testosterone is a major contributor to the building of muscle. Males and females both produce testosterone, with males having an approximately 15-fold higher circulating testosterone level compared to females (12). The primary production site for testosterone in males is the Leydig cells, located in the testes, while in females, testosterone is produced in smaller quantities within the ovaries and the zona reticularis of the adrenal cortex. Testosterone is an anabolic hormone, meaning it builds complex molecules from simple structures. For resistance training, this is particularly important within the muscles, where testosterone is released in response to resistance training, stimulates protein synthesis, and inhibits protein degradation, resulting in muscle hypertrophy (7, 18, 19). Growth hormone is another hormone released in a load-dependent manner during resistance training, with heavier loads producing larger growth hormone responses. Growth hormone increases muscle protein synthesis directly by binding to receptors on skeletal muscle or indirectly by facilitating the release of insulin-like growth factor 1 (IGF-1) (another hormone that is anabolic in skeletal muscle) from the liver (22).

Resistance training has also been demonstrated to release cortisol, a stress hormone essential to glucose availability and anti-inflammatory processes. In acute settings, such as when an athlete is in competition, cortisol will increase glucose availability within the body, providing more readily available energy to cells. However, cortisol has a sweet spot at which positive results are produced before it begins to have a negative effect on the athlete. Cortisol, when produced in excessive amounts, competes with testosterone for receptor availability and can therefore suppress testosterone (22). This can result in detrimental training effects, and if testosterone is suppressed for long periods, overtraining syndrome may result. Overtraining syndrome occurs when the training stress load outweighs rest and recovery. It can manifest as decreased physical performance, increased fatigue, disrupted sleep, poor mood, loss of motivation, and other negative effects (2, 20).

At a macrolevel, muscular adaptations occur in both structure and function with resistance training. Muscle hypertrophy, the enlargement of muscle fibers in a cross-sectional area, is the most notable muscle adaptation following resistance training. During resistance training in the form of mechanical loading, intracellular processes regulate gene expression and subsequently promote protein synthesis (via the aforementioned hormones). Anaerobic resistance training also results in reduction in muscle and blood pH, therefore increasing tolerance to the buildup of lactic acid. With consistent training, acute changes in pH improve the body's buffering capacity. This greater tolerance to metabolic acidosis can delay fatigue and increase muscular endurance (8).

Overall, improved neural, muscular, endocrine, and cardiovascular function contribute to enhanced muscle strength, power, endurance, and motor performance. The next section will address the more tangible changes that occur in the lacrosse athlete as a result of resistance training: increased strength, power, speed, and agility and reduced risk of injury.

INCREASED STRENGTH

Strength is defined as the ability to exert force on an object. As this relates to resistance training, it is the ability of a given muscle or muscle group to generate force under specific conditions, such as those that occur on the lacrosse field. Strength supports an athlete's ability to become faster, produce quicker changes in direction, create greater speed in shooting, etc. While skills specific to lacrosse, such as ball handling, foot speed, or game intuition, can only be improved with repetition and practice, an increase in strength will presumably translate to improved skill development and overall performance while also reducing injury rates (28). Resistance training for lacrosse can be performed through exercise with traditional weightlifting, resistance bands, body weight, aquatic exercises, or other means.

As previously discussed in this chapter, resistance training results in muscle hypertrophy (increase in skeletal muscle mass), which allows muscle groups to produce greater force. Physical adaptations will occur throughout resistance training, with an exponential increase in strength occurring when an athlete first begins resistance training. However, as athletes continue to progress with resistance training, they will experience less significant improvements in strength and may even experience plateaus in their training. Russian physiologist Leo Matveyev proposed the theory of periodization, in which manipulations and variations in training variables (i.e., changes in exercise volume and loading) are carefully made across training segments (11). American exercise physiologists took Matveyev's theory and applied it to the training of strength and power athletes. Periodization can be used by the lacrosse athlete with manipulation of training load and intensity built around the athlete's season. Different resistance training programs should be implemented in the off-season, preseason, in-season, and postseason.

Strength is exhibited when muscles act to produce force. There are three types of muscle actions with the development of muscular tension: isometric, eccentric, and concentric (21). An isometric action is when muscle length does not change, because the muscular torque is equal to the resistive torque acting in opposing directions on a joint. An example of an isometric muscle action is when an athlete holds a lunge in a static posture. An eccentric action is when a muscle lengthens because muscular torque is less than resistive torque. This occurs during the lowering phase of any resistance exercise, such as the lowering movement in a bench press. A concentric muscle action is when a muscle shortens (i.e., contracts) because the muscular torque is greater than the resistive torque; forces generated within the muscle and acting to shorten it are greater than the external forces to lengthen it. An example of a concentric action is performing a biceps curl, when the elbow is flexed to bring the weight up toward the biceps. All three types of muscle actions are performed by lacrosse athletes throughout all movements they perform.

Because of this, it is important for the lacrosse athlete to participate in resistance training that incorporates all three muscle actions. The simplest example is sprinting, the basis of movement for the lacrosse athlete. In its simplest form, the sprint can be broken down in the lower body to demonstrate isometric, eccentric, and concentric muscle actions occurring simultaneously. The action of flexing the hip to raise the thigh and flexing the knee involve concentric actions of both the hip flexor and hamstrings muscles. As the athlete straightens the planted leg to push off the floor, the hip extensors (i.e., hamstrings and gluteus maximus) and knee extensors (i.e., quadriceps) act concentrically. Contrast this with deceleration, such as that which occurs when a lacrosse athlete prepares to change direction or stop quickly; the quadriceps will act eccentrically to prevent the knee from flexing excessively and too quickly. Through this example, it is easy to understand why training muscles through concentric, isometric, and eccentric actions will benefit the lacrosse athlete while also reducing injury risk.

Plyometric actions are a coupling of eccentric and concentric muscle actions—that is, when a concentric action is immediately preceded by an eccentric action, taking advantage of a principle termed the **stretch-shortening cycle** (SSC). The SSC refers to an active stretch of a muscle (eccentric action) followed by immediate shortening of the same muscle (concentric action). It can be likened to a spring-like mechanism in which compressing and then releasing the coil causes the spring to rebound and jump off a surface or in a different direction. Increasing the speed at which the coil is compressed or how hard it is compressed (i.e., the amount of force applied) will result in higher or farther distances on the rebound (31). Increasing the SSC through resistance training can result in more explosive movements, which can be translated to the lacrosse field when performing sport-specific skills, such as shooting.

INCREASED POWER

In physics, **power** is defined as work accomplished per unit of time. As this pertains to resistance training, power can be defined as the ability to exert force at high speeds (25). The goal of power development in a lacrosse athlete is to increase the speed and quickness with which the athlete performs sport-related activities, such as shooting, defending, running, and changes in direction. Breaking it down further, power is equal to force multiplied by velocity. Therefore, increasing either force (i.e., strength) or velocity (i.e., speed) will result in increased power and explosiveness of the athlete. This can be further explained with the force–velocity curve (figure 1.1). The goal of strength and power training for lacrosse athletes can be reflected on this curve through working to shift the curve farther right. This results in the athlete theoretically being able to move larger loads at higher velocities. This can also be expressed as an improved rate of force development, which reflects how fast an athlete can develop force. An athlete with a greater rate of force development will be more explosive. The SSC is important in developing explosiveness and can be applied to the development of power.

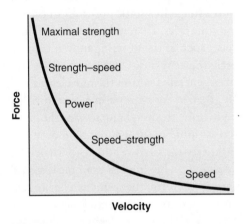

Figure 1.1   Force–velocity curve.

IMPROVED SPEED AND AGILITY

It is no surprise that speed and agility play a large role in the sport of lacrosse. The sport has been described as one of the fastest field-based games, characterized by intermittent high-intensity activity, collisions, and rapid changes of direction, all occurring while using a stick to handle a ball. Some will argue that the basis to improve overall lacrosse skill is the act of running or sprinting. While this book is not intended to examine proper running technique and form, biomechanics research has demonstrated the importance of strength development for running efficiency.

Running economy is a complex, multifactorial concept that represents the sum of metabolic, cardiovascular, biomechanical, and neuromuscular characteristics during running. These components can be improved through training, resulting in more efficient running mechanics (3). Biomechanical and neuromuscular components are the most relevant to this chapter. Strengthening muscles in isolation and progressing to more complex movements that simulate the act of running or sprinting can train muscle recruitment patterns that will result in quicker activation and enhanced efficiency when the lacrosse athlete runs. Similarly, resistance training has been suggested to increase type I and type II muscle fiber strength, which results in less motor unit activation to produce a given force. Type I muscle fibers, also known as slow-twitch muscle fibers, are resistant to fatigue, use oxygen, and are used in aerobic metabolism. Type II muscle fibers are known as fast-twitch muscle fibers and are largely used for anaerobic metabolism, resulting in bursts of power with rapid fatigue (15).

Sean M. Haffey/Getty Images

Lacrosse is a fast, field-based game filled with intermittent high-intensity activity, collisions, and rapid changes of direction.

Perhaps most important to the sport of lacrosse is speed. Due to the nonlinearity of lacrosse, it is important to understand the different properties of speed. Speed for lacrosse can be categorized into the following: acceleration, maximum velocity, deceleration, and transitions (i.e., changes of direction) (13). Each property requires different muscle activation patterns, and understanding the principles of each is important to understand what actions should be targeted with resistance training to improve speed and agility.

The initial phase of speed is acceleration. **Acceleration** is the name given to any process where the velocity increases. This is most notable when starting to run from a standstill position; however, acceleration occurs with changes in direction as well. A relatively large amount of force is required to initiate a sprint, and the more force athletes can generate relative to their body weight, the greater potential there is for acceleration. This relates back to strength and power. Derived from Newton's second law of motion, the equation for force is mass multiplied by acceleration. Therefore, increasing force will increase acceleration. Because sprinting is essentially a single-leg exercise (one leg is in contact with the floor at a given time), one can understand the importance of unilateral exercises in helping to develop force generation when sprinting. Exercises such as split squats, single-leg Romanian deadlifts, and single-leg explosive hops will contribute to increasing an athlete's acceleration potential.

At the peak of acceleration, the athlete has reached maximum velocity, or the fastest speed at which he or she is capable of running, albeit for a short amount of time. This is accomplished infrequently in lacrosse and for only seconds at a time. Following acceleration or maximum velocity, the athlete must slow down or change direction, known as deceleration. Deceleration is most notable in straightaway sprints, where a finish line is the end goal; once the athlete crosses the finish line, speed declines and deceleration occurs. However, in the sport of lacrosse, deceleration often occurs when there is an abrupt change in position or when a defender transitions from forward running to backward shuffling or the containment of an offensive opponent. Decelerations are also ripe for the potential for noncontact injuries, because braking forces are exerted on the floor with poor mechanics. Resistance and plyometric training can improve deceleration capabilities and therefore help reduce the risk of injury. The patterns demonstrated in decelerations are similar to and can be reinforced by exercises such as the depth jump, reverse lunge, and front squat.

Lacrosse involves many changes in direction, also known as **transitions**. In lacrosse athletes, various resistance training exercises and strategies can improve transitions (16). Training for strength and power with free weights can develop the force production required to maximize acceleration mechanics. Resistance movements with quick, eccentric demands, such as the kettlebell swing, power clean, jump squat, and reactive plyometrics, can support the development of force and power to execute transitions properly.

The combination of acceleration, transitions, and deceleration results in improved agility, which is an important skill in lacrosse. Resistance training can enhance a lacrosse athlete's agility. However, practicing the sport of lacrosse is the best way to translate improved agility into the athlete's game.

PREVENTION OF INJURY

While resistance training is important in improving the previously discussed characteristics, the athlete must first be assessed for mobility restrictions before embarking on a resistance training program. It is recommended that strength and conditioning professionals assess the athlete's ability to perform simple movements in full ranges of motion (e.g., a bodyweight squat with proper form, internal and external rotation about the hip, or shoulder mobility). The athlete should be able to achieve the full range of motion without compensation before adding resistance or weight to exercises. An increased injury of risk accompanies an athlete's inability to achieve an exercise position. An example would be an athlete performing a simple bodyweight squat who, due to a lack of mobility or to muscle imbalances, has an excessive valgus load to the knee joint. Inherently, there is now an increased risk of ligamentous injury within the knee.

Neuromuscular training is also used to identify underlying biomechanical dysfunction and muscular imbalances that can predispose an athlete to injury. Most of the literature has focused on neuromuscular training to prevent risk of noncontact anterior cruciate ligament (ACL) injury but can be applied broadly to other parts of the body. The principle in neuromuscular training is to strengthen deficient muscle groups and increase muscle activation for protective movements. An example of this principle is strengthening hip abductor muscles and the external rotators to balance hip adduction and internal rotation. This would then decrease knee valgus moments and subsequently decrease the risk of ACL injury.

When discussing injury prevention through resistance training, the **specific adaptation to imposed demand** (SAID) principle can also be followed. This principle states that when the body is placed under forms of stress through specific movements, it begins to make adaptations to better handle that stress. Injury risk may therefore be increased when athletes have not been adequately exposed to the demands of the sport and their tissues have not adapted to specific stresses. Resistance training is a great way to mimic the specific movement demands of the sport and gradually increase the load, allowing muscles to adapt to stresses.

SEX DIFFERENCES

While resistance training is important for both male and female lacrosse athletes, it is particularly important for females. There is a vast amount of literature assessing increased risk of noncontact injury in female lacrosse athletes, especially regarding the ACL (10, 30). This is largely due to anatomic factors that differ between men and women, such as a smaller femoral notch, wider quadriceps angle (more commonly referred to as the **Q-angle**), smaller ACL relative to body weight, and more muscle imbalances in women.

Ryan Hunt/Getty Images

Resistance training can reduce the risk of ACL injuries, especially in female lacrosse athletes.

The Q-angle is an anatomic feature to which increased risk of ACL injury in female athletes has been attributed. The Q-angle is defined as an angle created by a line from the anterior superior iliac spine to the patella center and a line from the patella center to the tibial tuberosity (figure 1.2). An increased, or wider, Q-angle has been associated with ACL injury. Females have wider Q-angles due to pelvic width, shorter femur length, and a more laterally placed tibial tuberosity when compared to males (24). Females with an increased Q-angle can be identified, and resistance training programs can be designed to assist in reducing the risk of ACL injury.

Studies have also suggested that compared to men, women have weaker hamstrings relative to the quadriceps and weaker gluteus medius and gluteus minimus muscles, resulting in greater hip internal rotation and knee abduction when jumping, landing, and cutting (23). This puts stress on the ACL and results in an increased injury risk. Resistance training should focus on strengthening these muscle groups to decrease muscle imbalance. Attention should also be

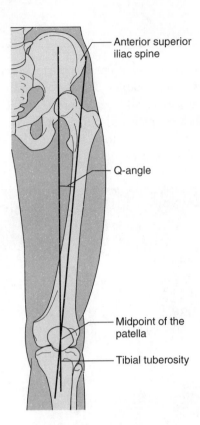

Figure 1.2 Q-angle.

focused on proper biomechanics when jumping, landing, and cutting (14). This relates back to the SAID principle, in which repetition of these stresses through resistance training can help the body better adjust to the stress. Strength and conditioning professionals should screen for muscle imbalances and mobility issues to personalize an athlete's resistance training program to aid in injury prevention; for women, specific attention should be focused on biomechanics of the hip and knee due to increased risk of injury to the ACL.

CONCLUSION

Resistance training has important implications for an athlete's physical ability. Through resistance training, an athlete's strength, power, and lacrosse-specific movements are developed. This is accomplished through positively stressing the metabolic, hormonal, muscular, and neurologic processes mentioned throughout this chapter. When these processes are stressed and adequately paired with rest and recovery, lacrosse athletes will improve their physical ability on the field. Strength and conditioning professionals must also be mindful of injury prevention and appropriately design a resistance training program that accounts for possible muscle imbalances, neuromuscular training, and gradual increases in load.

2

ANALYSIS OF THE SPORT AND SPORT POSITIONS

JOHN COLE AND JUSTIN KILIAN

Historically known by many names, the sport of lacrosse is a complex collection of skills requiring remarkable athleticism. The game has evolved substantially over the years regarding equipment, field dimensions, regulations, and popularity. The origin story of lacrosse traces back hundreds of years to the Indigenous people of North America. Despite the drastic changes since its inception, lacrosse has remained a sport that requires stamina, strength, and speed. As equipment has been influenced by modern technology, the exact biomechanics of the sport have adjusted. Still, even from the beginning, lacrosse required athletes to interact with some sort of ball via a stick. This chapter will focus on lacrosse athletes' physiological and biomechanical needs.

GENERAL BIOMECHANICAL ANALYSIS

Lacrosse requires a diverse range of skills minimally categorized as shooting, passing, checking, and picking up ground balls. These unique skills have numerous applications, but the fundamental aspects can be evaluated regardless of individual and situational deviations from textbook techniques.

Shooting

Shooting in lacrosse is dominantly an offensive skill, but defenders can be put in positions where shots are an acceptable strategy. Thus, most athletes should be familiar with and at least minimally competent in fundamental shooting techniques. Six phases characterize a lacrosse shot: the approach, crank-back, stick acceleration, stick deceleration, follow-through, and recovery (21). Various shots are necessary for different game situations (e.g., overhand, underhand, or sidearm), but each one follows the basics of these phases (17).

The **approach phase** is any movement that precedes floor contact with the drive leg, which is the back leg when shooting. This leg will be on the same side as the hand the athlete is using to shoot and allows for a forceful preparatory step. For example, when lacrosse athletes shoot right-handed, they grip the stick with the left hand toward the bottom of the stick and the right hand toward the head. They will step into the shot with their right leg as the drive leg. The muscular activity of the lower body may also create stiffness in the legs to provide the base necessary for explosive upper body movements (22). The approach phase can be basic sprinting, such as dodging down the alley or sweeping the middle of the field. During a time-and-space shot, the athlete may take a single step or perform a crow hop to get into optimal shooting position. As the athlete shifts weight toward the lead leg, there is a simultaneous **crank-back phase**, in which the torso rotates away from the goal and the top arm reaches maximal flexion at the elbow. A common error in this phase is lowering the bottom arm such that the elbow is pinned to the body; thus, it is important to acknowledge the need for a high elbow position in both arms. Mechanical errors limit the rotational ability of the stick acceleration phase, thus limiting the rotational velocity and shot speed (23). As the athlete's lead leg contacts the floor, there is a forceful pivot on this foot to allow the torso to rotate toward the goal and accelerate the stick (**stick acceleration phase**). Once the ball is released, the **stick deceleration phase** begins, then ends when the elbow of the top arm reaches maximal extension. The **follow-through phase** includes any compensatory movements the athlete completes after stick deceleration that lead to the next task. Therefore, the follow-through phase is relatively nonspecific and can look different in subsequent shots. During a powerful shot on the run, athletes often rotate far enough to take several steps while running backward, whereas a step-down shot may not have the same follow-through, based on the slower velocity of the approach phase.

Improper technique may be caused by a need for better learning but can also come from pain, so attention to biomechanical details of shooting form is an important part of coaching, whether in the weight room or on the field (32). Furthermore, lacrosse athletes tend to have reduced range of motion and rotational velocity in their nondominant hand compared to their dominant hand, which has implications for coaching sport-specific movement patterns in weight room settings (31). Muscular balance in training and practice may lead to more optimized shot biomechanics in both the dominant and nondominant hand. Overall, shot mechanics are largely dependent on lower body and torso rotational strength and power.

Passing

Passing mechanics are similar to those for shooting, particularly for the overhand position. As creativity in game play expands, alternative modes of passing—such as flips or backhand options—increase. The key to passing of any kind is the innate understanding of the stick's release point, which is determined by the characteristics of the pocket (6). Accuracy in passing is generally more critical than speed, due to the importance of maintaining possession by avoiding uncaused turnovers from wayward passes. Passing frequently occurs around the perimeter of the offensive formation, allowing a degree of separation from defenders and relatively less need for speed. Despite reduced velocity compared to shooting, precise passes can often find their mark when the receiving athlete moves in the proper manner to accept the pass. Whether a pass comes in a clearing situation or during an offensive possession, athletes on the same team should be able to get into positions that optimally set them up to receive the pass without interference from the defending team.

Despite the similarities in the mechanics of passing and shooting, the reduced ball velocity in a pass does not require the same degree of rotation used to enhance ball velocity when shooting (23). The push of the upper hand and pull of the lower hand are key mechanical aspects of passing that compensate for the reduced torso rotation, implicating the importance of arm strength for lacrosse athletes. Key coaching cues are to step into the pass to maintain complete control of the direction and power of the pass, along with snapping the wrist for a crisp and speedy release. Being off-balance decreases the likelihood of an accurate pass.

Checking

One of the key distinctions between men's and women's lacrosse is allowable contact. Both versions of the sport allow stick checks, although the exact definitions differ. Women are allowed to make stick-to-stick contact when the check is controlled and neither stick contacts an athlete. For men, contact during stick checks is allowed to be more aggressive due to the increased protective equipment worn. However, despite the extra protection, contact between the stick and the opponent's head, neck, back, or legs is penalized. Any stick check requires the athlete to have precise eye–hand (i.e., stick) coordination and fine-tuned motor control of the upper body. Some subtle torso rotation may occur, but excessive wind up through the torso is more likely to be deemed excessive and either flagged or carded. Therefore, the mechanics of a good stick check are generally dominated by the movement of the arms, with extension the dominant feature of the top arm and flexion the dominant feature of the bottom arm.

In men's lacrosse, body checks are an acceptable part of competition. The athlete doing the checking is allowed to make body-to-body contact with an opponent so long as this contact is not initiated with the head and the contact is above the waist from the front or side. Mechanically, the approach to a check is consistent with normal running mechanics, although before initiating contact, there is generally a dip into a more athletic stance to lower the center of mass for a more effective body check (i.e., the low athlete wins). Furthermore, the contact cannot be initiated with the stick, so athletes must bring their hands together before making contact. This pattern is considered to be within the category of horizontal push patterns, which can be effectively loaded in a weight room setting to increase the strength and power of this movement.

Ground Balls

No official rules limit an athlete's technique when picking up ground balls except in women's lacrosse, where covering the ball with the stick is prohibited. Flashy, one-handed pickups are sometimes necessary, depending on the relative position of the ball and the skill level of the athletes. However, a two-handed pickup of a ground ball creates a better angle between the head of the stick and the floor, helping the athlete to protect the ball with his or her body and thus increasing the likelihood of a successful pickup. The athlete may choose to scoop through the ball while continuing to run in the same direction. Men's lacrosse also allows athletes to rake the ball with the back of their stick to create momentum before rolling the ball around to the top side of the stick, where the momentum from the rake carries the ball into the pocket. Raking could be especially relevant when picking up ground balls close to the sideline, where there is a risk of deflecting the ball out of bounds during an unsuccessful attempt.

A standard ground ball pickup uses a modified lunge position, requiring the athlete to stay low and focused on the ball (15). For a right-handed pickup (i.e., with the right hand toward the top of the stick), the athlete will place the instep of the right foot next to the ball and flex the hips and knees to lower the body toward the ball. The top hand should be close to the head of the stick to optimize control, with the bottom hand toward the butt end of the stick. The front arm should be relatively straight and there should be some flex at the elbow of the back arm, but the shaft of the stick should be closer to parallel with the floor than perpendicular to it. Once the ball is in the stick, the front leg forcefully pushes into the floor, and the athlete extends the hips and knees to stand up and continue running, now in possession of the ball. Due to the strength and balance needed for ground ball pickups, lacrosse athletes should be exposed to ample unilateral resistance exercises.

GENERAL PHYSIOLOGICAL ANALYSIS

Lacrosse is a physically demanding, high-speed sport that encompasses many different physiological processes and requires strength, power, metabolic, and mental components (14). Like many field sports, lacrosse requires linear sprint speed, rapid changes of direction, quick application of force production, and reactive application of force (i.e., force absorption) in multiple directions. Strength, speed, agility, power, and complete metabolic conditioning are some of the aspects that must not be overlooked for lacrosse athletes.

Jaime Crawford/Getty Images

Lacrosse demands linear sprint speed, rapid direction changes, quick force application, and multi-directional force absorption.

Although strength and conditioning professionals should focus on sound athletic movement, reactive qualities, strength, and power when constructing programming, position demands of the lacrosse athlete must also be taken into account. There are five distinct positions that the strength and conditioning professional must consider when establishing a well-rounded training program for lacrosse. The specific positions, descriptions of their requirements, and their corresponding locations of operation on the field are as follows:

1. *Attackers.* In men's lacrosse, a team of three athletes operates with midfielders on offense. Attackers are required to stay in a 35-yard × 60-yard (32 m × 55 m) offensive zone, with the goal of rapid ball movement and scoring against the opposing defense. In women's lacrosse, the attack group is referred to as *first, second, and third home.*

2. *Midfielders.* A team of three midfield athletes operates in both the offensive and defensive space. They are open to move the entire field of play (110 yards × 60 yards [101 m × 55 m]). The midfield positions are often separated into offensive and defensive midfielders, who

substitute on the fly depending on the possession of the ball. In men's lacrosse, defensive midfielders are often separated into long-stick midfielders (LSMs) and short-stick defensive midfielders (SSDM) who use two different lengths of sticks depending on position requirements. These positions are similar in women's lacrosse, with the notable exception of stick length, which is a standard size.

3. *Defenders.* A team of three athletes is responsible for protecting the defensive zone and goal area. They work in concert with the defensive midfielders with the goal of defending the defensive zone, and they attempt to turn the ball over to change possession. Like the attackers, they are required to operate in a 35-yard by 60-yard (32 m × 55 m) space. In field lacrosse, defenders (LSMs and close defenders) will often use lacrosse sticks that are longer (52-72 in. [132-183 cm]), which allows a defender to keep the offensive athletes farther away and potentially check the ball loose for a potential change of possession. In box lacrosse, athletes use a standard stick length (30 in. [76 cm]), because the game is played in a tighter space. These traits are similar in women's lacrosse, with the notable exception of stick length, which is a standard size.

4. *Goalies.* The goalie in lacrosse has the job of protecting the goal from the opposing offense. The goalie mainly operates within the crease (9 yd [8 m] in diameter), which cannot be entered by any opposing offensive athlete unless the ball has crossed the goal line. Once a save by the goalie has been made, the goalie may leave the crease and sometimes operates in a half- or full-field capacity, although another athlete on the team must remain onside if the goalie crosses the midfield line. The goalie in women's lacrosse follows the same standards and rules as in men's lacrosse.

5. *Face-off specialists, or face off, get off (FOGO) (men's lacrosse).* The FOGO is a specialized position played by a midfielder who meets another face-off specialist at the midfield X to attempt to clamp and retain possession of the ball upon the whistle from the referee. If the FOGO gets possession of the ball, he then becomes an offensive midfielder who aims to get the ball into the offensive zone. Once possession is established, the FOGO will usually pass off the ball to the offense and immediately leave the field to be substituted by an offensive midfielder; in some cases, the FOGO will attempt to score or stay in the offensive zone. If the opposing face-off specialist does not achieve possession of the ball, then he becomes a defensive midfielder or leaves the field to be replaced by a defensive midfielder. In women's lacrosse, the face-off procedure is different, with a standing lateral rake upon the referee's whistle. The athlete taking the face-off usually does not leave the field and immediately becomes a field athlete after the face-off.

Each of these positions has similar physiological requirements, with some minor differences depending on the area of operation on the field. All lacrosse athletes should be trained with the basic physiological requirements and sound athletic principles of strength, speed, power, change-of-direction and multidirectional agility, and a high level of metabolic conditioning. Goalies and face-off specialists will additionally require quick visual and auditory reaction skills as well as close-proximity agility skills for the ability to operate rapidly in a small space.

Physical fitness assessments should be conducted before programming for all positions. In a study that compared National Collegiate Athletics Association (NCAA) Division I starters versus nonstarters in attack (A), midfield (M), and defense (D) athletes, all athletes were analyzed using age; height; body composition; handgrip strength; 20- and 40-yard (18 and 37 m) sprint times; the pro agility test; the 3-cone drill; vertical jump; 1-repetition maximum (1RM) bench press, squat, and hang clean; and a 1.5-mile (2.4 km) run (27).

In the study, it was determined that athletes in all three positions had similar pro agility test scores, but attackers and midfielders were generally quicker than defenders in the 3-cone drill (A: 7.08 seconds to the left, and 7.13 seconds to the right; M: 7.13 seconds to the left, and 7.13 seconds to the right; D: 7.21 seconds to the left, and 7.14 seconds to the right). However, attackers had slightly lower 1RM strength and power results compared to midfielders and defenders. Midfielders also scored higher on 1RM strength and power tests than attackers. Defenders scored the highest on strength and power tests (1RM bench press: D, 109.1 kg [240.5 pounds]; M, 108.4 kg [239.0 pounds]; A, 95.5 kg [210.5 pounds]; 1RM squat: D, 134.4 kg [296.3 pounds]; M, 122.1 kg [269.2 pounds]; A, 116.2 kg [256.2 pounds]; and 1RM hang clean: D, 105.4 kg [232.4 pounds]; M, 98.2 kg [216.5 pounds]; A, 91.7 kg [202.2 pounds]). These differences in test results speak to the overall demands and differences between attack, midfield, and defense positions (27).

As noted in the previously mentioned study, typical body composition for lacrosse athletes usually varies based on their position on the field. NCAA Division I male lacrosse athletes typically have a similar body composition across all positions. However, it has been noted that lacrosse defenders tend to have a greater overall body composition (i.e., a higher percent body fat) than midfielders or attackers. Based on the demands of the defensive positions, the ability to defend against opposing midfielders and attackers in the area around the defensive zone may benefit from higher body fat levels as long as there is no sacrifice in speed, agility, or quickness.

Strength and Power

Strength is considered the fundamental foundation for success in lacrosse. Building strength provides the platform for injury reduction and skill-specific enhancement.

Lacrosse athletes who have well-developed strength qualities may be more resistant to injury and are better prepared for the stress of games and game-speed practices over the length of a season. Additionally, athletes who are stronger and have explosive abilities have more success in practices and games. Execution of acceleration, agility, stick handling, and physical contact all begin with a comprehensive foundation of strength (14).

The strength and conditioning professional should be cognizant of these sport demands when building programming for lacrosse athletes. Muscle-isolation, bilateral-plane, and single-plane exercises, while effective in some realms (bodybuilding or powerlifting), can be ineffective for the field sport athlete. True functional resistance training that uses unilateral, multijoint, and rotation-based (or resisted-rotation) exercises are far more effective for the transfer of resistance training to the sport environment. Exercises that use changing time under tension, full range of motion, multiple planes of motion, balance, and trunk activation can often be more effective for the lacrosse athlete.

Power is another important trait related to lacrosse. This is loosely defined as the **speed–strength qualities** of the lacrosse athlete (i.e., the ability to use strength and speed in quick-movement skills). Developing power in athletes should be a focus of the strength and conditioning professional after the foundations of strength, movement, and speed have been established. The force production of an athlete will affect shot speed, sprint speed, and speed of multidirectional movement skills. Fast-twitch (type II) muscle actions based on strength and speed should include acceleration, deceleration, multidirectional movement, change of direction, and shooting and dodging techniques.

Speed and Agility

The game of lacrosse is largely based on speed. Quick turnovers with changes of possession, offensive and defensive sets, substitutions, clearing, and riding are aspects of the game that require a high level of speed and agility.

Lacrosse, similar to most sports, requires the athlete to execute explosive changes of direction, repeated sprinting, and application of force through the kinetic chain in multiple planes of motion (29).

Speed and agility are often overlooked elements on which strength and conditioning professionals should focus on in their programming. Aspects of speed and agility training include but are not limited to balance, foot speed, top-end speed, acceleration and deceleration, and multidirectional agility. Fast-twitch muscle fibers should be enhanced through effective training modalities. Sprint mechanics and lateral and multidirectional movement skills should be part of the strength and conditioning professional's program during off-season and preseason training. A well-rounded program should include this type of training on a daily, weekly, and monthly basis to prepare lacrosse athletes for the demands of their sport.

Metabolic Capacity

Training to improve the metabolic capacity of lacrosse athletes is similar to that for many other field sport athletes. Depending on the specific position of the lacrosse athlete, metabolic demands may be different. However, all positions in lacrosse arguably require a strong metabolic component to enable the athlete to maintain a high level of intensity through four quarters of play.

The metabolic stress of lacrosse requires the involvement of all three metabolic energy systems (phosphagen, glycolytic, and oxidative). This creates a challenge for the strength and conditioning professional to simultaneously build a cardiovascular foundation and improve the strength and power components that will lead to successful outcomes in practices and games (14).

The strength and conditioning professional should design off-season and preseason training programs that rely on a moderate to sometimes heavy metabolic component. The foundational components of aerobic training, sprint-recovery management, and muscular strength will assist athletes in decreasing game fatigue and increasing time to exhaustion between bouts of anaerobic sprint load. Baseline times for 1.5-mile (2.4 km) runs; 20-, 40-, and 60-yard (18, 37, and 55 m) sprints; and recovery between sprint efforts will assist the strength and conditioning professional in the design of the metabolic component for these programs. In addition, the strength and conditioning professional can incorporate high-intensity interval training in the weight room to increase metabolic qualities. Circuit training is an excellent method to increase the metabolic work capacity in a small space. An example is using 30 seconds of work in a resisted-movement exercise followed by 30 seconds of rest while moving through a circuit of different exercises for several rounds. This can progress to 40 seconds of work followed by 20 seconds of rest as athletes adapt to the metabolic demands of the workouts over time.

Once the strength and conditioning professional has baseline data from testing, incorporation of base-building sessions (short- to medium-length aerobic programming), repeated sprint interval sessions, and repeated multidirectional sessions that use acceleration–deceleration, lateral, and multidirectional movement can increase the metabolic capacity in a sport-specific method for better outcomes.

In addition, the strength and conditioning professional should analyze the lacrosse athlete's running and agility mechanics for energy efficiency. Dynamic warm-ups incorporating speed, agility, and quickness drills such as ankling, ankle pops, straight-leg runs, skipping patterns, and multidirectional movement patterns should be included in the programs. These drills should be incorporated before the session's strength exercises, when athletes are able to use their highest level of neuromuscular actions for the session. Speed, agility, and quickness sessions to improve the lacrosse athlete's ability to move efficiently will decrease time to exhaustion and lead to better energy-conservation and performance outcomes during the length of a game.

POSITION-SPECIFIC ANALYSIS

Attackers, midfielders, defenders, and goalies have unique performance attributes and game-play responsibilities. Strength and conditioning professionals need to understand these position-specific aspects when designing a training program.

Attackers

The attack positions are offensively minded, although there are some defensive responsibilities after turnovers where the attackers are a part of the play. Regardless, passing and shooting are critical skills for attackers to master. Balance and selective attention are specific characteristics of shooting that may increase the accuracy needed by attackers. In a group of NCAA Division III female lacrosse athletes, Marsh and colleagues discovered a relationship between athletes' ability to balance, their visual search and attention, and their shooting accuracy (19). While shooting mechanics are essential, other physical characteristics may need to be trained in addition to shooting technique. Sport-specific balance training that mimics shooting mechanics (e.g., unilateral movements with hip flexion and torso rotation) may be a critical addition to the training programs of attackers. Similarly, visual focus and attention drills may help shooters focus more on task-relevant cues, such as the handedness of the goalie, whether or not the goalie is baiting, or if the goalie is out of position.

Similarly, motor imagery training may be another vital aspect of offensive athletes that directly influences their scoring ability (12). Because similar regions of the brain are activated during physical tasks and visualized tasks, there may be some positive transfer from computer-based training to on-field performance. Hirao and colleagues (12) found that scoring abilities were increased in male lacrosse athletes following stimulus–response compatibility training (computer-based training that required the athletes to quickly point in the opposite direction when a character was presented on one side of the screen) and motor imagery (computer-based visualization of shooting in the opposite direction of a goalie's movement during a video clip). Therefore, shooting mechanics must be practiced in the context of responding to the environment—namely, reading the movements of the defenders and the goalie.

Another unique decision shooters have to consider is the type of shot. In many ball sports, speed and accuracy have an inverse relationship (19). In lacrosse, the sidearm shot was measured as the fastest shot, yet no differences were observed in accuracy compared to overhand and underhand shots (18). Based on situational needs, attackers may need to make in-game judgments regarding the style of shot that enhances the likelihood of scoring. Personal preference may also influence the style of a particular athlete. Standardized rules are in place that prevent the ball from being retained in the stick. However, the exact style of stringing is different for each stick; this is especially true for men but is becoming increasingly true for women due to rule changes and alterations in stick design (i.e., the offset head). The amount of hold—colloquially known as *whip*—positively correlates with shot speed and accuracy (6). However, the authors concluded that experience and individual ability should also be considered when selecting the right amount of whip for each athlete (6). Due to variations in the release point depending on the amount of whip, strength and conditioning professionals need to be aware of subtle changes in shooting mechanics that may—for better or worse—influence the accuracy of shooting.

Strength and conditioning professionals also need to consider the mechanical demands of shooting and select weight room exercises likely to facilitate a positive transfer of force. The importance of a stiff and stable lower body is evidenced by the greater muscle activity measured during an overhand shot in female lacrosse athletes. Greater EMG activity was apparent for the biceps femoris, rectus femoris, and gastrocnemius during fast shots compared to slow shots (21, 22). The lead leg is especially relevant because it initiates the impulse (i.e., force × time) that can be translated through the torso and into the upper extremities and stick. To avoid inefficient transfer of force, minimal knee flexion should be present during initial ground contact to create a stiff limb that efficiently transfers the braking impulse into usable force for shooting. To capitalize on the impulse transfer through the kinetic chain, slight knee extension during the stick acceleration and ball release phases is recommended (25). This sequence of force transfer is consistent with the measurements of torso velocity during overhand shooting that shows peak thoracic rotational velocity occurring approximately 2 seconds into a shot attempt (18). This delay in peak rotational velocity is likely explained by greater torso-to-pelvis separation, which has been associated with greater ball velocity in other rotational sports such as golf, tennis, and baseball (pitching). Therefore, lacrosse attackers and other shooters should participate in technical training to emphasize this sequence of force transfer from the lower body to the upper body via the torso. Additionally, specific rotational activities in the weight room (see chapter 8 for examples) may be warranted to enhance the ability to develop rotational force and velocity through mechanically similar exercises.

In addition to the technical abilities unique to attackers, physiological characteristics allow them to get into a tactically advantageous field position and outmaneuver defensive opponents. Generally, top speed is greater in games than in practice, yet relatively little of the total travel distance is covered at high speed (26). Direct comparisons among studies are challenging because of differences in reporting metrics, such as different cut points for running zones or relative versus absolute methods of quantifying high-speed effort (30). Regardless, it is prudent to evaluate the available literature to determine ranges for expected in-game demands so that lacrosse athletes can be appropriately trained to meet the rigors of competition.

In men's lacrosse, attackers have been reported to cover an average of approximately 4,000 to just over 7,000 meters (4,374-7,655 yd) per game, with approximately 200 to 900 meters (218.7-984.3 yd) of that distance at speeds faster than 12 km/h (7.5 mph) (1, 8, 24). On average, nearly 90 high-intensity (>2 m/s^2 [2.2 yd/s^2]) accelerations and decelerations were reported per game in Japanese international lacrosse athletes (1). In a sample of Australian national-level men's lacrosse competitors, Polley and colleagues reported a greater number of high-intensity decelerations than accelerations, suggesting the pattern of play may differ profoundly from one game to another (24). There also tends to be a difference between practices and games, with higher loads and intensities during competitions (8). Increases in load may play a role in fatigue, with attackers tending to decrease the overall intensity of their efforts with each progressing quarter (1, 8, 24). Based on the pattern of play and in-game demands, it is clear that attackers require a great deal of strength and power in the context of repeated sprint ability, characterized by frequent accelerations and decelerations.

While there is a point of diminishing returns, a certain level of physiological preparedness is necessary to support the activity profiles required for lacrosse practices and competitions.

Generally, attackers have above-average aerobic fitness, with 55 ml/kg/min as a reasonable target (10). Based on the faster speed and agility times for starters compared to nonstarters in a sample of NCAA Division I lacrosse athletes, it can be concluded that both of these metrics transfer to in-game performance (27). The average values for attackers in a study by Sell and colleagues were 2.8 seconds for the 20-yard (18 m) sprint, 4.98 seconds for the 40-yard (37 m) sprint, 4.36 seconds for the pro agility test, and 7.08 seconds for the 3-cone drill (27). Strength metrics were also assessed, with relative abilities of starting athletes being 1.2 times body weight for the bench press, 1.5 times body weight for the squat, and 1.2 times body weight for the hang clean. These performance measures tended to be similar to those for defenders but lower than those for midfielders. Physiological benchmarks should also be considered in light of the level of competition. The higher the level of competition, the higher the expected performance should be. For example, in the context of NCAA Division III lacrosse athletes, a 40-yard (37 m) sprint time of 5.5 seconds was recommended as the benchmark (10).

More data are available for women's lacrosse. With a larger field, total distances per game are often higher in women's lacrosse compared to men's lacrosse, with values ranging from 3,500 meters (3,828 yd) to over 8,000 meters (8,949 yd) (3, 16). The specific thresholds for defining sprint distances vary greatly among studies, but female attackers have been reported to achieve top speeds of 24 to 26 km/h (14.9-16.2 mph), which tends to be slower than midfielders and defenders, despite the fact that the total number of sprints is similar among positions (5, 16). For a sample of female NCAA Division I athletes, total unique high-intensity sprint efforts (>20 km/h [12.4 mph]) ranged from 1 to 11 per game, with total sprint efforts (>10 km/h [6.2 mph]) ranging from 37 to 199 per game (5). Sustained, short-duration, high-intensity sprints are essential, but changes of direction may be even more important based on the much higher average frequency of high-intensity (>3 m/s^2 [3.3 yd/s^2]) accelerations and decelerations per game (51 and 41, respectively). All of these high-intensity efforts tend to accumulate a wide range of sprint distances (distance covered at speeds >15 km/h [9.3 mph]) per game for attackers, with one study reporting a range of 205 to 1,318 meters (224-1,441 yd) (5) and another study reporting an average distance of 762 meters (833 yd) covered at speeds greater than 18 km/h (11.2 mph) (16).

External load can only be successfully achieved when physiological performance thresholds are met. Based on the substantial duration of effort combined with repeated high-intensity sprints, it is easy to conclude that women's lacrosse athletes require both anaerobic and aerobic capacity, as well as speed and agility (20). In a sample of NCAA Division I college athletes, aerobic performance on the 1-mile (1.6 km) run test was 7:01 minutes on average for the team, supported by average $\dot{V}O_2$max values of 45.7 ml/kg/min (7). These values align with another study of NCAA Division I athletes with estimated average $\dot{V}O_2$max values of 47.6 ml/kg/min for attackers (30). This same sample also recorded pro agility test scores of 5.05 seconds on average and Illinois Agility Test scores of 10.49 seconds on average. These athletes were also measured with average 40-yard (37 m) dash speeds of 6.2 seconds, with an average 20-yard (18 m) split of 3.39 seconds. These values resemble those for other women's sports, such as soccer, basketball, and field hockey (30). In a sample of NCAA Division III female lacrosse athletes, a slightly higher $\dot{V}O_2$max was found with an average of 51.2 ml/kg/min for attackers (13). The pro agility test averages were slightly faster at 4.96 seconds, as was the 40-yard (36.6 m) dash average of 5.56 seconds. This study also reported average strength levels for attackers of 44 kg (97 pounds) on the bench press and 73.7 kg (162 pounds) for the squat (13). Overall, it is clear that physiological abilities are important to support on-field performance, though more research on the exact benchmarks is needed to clearly establish minimal thresholds.

Due to the lack of robust normative data across competitive levels, it is prudent for each strength and conditioning professional to establish his or her own normative values and patterns of physiological preparedness and external load requirements to best fit the needs of each attacker. Furthermore, different styles of play may allow athletes to capitalize on their strengths despite their weaknesses, making normative comparisons challenging. For example, a stronger and more powerful athlete may focus on a more direct downhill dodge tactic, whereas a smaller, faster athlete may rely more on change of direction and finesse. Regardless of the exact use of these physiological parameters, each attacker should have a metabolic foundation of both aerobic and anaerobic capacity and an advanced level of strength, speed, and agility. In any context, all attackers should seek to improve strength and power metrics in a weight room setting to support the in-game demands of their position.

Midfielders

Similar to attackers, midfielders have offensive responsibilities. Some teams have two-way middies (slang for *midfielders*) with offensive and defensive duties. In contrast, other teams opt to substitute their middies with each change of possession, so athletes can be either offensive or defensive specialists. With onside requirements, the goalies and defenders generally stay on the defensive half of the field, while attackers remain on the offensive half. Midfielders are free to go back and forth as the need arises. For this reason, more open-field running is typical of the midfield position. However, midfielders are more frequently strategically substituted to manage fatigue due to the greater distance covered during a possession.

In men's lacrosse, NCAA Division III midfielders were found to have a range of total distance from 4,660 to 5,251 meters (5,096-5,743 yd) per game, which was an average of approximately 2,000 meters (2,187 yd) less than attackers and defenders (8). In this sample, an average of 446 meters (488 yd) was covered by midfielders at speeds greater than 18 km/h (11.2 mph), which was considerably more than by defenders but less than by attackers. However, with the lower distance covered, midfielders spent a higher percentage of their total distance (approximately 9%) at sprint speeds and had more unique sprint efforts (range: 12-16) compared to defenders (range: 7-11) but fewer than attackers (range: 15-21). More data are needed for men's lacrosse activity profiles at the youth and collegiate levels, but in a sample of national-level Australian athletes, midfielders covered the lowest total distance on average at 3,591 meters (3,927 yd), with a total of 1,338 meters (1,463 yd) covered at speeds faster than 12 km/h (7.5 mph), which was more than covered by defenders but slightly less than by attackers (24). However, at speeds greater than 21 km/h (13.0 mph), midfielders had the highest average coverage of the positions at 200 meters (219 yd). An important consideration when interpreting these numbers is that despite the similarities among positions, midfielders were measured to play an average of approximately 12 minutes less than attackers and approximately 23 minutes less than defenders. This conclusion about relative load was also supported in a sample of Japanese international-level competitors, with midfielders covering 110 m/min (120 yd/min) compared to the 81 m/min (89 yd/min) for attack and 87 m/min (95 yd/min) compared to defenders (1). However, caution should be used when applying the data from international competitions due to the longer (i.e., 20-minute) quarters (24). Regardless, the work density of midfielders is consistently higher than that of the other positions, despite the total workload often being lower.

Complementing in-game external load requirements, midfielders also need to be adequately trained with at least minimal proficiency for physiological parameters. Minimal data exist for normative physiological performance values for midfielders in men's lacrosse, but based on the external load variables, the fitness metrics should include metabolic capacity testing as well as strength, power, speed, and agility. NCAA Division I collegiate lacrosse midfielders have been measured with above-average aerobic capacity with 1.5-mile (2.4 km) run times of 9:46 minutes on average, which is the same as for defenders but slightly slower than for attackers (27). In general, men's lacrosse athletes are recommended to have aerobic capacity values of approximately 55 ml/kg/min (10). Based on the repetition of high-intensity efforts during game play, the aerobic system is likely more of a supplemental system that supports recovery than a performance system. Due to the lack of significant differences in aerobic performance between starting and nonstarting athletes and the concomitant lack of significant differences among positions, it may be concluded that aerobic capacity is an important foundational fitness attribute that ought to be above average but not targeted for improvement at the expense of anaerobic characteristics, such as muscular fitness and anaerobic capacity. While not separated by position, 300-yard (274 m) shuttle run tests have been used as markers of anaerobic fitness, with NCAA Division III athletes scoring an average of 58 seconds (4). For other anaerobic attributes, starters tended to have faster 20- and 40-yard (18 and 37 m) sprint speeds as well as faster pro agility test and 3-cone drill scores, further supporting the importance of these speed and agility characteristics for in-game performance (27). NCAA Division I midfielders tended to be faster than defenders and attackers, with average 20-yard (18 m) split times of 2.76 seconds and average 40-yard (37 m) times of 4.9 seconds. Agility scores were also faster than other positions, with an average score of 4.37 seconds on the pro agility test and an average score of 7.13 seconds on the 3-cone test (midfielders were slightly slower than attackers on the 3-cone test). Other options from the literature for agility assessment include the T-test, the 5-cone agility run test, and the 4-cone box run (10). Recommended times for these assessments (based on a NCAA Division III sample) are 9.5 seconds, 20 seconds, and 8.5 seconds, respectively.

Another aspect of testing is power production, often measured as jump performance. In a sample of NCAA Division I athletes in which the positions were not specified, preseason countermovement jump performance was reported to be 40.65 centimeters (16.0 in.), on average (28). Depth jump heights were slightly lower, at an average of 31.17 centimeters (12.3 in.). Of note, this study reported no significant decline in jump performance from preseason to postseason, but there was a significant decline in relative peak power and relative peak force. These findings may support the importance of metabolic conditioning to enhance work capacity and recovery, or they could indicate the need for load management strategies across the season to minimize the accumulating effects of fatigue on power and rate of force development (28).

In women's lacrosse, NCAA Division I midfielders have been reported to have average total distances ranging from 4,952 meters to 8,620 meters (5,416-9,427 yd) per game (2, 3, 5, 16). Midfielders have also been reported to have a larger amount of high-speed running, with an average of seven unique efforts over 20 km/h (12.4 mph) per game (5) and an average of 912.4 meters (998 yd) at speeds above 18 km/h (11.2 mph), which includes an average of 55.8 accelerations that occurred at rates faster than 3 m/s^2 (3.3 yd/m^2) (16). Midfielders also accumulated an average of 50 high-intensity accelerations and 36 high-intensity decelerations per game as well as edging out attackers and defenders for the highest top speeds, with an average of 25 km/h (15.5 mph) (5). Similar to men's lacrosse, female midfielders averaged fewer total minutes of playing time compared to the other positions, although the differences were not significant (3). Different than the men's game is a report that female midfielders covered more total distance per game than the other positions, suggesting less in the way of positional differences for women's lacrosse compared to men's lacrosse (5). Overall, the rolling average for running speed was quite low, which supports the importance of characterizing lacrosse as an intermittent sport that requires rapid changes of direction more than relying on top speeds (3). However, the strongest predictors of in-game performance for offensive productivity from midfielders were total distance, work capacity, and decelerations (2). Therefore, external workload can be assumed to have low to moderate correlations with in-game performance metrics, but other factors should also be assumed to play a role, such as sport-specific skills, tactical aspects, and physiological preparedness.

In terms of physiological preparedness, women's lacrosse athletes have been categorized with an above-average level of aerobic fitness. As a whole, NCAA Division I lacrosse athletes achieved average measured $\dot{V}O_2$max values of 45.7 ml/kg/min (7), which is slightly lower than the estimated $\dot{V}O_2$max values from a 20-meter (22 yd) shuttle run test, where midfielders reached average estimates of 47.3 ml/kg/min (30). In a sample of elite collegiate female lacrosse athletes from the United Kingdom, Yo-Yo intermittent recovery test estimates of $\dot{V}O_2$max for midfielders were 45.3 ml/kg/min, which was higher than for the other positions (20). These values are comparable to those in other team sports but lower than values expected for aerobic endurance athletes, supporting the importance of an aerobic foundation for recovery and sustaining performance while achieving the relatively high total distances in lacrosse and still relying on anaerobic attributes that contribute to success in accumulating the necessary sprint volume. For example, in the sample from the United Kingdom, midfielders were faster on average for 9.1-meter (10 yd) sprints (1.69 seconds), 36.6-meter (40 yd) sprints (5.46 seconds), and pro agility tests (4.95 seconds) than other positions (20). Positional differences in speed and agility were marginal in a sample of NCAA Division I athletes, although the absolute values were lower than in their U.K. counterparts: 1.99 seconds for the 9.1-meter (10 yd) and 5.90 seconds for the 36.6-meter (40 yd) sprints (30). As a measure of explosive power, countermovement jump scores were also higher in midfielders (27.9 cm [11 in.]), which were notably lower than the performances of NCAA Division I teams (39.7-44.0 cm [15.6-17.3 in.]) (7, 30). These explosive capabilities at least partially support in-game performance, because positive correlations were found between high-intensity accelerations and goals, assists, and shots in several NCAA Division I games (9).

Based on the limited evidence available, it seems midfielders may have a greater work density than the other lacrosse positions, relying heavily on repeated sprint ability. Load management is important for male and female midfielders based on the decline in performance from the first to the second half for women (16) and from one quarter to the next for men (24). Underpinning each of these in-game load metrics are the fundamental qualities of muscular strength and power.

Defenders

Lacrosse defense athletes have demands (lateral and multidirectional movement, sprint mechanics, and opposing force production to the opponent) similar to the other positions on the field, while goalies must execute explosive reactions in a smaller space to cover the defensive zone and the 6-foot × 6-foot (1.8 × 1.8 m) goal mouth. These positions are similar in demands for the men's and women's game, with differences in stick length. It should be noted that certain forms of contact are allowed in women's lacrosse, while certain forms of both contact and collision are allowed in the men's game.

The position demands of lacrosse defense athletes usually benefit from a slightly larger body composition (33), but this is not always common across the defense positions. Defense athletes operate in the defensive zone of the field during practices and games, with occasional breakouts to the offensive zone during changes of possession. Groups of six athletes (plus one goalie) operate in the defensive zone.

Defenders, like other players, need lateral agility, sprinting ability, and force against opponents, while goalies require explosive reactions in confined spaces to defend their zone effectively.

When operating in the defensive zone, the close-defense athletes use a group of three to defend a closer proximity to the goal and must use the performance qualities of lateral and multidirectional movement, changes of direction, and body-to-body contact matchups to push opponents out of the attacking goal area and cause turnovers through stick checking and legal body contact.

Additionally, the defensive zone is also defended by LSMs and SSDMs. These are also a group of three to complete the total of six athletes (plus one goalie) protecting the defensive zone. The LSMs and SSDMs have a slightly different requirement of operation in the defensive zone. While the close-defense athletes usually cover the close proximity of the goal area, termed *staying home*, LSMs and SSDMs operate in the entire defensive zone, covering a larger area from sideline to sideline and endline to midfield. These athletes must have the performance qualities of the close-defense athletes coupled with a higher metabolic component due to the larger coverage requirement.

Goalies

Lacrosse goalies present a different challenge for the strength and conditioning professional. Although goalies typically follow the same strength and conditioning programming as the rest of the athletes, the performance demands for the position differ slightly from other positions. Goalies are required to operate in the crease, which is a ring 18 feet (5.5 m) in diameter around the 6-foot × 6-foot (1.8 m × 1.8 m) opening of the goal mouth and a triangular area with a footprint of 6 feet × 7 feet (1.8 m × 2.1 m). The crease may not be entered by any athlete from the opposing offense unless the ball crosses the goal line. The crease area is the goalie's home base unless a turnover takes place in the defensive zone. In that circumstance, the goalie may leave the crease area and can operate in the total defensive zone to assist in clearing the ball downfield.

A lacrosse goalie may not be required to have a metabolic training component with similar intensity as that of the attack, midfield, and defensive positions. However, breakouts and clears will require some short-burst metabolic components, and goalies may benefit from metabolic training to enhance mental focus and stamina. Goalies are required to have the highest level of fast-twitch muscle reactions in the defensive zone. They are required to cover the entire 6-foot × 6-foot (1.8 m × 1.8 m) goal mouth from the floor to the top crossbar and post to post from left to right. Goalies must react to potential shots with an average speed of 80 to 90 mph (128.7-144.8 km/h) at the NCAA Division I level. Although the shooting athlete's distance from the goal may vary, lacrosse goalies have an extremely limited window of time to react to the direction and speed of the incoming shot. Therefore, it is recommended that the strength and conditioning professional add high-level components of reaction training to existing programs for goalies to enhance these qualities.

All lacrosse defenders (including goalies) may benefit from a solid foundation of strength and power that require the strength and conditioning professional to combine both upper and lower body strength and power qualities using upper and lower body pushing and pulling exercises, multidirectional movement and reaction skills, and repeated bouts of conditioning work to enhance aerobic and anaerobic work with recovery bouts in between. Once the strength foundations are established in off-season work, it is recommended that the strength and conditioning professional build on the strength foundation with more speed–strength and power work that includes speed and agility programming as the athletes transition from off-season to preseason.

CONCLUSION

Based on the general physiological and biomechanical analysis of lacrosse athletes, it is recommended that the strength and conditioning professional begin the process of programming with general baseline testing. Keeping in mind that the sport of lacrosse requires the athletes to run, cut, pass, shoot, defend, check, and cover off-ball areas of the field based on their positional assignments, standardized testing protocols outlined in chapter 3 are recommended.

The results of testing should drive the type of off-season, preseason, and in-season maintenance programming for the lacrosse athlete. Understanding that lacrosse involves the elements of high-speed sprinting, changes of direction, explosive upper and lower body movements, and quick acceleration and deceleration, the strength and conditioning professional should be aware of the risk of upper and lower body injuries.

In most cases, modern high school and NCAA lacrosse strength and conditioning prescriptions seem to be founded on a strength-training-only style of programming. This could be due to a lack of education, knowledge base, or experience in teaching field-based movement skills on the part of the strength and conditioning professional. However, programming should not be limited to resistance training only. While foundational strength remains a priority in training for the demands of lacrosse, explosive power, sprint mechanics, training for multidirectional and rotational movement, and acceleration and deceleration training should be incorporated in the strength and conditioning professional's weekly programming prescriptions.

Normative data regarding the sport of lacrosse remain somewhat scarce because lacrosse is a relative newcomer on the global stage. Due to differences in the biomechanical and physiological demands spread out over the different position requirements, observational analysis and input from sport-specific coaches may provide the strength and conditioning professional with a greater understanding of the sport's demands and how to program for lacrosse athletes. This will assist the strength and conditioning professional in designing prescriptions that will enhance all the qualities of the lacrosse athlete.

3

TESTING PROTOCOLS AND ATHLETE ASSESSMENT

THOMAS NEWMAN

Lacrosse, by definition, is a territorial possession game in which athletes continuously strive to gain or deny advantageous field positions to the opposing team. This dynamic sport takes place in a semistructured, free-flowing environment governed by a set of rules that emphasize fine motor skills and cognitive abilities. This chapter describes key assessments to evaluate a lacrosse athlete and provide insights a strength and conditioning professional can use to design an effective program that enhances performance and success on the field.

When reviewing the following protocols, strength and conditioning professionals must understand one crucial concept: Every athlete possesses a unique genetic endowment that can be enhanced but cannot be completely rewritten. In this chapter, traits are classified as either **mutable** (aspects that can be modified to some degree) or **nonmutable** (attributes that cannot be changed and therefore should be considered during recruitment, such as height).

GENERAL TESTING GUIDELINES

Regardless of the available technology, testing should be examined using an **output, driver, and strategy (ODS) model** (9). The ODS model, described by Dr. Jason Lake, is an effective paradigm when collecting and analyzing any kind of metric associated with performance in a program. While this approach was originally developed to help identify which metrics were most important in the depth jump, this thinking and approach has now expanded far beyond force plates (2). Since the initial application of the ODS model, strength and conditioning professionals worldwide have used this approach to efficiently streamline and prioritize a wide range of sport science metrics and test data, effectively driving decision-making within their programs.

Output describes a desired end state or outcome, such as increasing a vertical jump by a certain amount. **Drivers** are the various elements that can be manipulated to change the output, such as increasing total force, lean body mass, or relative strength. This framework provides a performance model that clarifies the proverbial "it depends" paradox. In reality, athlete development does not have fixed solutions but is rather a moving target with optimal training windows that open and close throughout an athlete's career. This concept, described by Newton and Kraemer (13), serves as a valuable resource to effectively explain to athletes the importance behind a particular block of training.

Lastly, **strategy** accounts for the biomechanical sequence of events that occurs when an output is performed, and it is largely associated with the likelihood and longevity or sustainability of an output. Using the previous example, if an individual successfully achieves an increase in his or her vertical jump by a certain amount but does so at the cost of creating a major valgus collapse at the knee joint upon takeoff, this improved output may come at a long-term cost. In other words, this newfound ability is achieved through what would be considered a poor mechanical strategy at the knee joint.

By using the ODS model, strength and conditioning professionals can develop a more comprehensive understanding of the factors affecting an athlete's performance and use this knowledge to make informed decisions about the training program. In turn, this allows athletes to reach their full potential while minimizing the risk of injury. Also, by incorporating the concepts of the ODS model, training plans can be tailored to individual athletes, taking into account each athlete's unique strengths and weaknesses. This approach encourages a more nuanced understanding of athletic development, helping both strength and conditioning professionals and athletes to navigate the complex world of sport performance.

TESTING PROTOCOLS

Establishing testing baseline protocols is the first step in developing a strength and conditioning program. Great care must be taken to ensure that all testing protocols adhere to scientific method principles of being accurate and reliable (or, within the context of testing, valid and repeatable). With the emergence of various commercial technologies, it is crucial that any measurement intended for decision-making is clearly understood by the staff implementing the testing. The good-enough or close-enough mindset will ultimately lead to useless data, poor decision-making, and wasted time that could have been more productively used elsewhere. The temptation to test for the sake of testing because everyone else is doing it typically does not lead to effective results and ultimately undermines confidence in the test itself. It is imperative that coaches and strength and conditioning professionals effectively explain and communicate the purpose of testing to athletes in an effort to increase intentionality and commitment to the subsequent prescribed program.

TEST FINDER

STRENGTH TESTS

1RM Barbell Back Squat 29
1RM Barbell Bench Press 31
1RM Chin-Up 32
Loaded Farmer's Carry 33

POWER TEST

Vertical Jump Test 35

SPEED AND AGILITY TESTS

10-Yard (9 m) Dash 38
Pro Agility Test 36

CONDITIONING ENDURANCE TESTS

Andy Shay's Box Passing Drill 43
Assault Bike Tabata Protocol 40
High-Velocity 300-Yard (274 m) Shuttle 42

STRENGTH TESTS

Strength is the fundamental physiological factor underpinning all human movement. Traditionally, **strength** has been described as an expression of maximal force capacity. However, it is now more commonly explained as force across a continuum of velocity. Regardless of the specific definition, strength is one of the traits that can be developed significantly by an effective resistance training program. In general, early emphasis should be placed on developing the neurological coordination to perform major exercises that become the launching point for a hypertrophy, acceleration, or top-end speed-training program. It is imperative to understand that at no point in the training program should technique and movement quality be sacrificed for the sake of inflating test numbers. A poorly performed assessment would be a **null test**, because the output was not achieved using the designated protocol.

1RM BARBELL BACK SQUAT

Purpose

In lacrosse, the back squat is a critical exercise to develop a strong foundation of strength that carries over to improving speed, power, and quickness (5). This effect appears to be most significant until the force output (i.e., the load lifted) approximately equals double the athlete's body mass (4, 15, 21). At this level of strength, a decision must be made to shift focus to increasing power or muscle hypertrophy.

Equipment

- Olympic barbell
- Weight plates
- Locks (2)
- Squat rack

Testing Protocol

An athlete's 1-repetition maximum (1RM) is most commonly assessed using multijoint exercises such as the squat, bench press, deadlift, and power clean. Although many 1RM testing protocols are effective, one that has been used successfully (8) is as follows:

1. Perform a general warm-up and specific warm-up using dynamic flexibility or callisthenic exercises, foam rolling, core facilitation and potentiation exercises, and an unloaded bar.

2. Do a light warm-up of 5 to 10 repetitions at 40% to 60% of the perceived or estimated 1RM.

3. Rest for 1 minute. For very strong athletes attempting a heavy 1RM, 1 to 3 additional warm-up sets may be needed.

4. Do 3 to 5 fast repetitions at 60% to 80% of the perceived or estimated 1RM.

5. Rest 1 to 2 minutes and perform a set of 1 repetition with approximately 90% to 95% of the perceived or estimated 1RM.

6. Step 5 will be performed close to the 1RM. Make a conservative increase in weight, and attempt another 1RM.

7. Allow a 3-minute rest period if the attempt is successful before making another attempt. It is important to allow enough rest before the next maximum attempt.

8. Obtain a 1RM within three to five attempts to avoid excessive fatigue. The process of increasing the weight up to a true 1RM can be enhanced by prior familiarization and experience. This process continues until a failed attempt occurs; then the weight is adjusted accordingly.

9. Record the 1RM as the weight of the last successfully completed attempt.

Coaching Tips

- Ideally, the athlete's 1RM should be within 3% to 5% of the projected 1RM based on the previous week's training. This estimation should provide an idea of the accuracy and efficacy of the training plan and also serve as a guide to the anticipated 1RM on testing day.

- During 1RM testing, resist the urge to have the athlete strive for one more attempt or make attempts until failure. There is a great risk—especially in programs that use multiple-repetition protocols—associated with athletes attempting to squeeze out one additional repetition by using any strategy possible and potentially sustaining an injury. Athletes should complete at least one month of regular resistance training before being tested for 1RM.

- If velocity-based testing is available, it is important to note that as the loads approach the 1RM, movement velocity decreases. Several studies have attempted to quantify a true maximal effort in compound (multijoint) exercises approaching 0.3 m/s; at these slower speeds, there typically is a breakdown of technique (6, 7).

Descriptive Data

See table 3.1 for target **relative strength values** (i.e., the 1RM divided by the athlete's body weight) based on playing position for male college lacrosse athletes (17).

Table 3.1   Relative Bodyweight Strength Values for 1-Repetition Maximum Barbell Back Squat

Position	Below average	Average	Above average
Defense	1.3	1.5	1.7
Midfield	1.1	1.5	1.9
Attack	1	1.5	2

Data from K.M. Sell, J.M. Prendergast, J.J. Ghigiarelli, et al., "Comparison of Physical Fitness Parameters for Starters vs. Nonstarters in an NCAA Division I Men's Lacrosse Team," *Journal of Strength and Conditioning Research* 32, no. 11 (2018): 3160-3168.

1RM BARBELL BENCH PRESS

Purpose

The barbell bench press is the primary exercise used to measure upper body horizontal press strength.

Equipment

- Olympic barbell
- Weight plates
- Locks (2)
- Bench with uprights (to rack the bar)

Testing Protocol

Follow the 1RM testing protocol described for the back squat (8).

Coaching Tips

- The bench press is a touch-and-go exercise. The spotter may assist in both the unracking and reracking of the weight upon completion. If at any point the barbell is touched, assisted, or guided during the exercise, it is considered a null test, and the load used in the previous attempt will be the 1RM.

- The bench press is an excellent tool to spark initial interest in resistance training. However, it loses application to lacrosse as strength levels increase, and in some instances, it becomes a detrimental factor in the structure and orientation of the shoulder joint.

- Ideally, the athlete's 1RM should be within 3% to 5% of the projected 1RM based on the previous week's training. This estimation should provide an idea of the accuracy and efficacy of the training plan and can also serve as a guide to the anticipated 1RM on testing day.

- During 1RM testing, resist the urge to have the athlete strive for one more attempt or make attempts until failure. There is a great risk—especially in programs that use multiple-repetition protocols—associated with athletes attempting to squeeze out one additional repetition by using any strategy possible and potentially sustaining an injury. Athletes should complete at least one month of regular resistance training before being tested for 1RM.

- Ideally, an athlete's 1RM should be within a predictable range of 10 pounds to 20 pounds (4.5-9.1 kg) of the loads used for a heavy training set composed of 2 to 3 repetitions.

Descriptive Data

In lacrosse, the ability to bench press is recognized as a peak performance indicator (17). However, the ultimate objective is not merely to achieve the heaviest bench press but rather to ensure that athletes are not deficient in upper body strength. Research and coaching insights indicate that once athletes reach these strength thresholds, training programs often redirect their focus away from the bench press to address other areas (17). Given the high incidence of shoulder injuries in lacrosse, it is crucial to strengthen the back muscles—both vertically and horizontally—as athletes approach the bench press benchmark. This strategy promotes a balanced development of pushing and pulling movements, which helps prevent muscular imbalances and reduce the risk of injuries (1). Moreover, the body's limitations on force production during bench pressing might be linked to its adaptive mechanisms, which, over time, could cause a shift in shoulder positioning that is disadvantageous during gameplay. Therefore, training strategies should prioritize maintaining health and preventing injuries that could arise from training adaptations not well suited to the demands of lacrosse.

See table 3.2 for target relative strength values (i.e., the 1RM divided by the athlete's body weight) based on position for male college lacrosse athletes (17).

Table 3.2   Relative Bodyweight Strength Values for 1-Repetition Maximum Barbell Bench Press

Position	Below average	Average	Above average
Defense	1.0	1.2	1.4
Midfield	1.1	1.3	1.5
Attack	0.9	1.2	1.5

Data from K.M. Sell, J.M. Prendergast, J.J. Ghigiarelli, et al., "Comparison of Physical Fitness Parameters for Starters vs. Nonstarters in an NCAA Division I Men's Lacrosse Team," *Journal of Strength and Conditioning Research* 32, no. 11 (2018): 3160-3168.

1RM CHIN-UP

Purpose

The supinated chin-up is a primary exercise to develop strength in the musculature of the back. The chin-up and its variations are vital components for ensuring long-term health and stability of the shoulder joint.

Equipment

- Chin-up bar
- Weight belt with a light chain or rope
- Weight plates

Testing Protocol

As a general rule of thumb, strength and conditioning programs should use the chin-up maximum as a regulator of the bench press. The old mantra that athletes should bench what they chin is a great maxim for them to understand that the shoulder complex works together in every moment, and overdevelopment (commonly anteriorly) creates a less optimal position of the shoulder during impact. This concept was originally discussed in the work of Baker and Newton (1), which analyzed the pushing and pulling ratios that determine shoulder strength and provided the following testing protocol:

1. Perform a general warm-up of calisthenic exercises and dynamic stretching.
2. Perform 3 repetitions of a bodyweight supinated chin-up.
3. Rest for 1 minute. Wrap a weight belt around the waist, feed a chain or rope through weight plates (starting with 10 kg [22 pounds] for weaker athletes or 20 kg [44.1 pounds] for stronger athletes), and attach the end of the chain or rope to the weight belt.

4. Prepare to do 1 repetition that begins with the eccentric (lowering) phase by beginning with the chin in line with the chin-up bar. Recruit spotters to support the attached weight in the beginning position.

5. On command, direct the spotters to release their support, then lower the body in a controlled manner until the elbows are fully extended.

6. Pull the body back to the beginning position. The attempt is successful if the chin is in line with the chin-up bar.

7. Allow a 3-minute rest period if the attempt is successful.

8. Increase the weight by 2.5 kg (5.5 pounds) to 10 kg (22 pounds) and repeat steps 4 through 8 until the chin does not reach the chin-up bar.

9. Record the 1RM as the weight of the last successfully completed attempt.

Coaching Tips

- There should be no movement in the legs or other parts of the body, and the lowering phase should be controlled.

- The chin-up can be especially challenging for weaker athletes and often gets overlooked or modified to the point of limited use. Rather than ignoring this challenge, strength and conditioning professionals should emphasize a variety of pulling exercises, because they act as a major protective mechanism to the back and shoulder complex.

Descriptive Data

The chin-up 1RM, when adding in the athlete's body weight and expressed relative to body weight, should equal or even exceed the relative strength level of the athlete's bench press. There do not appear to be any detrimental effects of further development of this attribute.

LOADED FARMER'S CARRY

Purpose

Grip strength is an often underrated yet essential marker of functional strength in athletics. During a meta-analysis, Cronin and colleagues explored the role of grip strength and found a positive correlation regarding fine-motor-skill coordination for precise tasks in hand-to-implement sports, such as lacrosse (4). Grip strength has also been measured in studies assessing central nervous system fatigue (12).

While some school programs may not have access to lab-grade dynamometers to measure absolute force production, the farmer's carry can serve as an effective field test. Once sufficient force production has been achieved using conventional barbell or dumbbell exercises, the protocol can be adapted to various shapes, sizes, and contraction types to better tailor the sport-specific transfer to lacrosse. Furthermore, the farmer's carry is an excellent training exercise to develop coordinated core stability under load and can be a valuable tool for promoting strength development, particularly during early stages of development when traditional exercises may not be feasible due to growth spurts.

Equipment

Dumbbells or kettlebells

Testing Protocol

1. Perform a general warm-up and specific warm-up using dynamic flexibility or callisthenic exercises, foam rolling, core facilitation and potentiation exercises, and an unloaded bar. (Consult the exercise directions provided on page 140.)

2. Select a weight that can easily be carried 100 feet (30 m) at a walking pace. A safe starting point for initial testing is a range between 40% and 60% of body weight in each hand.

3. Rest 1 to 2 minutes, then add between 10 and 20 pounds (4.5-9.1 kg) to each hand and repeat steps 2 and 3, with 5 minutes of rest between attempts.

4. If the full distance cannot be covered without setting the weights down, the test is concluded and the last successful weight is recorded.

5. This process can be repeated up to three times. If three attempts cannot be completed, the final weight becomes the starting point for future tests (14).

Coaching Tips

- Special attention should be given to making sure that when the grip begins to fail, the athlete is instructed not to drop the weight on the feet.
- This test may not be performed with a bilateral implement (e.g., a trap bar).
- Grip may be the significant limiting factor in this test via the nondominant hand.
- Regardless of the load being moved, proper bracing and trunk stability should be emphasized throughout the entire effort.
- This exercise serves as a great teaching opportunity to tell athletes that it is okay to fail and how to properly fail. This is essential in early development, because the same principles will be in effect with Olympic lifts and higher-intensity multijoint exercises. Teaching athletes how to safely miss before technique failure is an essential training milestone.

Descriptive Data

The loaded farmer's carry is used for a wide range of adaptations and applications. For the purposes of this book, this exercise serves as a primary strength marker for the forearm complex. The distance covered was originally discussed in Charles Poliquin's applied strongman training book (14) and has proven to be highly effective at both the high school and collegiate levels. Athletes should strive for loads that combine to a total of approximately their 5RM barbell back squat; see table 3.3 for relative values for three levels of play.

Table 3.3 Percentage of Body Weight in Each Hand for 100-Foot (30 m) Farmer's Carry

Level	Below average	Average	Above average
High school	40	50	60
College	50	60	70
Professional	60	70	90+

Data from C. Poliquin and A. McDermott, *Applied Strongman Training for Sport: Theory and Technical* (Nevada City, CA: Ironmind Enterprises, Inc., 2005).

POWER TEST

VERTICAL JUMP TEST

Purpose

The vertical jump has long been recognized as an ideal measure for determining maximum power output. This crucial metric takes into account both body mass and the vertical displacement achieved by the athlete, providing a convenient, comprehensive assessment of one's physical capabilities. In lacrosse, physical contact underscores the importance of accounting for body mass. Relying solely on vertical height as an indicator of performance could inadvertently skew results in favor of athletes with a smaller mass. The vertical jump test, therefore, serves as an exceptional tool for evaluating the critical balance between size and speed, ensuring a more accurate representation of an individual's athletic prowess.

Equipment

Vertec vertical jump apparatus (or a tape measure, chalk, and an unobstructed wall)

Setup

- If using a Vertec, adjust the height of the vanes to be within the athlete's standing reach height and the anticipated jump apex.
- If using a wall, rub chalk on the tips of the middle fingers of the dominant hand.

Testing Protocol

1. If using a Vertec, stand flat-footed under the vanes (with the Vertec to the outside of the dominant side of the body). Reach the dominant hand fully overhead and swipe the vanes to mark the standing reach height.
2. If using a wall, stand flat-footed next to the wall (with the wall to the outside of the dominant side of the body). Reach the hand fully overhead to make a mark on the wall and mark the standing reach height.
3. Stand approximately 4 inches (10 cm) away from the Vertec or the wall, with the Vertec or wall to the outside of the dominant side of the body.
4. Perform a vertical jump—with a countermovement but without a preparatory or stutter step—using the dominant hand to displace the highest vane at the apex of the jump.
5. Measure or calculate the difference between the height of the vane tapped during step 1 and the height of the vane tapped during step 3 and record it; this is the jump height.
6. Perform three jumps and record the best outcome to the nearest 0.5 inch or 1 centimeter. Allow sufficient time between jumps for full recovery.

Coaching Tips

- Do not overcue this test. Simply instruct the athlete to jump as high as possible.
- For younger athletes, the standing reach height should be periodically updated to account for growth.

- An article by Buckthorpe and colleagues (3) is a great resource on how to properly evaluate jump metrics from various devices.

Descriptive Data

After determining an athlete's jump height, use the following formula to calculate total peak power output (16):

$$\text{Peak power (in watts)} = (60.7 \times [\text{jump height in cm}]) + (45.3 \times [\text{body weight in kg}]) - 2{,}055$$

Athletes can then be divided into two corresponding groups: those who need to jump higher and focus on strength and acceleration and those who need to add body mass in an attempt to increase resilience during on-field contact. See table 3.4 (10) and table 3.5 (18, 19) for peak power values based on sex and position.

Table 3.4   Peak Power (in Watts) for College Female Lacrosse Athletes

Position	Below average	Average	Above average
Position athletes	2,581	3,220	3,859
Goalkeepers	3,870	4,584	5,298

Data from R.G. Lockie, S.A. Birmingham-Babauta, J.J. Stokes, et al., "An Analysis of Collegiate Club-Sport Female Lacrosse Players: Sport-Specific Field Test Performance and the Influence of Lacrosse Stick Carrying," *International Journal of Exercise Science* 11, no. 4 (2018): 269-280.

Table 3.5   Peak Power (in Watts) for College Male Lacrosse Athletes

Position	Below average	Average	Above average
Position athletes*	4,760	5,565	6,370
Goalkeepers	5,600	5,957	6,314

*Contributing athletes.

Data from S.W. Talpey, Personal communication, April 15, 2024; S.W. Talpey, R. Axtell, E. Gardner, and L. James, "Changes in Lower Body Muscular Performance Following a Season of NCAA Division I Men's Lacrosse," *Sports* 7, no. 1 (2019): 18.

SPEED AND AGILITY TESTS

PRO AGILITY TEST

Purpose

The pro agility test, also called the 20-yard (18 m) shuttle, is a vital assessment in lacrosse, acting as a measure of an athlete's ability to change direction quickly, incorporating acceleration and deceleration with proper technique. This capability is critical across all lacrosse positions. It not only assesses the power generated by the central nervous system, akin to what is observed in a vertical jump, but it also combines assessments of power, mobility, and balance into a single test. This makes the pro agility test a comprehensive indicator of an athlete's physical development and it can determine whether the strength and power developed in the weight room is being effectively translated to on-field performance or pinpoint areas for potential improvement in their athletes' development programs.

Mitchell Leff/Getty Images

The pro agility test accurately replicates the rapid demands of direction change, acceleration, and deceleration seen in lacrosse.

Equipment

- Stopwatch or electronic timing device (if available)
- Three field or court lines 5 yards (4.6 m) apart

Testing Protocol

1. Perform a warm-up.
2. Complete at least two practice runs at submaximal speed.
3. Straddle the center line in a three-point stance.
4. On command, sprint 5 yards (4.6 m) to the line on the right (touching the line with the right hand), then sprint left for 10 yards (9 m) to the farthest line (touching the line with the left hand), then sprint right for 5 yards (4.6 m) through the center line.
5. Perform two trials and record the best outcome to the nearest 0.01 second. Allow sufficient time between trials for full recovery.

Coaching Tips

- This test can be performed with athletes starting by going to the left or right direction, but commonly athletes go to the left first. However, it is important to note which movement direction was used to be able to compare times from different testing sessions.
- This test must be performed on the same surface for both pretesting and posttesting, because surface conditions drastically affect the intertest reliability and validity.

- Athletes of all heights must demonstrate the capacity to bend down and touch the line with their hands. Failure to have adequate hip mobility will be on clear display in the form of missed touches.
- As times approach and go below 4.4 seconds, testers will be required on both sides to ensure that the athlete touches the outer lines, because the athlete's speed makes it hard to check that from the center testing position.

Descriptive Data

See tables 3.6 and 3.7 for times based on movement direction (17).

Table 3.6 Pro Agility Test Times (in Seconds) for College Male Lacrosse Athletes—Moving Left First

Position	Below average	Average	Above average
Defense	4.69	4.45	4.21
Midfield	4.53	4.38	4.23
Attack	4.79	4.49	4.19

Data from K.M. Sell, J.M. Prendergast, J.J. Ghigiarelli, et al., "Comparison of Physical Fitness Parameters for Starters vs. Nonstarters in an NCAA Division I Men's Lacrosse Team," *Journal of Strength and Conditioning Research* 32, no. 11 (2018): 3160-3168.

Table 3.7 Pro Agility Test Times (in Seconds) for College Male Lacrosse Athletes—Moving Right First

Position	Below average	Average	Above average
Defense	4.57	4.31	4.05
Midfield	4.5	4.36	4.22
Attack	4.5	4.36	4.22

Data from K.M. Sell, J.M. Prendergast, J.J. Ghigiarelli, et al., "Comparison of Physical Fitness Parameters for Starters vs. Nonstarters in an NCAA Division I Men's Lacrosse Team," *Journal of Strength and Conditioning Research* 32, no. 11 (2018): 3160-3168.

10-YARD (9 M) DASH

Purpose

The 10-yard (9 m) dash measures acceleration, crucial for lacrosse athletes who need to excel in both offensive and defensive roles. This test, highlighting an athlete's ability to accelerate from a complete stop, combines mobility, strength, and proper sprint mechanics. Effective training in these areas translates directly into improved performance in lacrosse, a sport characterized by frequent starts and stops.

Equipment

- Stopwatch or electronic timing device (if available)
- Cones (2)

Setup

Place the cones on a line 10 yards (9 m) apart.

Testing Protocol

1. Perform a warm-up.

Jacob Kupferman/Getty Images

The 10-yard (9 m) dash assesses acceleration, which is vital for lacrosse players performing effectively in offensive and defensive positions.

2. Complete at least two practice runs at submaximal speed.
3. Assume a three- or four-point stance at the starting line.
4. On command, sprint through the finish line.
5. Perform two trials and record the best outcome to the nearest 0.01 second.
6. Allow at least 2 minutes of active recovery or rest between trials.

Coaching Tips

- Acceleration from a dead stop is a massive competitive advantage in lacrosse.
- Resist the temptation to use flying start tests, because these incorrectly place a greater emphasis on top-end velocity versus linear acceleration.
- Regardless of the final time, the goal is to optimize the first three to four initial strides from a crouched start.

Descriptive Data

See table 3.8 for times for college athletes based on sex (23). Note that the data are for basketball athletes rather than lacrosse athletes, however.

Table 3.8 10-Yard (9 m) Dash Times (in Seconds)

Sex	Below average	Average	Above average
Women	2.0	1.9	1.8
Men	1.8	1.7	1.6

Data from J.A. Zaragoza, Q.R. Johnson, D.J. Lawson, et al., "Relationships Between Lower-Body Power, Sprint and Change of Direction Speed Among Collegiate Basketball Players by Sex," *International Journal of Exercise Science* 15, no. 6 (2022): 974-984.

CONDITIONING ENDURANCE TESTS

Lacrosse, a sport experiencing rapid growth, lacks comprehensive original research on its metabolic demands and the effectiveness of related training programs, which are still in their early stages of development. Most existing studies have tried to modify testing protocols from sports such as soccer, football, and basketball to fit lacrosse's needs. Although these adapted protocols offer a basic framework for metabolic conditioning, they fall short of capturing the unique, rapidly evolving energetic requirements of lacrosse, particularly with the introduction of the shot clock. Consequently, there are no established benchmarks for evaluating and interpreting these tests, underscoring the need to create benchmarks from the tests presented in this chapter.

While setting testing goals and targets is beneficial, strength and conditioning professionals are encouraged to prioritize the continuous improvement of individual athletes' scores over time. While performance standards may vary across different levels, these tests determine which training programs yield the most significant improvements for both individuals and the team. The selected tests are particularly valuable because of their direct relevance to enhancing on-field performance: they assess cardiovascular endurance, pulmonary function, and bicarbonate buffering capacity; evaluate high-speed agility under metabolic stress; and simulate conditioning in game-like scenarios.

ASSAULT BIKE TABATA PROTOCOL

Purpose

The assault bike is a tremendous conditioning tool to develop conditioning and metabolic capacity without the detrimental effects of eccentric loading associated with traditional run conditioning. While this does not replace the need for on-field change-of-direction drills, this tool can effectively evaluate conditioning levels year-round and prevent athletes from getting out of shape. One meta-analysis concluded that Tabata conditioning may provide similar benefits to traditional aerobic training with far less time commitment (22).

Equipment

Assault bike

Setup

Adjust the vertical and horizontal location of the bike seat to allow 10 to 15 degrees of knee flexion at the bottom of the pedal stroke.

Pretest Peak Power Assignment

1. Perform a warm-up.
2. Pedal while pushing and pulling on the handles for 3 to 5 minutes to become familiarized with the equipment.
3. Rest for 1 minute.
4. Perform a maximal-effort burst for 20 seconds.
5. Record peak wattage.

Testing Protocol

1. Calculate each athlete's cutoff point for the test (i.e., the minimal threshold that needs to be maintained during the test to advance to the next round). Use 80% of the peak power (in watts) attained during the pretest to ensure athlete safety.

2. Perform eight 20-second rounds of maximum effort with 10 seconds of rest between rounds. If nausea occurs or if power output drops below the minimum threshold, discontinue the test.

3. Document the following data points (see table 3.9 for an example):
   - Pretest peak power output (in watts)
   - Calculated cutoff point (minimum threshold, in watts)
   - Number of rounds completed
   - Peak power (in watts) for each round
   - Drop-off in peak power from the first round to the last round

Table 3.9   Sample Testing Data for the Assault Bike Tabata Protocol

	Pretest peak power (W)	Cutoff point (W)*	Round 1 (W)	Round 2 (W)	Round 3 (W)	Round 4 (W)	Round 5 (W)	Round 6 (W)	Round 7 (W)	Round 8 (W)
Athlete 1	1,500	1,200	1,500	1,475	1,385	1,350	1,341	1,300	1,275	1,270
Athlete 2	1,610	1,288	1,610	1,410	450	—	—	—	—	---
Athlete 3	1,100	880	1,100	1,058	1,000	955	944	850	—	—

	Rounds completed	Drop-off in peak power
Athlete 1	8	15%
Athlete 2	3	72%
Athlete 3	6	23%

*The cutoff point is 80% of the pretest peak power; a round's wattage lower than the cutoff point indicates the final round was completed.

Coaching Tips

- This is not a conditioning test, and only one attempt is allowed.
- This test should not be performed without sufficient familiarization with the required effort and physiological effects associated with this type of testing.
- It is imperative to pay close attention to the calculated cutoff point for each athlete.
- The goal of this test is to demonstrate the underlying physiology to produce maximum power under metabolic distress.
- This is not a mental toughness drill; allowing or encouraging athletes to push through at lower wattages is counterproductive and can affect athlete safety.
- Especially for larger, more powerful athletes, make sure the equipment is commercial-grade strength and not unstable, especially at higher outputs.

Descriptive Data

See table 3.10 for peak power output values during the assault bike Tabata protocol for college and high school lacrosse athletes.

Table 3.10   Assault Bike Peak Power Output

Group	Peak watts
College males	1,500+
College females	1,100+
High school males	1,100-1,500
High school females	800-1,100

HIGH-VELOCITY 300-YARD (274 M) SHUTTLE

Purpose

The 300-yard (274 m) shuttle is an effective method for assessing anaerobic work capacity and the ability to sustain repeated efforts. Historically, the test involves completing 12 intervals of 25 yards (23 m) each (i.e., six 50-yard [46 m] round-trip laps with 11 changes of direction). However, within the context of lacrosse, a modified version of five 60-yard [55 m] intervals (i.e., two-and-a-half 120-yard [110 m] round-trip laps with four changes of direction) places a greater emphasis on the high velocities sustained throughout the entire duration of the assessment rather than a strength bias toward acceleration going into and out of the turns. This adaptation, developed at the University of Connecticut by Gerry Martin and Dr. William Kraemer (11), provides a more accurate evaluation of anaerobic demands at high velocities common to lacrosse, especially in the open-field nature of the women's game and the post–shot clock era in the men's game.

Equipment

- Stopwatch or electronic timing device (if available)
- Cones (2)

Setup

Place the cones on a line 60 yards (55 m) apart.

Testing Protocol

1. Perform a warm-up.
2. Assume a two-point stance at the starting line.
3. On command, sprint back and forth nonstop, touching the line with a foot at each change of direction.
4. Sprint five lengths with four changes of direction.
5. Sprint through the finish line at the cone opposite to the starting line.
6. Perform two trials with a 3-minute interim rest period.
7. Record the two times and calculate the average to the nearest 0.01 second.

Coaching Tips

- Ensure that the athletes are properly warmed up and have experienced high-velocity running prior to this test.

- Running this test for the purpose of demonstrating lack of conditioning is not advised.
- Athletes fail this test either because they lack the top-end velocity and speed or they lack the buffering capacity to facilitate muscular endurance at the appropriate velocity.

Descriptive Data

See table 3.11 for maximum (i.e., slowest) times for college (11) and high school lacrosse athletes.

Table 3.11   High-Velocity 300-Yard (274 m) Shuttle Times

Group	Maximum time
College defensive and attack athletes	49 s
College midfield athletes	47 s
High school athletes	Add 3 s based on position

Data from G. Martin and W.J. Kraemer, *300 Conditioning* (n.d.).

ANDY SHAY'S BOX PASSING DRILL

Purpose

The box passing drill developed by Andy Shay (18) is used in the final weeks before the season starts, aiming to assess the physical and cognitive abilities honed during the off-season. This drill serves as an excellent method to measure the success of the off-season program. Through this assessment, the coaching staff can pinpoint areas that need further development in the in-season training plan and perform an annual review of the training program's overall effectiveness.

Equipment

- Stopwatch
- Cones (4)
- Lacrosse stick (3)
- Ball

Setup

- Place the 4 cones 10 yards (9 m) apart in a box formation.
- Position three athletes of an equivalent skill level at 3 of the cones (1 cone remains empty).
- Give the ball to the athlete who has the open cone to the left.

Testing Protocol

1. Perform a warm-up.
2. On command, the athlete holding the ball throws it to the athlete to the right and then immediately sprints to the open cone to the left.
3. The athlete who receives the pass catches the ball and immediately passes it to the athlete at the cone to the right, then sprints to the open cone (where the previous athlete just passed from), and the box begins to "spin." The objective of this test is to successfully rotate through the corners of the box as fast as possible for 90 seconds.

Coaching Tips

- Coaches should evaluate who can catch and throw.
- Strength and conditioning professionals should evaluate who cannot make it to the open cone before the ball arrives.
- Both coaches and strength and conditioning professionals should evaluate who becomes fatigued and stop the test due to a drop, lack of speed, or lack of conditioning.
- The test needs three athletes who have both the stick skill and conditioning to achieve optimal results.

Descriptive Data

The box passing drill is designed to objectively assess an athlete's athletic prowess in lacrosse by combining key skills such as passing and catching. This drill categorizes athletes into three main groups based on their performance: underpowered, underconditioned, or lacking in skill. These evaluations are vital for coaching staff to monitor and improve their year-round development program throughout the year. An athlete who arrives at the cone ahead of time but fails to catch and throw accurately is just as disadvantaged as one with high athletic IQ but poor buffering capacity and motor control. Addressing these issues can lead to significant improvements in on-field performance. The drill's purpose is to offer a method to gauge each athlete's progress. The aim is to observe gradual improvements and, using the guidelines below, tailor a program that propels athletes toward elite levels of performance (18):

- Elite time goal: Achieving a time of 90 seconds indicates optimal buffering capacity.
- Passing proficiency: Completing 15 passes demonstrates elite-level stick skills.
- Physical power and speed: Performing 45 spins signifies elite physical strength and agility.

CONCLUSION

The development of lacrosse athletes necessitates a comprehensive strength and conditioning program, with effective testing protocols serving as a vital component. Because lacrosse is a dynamic and physically demanding sport, athletes must acquire a diverse range of physical and cognitive abilities. Using testing protocols that accurately assess these attributes enables coaches and strength and conditioning professionals to design customized training programs, optimizing athlete development.

Ensuring that testing protocols are accurate, reliable, and repeatable is essential. Coaches and strength and conditioning professionals must remain focused on the underlying purpose of each test and effectively communicate this to athletes. This fosters intentionality and commitment to the training programs developed as a result of the testing.

Using the testing protocols from this chapter, coaches and strength and conditioning professionals can facilitate the development of lacrosse athletes with superior physical attributes and cognitive abilities. As lacrosse becomes increasingly competitive, honing these skills is of paramount importance. Through the application of these scientific principles, coaches and strength and conditioning professionals can design customized training programs that enable athletes to reach their full potential, ultimately elevating the game of lacrosse.

4

SPORT-SPECIFIC PROGRAM DESIGN GUIDELINES

NICOLE SHATTUCK AND JL HOLDSWORTH

Lacrosse is a dynamic, fast-paced sport characterized by maneuverability, change of direction, and high-intensity intervals. It combines the speed of football, the contact of hockey, the hand–eye coordination of baseball, the aerobic endurance of cross country, and the dynamic movement and strategy of basketball. Therefore, lacrosse athletes must possess an extremely wide range of physical abilities to excel in their sport. Teams are made up of field athletes and goalkeepers. Field athletes are either attackers, defenders, or midfielders; there are additional considerations for face-off and draw specialists. Indoor athletes are classified as forwards or defenders, with transition athletes similar to a midfielder in field lacrosse. Strength and conditioning professionals should sequence resistance training to improve athletic qualities in a way that will correspond to lacrosse performance; however, different positions dictate certain field constraints and specific physical demands. Therefore, resistance training for lacrosse athletes should progress from general to specific based on the respective field positions.

Programming for lacrosse is just as dynamic as the sport itself. The strength and conditioning professional needs to build all the aforementioned physical qualities and also program for the unique demands of the various positions within the sport.

SPECIFICITY, OVERLOAD, AND ADAPTATION

Lacrosse-specific programs must start by building a solid base of **general physical preparation (GPP)**. All lacrosse athletes will have similar, general needs before specific needs are addressed. Research indicates a need for upper body muscular endurance along with upper and lower body strength and power for the high-intensity shots, passes, cuts, accelerations, decelerations, and body contact and the rapid, repetitive nature of the game (1, 3). Common injuries are knee and ankle sprains, strained hip and groin muscles, anterior cruciate ligament tears, and concussions (3). Additionally, women and girls should be physically prepared for contact but men and boys for collisions. A thoughtful resistance training program, researched and supported by evidence-based practice, can support and enhance common lacrosse actions while reducing the risk of injuries. Programming should start with progressive overload of basic movement patterns in the sagittal, frontal, and transverse planes to improve the general athletic abilities and safety of all lacrosse athletes (1, 3, 4, 15). Once a foundational level of GPP has been reached,

Kevin Hoffman/Getty Images for NLL

Lacrosse requires muscular strength, power, and endurance and strength for shots, passes, cuts, accelerations, decelerations, body contact, and rapid, repetitive movements.

training can then be focused on lacrosse-specific qualities. The lacrosse-specific aspects of the program should be based on the needs determined by the information presented in chapter 2.

Core, Assistance, and Special Exercises

Next, it is important to know the exercises that will structure a resistance training program. The National Strength and Conditioning Association (NSCA) classifies exercises as core, assistance, and special exercises (13). **Core exercises** are primary or main multijoint movements, not to be confused with exercises for the anatomical core area of the body. The two different core exercise types are structural and power movements. **Structural exercises** are multijoint movements, such as squats or deadlifts, that involve direct or indirect axial loading to challenge posture with the greatest number of muscles. **Power exercises** are like structural exercises in that they are multijoint movements that recruit many muscle fibers, but they are performed faster due to the explosive nature of the movements (4, 13, 14). **Assistance exercises** involve less muscle mass and are single-joint movements, such as hamstring curls or single-arm rows. **Special exercises** can sometimes resemble the more widely used core and assistance exercises. The difference is that special exercises have execution modifications that create sport-specific physical adaptations. These adaptations allow athletes to achieve larger performance improvements in their sport or position. Examples are a rotational medicine ball toss or certain cable machine movements for a face-off or draw specialist. These will be discussed in the position-specific section of this chapter.

Sagittal, Frontal, and Transverse Planes

Because strength and conditioning professionals select resistance training exercises, they must identify spaces in which lacrosse athletes will move. Lacrosse athletes run forward and laterally and rotate in coordinated patterns; it is unlikely that an athlete will be isolated to one plane of movement. The three planes are referred to as the sagittal, frontal, and transverse planes based on the standard anatomical position of standing upright with the palms forward (supinated) (13). Resistance training exercises are typically classified as linear (sagittal plane), lateral (frontal plane), and rotational (transverse plane) patterns. It is important to account for all planes to build a balanced program that will support an athlete's strength and power and the proper application and direction of forces.

A program's exercises must also create an effective and balanced line-of-movement profile. A line of movement refers to the musculature and directionality of movement being trained in an exercise. A program with imbalanced lines of movement produces a higher likelihood of injury. For example, training that uses only upper body pushes and neglects upper body pulls may lead to a higher potential for shoulder injuries.

Sport-Specific Resistance Training

According to the **specific adaptation to imposed demand** (SAID) principle, an athlete's body will adapt to a stimulus given the muscle group, intensity, and joint angles involved (9, 13). The more closely resistance training mimics the biomechanics, direction and intensity of force application, and energy systems of the sport, the greater the transfer will be to athletic performance (10, 15). Simply put, a lacrosse-specific program must effectively train the entire body, from feet to fingers, to be strong, powerful, and mobile.

To produce higher-performing lacrosse athletes, the overload must be high enough to create a training stimulus without injuring the athlete. Hans Seyle identified the **general adaptation syndrome** (GAS) in the 1930s. There are four phases to consider for resistance training: alarm, resistance, supercompensation, and overtraining (13). Intentional increases and reductions of volume, intensity, and frequency of resistance training allow athletes to realize the gains of their training and perform at a high level at specific times; this is known as periodization. The GAS indicates how the athlete's body will respond to physical stressors, and it can be applied to periodization models (figure 4.1).

The alarm phase occurs when training is introduced to an athlete at baseline. Fatigue and soreness from the novel stimulus will usually decrease performance until the system reaches either the resistance or overtraining phase. Planned adjustments of training stresses will allow adaptations to occur so that the individual can return to baseline (13). Supercompensation is achieved once adaptations have been realized, but pushing past the point of adequate recovery or adding too much work before the individual is ready will result in overtraining or injury. Recovery is necessary for a new baseline to be established; otherwise, training variables will need to be reduced. For example, beginner athletes have been shown to benefit from different training models than elite athletes (5), which is discussed later in this chapter.

Attributes to consider when deciding on the appropriate level of overloading include training age, biological age, and medical and injury history. Physical stress can be calculated with an understanding of metrics such as exercise load, volume, and intensity. While the general theory of overload is simple, accurately predicting overload requires understanding the stressors throughout the entire life of an athlete. Stressors resulting from a resistance training program are just a small part of the overall stressors that must be considered when planning the appropriate amount of overload. Unintentional overtraining or injury could occur without accounting for sport-skill practices, conditioning during practice, and life outside of the sport (6).

The appropriate level of overload will also vary by position. These variations are based on many factors, including typical body types, strength profiles, and metabolic demands. For

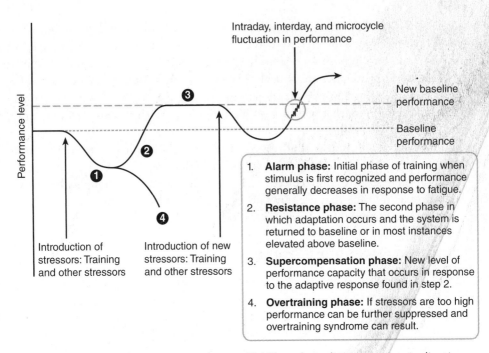

Figure 4.1   General adaptation syndrome (GAS) and application in periodization.

example, goalies can typically handle a higher amount of overload stress than midfielders. However, strength and conditioning professionals should be mindful of prescribing overload strategies based on position alone. A comprehensive needs analysis is the most accurate way to assess the needs of an athlete. In addition, the only way to know if the needs analysis and overload strategies were effective is by administering pretesting and posttesting for the desired training adaptations.

The NSCA and Collegiate Strength and Conditioning Coaches Association (CSCCa) have collaborated on a statement for introducing, or reintroducing, stress after an unknown or extended time off (2). For example, high school lacrosse athletes returning to activity after a winter break may require a more gradual reacclimatization than when returning from a summer break during which they were regularly playing for a club team. Following the frequency, intensity, and time (FIT) guidelines will provide athletes with a safe return to top lacrosse form (2).

Strength Adaptation for Lacrosse Athletes

Strength and conditioning professionals identify the role of strength in lacrosse movements and then implement resistance training protocols accordingly. The spectrum of strength qualities ranges from muscular endurance and size to strength abilities at different speeds (or rates) and maximal force production (4, 14, 15, 16). This chapter will focus on muscular strength, hypertrophy, and maximal strength to improve the direction, magnitude, and rate of force production.

The most common sport-specific movements for lacrosse athletes are cradling, catching, passing, or shooting the ball. The passing or shooting actions require a strong lower body to initiate the movement, a solid trunk to transfer the force, and strong arms to finish the motion as a mobile torso and shoulder joints allow the stick to follow through. Consider a long pass across the field from one defender to another. To accomplish this task, the athlete will benefit from full range of motion squats and Romanian deadlifts to address the lower body, heavy

Isaiah Vazquez/Getty Images

Passing requires a strong lower body to initiate movement, a solid trunk to transfer force, and strong arms to finish, while a mobile torso and shoulder joints enable follow-through.

dumbbell carries for a stable trunk, and pull-ups and push-ups for upper body strength and muscular endurance throughout the end ranges. Therefore, GPP for lacrosse athletes should include squat, hinge, push, pull, and rotational patterns along with loaded carries, with an emphasis on muscular endurance and size. Lacrosse movements require strength as well as quick, reactive outputs; therefore, improving the rate of force development (RFD) is critical for all lacrosse athletes (13).

Power Adaptation for Lacrosse Athletes

Power classification falls within the strength–speed and speed–strength qualities of the strength spectrum (4, 14, 16), which indicate that strength is being trained but account for the speed of the movement at various intensities. Power can be trained with structural exercises; however, power exercises, such as Olympic lifts, along with certain specialty exercises, such as medicine ball and kettlebell exercises, are ways to develop RFD and repetitive, explosive qualities for lacrosse athletes. These movements maximize mechanical power outputs when performed at low and medium loads (but not maximal loads), due to their ballistic nature (15, 16). The limitation to be aware of with medicine ball and kettlebell exercises is the ability to progressively overload, but these exercises are useful when incorporating rotational or coordinated patterns that mimic lacrosse movements. Plyometrics will also increase RFD for quick, powerful athletic movements (13). The foot and ankle complex should be strong yet mobile for both performance and injury-reduction purposes for lacrosse athletes; this will be discussed more in the section on plyometrics in chapter 6.

SPORT-SPECIFIC GOALS OF A RESISTANCE TRAINING PROGRAM

The goal of a lacrosse-specific resistance training program should be to build muscular endurance, size, strength, and power qualities that will enhance lacrosse actions and transfer to the field. Some exercises may resemble the sport's actions but will not involve equipment such as a stick, ball, goggles, or helmet in the same way. Some exercises may look nothing like the sport itself but are used to achieve certain physiological adaptations that can improve athletic qualities (e.g., force, rate, or frequency of muscle contractions), progress range of motion, or fortify an area of the body that may be at risk for injuries (4, 12, 13, 15). An effective lacrosse training program uses appropriate exercises to train all planes of motion (sagittal, frontal, and transverse). It is important to account for all three planes to build a balanced program that will support an athlete's strength and power and include the proper application and direction of forces.

A program's exercises must also create an effective and balanced line-of-movement profile. The line of movement refers to the musculature and directionality of movement being trained in an exercise. As previously explained, a program with imbalanced lines of movement produces a higher likelihood of injury.

Programs for female and male athletes will have some different goals as well. The primary difference in the resistance training goals stems from the need for female athletes to be physically prepared for contact and for male athletes to be physically prepared for collisions. Collisions require more hypertrophy, neck strength, and trunk stability work than contact alone.

The goal of this chapter is to equip strength and conditioning professionals with the understanding, tools, and ability to address lacrosse athletes' needs. The effective application of the various strength qualities and the implementation of special exercises is one of the paramount aspects of achieving maximal results. The next section will discuss the other paramount aspect: position-specific exercise selection.

POSITION-SPECIFIC EXERCISE SELECTION

The notion of position-specific exercises stems from the SAID principle; there are tissue needs and joint angles specific to certain field positions, because positions have particular roles and designated areas in the field of play. When the physical requirements are different, the strength and conditioning program must also be different to be effective. A strength and conditioning professional can assign position-specific resistance training exercises for the various positions by identifying differences in reaction needs, lateral movements, explosive acceleration and deceleration, balance, conditioning, and hand–stick–ball–eye coordination, as discussed in the previous section. The more similarly resistance training reflects the biomechanical actions and metabolic outputs of the sport, the greater the likelihood of transfer and improvement of performance variables (13, 15). The velocity, intensity, volume, and rest periods assigned to each of the following exercise descriptions are determined by the sport and position analysis from chapter 2.

Attackers

Attackers need to accelerate and reach high speeds quickly within approximately 5 to 20 yards (4.6-18 m). They move around other athletes or the crease and are sometimes needed in defensive plays when pressing an opponent who is clearing the ball. Attackers use passing, catching, and shooting, which call for upper body muscular endurance, strength, power, and trunk mobility.

An attacker's lower body movements are classified as dodging and off-ball cuts. Various dodges include the split dodge, which is a lateral movement into a sprint; the face dodge, which involves advancing and evading by reaccelerating; and the roll dodge around a defender. Off-ball cuts can be linear or curvilinear or include a quick change of direction to evade a defender.

Due to the force demands placed on attackers' bodies in end-range positions, attackers are best served by loaded hip and trunk mobility exercises. These exercises not only improve the resilience at end ranges but also increase the ability to create space while shooting or passing. Some examples of this exercise group are full range of motion front squats, T-spine mobility drills, and Turkish get-ups.

The ability of an attacker to explode laterally out of a cut or dodge can be a game changer. Single-leg, lateral-drive exercises are just what attackers need to create that game-changing speed. Squats and deadlifts, while beneficial for training the hip muscles, are primarily done on two legs and often in a linear manner. In single-leg, lateral-drive exercises, such as an LAX lunge or crossover step-up, not only is the athlete on a single leg but the working leg is actively driving the body laterally or angularly. This combination of attributes makes it an ideal exercise for attackers.

High-velocity, single-leg plyometric exercises are not for beginner athletes. However, for attackers with a solid foundation and training age, these exercises can help take their game to the next level. Many variations of these exercises can be used. Adding a foam crash pad to dive onto at the end of a plyometric exercise makes the exercise more attack-specific, requiring the greater proprioception and body control needed for diving into the crease to score.

Strength and conditioning professionals should program resistance training movements with full range of motion to promote strength and mobility, power exercises for explosive movements and first-step acceleration, and both intensive and extensive plyometrics for lacrosse attackers.

Midfielders

Midfielders typically run faster and more than other field positions (1, 3). A midfielder might play on one or both sides of the field, so the position requires attention to attack- and defense-specific resistance training as well as a developed aerobic capacity for transitioning between zones or for substitution purposes. The demands for more distance may fatigue midfielders differently, and strength and conditioning professionals should be aware of this during the training cycles.

Important movement styles used by midfielders are sprinting in one direction with the upper body turned another direction, linear acceleration, high-velocity deceleration, power snap rotations, and shoulder checking. There are three types of position-specific resistance training exercises that especially help midfielders to become more dynamic and, just as importantly, to stay healthy. These exercise types are rotational power exercises while moving, rapid force-yielding exercises, and contralateral exercises.

Midfielders must be able to shoot and pass the ball quickly, while moving, to be effective in their position. Rotational power exercises, such as rotational medicine ball throws, are important for all lacrosse athletes but even more so for midfielders. Furthermore, a midfielder must be able to execute the skills of the position while sprinting in various styles. Rotational power exercises for midfielders need to incorporate movement during the exercises. Many traditional rotational power exercises are performed from a stationary position. However, midfielders are rarely standing still when they quickly fire off a shot or pass. Therefore, incorporating some type of movement while executing rotational power exercises will greatly increase the training transfer from the resistance training to the midfielder's performance on the field. A simple way to do this is to have the midfielder run past a wall and do an explosive medicine ball throw into the wall while running, as opposed to standing still in front of the wall.

In the men's game, a midfielder contends with constant external forces being violently applied by opposing athletes. Rapid force-yielding exercises, which require a midfielder to decelerate loads quickly, help the athlete prepare for the types of physical stresses present during games and practices. It is essential that rapid force-yielding exercises are done for both the upper and lower body. An example of a rapid force-yielding lower body exercise is an altitude drop. An example of a rapid force-yielding upper body exercise is a throw/stop, which entails using a variation of a medicine ball throw but stopping the throw before the ball can leave the hands.

Power for shots and passes happens by transferring force from the leg opposite to the stick side. **Contralateral exercises** train the lower body on one side and the upper body on the opposite side. Strong contralateral systems are therefore crucial to ensuring powerful shots and passes. Common contralateral exercises are the Copenhagen plank, suitcase carry, and lateral bonding into a unilateral throw. Midfielders have the most dynamic position on the field. Therefore, their resistance training must prepare them accordingly.

Defenders

The ability to rapidly accelerate and decelerate can make or break a defender's ability to cut off an attacker or win out a ground ball; defenders will also need to reach high speeds within short distances. Back squats are one of the best ways to develop total and lower body strength, but split squats and other unilateral lower body movements are highly predictive for change-of-direction movements (8). Olympic lifts and derivatives support repeated high-intensity efforts and should also be included in defenders' position-specific resistance training.

Defenders cannot push an offensive athlete out of their intended path if they cannot maintain their own position. Trunk stability and strength allow defenders to maintain their position and stifle the offense. Stronger trunk stability also allows for a more efficient transfer of lower body power into the upper body. This increased force transfer makes for much more impactful checking by the defender.

Defenders also use their sticks to check or intercept passes. Although they may not pass as much as other positions, upper body muscular endurance is still an emphasis for defenders (1, 3). In the women's game, defenders bilaterally push (or check), approach, shift or slide laterally, and react to the opposing team's offensive advances. In the men's game, in addition to those skills, crossover running, checking, anchoring, and chopping are primary movements for defenders. Defenders in men's lacrosse need to be able to push and pull at the same time to use their stick most effectively against attackers. Traditional resistance training includes pushing and pulling exercises. These exercises will usually emphasize the push or pull more, depending on the exercise, but both actions build the strength that defenders need on the field. An example of a simultaneous pushing and pulling exercise is a single-arm dumbbell press with a unilateral row.

Goalies

Lacrosse goalies have the most unique needs out of all positions. Goalies maintain a 6-yard (5.5 m) crease and 2-yard × 2-yard (1.8 m × 1.8 m) cage and have significantly lower running volumes than the other positions (1, 3) (see the USA Lacrosse website, www.usalacrosse.com/field-diagrams). Although the position of the goal is different on a men's and women's field, the goal and circle are the same size. Goalies stand in an athletic, quarter-squat position while holding a goalie stick upright. They slide laterally within the frame of the cage to maintain position, react to a shot, drop or land in a split for low shots, or chase a wide shot, and they are often involved in a clear after a defensive stop. The density of a goalie's play is higher, but rest time during games and practices can be longer due to constraints of the position.

The unique demands of a goalie are best trained through using a few different types of position-specific exercises. Single-effort power repeats, ankle–foot complex strengthening, and hip abduction exercises are more essential to goalies than to other positions on the field.

Goalies must produce high power outputs in rapid succession. Exercises that train this quality will help goalies increase and maintain their quickness at the net. These exercises can be loaded with external resistance or body weight. An example of this type of exercise is a barbell push press to improve the ability to react to high shots. The exercises must have short rest intervals between the repetitions but a longer rest between sets. Using no rest between sets simply becomes a conditioning exercise instead of training the desired trait.

The ankle–foot complex is important for all lacrosse athletes. However, it is even more so for a goalie. A weak ankle–foot complex could make the difference between stopping a shot and the other team scoring a goal. All power transmission through the hips and legs must be supported and transferred by a strong ankle–foot complex. A weak ankle–foot complex could make the goalie's feet look like they are stuck in sand. One of the best ways to train the ankle–foot complex is to incorporate a floating heel in traditional lower body exercises. A floating heel means the heel is slightly elevated and unsupported during the exercise. This slight elevation of the heel requires the forefoot to support the load and force generated. Beyond building strength, goalies are well served to spend time on exercises that increase the mobility of the ankles as well.

Hip abduction powers a goalie from one side of the net to the other. Strengthening the hip abductor muscles is crucial to improving a goalie's power in the net. The ability of the goalie to explosively push laterally is drastically improved by training hip abduction. Many lower body exercises work hip abduction, but exercises that develop the maximal strength of hip abduction will help the goalie's performance most. Great examples of this type of exercise are landmine lateral acceleration single-leg squats and slide board activities.

Other Considerations

Face-off and draw specialists require training for the unique demands of their position. Men and boys initiate the face-off in a crouched position; therefore, loaded sled pushes that mimic the joint angles would be beneficial. Women and girls perform the draw in an athletic stance with the ball at chest level; the ball must be thrust into the air on the whistle. Machine-based pulley systems, suspension training attachments, and different cable machines can be used to assign special exercises that can mimic the reactive pulls and pushes of this skill. Overall, upper and lower body strength and power for reactivity and ball placement, as well as trunk stability, can make a difference in the success of this specialist position.

There are many differences between men's and women's lacrosse. These differences need to be considered when designing a program. For example, the increased contact of men's lacrosse requires more hypertrophy work to build more cross-sectional muscle that attenuates injury from impact. Preparing for body contact may be reflected in maintaining the upper body **general preparation phase** (also abbreviated as *GPP*) throughout the year, neck strengthening for both wearing helmets and protecting against concussions, and trunk training exercises using isometrics or with perturbations.

TRAINING FREQUENCY

Training frequency for lacrosse athletes, usually defined within a period of one week, will depend on the athletes' training age and time of year. Novice (untrained) athletes should do two or three resistance training sessions per week, intermediate-trained athletes should do three or four, and advanced (well-trained) athletes should do four to seven (13). It is recommended that resistance training be spaced out through the week to allow for recovery; more than three days between sessions could result in undertraining, but training too frequently could result in overtraining. However, it is not uncommon to train on back-to-back days. Strength and conditioning professionals who plan consecutive sessions should be aware of exercise selection and order. A split training model might make the most sense to provide enough stimulus and recovery between training exposures, especially with more advanced athletes. For example, grouping lower body exercises on Monday and Thursday and upper body exercises on Tuesday and Friday allows athletes to maintain their training status throughout the week, because the sessions stress different muscle groups. The concepts of training frequency are further outlined in the periodization section of this chapter and detailed throughout chapters 9 to 12.

EXERCISE ORDER

Strength and conditioning professionals should arrange exercises appropriately within a training session for safety and the best possible training outcomes. Exercise order is important, because some movements can affect an athlete's ability to perform subsequent exercises within a session. This is known as **priority training** (5, 13). Power exercises should precede structural movements, with single-joint movements and trunk stability exercises at the end of the session. For example, box jumps should be performed before back squats and back squats before a single-arm dumbbell row. This order allows athletes to perform the most difficult and metabolically taxing exercises first, with maximal effort (7, 11).

The exercise order recommended below is optimal for general training adaptation goals. Not all exercise categories need to be used in a single training session.

1. Performance preparation, injury prevention, and prehab-type of exercises
2. General warm-up exercises
3. Specific warm-up exercises
4. Activation or potentiation exercises to prepare for power or plyometric exercises
5. Plyometric exercises
6. Power (single or repeat) exercises
7. Structural exercises
8. Accessory and special exercises
9. Conditioning

Some strategies to manage a session involve grouping exercises in a certain way. A **compound set** is the pairing of two exercises that address the same muscle group, which can cause fatigue (13). Sometimes fatigue is the goal for single-joint exercises, but a more effective way to improve strength and power is to allow the muscles to fully recover. Supersets and circuits can manage rest periods efficiently (13). **Supersets** are two exercises targeting different muscle groups. **Circuits** combine three or more movements separated by a rest interval that must be completed in succession before the next block of exercise. This can also be a great way to manage larger groups of athletes.

INTENSITY

Exercise intensity in the weight room is usually quantified by weight. The weight is often based off a 1-repetition maximum (1RM) (13). **Load**, on the other hand, is the absolute expression of the weight lifted. For example, for one athlete, a heavy load in a squat could be 200 pounds (90.7 kg). However, that 200-pound (90.7 kg) squat would only be a 50% intensity exercise for an athlete who can squat 400 pounds (181.4 kg). Conversely, a body weight push-up has an intensity of 100% for an athlete who can only complete one push-up.

Therefore, this section suggests other means that may be used to quantify intensity, such as an **estimated 1RM** (e1RM), using velocity training guidelines, and educating athletes on autoregulation methods for intensity.

One-Repetition Maximum

Resistance training becomes more individualized and effective when it is more relative to the athlete's abilities. A 1RM is expressed as a percentage of the athlete's maximal, relative output for the exercise (13). For example, 80% of a 225-pound (102.1 kg) 1RM back squat is 180 pounds (81.6 kg), and that would be the suggested weight for training power qualities, depending on the sets and repetitions. Other repetition maximums, such as e1RM, 3RM, 6RM, and 10RM, may be preferred in certain situations, because 1RM testing can be taxing and time consuming and is not usually advised for novice athletes (13). The RM relationship indicates that a moderate number of repetitions at ≥85% will increase maximal and absolute strength, power ranges for strength–speed and speed–strength qualities are between 75% and 90%, hypertrophy is between 67% and 85%, and muscular endurance is 67% or less. Intensity, volume, and rest are shown collectively in table 4.1.

Power exercises, such as Olympic lifts and derivatives, have similar RM intensity parameters as structural and assistance exercises. The force–velocity (F-V) curve will be more useful for power exercise prescriptions and is discussed next.

The Force–Velocity Curve

The elicited adaptations from a program must be relevant to the physical qualities required to excel in lacrosse. If not, then the time spent training for those adaptations was wasted. For example, a program that focuses solely on absolute strength will likely decrease speed and increase movement stiffness, neither of which is good for lacrosse. This is why a lacrosse program is not just about getting an adaptation but also about programming for the right adaptations.

The **F-V curve** represents the relationship of higher loads with lower velocity and lower loads with higher velocity. The F-V curve relationship guidelines can provide more specific goals based on percentages of the 1RM (4, 15). Structural exercises can also fall on the curve but should be evaluated by measuring average velocity, whereas peak velocity is the appropriate metric for evaluating Olympic lifts and their derivatives. The goal of a resistance training program should be to make improvements across all intensities, velocities, and muscular contractions. Eccentric, concentric, and isometric F-V relationships provide additional insights, but they are beyond the scope of this chapter.

Velocity-Based Training

Coaches and strength and conditioning professionals can use **velocity-based training** (VBT) to improve power outputs by developing RFD. There are VBT technologies, such as TENDO Units, Perch, or EliteForm, that can give direct feedback on intensity and the set–repetition scheme while an athlete is lifting. Strength and conditioning professionals should research the validity and reliability of any technology before purchasing it to ensure that the device will accurately and consistently measure what it says it will (5). VBT can be used year-round but is especially useful in-season when high-minute athletes are more fatigued and low-minute athletes can have an opportunity to develop; athletes can still achieve resistance training goals without overdoing or underdoing it by adjusting during their resistance training sessions.

Olympic Weightlifting Derivatives

Due to the complexity of a clean or snatch, an athlete's ability to gain the full benefits may be impaired when the exercise is performed incorrectly. Olympic weightlifting derivatives are variations that remove part of the movement and can be a safer, more efficient option when implemented within a team setting (14). Additionally, by removing the catch of a heavy barbell in a clean pull, strength and conditioning professionals can accommodate athletes with restrictions such as limited shoulder or wrist mobility. Because Olympic weightlifting derivatives still involve triple extension and will recruit high amounts of muscle fibers, they can be just as effective as the full movement when programmed appropriately (4, 14). Percentage guidelines still apply to Olympic weightlifting derivatives; however, changing the start position (hang, midthigh, or floor) creates some overlaps in the F-V relationship (4, 14). The NSCA's position statement suggests effective programming guidelines that are shown in figure 4.2.

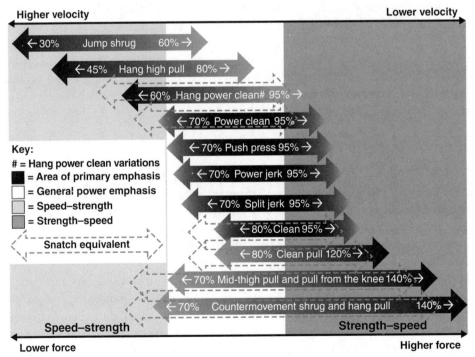

Figure 4.2 F-V characteristics for Olympic weightlifting derivatives.

Reprinted by permission from P. Comfort, G.G. Haff, T.J. Suchomel, et al., "National Strength and Conditioning Association Position Statement on Weightlifting for Sports Performance, "*Journal of Strength and Conditioning Research* 37, no. 6 (2023): 1163-1190.

Autoregulating Progressive Resistance Exercise

Estimating a 1RM may be helpful, but **autoregulating progressive resistance exercise** (APRE) methods quantify intensities based on a subjective scale. They can give more flexibility within a resistance training program and are shown to be more effective than linear periodization for NCAA Division I athletes (9). Using their 3RM, 6RM, and 10RM, athletes will have some autonomy by managing their weights based on their performance using 4-set protocols. Athletes then carry over the weight to the next training session. The benefit to using APRE is that technology is not necessary; athletes and coaches get direct feedback. However, APRE may be more appropriate for intermediate and advanced athletes.

VOLUME

Volume refers to the total repetitions and sets performed during a training session. Sets are separated by a rest period. Repetitions are the number of times an exercise is performed within a set before a rest. **Training volume** can be calculated as repetitions × sets. The athlete's training age, strength levels, sex, current nonresistance training stressors, current health status, and program goals are just some of the factors considered when prescribing volume. While all of these factors are important, the primary variable used to determine training volume for lacrosse athletes is the time of year relative to the lacrosse season.

During the preparatory phase, an athlete generally engages in high-volume, low-intensity exercise to increase work capacity during the off-season. This is important for developing muscular endurance and cross-sectional areas of the muscles, which will prepare the athlete to take on greater loads during preseason and in-season training (13, 16). Low-volume, high-intensity resistance training should be prescribed in-season to maintain adaptations while limiting fatigue. Strength and conditioning professionals can align the desired adaptations with a combination of repetitions and sets, as shown in table 4.1.

REST PERIODS

Rest periods between sets are necessary to resistance training. Intensity and volume are inversely related; high-intensity exercises require a lower volume and more rest time, whereas low-intensity exercises involve a higher volume and less rest time. Therefore, back squats at 85% of the 1RM require enough rest between sets to maintain the exercise intensity necessary for muscle growth and strength adaptation (7, 13). Muscular endurance requires 30 seconds or less of rest, because the intensity is relatively low and the number of repetitions will be somewhat higher;

Table 4.1 Resistance Training Guidelines: Intensity, Volume, and Rest

Training emphasis	Intensity (%1RM)	Ideal reps per set	Ideal sets per session	Rest period
Strength	≥85%	1-6	2-6	2 to 5 min
Power: single effort	80%-90%	1-2	3-5	2 to 5 min
Power: repeated effort	75%-85%	3-5	3-5	2 to 5 min
Hypertrophy	67%-85%	6-12	3-6	30 s to 1.5 min
Muscular endurance	≤67%	≥12	2-3	≤30 s

Adapted by permission from J.M. Sheppard and N.T. Triplett, "Program Design for Resistance Training," in *Essentials of Strength Training and Conditioning*, 4th ed., edited for the National Strength and Conditioning Association by G.G. Haff and N.T. Triplett (Champaign, IL: Human Kinetics, 2016), 458.

for hypertrophy, athletes need 30 to 90 seconds of rest between sets; and for strength and power, they need longer rest periods, ranging from 2 to 5 minutes (7, 13). Table 4.1 provides a summary of resistance training guidelines. Of note, supersets and circuits may not need the same amount of rest between exercises if the movements target different muscle groups.

PERIODIZATION

Periodization is defined as planned changes in load, intensity, and frequency of training that allow athletes to realize the gains of training and perform at a high level at specific times. Linear periodization involves planned increases and decreases in training load. However, in-season, lacrosse athletes need to peak for every game, making nonlinear (undulating) periodization models more appropriate; these are discussed later in this section (6, 14).

The annual plan is separated into *preparatory, competition*, and *transition* phases. The phases contain smaller training blocks, referred to as *macrocycles, mesocycles, microcycles, training days,* and *training sessions* (13). Planning out the variables of each cycle starts with the end in mind and requires regular evaluation to see if the athletes are responding appropriately to the stimuli. The following are the two most important things to ask: "Where are the athletes now?" and "Where do they need to be by the end of the next six weeks? Semester? Year?" Once the strength and conditioning professional evaluates the athletes, training can be sequenced from assessments, training age, and history based on the time of year. A logical progression from muscular endurance to hypertrophy to strength to power can guide the planning process for preparatory, transition, and competition phases (15). There are several practical training models to consider when putting all or several pieces of an annual plan together. Periodization terms are found in table 4.2 at the end of this section.

Training Phases

The **preparatory phase** is made up of GPP and involves a variety of higher-volume, lower-intensity resistance training exercises to physiologically prepare the athletes. Higher volume muscular endurance and hypertrophy resistance training are a focus of the preparatory phase for lacrosse. Much of the preparatory phase makes up the lacrosse off-season. Developing muscular endurance and size improves the magnitude and rate of force production; accomplishing this early on in an annual plan will allow for greater strength and power adaptations later (14). The frequency of resistance training sessions will be highest during this phase.

The **competition phase** may last several months. It can be broken into several smaller cycles (macrocycles, mesocycles, or microcycles) to complement practices and game demands as the season progresses, but the overall goal is to maintain strength and power adaptations from previous phases while reducing the risk of injuries. Improvements can be made during the competition phase, but these are harder to achieve. Resistance training sessions will likely drop to once or twice per week, depending on the competition schedule. Feedback from athletes is important for managing stressors throughout the phase using e1RM, APRE, or VBT and improving recovery habits to keep the athletes healthy.

There are typically two **transition phases** within an annual plan, commonly referred to as the preseason and postseason by lacrosse athletes and coaches. A strength and conditioning professional may include another transition phase as needed. Preseason transition phases carry over the strength and power developments from previous cycles with an emphasis on overreaching before the season begins. Postseason transition phases are notably different and should be focused on active recovery for the athletes (13). Reduced volume, intensity, and frequency of training will be necessary after the competition phase. Lacrosse is physically demanding, which is why athletes should be encouraged to stay active to limit complete detraining and longer reacclimatization.

One nuance to consider for every lacrosse training phase is team building. Success in lacrosse is much easier with great team culture and cohesion. During certain phases of the year, coaches and athletes may spend little time together. During these times, team building is crucial for maintaining the integrity of the team.

Training Cycles

Training cycles are blocks of training that have a specific progression and structure. The annual cycle is the standard one-year plan, although multiyear cycles would make sense for college athletes. Macrocycles last several months, mesocycles last several weeks, and microcycles are usually represented as 7-day periods but can range from 2 to 14 days. Training days can involve multiple training sessions (14). How the training cycles are organized will be determined by the periodization training model.

Periodization Training Models

A periodization training model will define how cycles and phases are structured to achieve certain outcomes (10). Training models that allow for one quality to be the focus of a training block before progressing to the next are called **sequential training** (5). This seems great in theory, but the practical outcomes are not guaranteed. Focusing on a single quality, such as hypertrophy, could lead to loss of other strength and power adaptations, especially if the athletes are training concurrently in the weight room and on the field (9). Thus, sequential training models are less ideal for lacrosse.

The **parallel training model** exposes athletes to various stimuli within a training session, day, or microcycle (5). It is easy to overtrain athletes with low training age. Fewer training sessions are needed but more types of training can be included in a session, which is why the parallel training model may be useful in some lacrosse resistance training instances. Developmental athletes, such as novices or youths, respond better when skills or qualities are trained simultaneously due to their lower tolerance for training load. Consideration of appropriate load, intensity, and volume is important to reduce the risk of overtraining and burnout.

The **emphasis training model** is ideal for intermediate- to high-level athletes with busy training and competition schedules, because they need greater stimuli to improve performance (5). This type of training, popularized by Charlie Francis, is preferred for team sports that need to peak throughout the season. When planning a block of training, there will be a main emphasis with secondary and tertiary goals. The emphasis training model allows athletes to improve strength without neglecting muscular endurance or power. The programming can progressively overload the muscles in an efficient and effective way from one block to the next, decrease the likelihood of detraining of adaptations from previous phases, and limit disruption to any field training. For example, certain exercises, such as high-intensity squats or explosive Olympic movements, pair well with sprinting, plyometric activities, or a practice that involves one-on-one drills and small-sided games (7). Bench presses, assistance movements, and medicine ball exercises complement practices or conditioning that have more full-field or strategic install days. Most importantly, the emphasis training model is useful for planning undulating cycles of training. Consecutive training days can occur while promoting recovery because the model groups high-stress activities and lower-stress activities, which is why it has become common within collegiate sport performance programs and is appropriate for lacrosse resistance training programs.

The best approach is to coordinate resistance training and conditioning elements with the coach, but this is not always possible (6, 7). A coach may plan training sessions that range from high-speed, game-like practices to slower, skill-development practices. There are infinite possibilities of load generated by a coach's practice plan. On top of this, the practice may deviate from the coach's intended plan. The resulting physical demands must be considered when planning the appropriate amount of overload.

Collaboration can help achieve desired adaptations by overloading the more advanced athletes on certain days while using other training days as part of the recovery process, as discussed in the Training Frequency section of this chapter. Strength and conditioning professionals should take time to learn the athletes' daily, weekly, and monthly plans to best prepare resistance training protocols. It should be noted that although recovery is important, full recovery is not always necessary. The science can provide a road map, but the art is knowing when to push athletes to the next level.

Table 4.2 Periodization Terms

	Period	Duration	Description
Phase	Preparatory	Several months	Aligns with the off-season with a goal of developing a base level of strength and conditioning and GPP. Involves higher volume, lower training intensities, and a greater variety of training modes.
	Competition	Several months	Lacrosse athletes and teams will need to perform in practices and on game day. Resistance training should aim to reduce the risk of injuries by maintaining strength and power gains from previous training cycles.
	Transition	2 to 4 weeks	Occurs before and after the competition period, usually referred to as "preseason" or "postseason." Preseason transition is used to elevate strength and power adaptations. Postseason transition is marked by active rest and unloading.
Cycle	Multiyear plan	2 to 4 years	Multiple annual plans linked together.
	Annual plan	1 year	Divided into preparatory, competitive, and transition cycles as the various macrocycles.
	Macrocycle	Several months, up to a year	Composed of several mesocycles.
	Mesocycle	2 to 6 weeks	Commonly known as a "training block"; usually lasts 4 weeks.
	Microcycle	Several days, up to 2 weeks	Shorter, day-to-day planning of training sessions within a 2- to 14-day period. Typically lasts 7 days (1 week).
	Training session	Several hours	Resistance training, lacrosse practice, or both. A training day could have multiple training sessions, separated by 30 min or more of rest.

Adapted by permission from G.G. Haff and E.E. Haff, "Training Integration and Periodization," in *NSCA's Guide to Program Design*, 2nd ed., edited for the National Strength and Conditioning Association by Margaret T. Jones (Champaign, IL: Human Kinetics, 2025), 265.

CONCLUSION

Lacrosse athletes need to be strong and powerful to acquire possession of the ball and score more goals than the opposition. The elements of sport- and position-specific resistance training must support the athlete's development throughout the year and his or her playing career. To achieve this, a strong foundation of general physical preparedness must be established before progressing to more sport-specific programming. This foundation includes basic movements that can be progressed for the strength and power needed in practices and games. The combination of the foundational and sport-specific knowledge needed to build a high-performing lacrosse athlete demonstrates why resistance training for lacrosse is as dynamic as the sport.

PART II

EXERCISE TECHNIQUE

5

TOTAL BODY EXERCISE TECHNIQUE

JL HOLDSWORTH AND EDWARD R. SMITH, JR.

The game of lacrosse is fast and explosive. Whether in an out-the-front face-off win by a team's face off, get off (FOGO), a game-winning shot diving across the crease from an attacker, a loose ball pickup, or a double rebound shot save by a goalie, lacrosse athletes must be able to absorb and generate force at a high level to be successful. They must use their whole body proficiently, whether they are offensive or defensive-minded. Generating force through the floor and transferring it to the upper body must be effective in all planes of motion. All of the aforementioned scenarios use the kinetic connection between the lacrosse athlete's upper and lower body.

The exercise selection and modalities should vary based on a lacrosse athlete's ability and developmental level and the strength and conditioning professional's competency toward the exercises. This chapter will present a series of progressive exercises, with additional variations, that build upon the general physical preparedness of lacrosse athletes when it is developmentally appropriate to do so. According to Mel Siff, general physical preparation (GPP) training focuses on general conditioning to improve strength, speed, and power (1). This underlying work is critical for continued growth of any lacrosse athlete. Without this foundational element, more complex exercise variations could be less effective for the athlete's overall development. Thus, this chapter begins with a section of GPP total body exercises.

Specific physical preparation (SPP) training focuses on the specific movements required for the game of lacrosse (1). Ten additional exercise variations have been broken down into two categories: SPP accessory exercises (often called **assistance exercises**) and SPP specialized exercises. This model of exercise organization will also be used in chapters 6 and 7.

Most total body exercises trend toward the **strength–speed** development of the lacrosse athlete in the weight room (see figure 4.2 on page 56). In addition, the **speed–strength** development of a lacrosse athlete comes from exercises that typically have a plyometric component. This plyometric element is seen in numerous aspects of the game, including running, shooting, attacking, and defending. Both plyometric and **force-yielding** exercises can be found in each of the next two chapters as they pertain specifically to the lower and upper body.

Please note that a lacrosse athlete's ability in the weight room and technical sport skills may differ. The ability to grow both aspects congruently depends on a well-thought-out and progressively designed approach among the coach, athletic training staff, strength and conditioning professional, nutrition staff, and other qualified staff members associated with the lacrosse athlete. It is also important to note that one can augment the weight, change the speed or tempo of the movement, or even add an oscillating component to exercises to change the stimuli and create progressive variations in the programming.

EXERCISE FINDER

GPP TOTAL BODY EXERCISES

Barbell Hang Clean (BBHC) 64
    Barbell Clean (BBC) 66
    Barbell Hang Power Clean 66
    Barbell High Pull / Barbell Hang High Pull 66
Barbell Hang Power Snatch (BBHPS) 66
    Barbell Hang High Pull (With Snatch Grip) 68
    Barbell Hang Snatch (BBHS) 68
    Barbell Snatch 68
    Dumbbell Single-Arm Snatch 68
Kettlebell Swing 68

SPP ACCESSORY EXERCISES

Elevated Push-Up Position Single-Arm Row 70
Farmer's Handle Suitcase Carry 72
Landmine Row to Press 74
Medicine Ball Squat to Vertical Throw 73
Sandbag Over the Shoulder Toss 71

SPP SPECIALIZED EXERCISES

Anti-Rotation Single-Arm Kettlebell Swing 75
Kettlebell Windmill 78
Lateral Bound Into Rotational Shot-Put Throw 76
Medicine Ball Single-Leg Snap Down 79
Sled Throw 80

GPP TOTAL BODY EXERCISES

BARBELL HANG CLEAN (BBHC)

Primary Muscles Trained

Gluteus maximus, semimembranosus, semitendinosus, biceps femoris, vastus lateralis, vastus intermedius, vastus medialis, rectus femoris, soleus, gastrocnemius, deltoids, trapezius

Beginning Position

- Stand with the feet about hip-width apart and the toes slightly turned out.
- With the arms at the sides, tightly grasp the bar with a double overhand grip just outside the hips and with the knuckles pointed toward the floor *(a)*.
- Keeping the bar on the thighs, slowly hinge at the hips and allow the chest to move over the bar until the bar is just above the knees *(b)*.

Movement Phases

1. Begin by initiating force through the floor in an explosive manner.
2. Keeping the back flat, extend explosively through the ankles, knees, and hips (triple extension) while keeping the elbows fully extended and the bar close to the body *(c)*.
3. During triple extension, pull the bar upward, keeping the elbows high until dropping underneath to a full squat position while shooting the elbows under the bar and allowing the bar to land on the upper deltoids and chest *(d)*. The bar may roll back onto the fingers for a more stable and comfortable catch.
4. Stand up entirely with the barbell resting on the shoulders *(e)*.
5. Return the bar to the beginning position.

Breathing Guidelines

Inhale and use the air to brace before beginning the exercise. After the catch, exhale while standing up.

Figure 5.1   Barbell hang clean: *(a)* beginning position; *(b)* hinge at the hips; *(c)* extend explosively through the ankles, knees, and hips; *(d)* catch; *(e)* end position.

Spotting Guidelines

Spotters are not required when performing this exercise. Be sure the area is clear and free of loose weights.

Exercise Modifications and Variations

Barbell Hang Power Clean

This variation includes all of the aforementioned positions and movements, with the exception of the depth in the catch, which is a *quarter squat* in a power (athletic) position.

Barbell Clean (BBC)

This variation has a similar movement and catch to the BBHC. The significant change is in the initial setup. The barbell will start on the floor, and the "first pull" is initiated to get the bar back to the hang position of the BBHC.

Barbell High Pull / Barbell Hang High Pull

This variation is similar to the BBC or BBHC except for the catch. Instead, complete the explosive high pull of the bar to shoulder height and return to hip level with control.

Coaching Tip

This exercise should be as explosive as possible; keep the bar as close to the body as possible and allow the bar to land on the shoulders and roll back onto the fingers.

BARBELL HANG POWER SNATCH (BBHPS)

Primary Muscles Trained

Gluteus maximus, semimembranosus, semitendinosus, biceps femoris, vastus lateralis, vastus intermedius, vastus medialis, rectus femoris, soleus, gastrocnemius, deltoids, trapezius

Beginning Position

- Stand with the feet about hip-width apart and the toes slightly turned out.
- The hands should be spaced widely when gripping the bar, roughly the width of the elbows if standing with the arms out to make a *T*.
- Tightly grasp the bar with a double overhand grip and the knuckles pointed toward the floor *(a)*.
- Keeping the bar on the thighs, slowly hinge at the hips and allow the chest to move over the bar until the bar is just above the knees *(b)*.

Movement Phases

1. Begin by initiating force through the floor in an explosive manner.
2. Keeping the back flat, extend explosively through the ankles, knees, and hips (triple extension) while keeping the elbows fully extended and the bar close to the body *(c)*.
3. During triple extension, pull the bar upward, keeping the elbows high *(d)* until dropping underneath the bar into a power position while punching the knuckles toward the ceiling with the arms fully extended overhead *(e)*.

Figure 5.2 Barbell hang power snatch: *(a)* beginning position; *(b)* hinge at the hips; *(c)* extend explosively through the ankles, knees, and hips; *(d)* pull the bar upward and keep the elbows high; *(e)* catch; *(f)* end position.

4. Stand up entirely with the barbell overhead *(f)*.
5. Return the bar to the beginning position.

Breathing Guidelines

Inhale and use the air to brace before beginning the exercise. After the catch, exhale while standing up.

Spotting Guidelines

Spotters are not required when performing this exercise. The area around the movement should be clear and free of loose weights.

Exercise Modifications and Variations

Barbell Hang Snatch (BBHS)

This variation includes all of the positions and movements of the BBHPS with the exception of the depth in the catch, which is a full deep squat position with the bar overhead.

Barbell Snatch

This variation has a change in the initial setup. The barbell will start on the floor, and the first pull is initiated to get the bar back to the hang position of the BBHPS. With the bar overhead, catch the bar in a full deep squat position.

Barbell Hang High Pull (With Snatch Grip)

This variation is similar to the BBHPS except for the catch. This movement has no catch. Instead, complete the explosive high pull of the bar to shoulder height and return to hip level with control.

Dumbbell Single-Arm Snatch

In this variation, grasp the dumbbell (DB), hinge at the hips, and let the DB drop between the legs. Initiate the exercise with explosive hip extension. Keep the DB close to the body throughout the movement into the landing position overhead.

Coaching Tip

This exercise should be as explosive as possible with the bar caught over and slightly behind the head.

KETTLEBELL SWING

Primary Muscles Trained

Gluteus maximus, semimembranosus, semitendinosus, biceps femoris, vastus lateralis, vastus intermedius, vastus medialis, rectus femoris

Beginning Position

- Stand over a kettlebell with the feet between hip- and shoulder-width apart with the toes pointed forward.
- Grab the kettlebell across the top of the handle with a double overhand grip.
- Stand up with the kettlebell and hold it between the legs (a).

Movement Phases

1. Initiate the movement in the swing by flexing the hips with a slight knee flex (hinge) and forcefully pushing the kettlebell between the legs.
2. Keeping the back flat, allow the kettlebell's momentum to pull the chest down parallel with the floor while keeping the shoulders back (b).

Figure 5.3 Kettlebell swing: *(a)* beginning position; *(b)* bottom position; *(c)* top position.

3. After the kettlebell goes back between the legs, explosively extend the hips and knees to full extension.

4. Allow the momentum created with the hips to carry through the torso into the upper extremities and carry the kettlebell up to chest height *(c)*.

5. Allow gravity and momentum to reverse the motion of the kettlebell back between the legs into the next repetition.

Breathing Guidelines

Inhale before initiating the movement and exhale while swinging the kettlebell upward.

Spotting Guidelines

Spotters are not required when performing this exercise.

Exercise Modifications and Variations

A kettlebell swing can be done with a dumbbell if kettlebells are not available.

Coaching Tip

Be explosive with the hips; broken down, the hips move forward, then back. The knees will only move slightly. The kettlebell does not need to go overhead.

SPP ACCESSORY EXERCISES

ELEVATED PUSH-UP POSITION SINGLE-ARM ROW

Primary Muscles Trained

Latissimus dorsi, rectus abdominis, external and internal obliques, psoas major, iliacus, anterior deltoid, serratus anterior

Beginning Position

- Assume a push-up position with one hand on a slightly (4-8 inches [10-20 cm]) elevated surface.
- In the opposite (unelevated) hand, hold a weight.
- Bring the weight off the floor to the same distance off the floor as the hand on the elevated surface (a).

Movement Phases

1. Begin the movement by pulling the weight vertically toward the torso (b).
2. As the weight moves upward, ensure the rest of the body remains motionless.
3. Once the weight reaches the torso, return the weight to the beginning position.
4. When the weight reaches the beginning position, begin the next repetition.
5. At the end of the set, switch the hand positions and repeat the movement.

Figure 5.4   Elevated push-up position single-arm row: (a) beginning position; (b) end position.

Breathing Guidelines

Inhale as the weight is lifted. Exhale as the weight is lowered.

Exercise Modifications and Variations

This movement can be done with a dumbbell or a kettlebell. The farther apart the feet are positioned, the easier it is to resist rotation in the hips. Lift the leg on the opposite side of the rowing arm to significantly increase the difficulty of the exercise.

Coaching Tip

The elevation height is determined by the height required to have the weight implement off the floor with the arms fully extended. Maximally contracting the gluteal muscles on the same side as the rowing arm helps prevent the hips from rotating as the weight is being raised and lowered.

SANDBAG OVER THE SHOULDER TOSS

Primary Muscles Trained

Gluteus maximus, erector spinae, quadratus lumborum, latissimus dorsi, rhomboids, biceps femoris, semitendinosus, external and internal obliques

Beginning Position

- In a standing position, place each foot on one side of the sandbag.
- Squat down until the knees are flexed at an approximately 100-degree angle.
- Flex forward at the waist and place one hand on each side of the sandbag (a).

Movement Phases

1. Initiate the movement by using a squat motion to stand up enough for the sandbag to reach midshin height.
2. Row the sandbag into the body while bringing the knees closer together to create a shelf with the thighs.
3. Place the bottom of the sandbag on the thighs and allow it to rest there while repositioning it for the throw (b).
4. Reposition the arms around the entire sandbag, hugging it tight against the torso (c).
5. Explosively extend the hips, knees, ankles, and back as when reaching maximal total body extension.
6. Finish the movement by throwing the sandbag back over one shoulder (d).
7. Turn around and place each foot on one side of the sandbag to begin the next repetition.

Figure 5.5   Sandbag over the shoulder toss: (a) beginning position; (b) stand and row the sandbag to the body; (c) hug the sandbag; (d) throw the sandbag over one shoulder.

Breathing Guidelines

Inhale before picking the sandbag up. Exhale while the sandbag is resting on the thighs. Inhale before the explosive extension of the hips. Exhale while finishing the throw.

Exercise Modifications and Variations

A heavy medicine ball can be used instead of a sandbag. Numerous rows to the chest can be done before repositioning the sandbag. This adds a grip-training element and increases the latissimus dorsi and rhomboid training volume.

Coaching Tip

Ensure the weight of the sandbag is evenly distributed above and below the hand placements before picking it up. Ensure the highest arm on the sandbag is on the same side as the shoulder over which the sandbag is being tossed. The athlete must create the force from the hips, not by hyperextending the back. The sandbag must be launched from the powerful extension of the hips and legs, not just by using the arms to lift and throw the bag over the shoulder. This movement cannot be executed slowly once the sandbag leaves the thighs and has begun to be thrown.

FARMER'S HANDLE SUITCASE CARRY

Primary Muscles Trained

External and internal obliques, flexor digitorum superficialis, flexor digitorum profundus, trapezius, sternocleidomastoid, quadratus lumborum, gluteus medius, adductor magnus

Beginning Position

- Stand with the feet shoulder-width apart.
- Start with the farmer's handle outside the frame of the body, to the side of the hand that will hold the implement.

Movement Phases

1. Squat down and close one hand around the farmer's handle.
2. Stand up with the farmer's handle, ensuring the body is perfectly erect and not flexing to one side.
3. Begin walking while maintaining an erect posture.
4. Once the specified distance or time has been met on one side, set the implement down and repeat on the other side.

Breathing Guidelines

Inhale before picking the handle up. Exhale when standing fully erect. Diaphragmatically breathe while walking.

Exercise Modifications and Variations

If farmer's handles are not available, a dumbbell, kettlebell, farmer's carry strap handle, or loading pin are other options. This hold can be done in place instead of while walking. A shrug can be added to the farmer's carry to increase trapezius work in the exercise. A lifting strap can be added to eliminate grip as the limiting factor.

Figure 5.6 Farmer's handle suitcase carry.

Coaching Tip

When changing directions, while keeping the implement in the same hand, allow the athlete to set down the farmer's handle and turn around. Spinning the weight around in the air can create extra rotational torque not intended to be a part of this movement. Suitcase carries put more shearing force on the spine than bilateral carries; be aware of this for athletes with a history of lower back issues.

MEDICINE BALL SQUAT TO VERTICAL THROW

Primary Muscles Trained

Gluteus maximus, semimembranosus, semitendinosus, biceps femoris, vastus lateralis, vastus intermedius, vastus medialis, rectus femoris, anterior deltoids

Beginning Position

- Start with the feet shoulder-width apart.
- Hold the medicine ball at chest height just below the chin, ready to press it vertically (a).

Movement Phases

1. Initiate the movement by pushing the hips back and dropping into a squat position (b).
2. Explosively press through the floor to stand up.
3. As the lower body fully extends, carry the force created through the body into the medicine ball.
4. Explosively press the medicine ball off the chest into the air (c).
5. Allow the medicine ball to drop to the floor.

Figure 5.7   Medicine ball squat to vertical throw: (a) beginning position; (b) drop to squat position; (c) explosively press ball up.

Breathing Guidelines

Inhale before squatting and exhale as the medicine ball is being pressed overhead.

Exercise Modifications and Variations

Jumping during the up portion of this exercise is an added variation.

Coaching Tip

Keep the chest upright and make this exercise as explosive as possible. A heavier medicine ball is not necessarily better.

LANDMINE ROW TO PRESS

Primary Muscles Trained

Gluteus maximus, semimembranosus, semitendinosus, biceps femoris, hip rotators, latissimus dorsi, deltoids

Beginning Position

- Stand perpendicular to the barbell, with the far end placed in the landmine attachment.
- Hip hinge down to the barbell, keeping the back flat.
- With the inside hand, grasp the barbell about a hand's width from the end (a).

Figure 5.8 Landmine row to press: (a) beginning position; (b) row the barbell across the body; (c) grasp bar with the opposite hand; (d) press the bar overhead.

Movement Phases

1. Begin by explosively pressing through the floor and rowing the barbell across the body (b).
2. When the barbell crosses the chest from the row, grasp it with the opposite hand (c).
3. With the opposite hand, explosively press the barbell across the body to over the head, rotating off the back foot (d).
4. Slowly reverse the motion back to the floor.

Breathing Guidelines

Inhale before rowing and exhale as the landmine is being pressed across and overhead.

Exercise Modifications and Variations

This exercise can be performed using only the row or the pressing motion. Additionally, those variations could be performed with a band or rack-attached jammer arms.

Coaching Tip

Be explosive and allow the feet to rotate through the finish of the movement.

SPP SPECIALIZED EXERCISES

ANTI-ROTATION SINGLE-ARM KETTLEBELL SWING

Primary Muscles Trained

External and internal obliques, erector spinae, quadratus lumborum, gluteus maximus, biceps femoris, semitendinosus, latissimus dorsi

Beginning Position

- Begin in a standing position with the feet shoulder-width apart and the toes pointed straight ahead.
- Hold a kettlebell in one hand, outside the frame of the body (a).

Movement Phases

1. Initiate the movement by pushing the hips back and flexing the knees slightly.
2. Flex forward at the waist, keep the back flat, and allow the kettlebell to swing backward with movement generated from the hips (b).
3. Upon reaching the end range of the swing, rapidly accelerate the hips forward.
4. Extend the hips to the start position and allow the kettlebell to swing out in front of the body (c).
5. Keep the hips fully extended until the kettlebell swings back and reaches the start position.
6. As the kettlebell reaches the start position, begin the next repetition of swings so the kettlebell has no loss of swing momentum.
7. At the end of the set, repeat the movement with the other hand holding the kettlebell.

Figure 5.9 Anti-rotation single-arm kettlebell swing: *(a)* beginning position; *(b)* flex forward and swing the kettlebell backward; *(c)* extend the hips to swing the kettlebell forward.

Breathing Guidelines

Inhale at the initiation of the swing. Exhale just before full extension in the swing.

Exercise Modifications and Variations

Add a band to accelerate the kettlebell and increase the difficulty of maintaining a neutral trunk position.

Coaching Tip

Keep a neutral pelvic position and do not allow the trunk or hips to rotate throughout the entire motion. Ensure the hips generate force and the arms do not assist or resist in the swing. Initiating the next swing before the kettlebell reaches the beginning position will create poor timing in the swing.

LATERAL BOUND INTO ROTATIONAL SHOT-PUT THROW

Primary Muscles Trained

Gluteus medius, gluteus maximus, external and internal obliques, quadratus lumborum, pectoralis major, gastrocnemius, tibialis posterior, peroneals

Beginning Position

- Stand holding a medicine ball at chest level with the forearms parallel with the floor.
- Flex the hips and knees, load the ankles, and hinge slightly to load the hips *(a)*.

Movement Phases

1. Explosively push laterally with the outside leg *(b)*.
2. Immediately upon landing on the opposite leg *(c)*, explosively push back laterally to the beginning position *(d)*.
3. Upon landing with the initiating leg *(e)*, immediately drive laterally in the opposite direction.
4. As the lateral-bounding leg is extending, externally rotate the hip to initiate a rotational throwing motion through the body.
5. As the hips rotate, transfer that power through the trunk and into an explosive shot-put–style throw with the medicine ball *(f)*.
6. Retrieve the ball to get set for the next repetition.

Figure 5.10   Lateral bound into rotational shot-put throw: *(a)* beginning position; *(b)* lateral jump; *(c)* land; *(d)* lateral jump back; *(e)* land; *(f)* shot-put–style throw the ball.

Breathing Guidelines

Inhale before the initial bound. Exhale as the shot-put throw is being completed. For higher-repetition bounding drills, several breaths may be needed.

Exercise Modifications and Variations

The addition of a band around the waist, pulling against or accelerating the lateral bounding, adds difficulty to the drill. Lines on the floor can be used to give athletes a target to bound over. A slant board can be added on one side to increase the foot and ankle complexity. The number of bounds can be changed before the throw. Randomizing when the bound throw will occur can be done by adding a reactionary signal.

Coaching Tip

Cue the athlete to cover as much floor as possible while maintaining control when bounding. The athlete must land with the hip, leg, and ankle loaded to be able to immediately accelerate back in the opposite direction. Ensure the athlete does not use both arms, or worse yet, a baseball-throwing motion to throw the ball. This is an advanced drill that must be done explosively; it cannot be done slowly.

KETTLEBELL WINDMILL

Primary Muscles Trained

Gluteus maximus, semimembranosus, semitendinosus, biceps femoris, erector spinae, serratus anterior, external oblique, quadratus lumborum

Beginning Position

- Hold a kettlebell in a front rack position.
- The feet should be double hip-width apart, both pointing 45 degrees in one direction (more than what is shown in *a*).

Movement Phases

1. Load the back heel on the kettlebell side, pushing the hip out (*b*).
2. Raise the hand holding the kettlebell, keeping the elbow fully extended (*c*).
3. Keep the knees extended while lowering, reaching the bottom hand toward the floor (not shown).
4. Push through the kettlebell, standing up to return to the top position.
5. At the end of the set, repeat the movement with the other hand holding the kettlebell or alternate hands during the set.

Breathing Guidelines

Inhale before starting to lean over. Exhale as needed in the process of standing.

Exercise Modifications and Variations

This exercise can be done with a dumbbell.

Coaching Tip

Control the descent and watch the kettlebell as the lower hand touches the floor. If flexibility does not allow for touching the floor, place something on the floor to bring the level slightly higher, or slightly flex the knee of the front leg (but strive over time to do the exercise with the knee fully extended).

Figure 5.11   Kettlebell windmill: *(a)* beginning position; *(b)* push hip out; *(c)* raise kettlebell.

MEDICINE BALL SINGLE-LEG SNAP DOWN

Primary Muscles Trained

Gluteus maximus, semimembranosus, semitendinosus, biceps femoris, vastus lateralis, vastus intermedius, vastus medialis, rectus femoris, latissimus dorsi

Beginning Position

- Stand on one leg.
- Hold the medicine ball held overhead with the hands behind it, prepared to throw it at the floor *(a)*.

Movement Phases

1. Begin the movement by forcefully hinging at the hips, moving the chest toward the floor.
2. Forcefully snap the medicine ball to the floor *(b)*. (*Note:* A nonreactive slam ball version of a medicine ball is recommended.)
3. Absorb the speed of the movement into the hip of the single leg on the floor.
4. Decelerate the body before falling over or moving forward.
5. At the end of the set, repeat the movement on the other side or alternate sides during the set.

Breathing Guidelines

Inhale before initiating the movement. Exhale as the medicine ball is being snapped down to the floor.

Figure 5.12 Medicine ball single-leg snap down: *(a)* beginning position; *(b)* snap down to slam the ball into the floor.

Exercise Modifications and Variations

Add movement with the medicine ball to change where it lands (inside or outside the foot). Additional hanging on the medicine ball by decelerating the lower body will stimulate the movement.

Coaching Tip

Be explosive through the movement. Absorb the force explosively.

SLED THROW

Primary Muscles Trained

Gluteus maximus, semimembranosus, semitendinosus, biceps femoris, vastus lateralis, vastus intermedius, vastus medialis, rectus femoris, soleus, gastrocnemius, deltoids, triceps brachii

Beginning Position

- Crouch down behind the high handles of a weighted or resistive sled.
- Lean with the body weight onto the arms of the sled *(a)*.

Movement Phases

1. Initiate the movement by generating force through the foot and ankle complex.
2. Explosively press and throw the sled away from the body as every major joint fully extends *(b)*.

Breathing Guidelines

Inhale before the movement. Exhale as force is being applied through the arms of the sled.

Exercise Modifications and Variations

This can be done with a medicine ball and jumping out horizontally with a broad jump.

Coaching Tip

The weight or resistance of the sled does not need to be super heavy, but it needs to be heavy enough that the sled does not turn when it is tossed.

Figure 5.13 Sled throw: *(a)* beginning position; *(b)* explosive push.

6

LOWER BODY EXERCISE TECHNIQUE

JL HOLDSWORTH AND EDWARD R. SMITH, JR.

Lacrosse is a ground-based sport with many starts, stops, and directional changes. General physical preparation (GPP) resistance training exercises are a part of an effective program. It is important to know how strength transfers to sport performance to avoid training that may lead to excessive stress on portions of the body that are used dynamically in the sport. Testing can determine an athlete's strengths and weaknesses to be considered in program design. Does the athlete have a strength deficit? Is he or she in a **strength association zone** (characterized by a nearly linear relationship between relative strength and performance capability), where increases in strength directly affect performance? Or has the athlete reached a **strength reserve zone** (characterized by a limited return on investment to maximum strength) where further increases show a much smaller effect on performance (2)? Understanding these dynamics paints a picture of progressive development. For example, if an athlete has a strength deficit in the squat, then developing this quality is paramount in training. As the athlete becomes stronger, performance on the field will improve. As this same athlete reaches his or her strength reserve, progressing the exercise to a more specific physical preparation (SPP) exercise can allow for further growth and transfer while maintaining the base movement quality of general squat strength. Focusing too heavily on GPP exercises can affect a lacrosse athlete's continued development. Not only will SPP exercises give a high-value return by helping the lacrosse athlete maintain dynamic athleticism, but there is also a progressive component that will enable growth in a developmentally appropriate fashion as a result of adaptations to the foundational GPP exercises.

Although plyometrics are not typical resistance training exercises, they are important in a quality resistance training program for lacrosse. As such, a plyometrics overview is included as part of this chapter. As a reminder, jumps, hops, and bounds can have added resistance or assistance to drastically increase difficulty. These changes must be implemented by a strength and conditioning professional, because they are highly taxing on an athlete.

In any great program, attention must be paid to creating a balanced line of movement distribution. This was done when developing the list of exercises in this chapter. There are balanced selections of knee- and hip-dominant exercises. In addition, the dynamic nature of lacrosse makes it essential to include some specialty exercises to ensure the body is prepared for the rigorous demands of the sport.

This chapter does not describe GPP lower body exercises (it only lists them), because these large-muscle, multijoint, compound movements can be found in the NSCA's *Exercise Technique*

Manual for Resistance Training (1). Instead, this chapter includes SPP lower body exercises and associated variations that progress from the GPP exercises to move a lacrosse athlete to the next level.

EXERCISE FINDER

GPP LOWER BODY EXERCISES

Back Squat

Deadlift

Front Squat

Lateral Squat

Lunge (Linear and Lateral)

Nordic Hamstring Curl

Romanian Deadlift (RDL)

Single-Leg Rear Foot
  Elevated (RFE) Squat

Split Squat

Step-Up

SPP PRIMARY LOWER BODY EXERCISES

Deadlift Variation: King Deadlift 88

High Acceleration Force (HAF) Sled March 89

Lunge Variation: LAX Lunge 86

RDL Variation: Dumbbell Contralateral Kickstand RDL 87

Split Squat Variation: Dumbbell Heel-Floating Split Squat 85

SPP ACCESSORY LOWER BODY EXERCISES

Copenhagen Plank. 91

Heavy Reverse Sled Drag 94

Lateral Squat Variation: Landmine Sway Squat. 92

Single-Leg Squat With Slider 90

Step-Up Variation: Crossover Step-Up 95

SPP SPECIALIZED LOWER BODY EXERCISES

Banded Maximum-Sprint Posture March. 99

Band Tantrum Kick. 101

RDL Variation: Cable Dipping Bird 100

Single-Leg Hip Thrust Drop 98

Squat Variation: Landmine Lateral Acceleration Single-Leg Squat 96

LOWER BODY PLYOMETRIC EXERCISES

Landings 102

Multidirectional Jumps, Hops, and Bounds. 103

Multiresponse Jumps, Hops, and Bounds 103

Single-Response Jumps, Hops, and Bounds 103

SPP PRIMARY LOWER BODY EXERCISES

SPLIT SQUAT VARIATION: DUMBBELL HEEL-FLOATING SPLIT SQUAT

Primary Muscles Trained

Tibialis posterior, gastrocnemius, soleus, flexor digitorum (longus and brevis), vastus lateralis, vastus medialis, rectus femoris, gluteus maximus, flexor digitorum superficialis, flexor digitorum profundus

Beginning Position

- Stand with the feet shoulder-width apart.
- Hold dumbbells in the hands.
- Take one step forward, placing one foot in front of the other.
- Lift the front foot's heel so there is about 1 inch (2.5 cm) of distance from the floor to the heel *(a)*.

Movement Phases

1. Initiate the movement by flexing the hips and knees to lower the body.
2. Keeping the torso erect, lower the body until the back leg's knee until it is about 1 inch (2.5 cm) from the floor, or as low as it is possible to go while maintaining control *(b)*.
3. Once the controlled end range of movement has been reached, extend the hips and knees to return to the beginning position.
4. At the end of the set, switch the position of the feet and repeat the movement.

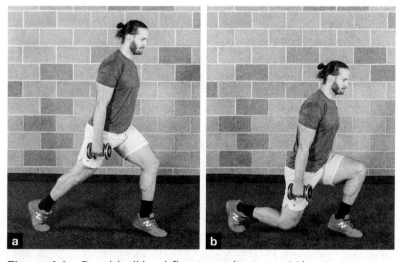

Figure 6.1   Dumbbell heel-floating split squat: *(a)* beginning position; *(b)* end position.

Breathing Guidelines

Inhale while lowering the body. Exhale at the top of the movement.

Exercise Modifications and Variations

Using a barbell eliminates the limiting factor of grip strength and allows for much heavier loads. Using a contralateral dumbbell increases the stability component of the exercise. The toes can be placed on a surface elevated 2 to 3 inches (5-8 cm) to achieve the heel-floating requirement of the exercise.

Coaching Tip

Do not allow the athlete to forcefully contact the floor with the knee. For some, the ankle–foot complex may be the limiting factor in this exercise. Ensure the feet maintain a shoulder-width distance apart when the initial split-squat stance is set. A narrow stance may create a stability issue.

LUNGE VARIATION: LAX LUNGE

Primary Muscles Trained

Gluteus medius, external and internal obliques, tensor fasciae latae, vastus lateralis, biceps femoris, semimembranosus, semitendinosus

Beginning Position

- Stand with the feet shoulder-width apart.
- Hold dumbbells in the hands (a).

Movement Phases

1. Step one leg behind and across the other leg, placing the toes on the floor.
2. Push the hips back, flex the hips and knees, and lower the body; place the back knee just behind the heel of the front leg, 1 inch (2.5 cm) off the floor (b).
3. From the bottom position, drive up with the front leg and laterally from the hip on the same side.
4. While coming up, bring the back leg from behind the body and return to standing with the feet shoulder-width apart.

Figure 6.2   LAX lunge: (a) beginning position; (b) end position.

5. At the end of the set, repeat the movement with other leg as the front leg or alternate legs during the set.

Breathing Guidelines

Inhale while lowering the body. Exhale at the top of the movement.

Exercise Modifications and Variations

Using a barbell eliminates the limiting factor of grip strength and allows for much heavier loads. Using a contralateral dumbbell increases the stability component of the exercise. A band can be added for lateral resistance while moving out of the bottom position.

Coaching Tip

The step cannot be too far back or too far across the body. The hips should remain square and the back knee behind the heel when in the bottom position. The torso and shin will be at acceleration angles, not vertical. The athlete should not allow the back knee to forcefully contact the floor.

RDL VARIATION: DUMBBELL CONTRALATERAL KICKSTAND RDL

Primary Muscles Trained

Gluteus maximus, biceps femoris, semimembranosus, semitendinosus

Beginning Position

- Place the feet just less than hip-width apart with a slightly staggered stance.
- Distribute weight toward the front leg.
- Hold the dumbbell in the hand opposite to the active (front) leg *(a)*.

Movement Phases

1. Begin the movement by hinging at the hips with the knees slightly flexed.
2. Keep the shoulders back and flat as the chest descends toward the floor.
3. When the chest is approximately parallel with the floor *(b)*, pull back through the hamstrings and return to standing vertically.

Figure 6.3   Dumbbell contralateral kickstand RDL: *(a)* beginning position; *(b)* end position.

4. At the end of the set, repeat the movement in the opposite staggered stance or alternate the foot positions during the set.

Breathing Guidelines

Inhale before the descent. Exhale during the upward movement phase.

Exercise Modifications and Variations

An exercise variation can be done with bands or moving the dumbbell to an ipsilateral hold.

Coaching Tip

The athlete should move through the hip and pull through the hamstring to stand up. More weight should be kept on the front foot.

DEADLIFT VARIATION: KING DEADLIFT

Primary Muscles Trained

Gluteus maximus, semimembranosus, semitendinosus, biceps femoris, vastus lateralis, vastus intermedius, vastus medialis, rectus femoris

Beginning Position

- Hold dumbbells to the sides of the body.
- Balance on a single leg with the knee of the other leg flexed to 90 degrees and with the foot behind the body (a).

Movement Phases

1. While balancing on one leg, flex the hip and knee of the supporting leg to lower the body until the knee of the suspended leg touches the floor just slightly behind the foot of the supporting leg (b).

2. Stand back up by pressing through the floor to extend the hip and knee of the supporting leg.

3. At the end of the set, repeat the movement with other leg as the balancing leg or alternate legs during the set.

Figure 6.4 King deadlift: (a) beginning position; (b) end position.

Breathing Guidelines

Inhale before the decent. Exhale as the knee and hip are extended.

Exercise Modifications and Variations

To make this exercise more knee dominant, reach back farther with the knee that touches the floor and keep a more upright torso position. This is often referred to as a **skater squat**.

Coaching Tip

If balance becomes an issue, have the athlete find a spot on the floor to stare at during the whole exercise or slightly increase the height of the surface where the knee touches, lowering it periodically to increase the range of motion.

HIGH ACCELERATION FORCE (HAF) SLED MARCH

Primary Muscles Trained

Gluteus maximus, biceps femoris, semimembranosus, semitendinosus

Beginning Position

- Load a sled or adjust the resistance so that significant force is needed to move it across the floor.
- Grasp the sled with both hands and lean out onto it *(a)*.

Movement Phases

1. While leaning forward, pick up one leg and begin to push the floor back away from the sled *(b)*.
2. March with force. With each step, drive the opposite knee toward the sled.
3. March the desired number of steps or total distance.

Breathing Guidelines

Diaphragmatically breathe throughout the entire exercise.

Coaching Tip

Keeping the elbows fully extended with the arms in front of the body will add a shoulder

Figure 6.5　HAF sled march: *(a)* beginning position; *(b)* end position.

stability component. The athlete should push force through the floor and not try to pull with his or her heel (if this can occur, there is not enough weight on the sled).

SPP ACCESSORY LOWER BODY EXERCISES

SINGLE-LEG SQUAT WITH SLIDER

Primary Muscles Trained

Adductor magnus, adductor longus, rectus femoris, vastus medialis

Beginning Position

- Stand with the feet shoulder-width apart.
- Place one foot on an object that slides easily on the working surface (a).

Movement Phases

1. Begin by flexing the hip and knee of the leg not standing on the slider to lower the body.
2. While the body lowers, keep the knee of the leg on the slider fully extended and move the leg laterally away from the body at the same rate as the hip and knee of the other leg are flexing (b).
3. Once a full range of motion has been reached, pull the leg on the slider in (while keeping the knee still fully extended) as the hip and knee of the other leg extend to raise the body out of the single-leg squat position.
4. Once the body has returned to the beginning position, begin the next repetition.
5. At the end of the set, repeat the movement with other leg on the slider or alternate legs during the set.

Figure 6.6 Single-leg squat with slider: (a) beginning position; (b) end position.

Breathing Guidelines

Inhale while lowering the body. Exhale at the top of the movement.

Exercise Modifications and Variations

A band on the foot can be added to resist the adduction of the leg from the bottom position of the movement. Holding a stationary object may help with balance during the movement.

Coaching Tip

Start a tempo eccentric and concentric (see chapter 9) to teach the athlete how to control the movement. Ensure the adduction happens at the same pace as the lowering and raising of the squat. Ensure the knee of the slider leg stays fully extended throughout the entire movement.

COPENHAGEN PLANK

Primary Muscles Trained

Adductor magnus, adductor longus, quadratus lumborum, external and internal obliques

Beginning Position

- Lie on one side of the body with the legs stacked on top of each other.
- Place the forearm that is closest to the floor in a supporting position directly under the shoulder.
- Place the inside of the top leg on an elevated surface that is approximately as far off the floor as the top shoulder in the side-lying position. Place the bottom leg below the elevated surface, flexed at a 90/90 position at the knee and hip and holding no body weight (a).

Movement Phases

1. Elevate the entire body, keeping only the forearm on the floor and the top leg on the elevated surface (the bottom leg remains below the surface, holding no weight).

2. Maintain a perfectly vertical line from the shoulders through the hips and to the part of the leg on the elevated surface (b).

3. After the allotted duration, lower the body to the floor. Repeat for the desired number of repetitions or hold the top position for time.

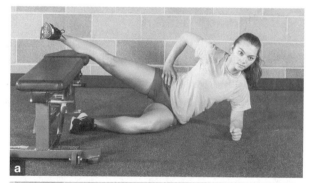

Figure 6.7 Copenhagen plank: (a) beginning position; (b) end position.

Breathing Guidelines

Breathe diaphragmatically throughout the entire exercise.

Exercise Modifications and Variations

Move the point of contact with the elevated surface out from the knee toward the ankle to increase the difficulty of the exercise. This exercise can be done repetitively or as an isometric hold in the lifted position. Extending the knee of the lower leg can add a maximal contraction of the bottom leg into the elevated surface for bilateral adduction work. Additionally, a load can be added to the top hip with chains or other pliable load sources.

Coaching Tip

For athletes new to the exercise, start with the knee on the elevated surface. If the involved musculature has not been trained, starting at the ankle could cause an adductor strain. Once the athlete shows competency contacting the surface at the knee, the point of contact can be moved farther down the leg toward the ankle.

LATERAL SQUAT VARIATION: LANDMINE SWAY SQUAT

Primary Muscles Trained

Gluteus maximus, semimembranosus, semitendinosus, biceps femoris, vastus lateralis, vastus intermedius, vastus medialis, rectus femoris

Beginning Position

- Stand with the feet more than shoulder-width apart and the toes pointed out (sumo position) while straddling the end of a bar that is in a landmine attachment.
- Squat down to the bar and grasp the barbell end with a double underhand grip.
- Maintain an upright posture and lift the bar between the legs to start in a squatted position (i.e., the knees flexed to approximately 90 degrees) (a).

Movement Phases

1. Remaining in the lowered position, transfer the weight to the left leg and sway to the left while fully extending the right knee (b).
2. Still remaining in the lowered position, transfer the weight to the right leg and sway to the right while fully extending the left knee (c).
3. Sway from side to side to complete the desired number of repetitions, place the bar on the floor, and stand up.

Breathing Guidelines

Breathe diaphragmatically while swaying side to side to increase demand on the mobility of the hips. Exhale when the weight is fully transferred to one side.

Exercise Modifications and Variations

A variation of this exercise is done with a dumbbell held in a goblet position. Additionally, the barbell can be moved from between the legs to chest level to place a higher demand

Figure 6.8   Landmine sway squat: *(a)* beginning position; *(b)* while squatted, sway to the left; *(c)* while still squatted, sway to the right.

on posture and range of motion. If the weight places too much demand on the range of motion, try rolling the weight on the floor side to side until mobility and strength are optimal to add resistance.

Coaching Tip

If the athlete is short in stature or has long arms, he or she may need to use smaller weights on the bar to keep it from touching the floor during the sway.

HEAVY REVERSE SLED DRAG

Primary Muscles Trained

Vastus lateralis, vastus intermedius, vastus medialis, rectus femoris

Beginning Position

- Load a sled or adjust the resistance so that force is needed to move it.
- With a strap attached to the sled, face the sled and wrap the strap around the waist.
- Slightly lean back into a quarter-squat position (a).

Movement Phases

1. Begin by stepping back with one foot.
2. Forcefully press through the toes and pull the sled with the body weight to force it backward (b).
3. Pull for the desired distance or number of steps on each side.

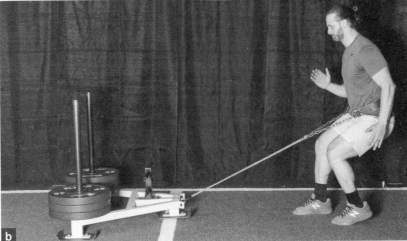

Figure 6.9   Heavy reverse sled drag: (a) beginning position; (b) step backward.

Breathing Guidelines

Breathe diaphragmatically throughout the entire exercise.

Exercise Modifications and Variations

If a sled is not present, use two bands looped together and walk backward and forward as a modification.

Coaching Tip

Make sure to extend the knee fully through each step.

STEP-UP VARIATION: CROSSOVER STEP-UP

Primary Muscles Trained

Gluteus maximus, semimembranosus, semitendinosus, biceps femoris, vastus lateralis, vastus intermedius, vastus medialis, rectus femoris

Beginning Position

- Stand with a step-up platform to the side of one foot.
- Hold dumbbells to the sides of the body (a).
- With the foot opposite to the one beside the platform, step across the body to place the foot on top of the platform (b).

Movement Phases

1. By pressing through the foot on top of the step-up platform, push the floor away from the body's center.
2. Stand up through the knee and hip of the leg on the platform while driving the opposite knee vertically through full hip flexion (c).
3. Step down to the opposite side of the platform.
4. At the end of the set, stand with the platform to the side of the other foot and repeat the movement.

Breathing Guidelines

Inhale before stepping onto the platform. Exhale as the knee and hip fully extend.

Exercise Modifications and Variations

Change to a single dumbbell held at chest level below the chin to aid in an upright posture. Alternatively, to add an explosive stimulus, remove the dumbbells and jump vertically with every step-up.

Coaching Tip

Be sure the foot that is placed on the platform is fully on the top of the platform and not too close to the edge that it could slip off. If the platform has a softer surface, place the foot farther away from the edge so the platform does not compress so much that the top surface becomes unstable.

Figure 6.10   Crossover step-up: *(a)* beginning position; *(b)* place outside foot on platform; *(c)* top position.

SPP SPECIALIZED LOWER BODY EXERCISES

SQUAT VARIATION: LANDMINE LATERAL ACCELERATION SINGLE-LEG SQUAT

Primary Muscles Trained

Gluteus medius, gluteus maximus, peroneals, tibialis posterior, erector spinae, quadratus lumborum, external and internal obliques, biceps femoris

Beginning Position

- Place a barbell inside of a landmine attachment that is fixed and will not move with force applied horizontally into the attachment.
- Place a large rubber plate on the barbell.
- Pick up the end of the barbell and place the collar of the barbell in the elbow joints, with the hands clasped together and the arms in front of the body.
- Press the outside of right shoulder and arm against the rubber plate.
- Place the feet next to each other and in a position on the floor away from the landmine (i.e., to the left) with the head, torso, and legs aligned to create a 45- to 65-degree body angle with the floor *(a)*.
- Flex the right knee to 90 degrees; the body will now be supported by the left leg at a lateral acceleration angle, with resistance from leaning against the rubber plate *(b)*.

Movement Phases

1. Push the left hip back and squat down on the left leg to lower the body.
2. Squat down until the right knee is approximately 1 inch (2.5 cm) from the floor (farther than what is shown in c).
3. Drive back up to the top position by extending the left hip and knee while pushing into the plate.
4. At the end of the set, switch the position of the feet and repeat the movement.

Figure 6.11 Landmine lateral acceleration single-leg squat: (a) beginning position; (b) lean against the plate with support from the outside leg; (c) end position.

Breathing Guidelines

Inhale while lowering the body. Exhale at the top of the movement.

Exercise Modifications and Variations

For weaker athletes, use a lighter bar in the landmine. If there is no landmine available, use a stability ball against the wall to mimic the movement.

Coaching Tip

Ensure the athlete loads the outside hip and ankle in this movement. The angles of the torso and the outside shin need to match; they should not be vertical.

SINGLE-LEG HIP THRUST DROP

Primary Muscles Trained

Gluteus maximus, erector spinae, quadratus lumborum, biceps femoris

Beginning Position

- Lie supine on the floor with the heel of one foot on a bench (or a similarly elevated surface) with the knee of the supporting leg flexed to approximately 90 degrees (a).
- Lift the hips off the floor and the other leg in the air (b).

Movement Phases

1. Explosively extend the hip of the supporting leg to drive the lower body, gaining as much height as possible (c).
2. Land, as stiffly as possible, back on the bench with the same leg that drove off the bench (i.e., back to b).
3. Lower the hips to the beginning position to begin the next repetition.
4. At the end of the set, repeat the movement with other leg as the supporting leg or alternate legs during the set.

Breathing Guidelines

Inhale before thrusting the hips in the air. Exhale after sticking the landing.

Exercise Modifications and Variations

The back can be put on another elevated surface to increase the difficulty of the exercise. Load the hips with bands for greater difficulty. Less experienced athletes can start with a bilateral version.

Figure 6.12 Single-leg hip thrust drop: (a) beginning position; (b) lift the hips off the floor; (c) end position.

Coaching Tip

This exercise is all about teaching how to create and stop force. The thrust must be explosive. The landing must create instantaneous stiffness. There can be no give in the body once the foot lands back down. The athlete must stop all the momentum as the foot lands. Any drop in the hips after landing is a leak in the system's ability to stop force.

BANDED MAXIMUM-SPRINT POSTURE MARCH

Primary Muscles Trained

Psoas major, iliacus, quadratus lumborum, rectus femoris, tibialis anterior, gluteus maximus

Beginning Position

- Start by placing a heavy resistance band around the waist. Have an additional person hold the band at its opposite end. (Make sure the band is fully gripped in the hands to avoid potentially snapping the active athlete.)

- Stand erect on one leg with the knee fully extended with the gluteal muscles maximally contracted.

- Raise the opposite leg above, or at least to, 90 degrees at the hip.

- Flex the knee past 90 degrees on the raised leg.

- Fully dorsiflex the ankle on the raised leg.

- Look straight forward.

- Place the arms in the sprint swing position (a).

Movement Phases

1. Drive the raised leg down.

2. Upon contact with the floor, drive the supporting leg up to match the beginning position of the opposite leg (b).

3. Alternate legs to repeat the action. Repeat for the desired number of repetitions or time.

Figure 6.13 Banded maximum-sprint posture march: (a) beginning position; (b) end position (of one leg).

Breathing Guidelines

Breathe diaphragmatically throughout the entire exercise.

Exercise Modifications and Variations

To increase difficulty, speed up the exercise and simultaneously switch legs in the air, making the exercise a sprint instead of a march. Hold on to a stable object to remove the need to balance during the exercise. Add small pushes and pulls to the body to increase the stability demand during the exercise.

Coaching Tip

At the beginning and ending positions, the athlete can be cued that he or she should be able to balance a bucket of water on the head, a bucket on the flexed knee, and the handle of a bucket on the lifted toes. This teaches neutral head, knee, and toe up positions.

RDL VARIATION: CABLE DIPPING BIRD

Primary Muscles Trained

Biceps femoris, semimembranosus, semitendinosus, gluteus maximus, quadratus lumborum

Beginning Position

- First, determine the correct position of the feet relative to the cable machine by holding the handle of a cable machine in one hand, flexing all the way forward with the elbow fully extended, and moving away from the machine until there is tension on the cable in the full-range-of-motion position of the exercise (not shown).
- Return back to a standing position and lift the contralateral leg off the floor. The supporting leg is the same side as the hand holding the cable. There should be forward tension on the cable. Slightly flex the knee of the supporting leg, just enough to come out of a locked knee position (a).

Movement Phases

1. Begin by flexing forward at the waist.
2. Allow the arm to come away from the body in an overhead position while flexing forward.
3. Keep the contralateral gluteal muscles contracted and the knee fully extended.
4. Flex forward until the elbow is fully extended and the back leg is parallel or slightly past parallel with the floor (b).
5. Return to the beginning position by pulling back on the floor with the supporting leg to begin to pull the body erect.
6. As the leg is pulling the body erect, pull the arm back into the body.
7. Finish in the beginning position, with the hamstrings fully contracted to maintain the position as the cable is working to pull the body forward.
8. At the end of the set, repeat the movement with other leg as the supporting leg.

Breathing Guidelines

Inhale while lowering the body. Exhale at the top of the movement.

Exercise Modifications and Variations

Bands can be used if a cable machine is not available. To emphasize a specific aspect of the hamstrings, use a partial range of motion in only the top or only the bottom portion of the movement.

Coaching Tip

The athlete should pull with the hamstrings to raise and lower the body. The latissimus dorsi should not be used to try to control the movement. Tell the athlete to think of the arm as a strap attaching the lower body to the weight.

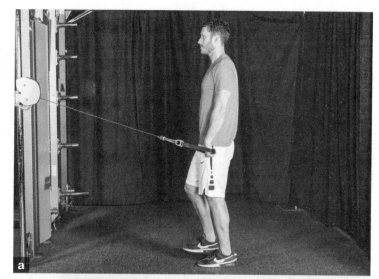

Figure 6.14 Cable dipping bird: *(a)* beginning position; *(b)* end position (of one leg).

BAND TANTRUM KICK

Primary Muscles Trained

Gluteus maximus, semimembranosus, semitendinosus, biceps femoris

Beginning Position

- Place a heavy resistance band across the J hooks or safeties of a rack at about midthigh height.
- Lie supine on the floor with the feet elevated on top of the resistance band.
- With the heels and Achilles tendons laying atop the resistance band, bridge the hips up with the knees fully extended.

Movement Phases

1. Begin by raising one leg off the band *(a)*.
2. Alternating legs, kick quickly and repetitively *(b)*.

Figure 6.15 Band tantrum kick: (a) beginning position; (b) kick legs.

3. Maintain the bridged hips while maintaining a rigid but flowing torso. Repeat for the desired number of repetitions or time.

Breathing Guidelines

Diaphragmatically breathe throughout the entire exercise.

Exercise Modifications and Variations

If large bands are unavailable, a variation would be to use a stability ball. Additionally, this exercise can be performed with flexed knees.

Coaching Tip

This exercise is a useful, controlled environment in a return-to-play process for hamstring injury.

LOWER BODY PLYOMETRIC EXERCISES

To talk about plyometrics, each type of plyometric exercise must first be defined. A **jump** is a bilateral takeoff and bilateral landing. A **hop** is a unilateral takeoff and unilateral landing on the same leg. A **bound** is a unilateral takeoff with a unilateral landing on the opposite leg. Intensive exercises with maximum effort or intensity (both in force absorption and force production) are neurologically taxing and are commonly performed in lower volumes. Extensive exercises at submaximal intensity are often used to develop and build repetitive tissue resiliency and are programmed using higher volumes.

Primary Muscles Trained

Gluteus maximus, semimembranosus, semitendinosus, biceps femoris, vastus lateralis, vastus intermedius, vastus medialis, rectus femoris

Landings

It is essential to teach athletes to land and absorb force while leading them to produce power. Some ways to teach force absorption include the following:

- *Snap down:* Athletes start with their feet hip-width apart, raised up on their toes and with their hands overhead, and then violently (i.e., abruptly and powerfully) snap themselves down into an athletic stance and brace.

- *Depth drop:* Athletes start on top of a box or weight bench, step off, and fall to the floor, absorbing the momentum gained by gravity. When landing, athletes should absorb the initial force but be ready to rebound from the floor. Athletes should begin low and increase height over time.

Single-Response Jumps, Hops, and Bounds

A single-response exercise has a reset between each repetition. Single-response exercises should be used early in a preparatory phase, when teaching and technique are vital. Vertical jumps, broad jumps, and pause bounds are exercises in this category.

Multiresponse Jumps, Hops, and Bounds

Extensive activities include line jumps, hops, jump rope, and mini-hurdles. Intensive exercises include high hurdle or box hops and jumps, high and far bounds, and repeat broad jumps.

Multidirectional Jumps, Hops, and Bounds

The demands of lacrosse require the body to perform in all planes of motion. Implementing multidirectional jumps, hops, and bounds may give athletes the most carryover to the sport. Multidirectional movements include rotational, lateral, and multiplanar jumps; hops; and bounds. All jumps, hops, and bounds can have resistance or assistance added by the strength and conditioning professional, if necessary.

7

UPPER BODY EXERCISE TECHNIQUE

JL HOLDSWORTH AND EDWARD R. SMITH, JR.

Although lacrosse is often called the fastest sport on two feet, the upper body is equally important for an athlete's success. As discussed in chapter 6, an athlete must be able to transfer force through the entire body. Athletes' upper body strength and power can make or break their ability to efficiently transfer force into a high-velocity pass or shot or defend at close proximity. Traditional upper body exercises are needed for general physical preparation (GPP) and to build the armor of the lacrosse athlete. Training the neck is also a vital piece of any lacrosse upper body program. Poor neck strength has been shown to be a significant predictor of experiencing more concussion-related injuries (1).

Due to the immense amount of rotational power needed in lacrosse, force transfer cannot be maximized by using only traditional resistance training exercises. Traditional upper body resistance training exercises only train the body in one plane of motion at a time. When considering these exercises, there are four major movement categories within the generalized upper body: vertical push, vertical pull, horizontal push, and horizontal pull. Traditional exercises are great for establishing a base level of strength development; however, lacrosse is a dynamic sport where all planes of motion are used in a single movement to create an athlete's performance. For this reason, a lacrosse-specific resistance training program also needs to include exercises—when developmentally applicable—that use all three planes of motion in one exercise. It is equally important to use exercises that generate force unilaterally and transmit or stabilize that force on the contralateral side. An effective program must also include mobility training through the upper body, specifically with regard to the thoracic spine and shoulder complex.

The exercises presented in this chapter are not meant to make up the entire resistance training program. They are to be used in addition to, not in place of, more general and traditional resistance training exercises, which can be found in the NSCA's *Exercise Technique Manual for Resistance Training* (2). This chapter also provides some variations of traditional exercises that increase their performance transfer to lacrosse. The following primary, accessory, and specialized exercises should build a strength and conditioning professional's knowledge base and ability to improve a lacrosse athlete's performance.

EXERCISE FINDER

GPP UPPER BODY EXERCISES: HORIZONTAL PUSH

Barbell Bench Press (BBBP) 108
   Dumbbell Bench Press (DBBP) 109
   Dumbbell Incline Bench Press 109
   Floor Press. 109
   Glute Bridge Press. 109
   Push-Up 109

GPP UPPER BODY EXERCISES: VERTICAL PUSH

Barbell Overhead Press (BBOHP) 110
   Barbell Push Jerk (BBPJ) 111
   Barbell Push Press (BBPP). 111
   Barbell Split Jerk. 111
   Dumbbell Overhead Press 111
   Landmine Rotational Press 111
   Landmine Single-Arm Press 111

GPP UPPER BODY EXERCISES: HORIZONTAL PULL

Barbell Bent-Over Row (BBBOR). 112
   Dumbbell Single-Arm Bent-Over Row (DBSAR) 113
   Inverted Row. 113
   Landmine Row. 113
   Lawn Mower Row 113
   Meadow Row 113
   Seated Row 113

GPP UPPER BODY EXERCISES: VERTICAL PULL

Pull-Up 114
   Cable Straight-Arm Row .115
   Chin-Up 114
   Dumbbell Pullover 115
   Lat Pulldown. 114

SPP PRIMARY UPPER BODY EXERCISES

Dumbbell Half-Kneeling Overhead Press 119
Kickstand Row (With Contralateral Load) 115
Landmine Single-Arm Push Press .117
Over–Under Pull-Up 116
Single-Arm Suspension Row 120

SPP ACCESSORY UPPER BODY EXERCISES

Banded Iron Cross Triceps Extension 122
Banded T-Spine Rotational Row .125
Dumbbell Suitcase Shrug 121
Single-Arm Dumbbell Muscle Snatch 124
Suspension Strap Jammer Press 123

SPP SPECIALIZED UPPER BODY EXERCISES

Biceps Drop Catch 125
Medicine Ball Altitude Drop, Catch, and Throw 127
Mini-Ball Shoulder Drop Catch 130
Offset-Load Bench Press 129
Sledgehammer Levers 131

NECK EXERCISES

Chin Lift: Protractions, Protractions With Rotation (Look Left and Right),
and Ear-to-Shoulder Protractions With Lateral Flexion 132
Four-Way Short-Lever Bench Neck Holds (Forehead, Left, Back, Right) . 132
Long-Lever Three-Way Isometric Neck Falls (Back, Left, Right) 132

GPP UPPER BODY EXERCISES: HORIZONTAL PUSH

BARBELL BENCH PRESS (BBBP)

Primary Muscles Trained

Pectoralis major, anterior deltoids, triceps brachii

Beginning Position

- Lie on the bench with the back, head, and hips in contact with the pad.
- Plant both feet firmly on the floor.
- The bar should be at eye level and lower than an arm's length away from the bench in the rack.
- Hand placement may depend on personal comfort, starting a thumb's width away from the inside of the knurling on the barbell.
- The hands, including the thumbs, should be fully wrapped around the bar.
- Remove the bar from the rack and hold it above the chest (a).

Movement Phases

1. Lower the bar with control to the midchest (b).
2. When the bar contacts the chest, reverse the motion and return the barbell to the beginning position.

Figure 7.1   Barbell bench press: (a) beginning position; (b) end position.

Breathing Guidelines

Inhale and brace before lowering the bar to the chest. Exhale as the bar returns to the extended position over the chest.

Spotting Guidelines

Stand at the athlete's head and grasp the bar with an alternating hand grip between the athlete's hands. Help lift the bar out of the rack and stabilize it over the athlete's chest. Let go of the bar and be actively engaged if the athlete needs assistance. Upon completion of the set, help the athlete put the bar back into the racking position.

Exercise Modifications and Variations

Push-Up

Lie prone on the floor. Place the hands wider than shoulder-width apart, with the feet together and the back straight. Push the floor away from the body while maintaining a streamlined posture from ear to ankle. Control the body during a descent back to the floor.

Dumbbell Bench Press (DBBP)

This exercise variation allows more control and movement variation at the shoulder joint. Holding a dumbbells in a neutral grip, assume the beginning position described for the BBBP and control the weight while bringing the dumbbells down to chest level. In contrast to the BBBP, the dumbbells will come down just to the outside of the chest.

Dumbbell Incline Bench Press

This variation is a slight variation of the DBBP, with the bench inclined. The amount of bench incline may vary, but 45 degrees is a typical angle. The dumbbells will come down slightly higher, just outside the chest.

Floor Press

In this variation, the exercise is performed the same as the BBBP but while lying on the floor. Subsequently, the range of motion is limited to when the elbows touch the floor.

Glute Bridge Press

Begin this exercise by lying supine on the floor. Glute bridge up and perform the BBBP; aim to contact the bar with the lower chest.

Coaching Tips

- While performing this movement, the athlete should generate force through the floor to help drive the barbell off the chest.
- Using a suicide grip (commonly called an **open grip**—i.e., the thumbs are not wrapped around the bar) is dangerous for the athlete and spotter.

GPP UPPER BODY EXERCISES: VERTICAL PUSH

BARBELL OVERHEAD PRESS (BBOHP)

Primary Muscles Trained

Anterior deltoids, medial deltoids, triceps brachii

Beginning Position

- With the barbell resting in a rack at chest level, grasp the bar with a double overhand grip with the hands slightly more than shoulder-width apart.
- Lift the barbell out of the rack, allowing it to rest across the front of the shoulders.
- Stand with the feet shoulder-width apart and the toes pointed straight ahead (a).

Movement Phases

1. Press the barbell over the head until the elbows are fully extended (b).
2. Reverse the motion, controlling the bar back to the front of the shoulders.

Breathing Guidelines

Inhale and brace before pressing the barbell. Exhale when the bar stops over the head.

Figure 7.2 Barbell overhead press: (a) beginning position; (b) end position.

Spotting Guidelines

Spotters are not needed for this exercise. Have safeties on the rack just below chest height to catch the weight if it falls, or use rubber bumper plates so that the bar will hit the floor without damaging equipment or the athlete.

Exercise Modifications and Variations

Dumbbell Overhead Press

This variation is the same as the BBOHP except that it uses dumbbells and different hand placement. The dumbbell hand placement should be in a neutral position just above the shoulders before the press.

Barbell Push Press (BBPP)

This variation is the same as BBOHP except that it initiates power through the floor with the legs to help press the weight overhead.

Barbell Push Jerk (BBPJ)

This variation is the same as the BBPP with an added catch in a power position.

Barbell Split Jerk

This variation is the same as BBPJ except for the catch position. The legs will go into a power split position when catching the bar.

Landmine Single-Arm Press

This variation is similar to the BBOHP but allows athletes to press more out in front of their body instead of fully overhead. Grasp the end of the barbell in one hand just off the front of the same shoulder. Standing with the feet shoulder-width apart, press the barbell away from the body until the elbow is fully extended up and out in front of the body.

Landmine Rotational Press

This variation using the landmine attachment begins with bringing the barbell across the body to the outside shoulder in one hand (while standing parallel to the barbell). To begin the exercise, initiate force through the floor and press the bar across the body. Rotate toward the front leg until the elbow fully extends and the arm moves over and outside the opposite shoulder.

Coaching Tips

- At full extension of the arm, make sure the bar is above the head (cue the athlete to imagine pushing the head "through the window").
- Use a dumbbell or landmine variation to assist a lacrosse athlete with a prior shoulder injury or use a standard progression or regression of exercises.

GPP UPPER BODY EXERCISES: HORIZONTAL PULL

BARBELL BENT-OVER ROW (BBBOR)

Primary Muscles Trained

Latissimus dorsi, middle trapezius, rhomboids, teres major, posterior deltoids

Beginning Position

- Position the feet slightly more than hip-width apart, with the knees slightly flexed.
- Use a double overhand grip, similar to the position described for the BBBP (or moderately wider, if preferred).
- Use proper deadlift mechanics to lift the bar off the floor.
- Allow the bar to hang at full elbow extension, resting on the front of the thighs.
- Hip hinge with a moderate knee flex, keeping the back flat (as in the bottom of a Romanian deadlift) to a bottom (beginning) position with the elbows fully extended (a).

Movement Phases

1. Initiate the movement by pulling the bar back toward the abdomen until it contacts the body (b).
2. Return the bar to the beginning position. Actively control the weight; do not just let it fall to the bottom.

Breathing Guidelines

Inhale at the start of the movement; this increases stability through the torso. Hold the breath and brace through the exercise. Exhale as the bar lowers.

Figure 7.3   Barbell bent-over row: (a) beginning position; (b) end position.

Exercise Modifications and Variations

Inverted Row

This bodyweight variation can be done using a barbell in a rack position or suspension strap trainers. Grasp the bar with a double overhand or underhand grip. Keep the torso rigid and maintain a streamline from ankle to ear for the entire exercise. Initiate the movement, pulling up toward the barbell until contact is made at midchest. Reverse the motion until the elbows are back to full extension.

Seated Row

This variation can be done with bands or a cable machine. Sitting upright with the arms held out in front of the body and the elbows fully extended, grasp the cable machine handle and pull the handle back toward the body until it contacts the body just below the sternum.

Dumbbell Single-Arm Bent-Over Row (DBSAR)

This variation allows an athlete to perform a unilateral row. The weight will start on the floor. Grasp the dumbbell, lean over with a slightly staggered stance, and support the body with the opposite hand on a bench. Keep the body parallel with the floor while pulling the weight back toward the hip. Once the weight is at hip level, control it while descending back to the beginning position.

Lawn Mower Row

This variation is very similar to the DBSAR, except it allows the torso to rotate downward in the bottom position and open upward in the top position. This exercise resembles someone starting a lawn mower with a pull string.

Landmine Row

This variation changes the implement back to the barbell and allows the strength and conditioning professional to choose whether the exercise is bilateral or unilateral. Grasp the bar below the barbell sleeve to perform this exercise. Maintaining a start position similar to that of the BBBOR, pull the bar toward the body and control it back to full elbow extension.

Meadow Row

The barbell will be in a landmine attachment for this variation. Grasp the end of a barbell while bent over with a staggered stance, bracing on the forward leg. Pull the end of the barbell toward the lower portion of the chest with the elbow abducted from the body over the top of the barbell. Pull up until the end of the barbell contacts the outer torso, and control the weight back to the start position with each repetition.

Coaching Tip

Athletes often cheat on these exercises by thrusting the weight up to the body. They should control the bar in all phases of this movement.

GPP UPPER BODY EXERCISES: VERTICAL PULL

PULL-UP

Primary Muscles Trained

Latissimus dorsi, teres major, rhomboids, middle trapezius, posterior deltoids

Beginning Position

- Grasp the pull-up bar overhead with a double overhand grip slightly more than shoulder-width apart.
- Hang with the back engaged, ready to begin the pull (a).

Movement Phases

1. With the back engaged, begin pulling the chest to the bar until the chin is above the bar while maintaining a rigid torso (b).
2. Once the chin has reached the top of the bar, lower back to the beginning position with a controlled movement.

Breathing Guidelines

Inhale before the pull-up begins, and exhale at the top. Continue to breathe on the descent back to resetting for the next repetition.

Figure 7.4   Pull-up: (a) beginning position; (b) end position.

Exercise Modifications and Variations

Chin-Up

A chin-up is the same as a pull-up, except the grip is double underhand.

Lat Pulldown

Sitting on a lat pulldown machine with the legs locked in, grasp the lat bar with a grip of choice. Pull the bar down, with the torso rigid and slightly leaned back, until the bar touches the upper chest. Control the bar back to the beginning position.

Dumbbell Pullover

Lying supine on a bench, grasp the end of a dumbbell and hold it directly above the chest. Control the dumbbell while beginning to lower it back over the head as far as comfortable. While maintaining a tight torso, reverse the motion and pull the dumbbell back to the beginning position.

Cable Straight-Arm Row

Stand facing a cable column machine set higher than face height. Grasp the end of the cable in one hand. The elbow should be straight. Pull the cable down (via shoulder extension, not elbow flexion) toward the side of the body and control it back to the start position to complete each repetition. It is essential to keep the shoulder back and down instead of allowing it to roll over while performing the pulldown. This variation is often used to train the lats and back when an athlete has a limitation that prevents vertical pulling.

Coaching Tip

Athletes often cheat on this exercise by kicking and not controlling the descent or pulling to the top. If necessary, use eccentric (lowering only) pulls or bands to ensure the movement is done with the correct form until strength is at a level where no assistance is needed.

SPP PRIMARY UPPER BODY EXERCISES

KICKSTAND ROW (WITH CONTRALATERAL LOAD)

Primary Muscles Trained

Latissimus dorsi, middle trapezius, rhomboids, teres major, biceps brachii

Beginning Position

- Stand with one foot in front of the other.
- Place a weight in the hand opposite to the front foot.
- Put most of the body weight onto the front foot, using the back foot for balance. Slightly flex the front knee and moderately flex the back knee.
- Hinge forward until the upper body is parallel or nearly parallel with the floor (hinge more than what is shown in *a*).
- Hold the weight with the elbow fully extended.

Movement Phases

1. Initiate the movement by pulling the dumbbell up to the side of the body *(b)*.
2. Lower the weight until the elbow is fully extended.
3. At the end of the set, place a weight in the other hand, switch the position of the feet, and repeat the movement.

Figure 7.5   Kickstand row: *(a)* beginning position; *(b)* end position.

Breathing Guidelines

Inhale before pulling the weight up. Exhale after returning the weight to the beginning position.

Exercise Modifications and Variations

A kettlebell can be used instead of a dumbbell. A barbell can be used, with the hand grip in the center, to train the shoulder's internal and external rotation stability during the movement. Chains or a band attached to the floor can be used if an accommodating resistance effect is desired. Tuck the elbow or abduct the arm 90 degrees (at the shoulder) to change the emphasis of the muscles trained.

Coaching Tip

The athlete should maintain a neutral spine throughout the exercise. Ensure the trunk remains level and does not rotate.

OVER–UNDER PULL-UP

Primary Muscles Trained

Latissimus dorsi, lower trapezius, brachialis, teres major, biceps brachii

Beginning Position

- Grasp the pull-up bar overhead with one hand in a pronated grip and the other in a supinated grip.
- Hang with the legs off the floor with the elbows fully extended *(a)*.

Movement Phases

1. Initiate the movement by depressing the shoulder blades and pulling upward.
2. Keep pulling until the chin is above the bar while maintaining a rigid torso *(b)*.
3. Once the chin has reached the top of the bar, lower back to the beginning position with a controlled movement.

Breathing Guidelines

Inhale before pulling. Exhale after returning the body to the beginning position.

Exercise Modifications and Variations

External resistance, such as chains around the neck or weights hanging from the waist, can be added. To add extra tibialis work, weights can be placed on top of the foot and the exercise performed by keeping the weights in place with dorsiflexion. If an athlete is not strong enough to do a pull-up, bands can be placed around the bar and used to reduce the load. The exercise can be done using a thicker bar to increase the grip component.

Coaching Tip

To create a consistent standard, the athlete's elbows must begin and end fully extended. The athlete should not swing the body while performing the exercise. Ensure the athlete controls his or her body weight on the way down and does not just drop to full elbow extension.

Figure 7.6   Over–under pull-up: *(a)* beginning position; *(b)* end position.

LANDMINE SINGLE-ARM PUSH PRESS

Primary Muscles Trained

Anterior deltoids, medial deltoids, triceps brachii

Beginning Position

- Stand with the feet shoulder-width apart at the end of a barbell in a landmine attachment.
- Grasp the end of the barbell in one hand just off the front of the same shoulder *(a)*.

Movement Phases

1. Perform a controlled dip by flexing the knees with a slight hip hinge *(b)*.
2. Without a pause between the dip and drive, reverse the dipping motion and drive the barbell upward by pressing it up and away toward the landmine attachment. The explosive nature of the exercise will result in full knee extension and moderate-to-significant plantar flexion *(c)*.
3. Control the weight while lowering the heels to the floor and returning the bar back to the front of the shoulder.
4. At the end of the set, grasp the barbell with the other hand and repeat the movement.

Figure 7.7 Landmine single-arm push press: *(a)* beginning position; *(b)* dip; *(c)* drive.

Breathing Guidelines

Inhale before pressing the barbell. Exhale as the elbow is fully extended.

Exercise Modifications and Variations

This exercise can be done by pressing the bar with both arms. Additionally, band tension can be added under the feet and around the bar. (Make sure the band is a manageable tension and is fully under the arch of the shoe.)

DUMBBELL HALF-KNEELING OVERHEAD PRESS

Primary Muscles Trained

Deltoids, triceps brachii

Beginning Position

- Kneel on one knee with the opposite leg out in front, keeping the body stable from left to right.
- Grasp the dumbbell in one hand and let it rest on the anterior shoulder (a).

Movement Phases

1. Begin by pressing the dumbbell overhead.
2. Keep an upright, rigid torso position (b).
3. Stabilize the weight overhead and control it while lowering it back down.
4. At the end of the set, grasp the dumbbell with the other hand, switch the position of the legs, and repeat the movement.

Figure 7.8   Dumbbell half-kneeling overhead press: (a) beginning position; (b) end position.

Breathing Guidelines

Inhale before pressing overhead. Exhale as the elbow and shoulder fully extend over the head.

Spotting Guidelines

A spotter could stand beside the athlete, spotting him or her at the wrist.

Coaching Tip

Do not load the exercise so heavily that the athlete cannot move the dumbbell without laterally bending. The athlete should keep the elbow in front of the body through the pressing motion to help with shoulder stabilization and comfort.

SINGLE-ARM SUSPENSION ROW

Primary Muscles Trained

Latissimus dorsi, middle trapezius, rhomboids, teres major, biceps brachii, posterior deltoids

Beginning Position

- Grasp the handle of a suspension strap in one hand and lean back to the desired resistance level.
- With a rigid torso, hold a streamlined posture from ear to ankle with the heels serving as the anchor point with the floor (a).

Movement Phases

1. Begin by pulling the body toward the handle.
2. Continue to pull until the body contacts the handle just outside the torso (pull farther than what is shown in b).
3. At the end of the set, grasp the handle with the other hand and repeat the movement.

Breathing Guidelines

Inhale before the pull. Exhale while lowering.

Figure 7.9 Single-arm suspension row: (a) beginning position; (b) end position.

Exercise Modifications and Variations

An additional variation prompts rotational work to allow a single-arm rotational row. At the bottom of the row, allow the torso to open upward. During the final portion of the pull, rotate the body toward the handle.

Coaching Tip

Controlling the descent is as crucial as the pulling portion of this exercise.

SPP ACCESSORY UPPER BODY EXERCISES

DUMBBELL SUITCASE SHRUG

Primary Muscles Trained

Upper trapezius, external and internal obliques, levator scapulae, sternocleido-mastoid, quadratus lumborum

Beginning Position

- Stand with the feet shoulder-width apart.
- Place a dumbbell in one hand, outside the frame of the body on the side holding the weight (a).

Movement Phases

1. Initiate the movement by elevating the shoulder in a straight line of pull.
2. Elevate the shoulder until a full range of motion is reached (b).
3. Lower the shoulder back to the beginning position.
4. At the end of the set, grasp the dumbbell with the other hand and repeat the movement.

Figure 7.10   Dumbbell suitcase shrug: (a) beginning position; (b) end position.

Breathing Guidelines

Inhale before pulling the weight. Exhale after returning the weight to the beginning position.

Exercise Modifications and Variations

Using grip straps to focus on training the trapezius without being limited by grip strength is highly advantageous for this exercise.

Coaching Tip

Ensure the athlete's shoulder elevates in a perfectly vertical direction and that there is no rolling of the shoulder.

BANDED IRON CROSS TRICEPS EXTENSION

Primary Muscles Trained

Triceps brachii, posterior deltoids, rhomboids, middle trapezius

Beginning Position

- With the shoulders abducted and elbows flexed to 90 degrees, hold a band directly in front of the deltoids without any slack in the band (a).

Movement Phases

1. Initiate the movement by extending the elbows through the full range of motion while keeping the palms down.
2. Contract the triceps brachii forcefully at extension while ensuring there is no movement in the shoulder joints (b).
3. Return the elbows back to their 90-degree beginning position without any movement occurring in the shoulder joints.

Figure 7.11   Banded iron cross triceps extension: (a) beginning position; (b) end position.

Breathing Guidelines

Breathe diaphragmatically throughout the entire exercise.

Exercise Modifications and Variations

Externally rotate the shoulders by moving the hands from in front of the chest to overhead to increase the difficulty of stabilizing the external rotation.

Coaching Tip

Ensure the athlete's elbows remain at the same level as the deltoids throughout the entire movement. There is a tendency to allow the elbows to drop as the difficulty increases with higher repetitions.

SUSPENSION STRAP JAMMER PRESS

Primary Muscles Trained

Anterior deltoids, triceps brachii

Beginning Position

- Stand with the knees slightly flexed and the feet between hip- and shoulder-width apart behind a bar that is hanging in the two handle ends of a suspension strap.
- Grasp the bar with an overhand grip at upper chest level (a).

Movement Phases

1. Press the bar away from the body forcefully; the explosive nature of the exercise will result in full knee extension and moderate plantar flexion.
2. The end position will be with the hands, shoulders, hips, knees, and ankles in a line (b).
3. Return to the beginning position by lowering the heels to the floor, slightly flexing the knees, and lowering the bar back down to the body, keeping the elbows in toward the body and behind the barbell.

Figure 7.12   Suspension strap Jammer press: (a) beginning position; (b) end position.

Breathing Guidelines

Inhale before pushing. Exhale upon the push.

Exercise Modifications and Variations

This exercise can be modified by switching hand positions, especially using a double overhand grip for face off, get off (FOGO) athletes. Also, if arm attachments are available, this exercise can be done without using suspension straps.

Coaching Tip

Have the athlete be explosive through the press.

SINGLE-ARM DUMBBELL MUSCLE SNATCH

Primary Muscles Trained

Deltoids

Beginning Position

- Place the feet between hip- and shoulder-width apart, with the toes pointed forward.
- Grasp a dumbbell in one hand and hold it between the legs with the knees moderately flexed (a).

Movement Phases

1. Begin the movement by forcefully pulling the dumbbell upward (b).
2. Continue pulling until the dumbbell is overhead with the elbow fully extended and the knuckles are punched to the sky (c).

Figure 7.13 Single-arm dumbbell muscle snatch: (a) beginning position; (b) pulling the dumbbell; (c) end position.

3. Slowly lower the dumbbell back to the shoulder and provide assistance with the opposite hand by grasping one side of the dumbbell to return it to the beginning position.
4. At the end of the set, grasp the barbell with the other hand and repeat the movement or alternate hands during the set.

Breathing Guidelines

Inhale before the initial pull. Exhale as the weight is punched overhead.

Coaching Tip

The athlete should pull hard, punch high, and keep the dumbbell close to the body as it is pulled upward and lowered past the body to the beginning position.

BANDED T-SPINE ROTATIONAL ROW

Primary Muscles Trained

Rhomboids, latissimus dorsi

Beginning Position

- Start in a quadruped position perpendicular to a low band attached to a rack.
- With the outside hand, reach across and underneath the body to grab the band (a).

Movement Phases

1. Begin the movement by pulling the band across and underneath the body.
2. Continue pulling while rotating toward the pulling side of the body (b).
3. Control the band back to the beginning position, rotating the outside shoulder underneath the body.
4. At the end of the set, reposition the body to pull the band with the other hand.

Breathing Guidelines

Inhale before the row. Exhale at the top of the rotation to increase rotation at the T-spine.

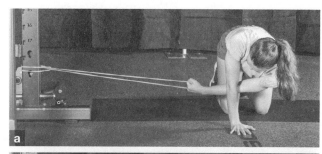

Figure 7.14 Banded T-spine rotational row: (a) beginning position; (b) end position.

Coaching Tip

The athlete should try to disassociate the lower and upper body and should try to maintain the hips parallel with the floor.

SPP SPECIALIZED UPPER BODY EXERCISES

BICEPS DROP CATCH

Primary Muscles Trained

Biceps brachii, brachialis, brachioradialis, anterior deltoids

Beginning Position

- Stand with a dumbbell in each hand.
- Flex the elbows to approximately 130 degrees (a).

Movement Phases

1. Release the dumbbells, allowing them to drop down.
2. Quickly extend the elbows to move the hands away from the dumbbells at a faster rate than the speed of the falling dumbbells *(b)*.
3. When the elbows reach 90 degrees, catch the dumbbells with the elbows fixed in the 90-degree flexed position. Do not allow any movement in the shoulders or elbows when the dumbbells are caught *(c)*.
4. Return the dumbbells to the beginning position.

Figure 7.15 Biceps drop catch: *(a)* beginning position; *(b)* extend the elbows while releasing the dumbbells; *(c)* catch the dumbbells in the fixed elbow position.

Breathing Guidelines

Inhale before releasing the weight. Exhale after returning the dumbbells to the beginning position.

Exercise Modifications and Variations

To increase the difficulty of the exercise, have a partner drop a dumbbell from an elevated position. For this variation, the athlete catching the dumbbell should begin the exercise with the elbow flexed at 90 degrees and keep that fixed position as the dumbbell is caught.

Coaching Tip

Stiffness of the joints upon catching the dumbbells is essential to attain the desired training effect. The dumbbells must be instantly stopped upon catching. Allowing the dumbbells to drop farther after catching them negates much of the desired training effect of this exercise.

MEDICINE BALL ALTITUDE DROP, CATCH, AND THROW

Primary Muscles Trained

Pectoralis major, anterior deltoid, triceps brachii

Beginning Position

- The athlete lies supine on the floor.
- A partner stands at the head of the athlete and holds a medicine ball above the athlete's chest.
- The athlete on the floor holds the arms in a ready position to catch the medicine ball *(a)*.

Movement Phases

1. The standing partner releases the ball to drop it straight down, directly over the athlete's chest *(b)*.
2. The athlete catches the ball *(c)* and immediately throws it back in the air as high as possible *(d)*.
3. The standing partner catches the ball and resets the ball position for the next repetition.

Breathing Guidelines

Upon catching the ball, the athlete should momentarily hold his or her breath until the release of the throw.

Spotting Guidelines

The standing partner must be sure to drop the ball directly over the athlete's chest. The ball must be dropped vertically with no movement horizontally. It is imperative that the standing partner catches the ball once it has been thrown.

Exercise Modifications and Variations

The partner may stand on an elevated surface to increase the velocity of the ball before it reaches the athlete. While this exercise is traditionally done with the athlete lying on the floor, it may also be done lying on a bench.

Coaching Tip

Ensure the athlete understands that he or she is to catch and stop the momentum of the ball as quickly as possible before throwing it back up into the air. The return throw by the athlete must be executed with as much force as possible. Having athletes compete to see who can throw highest helps elicit maximal force production.

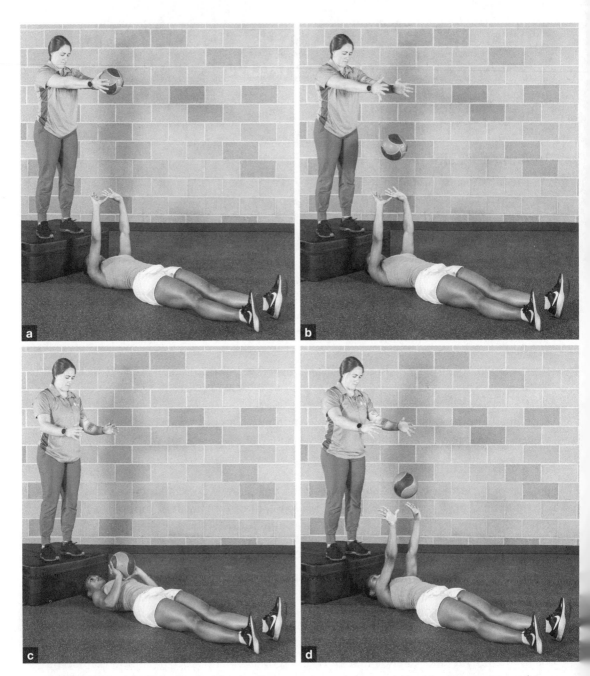

Figure 7.16 Medicine ball altitude drop, catch, and throw: *(a)* beginning position; *(b)* partner drops the ball; *(c)* athlete catches the ball; *(d)* athlete throws the ball.

OFFSET-LOAD BENCH PRESS

Primary Muscles Trained

Pectoralis major, anterior deltoid, triceps brachii, latissimus dorsi, external and internal obliques

Beginning Position

- For this exercise, load one side of a barbell with 10% to 25% more load than the other side.
- Lie on a bench with the loaded barbell in a rack directly above the eyes.
- Place both feet on the floor, creating pressure with the legs by pushing toward the head.
- While depressing the shoulder blades and tightening the latissimus dorsi, grip the bar with the hands wider than shoulder-width apart.

Movement Phases

1. Initiate the exercise by unracking the barbell. This is executed by pushing on the overloaded side and pulling on the underloaded side to maintain a level barbell.
2. Hold the barbell motionless directly above the upper chest (a).
3. Once the barbell is motionless, lower it toward the chest.
4. When the barbell is 1 inch (2.5 cm) from the chest, bring it to a complete stop (b).
5. Press the barbell upward until it reaches the beginning position.

Breathing Guidelines

Inhale before lowering the weight. Exhale after returning the weight to the beginning position.

Spotting Guidelines

A spotter must keep his or her hands close to the barbell at all times. The spotter should not touch the barbell unless the athlete can no longer

Figure 7.17 Offset-load bench press: (a) beginning position; (b) end position.

continue to press the bar and it begins to descend. Due to the uneven load, the spotter must understand the need to pull up with the hand on the overloaded side while maintaining downward pressure with the hand on the underloaded side. If the spotter pulls up hard on the underloaded side, it may cause the athlete to roll off the bench to the overloaded side.

Exercise Modifications and Variations
The offset load may be achieved by the use of chains. The chains can be used at different "link sets" to create the offset in the load.

Coaching Tip
This is an advanced exercise that should not be used with novice athletes. Begin the offset loading with a load offset by 10% to get the athlete accustomed to the exercise. Executing several weeks of slower tempo work before progressing the load or the movement speed is recommended.

MINI-BALL SHOULDER DROP CATCH

Primary Muscles Trained
Posterior shoulder, rotator cuff muscles

Beginning Position
- Grasp a mini-ball and lie prone with the chest supported on an incline bench.
- Abduct and flex (i.e., horizontally abduct) one shoulder to 90 degrees with the palm facing the floor (a).

Movement Phases
1. Allow the ball to drop out of the hand (b).
2. Quickly lower the arm and catch the ball before it falls to the floor with the palm still facing the floor (c).
3. Raise the arm to return to the beginning position quickly.
4. At the end of the set, switch the ball to the other side and repeat the movement or alternate hands during the set.

Figure 7.18 Mini-ball shoulder drop catch: (a) beginning position; (b) release the ball; (c) catch the ball.

Breathing Guidelines

Breathe diaphragmatically throughout the entire exercise.

Exercise Modifications and Variations

Three variations of this exercise include flexing the elbow to 90 degrees, keeping the elbow straight and flexing the shoulder up to a Y position, and standing and flexing the shoulder to 90 degrees in front of the body.

Coaching Tip

Start with lighter mini-balls and progress to heavier mini-balls slowly. Using a ball that is too heavy can lead to injury in the shoulder.

SLEDGEHAMMER LEVERS

Primary Muscles Trained

Extensor carpi ulnaris, flexor carpi ulnaris

Beginning Position

- Position the head of the sledgehammer behind the body.
- Grip the sledgehammer handle in one hand halfway between the end of the handle and the head of the sledgehammer.
- With the arm fully extended to one side of the body, lift the sledgehammer off the floor.
- The weight of the sledgehammer will put the wrist in a slight radial deviation for the beginning position.

Movement Phases

1. Initiate the movement by flexing the wrist to bring the pinky finger toward the forearm (ulnar deviation).
2. Flex the wrist through a full range of motion, lifting the head of the sledgehammer higher in the air.
3. Once the full range of motion has been achieved, slowly lower the sledgehammer back to the beginning position.
4. At the end of the set, grasp the sledgehammer with the other hand and repeat the movement or alternate hands during the set.

Breathing Guidelines

Breathe diaphragmatically throughout the entire exercise.

Exercise Modifications and Variations

Radial deviation can also be executed to work the other side of the forearm. This variation requires the head of the sledgehammer to be in front of the body.

Coaching Tip

Ensure that athletes gradually progress to moving their grip farther down the handle of the sledgehammer as they gain strength. The farther the grip from the head of the sledgehammer, the heavier the weight. Moving down the handle too quickly will result in a limited range of motion in the wrist, diminishing the effects of the exercise.

NECK EXERCISES

Exercises for the neck need to be a part of a well-designed resistance training program (3). Other than barbell, dumbbell, or kettlebell shoulder shrugs, a complete program for the neck muscles involves neck flexion, extension, and protrusion (4). The primary muscles trained include the following, based on the movement:

- Anterior (flexion): scalene, sternocleidomastoid, longus capitis, longus colli
- Posterior (extension): semispinalis capitis, splenius capitis, splenius cervicis
- Protrusion (terminal extension): suboccipital muscles, multifidus
- Upper back (stabilizes, absorbs forces): trapezius, scapularis, infraspinatus, teres minor, teres major

Chin Lift: Protractions, Protractions With Rotation (Look Left and Right), and Ear-to-Shoulder Protractions With Lateral Flexion

Lie supine with the shoulders abducted 90 degrees and the elbows flexed to 90 degrees. Begin by protracting the head off the floor, keeping the chin and forehead on the same plane while raising and lowering the head. The action is similar for protractions with rotation (looking left and right), with the addition of simply turning the chin toward one shoulder and then to the opposite shoulder. Lastly, for ear-to-shoulder protractions, begin with the initial protraction of the head off the floor but continue the exercise by moving one ear to the shoulder on the same side and then moving the opposite ear to that side's shoulder to finish one repetition on each side. During all of these exercises, it is important to actively keep the neck protracted toward the ceiling.

Four-Way Short-Lever Bench Neck Holds (Forehead, Left, Back, Right)

With the knees on the floor, place the forehead on a bench. Make sure to maintain a straight line from head to knee, as in the up position of a modified push-up but with the head on a bench. Remove the hands from the floor and hold isometrically for a short duration (5 to 15 seconds).

Long-Lever Three-Way Isometric Neck Falls (Back, Left, Right)

Stand with the body as straight as possible from heel to head, with the arms crossed in front of the body. Slowly fall backward as a partner holds the back of the head. End in a supine plank position with the heels touching the floor and the partner holding the head. It is important for the partner to have a strong established base of support. As strength improves, the partner can lower the athlete closer to the floor. When performing the exercise to the left and to the right, make sure the inside foot is stacked in front of the outside foot in relationship to where the partner is standing.

8

ANATOMICAL CORE EXERCISE TECHNIQUE

ANDREW SACKS AND JESSI GLAUSER

For athletes competing in sports featuring rotational movement patterns such as swinging, throwing, or—in the case of lacrosse athletes—shooting and passing, building strength and power in the anatomical core musculature is an integral part of the training process. A strong, powerful core enables these athletes to effectively transfer and amplify energy between their lower and upper body and generate high levels of torque through their midsection, leading to higher shooting and passing velocities. These increased velocities can make lacrosse athletes' shots on goal faster and therefore more difficult to defend and can improve their ability to throw passes over longer distances.

Core strength and stability also come into play during the more physical aspects of lacrosse, such as maintaining defensive positioning in one-on-one situations, battling for ground balls, and absorbing or delivering checks. The ability to control one's body and not allow an opponent to dictate the flow of one-on-one interaction can often make the difference between a successful outcome and failure in any contact sport, and lacrosse is no exception.

The anatomical core is composed of the axial skeleton—the spine, head, and ribcage—and the muscles that originate from the axial skeleton (1, 2). From a strength and conditioning perspective, core training more typically focuses on the muscles of the trunk between the pelvis and shoulders (and not, say, the muscles of the face), because these are the muscles that will contribute to athletic performance.

Traditionally, core training strategies have been designed to build isometric strength and endurance in the trunk musculature with plank variations and rotational holds (e.g., Pallof press variations) and concentric strength with exercises such as crunches and sit-ups. These basic exercises can still serve a purpose in a core training program, but they only train a small portion of the movement patterns involving the core. An advanced, comprehensive core training program will include exercises that build strength, power, stability, mobility, and neuromuscular coordination, improving the athlete's ability to resist movement, generate movement, absorb and transfer energy, stabilize the spine, and optimize kinetic sequencing during whole-body movements.

Kinetic sequencing is an important concept to understand when designing training programs to improve rotational power, because a properly sequenced rotation will produce higher rotational velocities than one that is poorly sequenced (3, 5, 7). To produce the highest level of force generation and transfer from the lower body to the upper body, athletes must learn to rotate their pelvis before rotating their upper torso, creating what is known as hip–shoulder separation. This separation stretches and loads the core musculature and fascia, priming the muscles to rapidly produce high levels of force via the stretch-shortening cycle (4).

Once the pelvis has reached peak rotational torque, the upper torso can then rotate powerfully and amplify the force generated from pelvic rotation. The combined rotational energy generated by the pelvis and torso can then be transferred to the arms, which will in turn transfer that energy into the stick and ultimately the ball, producing the highest level of rotational velocity at the point where the ball leaves the head of the stick. To fully transfer rotational energy through the kinetic chain, each section of the chain must also be able to decelerate and stabilize before acceleration of the next section (6). This creates a whip-like action through the body, culminating in a whip crack of energy at ball release.

This chapter will provide examples of exercises designed to optimize core function in lacrosse athletes. The exercise selection is not comprehensive but may serve as part of a systematic progression of core training that requires the athlete to respond and adapt to static and dynamic training stimuli. Within the progression, ground-based isometrics serve as an initial training stimulus for novice athletes and remain one of the foundational components within a more advanced training program. Before advanced acceleration and deceleration exercises are implemented, postural stabilization is addressed via statically braced positions followed by dynamic, stabilization-resisting sagittal and frontal plane movements. Postural modifications and variations for the selected exercises are included to provide sample progressions and regressions that fit an athlete's training age and periodization needs.

The two overarching categories in which the exercises are organized are braced exercises and movement exercises. The positions in the braced category include standard, rotational, and postural variations. The movement category includes variations of contract/relax, lifts and chops, and deceleration and acceleration exercises.

EXERCISE FINDER

BRACED EXERCISES

Farmer's Carry 140
Farmer's Carry Uneven 141
Pallof Hold 138
Prone Pull-Through 137
RKC Plank 136
Rollout 139
Suitcase Carry 142
Waiter's Carry 143

MOVEMENT EXERCISES

Cable Chop 147
   Downward Chop 147
   Half-Kneeling Cable Chop 147
   Split-Stance Cable Chop 147

Cable Lift. 148
  Half-Kneeling Cable Lift 150
  Split-Stance Cable Lift 150
Landmine Rotations 160
  Stationary Landmine Rotation 160
Medicine Ball Catch and Deceleration 153
  Half-Kneeling Medicine Ball Catch and Deceleration 153
  Split-Stance Medicine Ball Catch and Deceleration 153
Medicine Ball Chop and Rebound 151
Medicine Ball Chop Circuit 150
Medicine Ball Chop Toss 155
  Drop Step 156
  Shuffle Step 156
  Turn and Burn 156
Medicine Ball Shot Put 158
  Drop Step 159
  Shuffle Step 159
  Turn and Burn 159
Medicine Ball Side Toss 162
  Drop Step 162
  Shuffle Step 162
  Turn and Burn 162
Medicine Ball Slam 156
  Jump Slam 158
  Single-Leg Slam 158
PVC Contract, Relax, Coordinate (C-R-C) 144
PVC C-R-C Lateral 145

BRACED EXERCISES

RKC PLANK

Primary Muscles Trained

Transversus abdominis, external and internal obliques, rectus abdominis, gluteus maximus, quadriceps, pectoralis major, latissimus dorsi, scapulothoracic stabilizers

Beginning Position

- Position the body prone on the floor with the ankles dorsiflexed and the knees and hips extended.
- Position the feet approximately hip-width apart with the weight suspended on the toes.
- Flex the shoulders and elbows to 90 degrees with the palms facing each other.
- Position the cervical spine in a neutral position.

Movement Phases

1. The RKC plank is an isometric core exercise. Therefore, the only movement is transitioning from the floor to the supported, braced, and elevated prone position.
2. Maintain isometric tension throughout the whole body. Emphasis is on active tension of the external shoulder rotators, hip adductors, knee extensors, glutes, and hip extensors.
3. Additionally, actively generate abdominal tension without releasing the tension of the aforementioned muscle groups in an isometric attempt to pull the forearms toward the feet.

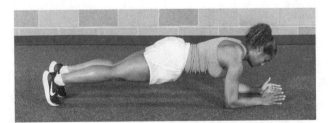

Figure 8.1 RKC plank.

Breathing Guidelines

- Inhale before the initial phase of the movement to generate intra-abdominal pressure.
- Use controlled inhalation and exhalation to maintain intra-abdominal pressure throughout the movement. Shallow breaths are suggested.

Exercise Modifications and Variations

Modifications and variations of the RKC plank may include adding load via external weight (e.g., a weight plate or vest). To amplify the tension and include an antirotational variation, lift one leg a few inches off the floor and retain tension as described previously. Side plank variations may also be implemented using the same tension strategies while holding the position on a single arm in a horizontal abducted position and on the lateral foot.

Coaching Tips

- The athlete should maintain total body tension.
- Maximal intent will allow for the RKC plank to be held for less than the usual plank duration. Strength and conditioning professionals should be aware of the isometric tension requirements and start with a duration of less than 30 seconds as a target time. Chronic adaptation to the stimulus may extend the duration of the exercise but should be prescribed based on seasonal demands and anatomical core training needs.

PRONE PULL-THROUGH

Primary Muscles Trained

Transversus abdominis, external and internal obliques, rectus abdominis, gluteus maximus, quadriceps, pectoralis major, latissimus dorsi, scapulothoracic stabilizers

Beginning Position

- Position the body prone on the floor with the ankles dorsiflexed, knees and hips extended, and the resistance load within reach.
- Position the feet approximately hip-width apart.
- Flex the shoulders and elbows to 90 degrees, creating an elevated prone position with the weight suspended on the toes and forearms.
- Position the cervical spine in a neutral position (a).

Movement Phases

1. Initiate the movement by reaching under the body and grasping the load (e.g., dumbbell, kettlebell, sandbag, weight plate).
2. Pulling across the body using horizontal abduction in the transverse plane, drag the load across the floor to the opposite side of the body (b).
3. Maintain tension throughout the whole body.
4. Repeat the movement for the prescribed number of repetitions or time, then switch to the opposite hand.

Figure 8.2 Prone pull-through: (a) beginning position; (b) end position.

Breathing Guidelines

- Inhale before the initial phase of the movement to generate intra-abdominal pressure.
- Use controlled inhalation and exhalation to maintain intra-abdominal pressure throughout the movement. Shallow breaths are suggested.

Exercise Modifications and Variations

The movement may also be performed with straight arms held at the top of the plank position. The load prescribed may vary to increase or decrease intensity.

Coaching Tips

- The athlete should maintain total body tension.
- The core should not rotate during the pull-through.

PALLOF HOLD

Primary Muscles Trained

Transversus abdominis, external and internal obliques, rectus abdominis, erector spinae, quadratus lumborum

Beginning Position

- Stand in an athletic position perpendicular to the resistance load (e.g., band or plate-loaded cable system).
- Grasp the band or handle of the cable system with the shoulders flexed and the elbows extended at sternum height.
- Stand in a position where tension on the band or cable system provides a rotational force to be resisted.

Movement Phases

1. The Pallof hold is an isometric core exercise. Therefore, the challenge is to maintain erect spinal alignment, resisting transverse rotation and lateral flexion.
2. During press variations, press the hands to full elbow extension and then return them to the sternum with each repetition.

Breathing Guidelines

- Inhale before the initial phase of the movement to generate intra-abdominal pressure.
- Use controlled inhalation and exhalation to maintain intra-abdominal pressure throughout the movement.

Figure 8.3 Pallof hold.

Exercise Modifications and Variations

Variations of the exercise may include stance changes—including tall-kneeling, half-kneeling, or split stance—and position changes (e.g., a slow lateral walk as the isometric position is held). Additionally, press variations provide progression and regression load changes.

Coaching Tips

- The athlete should stay standing tall.
- Have the athlete focus on maintaining a neutral spine to resist the rotation.

ROLLOUT

Primary Muscles Trained

Transversus abdominis, external and internal obliques, rectus abdominis, latissimus dorsi, pectoralis major, scapulothoracic stabilizers

Beginning Position

- Start in a tall-kneeling position with the hands on the front of a stability ball.
- Position the stability ball at a distance from the front of the thighs where the elbows are fully extended (a).

Movement Phases

1. In a slow and controlled manner, extend the knees and allow the shoulders to flex— while maintaining a braced core—to lean into the stability ball and roll it forward.
2. Keep the elbows fully extended as the stability ball rolls away from the body and the forearms, then the upper arms, roll along the top sides of the ball.
3. Continue the rollout until the stability ball approaches the face (b).
4. Maintaining a neutral spine, flex the knees and extend the shoulders to roll the stability ball back to the beginning position.

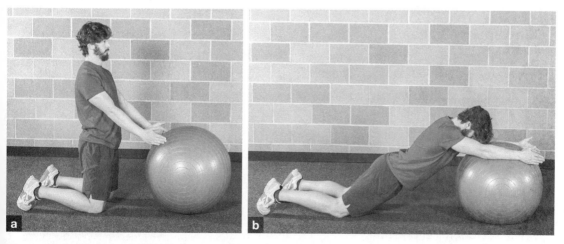

Figure 8.4 Rollout: (a) beginning position; (b) end position.

Breathing Guidelines

- Inhale before the initial phase of the movement to generate intra-abdominal pressure.
- Use controlled inhalation and exhalation to maintain intra-abdominal pressure throughout the movement. Inhalation during the eccentric phase of the movement and exhalation during the concentric phase may be necessary to progress through potential sticking points.

Exercise Modifications and Variations

The exercise may be completed using multiple apparatuses, including a stability ball, suspension trainer, or wheeled rolling equipment (e.g., ab wheel, glute–ham roller, or barbell with rotating plates or collars).

Coaching Tip

Ensure that the hips are held in the same stiff beginning position during the entire movement.

FARMER'S CARRY

Primary Muscles Trained

Transversus abdominis, external and internal obliques, rectus abdominis, gluteus maximus, wrist and hand flexors

Beginning Position

- The exercise may be loaded with multiple apparatuses, including dumbbells, kettlebells, a trap or hex bar, or specialized farmer's carry plate loaders.
- Use proper deadlift mechanics with the chosen apparatus to initiate the movement.
- The movement begins with an upright and standing posture with the chosen load in both hands. The shoulders, hips, knees, and ankles are stacked along the vertical axis.

Movement Phases

1. Initiate the movement by taking controlled walking steps for the prescribed distance or time.
2. It is imperative to maintain control of the loaded apparatus, minimizing sagittal and frontal plane movement.
3. Maintain a braced and erect posture throughout the movement. Do not allow spinal flexion, lateral flexion, or hyperextension.

Breathing Guidelines

- Inhale before the initial phase of the movement to generate intra-abdominal pressure.
- Use controlled inhalation and exhalation to maintain intra-abdominal pressure throughout the movement.

Figure 8.5 Farmer's carry.

Exercise Modifications and Variations

Progressions and regressions of the farmer's carry may include changes of intensity via load increases, distances covered, or variations in the gait cycle, such as marching or other knee-height variations.

Coaching Tips

- The athlete should maintain an upright posture.
- If the athlete cannot maintain posture or a normal gait cycle, assess the load, because a reduction may be required to maintain correct form during the movement.

FARMER'S CARRY UNEVEN

Primary Muscles Trained

Transversus abdominis, external and internal obliques, rectus abdominis, gluteus maximus, wrist and hand flexors

Beginning Position

- The exercise may be loaded with multiple apparatuses, including dumbbells, kettlebells, and specialized farmer's carry plate loaders.
- Initiate the movement using a hip hinge pattern to deadlift the chosen apparatus.
- The movement begins with a standing posture with a load in each hand, but with one load being substantially greater than the other load. The shoulders, hips, knees, and ankles are stacked along the vertical axis to create an erect posture.

Movement Phases

1. Initiate the movement by taking controlled walking steps for the prescribed distance or time.
2. It is imperative to maintain control of the loaded apparatus, minimizing excessive sagittal and frontal plane movement.
3. Maintain a braced and erect posture throughout the movement.

Breathing Guidelines

- Inhale before the initial phase of the movement to generate intra-abdominal pressure.
- Use controlled inhalation and exhalation to maintain intra-abdominal pressure throughout the movement.

Exercise Modifications and Variations

Progressions and regressions of the uneven farmer's carry may include intensity via load changes in one or both hands, distances covered, or variations in the gait cycle, including marching or other knee-height variations. Additionally, variations in load position may be used with the weight held in a front rack position while maintaining uneven loads between the hands.

Figure 8.6 Farmer's carry uneven.

Coaching Tips

- The athlete should maintain an upright posture. Careful attention should be given to compensation via lateral flexion of the spine due to variance between loads.
- If the athlete cannot maintain posture or a normal gait cycle, assess the load, because a reduction may be required to maintain correct form during the movement.

SUITCASE CARRY

Primary Muscles Trained

Transversus abdominis, external and internal obliques, rectus abdominis, gluteus maximus, wrist and hand flexors

Beginning Position

- The exercise may be loaded with multiple apparatuses, including a dumbbell, kettlebell, or a specialized farmer's carry plate loader.
- Similar to the farmer's carry, use a hip hinge pattern to deadlift the chosen apparatus to initiate the movement. However, the load is carried in only one hand.
- The movement begins with a standing posture with the chosen load in hand. The shoulders, hips, knees, and ankles are stacked along the vertical axis.

Movement Phases

1. Initiate the movement by taking controlled walking steps for the prescribed distance or time.
2. It is imperative to maintain control of the loaded apparatus, minimizing sagittal, frontal, and transverse plane movement.
3. Maintain a braced and erect posture throughout the movement.
4. At the end of the set, repeat the movement on the other side.

Breathing Guidelines

- Inhale before the initial phase of the movement to generate intra-abdominal pressure.
- Use controlled inhalation and exhalation to maintain intra-abdominal pressure throughout the movement.

Exercise Modifications and Variations

Progressions and regressions of the farmer's carry may include intensity via load increases, distances covered, or variations in the gait cycle, including marching or other knee-height variations.

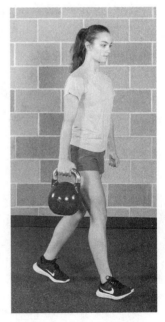

Figure 8.7 Suitcase carry.

Coaching Tips

- The athlete should maintain an upright posture. Careful attention should be given to compensation via lateral spine flexion due to variance between loads.
- If the athlete cannot maintain posture or a normal gait cycle, assess the load to regress the movement.

WAITER'S CARRY

Primary Muscles Trained

Transversus abdominis, external and internal obliques, rectus abdominis, gluteus maximus, wrist and hand flexors

Beginning Position

- The exercise may be loaded with multiple apparatuses, including a dumbbell or a kettlebell.
- Initiate the movement by holding the kettlebell, dumbbell, or other apparatus in one hand in a front-racked position and pressing it overhead.
- The wrist, elbow, and shoulder should be stacked, with the shoulder girdle maintaining a packed (depressed) position.

Movement Phases

1. Initiate the movement by taking controlled walking steps for the prescribed distance or time.
2. It is imperative to maintain control of the load, minimizing sagittal and frontal plane movement.
3. Maintain a braced and erect posture throughout the movement, with the elbow of the loaded arm fully extended.
4. At the end of the set, repeat the movement on the other side.

Breathing Guidelines

- Inhale before the initial phase of the movement to generate intra-abdominal pressure.
- Use controlled inhalation and exhalation to maintain intra-abdominal pressure throughout the movement.
- The contralateral unloaded hand may be used as feedback by placing the hand on the abdomen to assist in breathing and abdominal tension.

Figure 8.8 Waiter's carry.

Exercise Modifications and Variations

Progressions and regressions of the waiter's carry may include intensity via load increases, distances covered, or variations in the gait cycle, including marching or other knee-height variations. A load may be added to the contralateral side in either a suitcase, front-racked, or waiter's carry position.

Coaching Tips

- The athlete should maintain an upright posture. Careful attention should be given to compensation via lateral spine flexion due to variance between loads.
- If the athlete cannot maintain posture or a normal gait cycle, assess the load to regress the movement.

MOVEMENT EXERCISES

PVC CONTRACT, RELAX, COORDINATE (C-R-C)

Primary Muscles Trained

Transversus abdominis, external and internal obliques, rectus abdominis, erector spinae, latissimus dorsi, pectoralis major, deltoids, scapulothoracic stabilizers

Beginning Position

- Two athletes are required for this partner exercise (a).
- The first athlete assumes an athletic stance and grasps the stick shoulder-width apart with extended elbows to create movement.
- The second athlete assumes an athletic stance and grasps the stick outside the hands of first athlete to provide resistance.

Movement Phases

1. On the start command, the first athlete rotates the stick in a clockwise or counter-clockwise motion (b).
2. The second athlete braces in an attempt to maintain a stick position parallel with the floor.

Breathing Guidelines

- Inhale before the initial phase of the movement to generate intra-abdominal pressure.
- Use controlled inhalation and exhalation to maintain intra-abdominal pressure throughout the movement.

Exercise Modifications and Variations

The exercise may be completed using multiple apparatuses, including a wooden dowel, PVC pipe, or lacrosse stick.

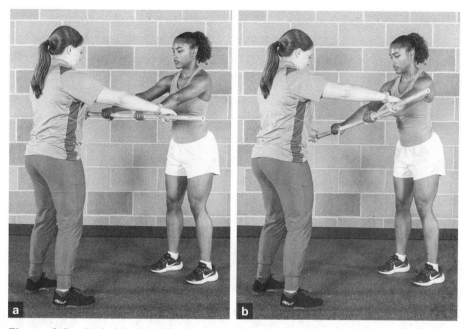

Figure 8.9   PVC C-R-C: *(a)* beginning position; *(b)* effort to create movement and effort to brace to counter the movement.

Coaching Tips

- Cue the athletes to brace before the movement.
- Instruct both athletes to maintain elbow extension during the exercise.
- If the athlete generating the rotation does not allow the second athlete to rotate back to the beginning position, cue the first athlete to provide enough resistance for a slow, controlled rotation back to the beginning position.
- Vary the time, angle, and resistance applied, being cautious. Pair athletes of similar strength levels.

PVC C-R-C LATERAL

Primary Muscles Trained

Transversus abdominis, external and internal obliques, rectus abdominis, erector spinae, latissimus dorsi, pectoralis major, scapulothoracic stabilizers

Beginning Position

- Two athletes are required for this partner exercise.
- The athletes stand side by side in an athletic stance with their shoulders flexed. Both athletes grasp the stick with their hands shoulder-width apart, using a double-pronated grip *(a)*.

Movement Phases

1. On the start command, both athletes drive the stick toward their partner.
2. Both athletes brace and attempt to maintain a stick position parallel to the floor without rotating in the transverse plane *(b)*.

Figure 8.10 PVC C-R-C lateral: *(a)* beginning position; *(b)* effort to create movement and effort to brace to counter the movement.

Breathing Guidelines

- Inhale before the initial phase of the movement to generate intra-abdominal pressure.
- Use controlled inhalation and exhalation to maintain intra-abdominal pressure throughout the movement.

Exercise Modifications and Variations

The exercise may be completed using multiple apparatuses, including a wooden dowel, PVC pipe, or lacrosse stick.

Coaching Tips

- Cue the athletes to brace before the movement.
- Instruct both athletes to maintain elbow extension during the exercise, remain balanced, and fight to maintain a forward-facing position.
- Vary the time, angle, and resistance applied. Carefully pair athletes of similar strength levels.

CABLE CHOP

Primary Muscles Trained

Transversus abdominis, external and internal obliques, rectus abdominis, latissimus dorsi, pectoralis major

Beginning Position

- Attach a rope or straight bar handle to a cable machine and set the pulley at chest height. An elastic band can also be used in lieu of a cable machine.
- Assume an athletic stance facing 90 degrees away from the cable machine, perpendicular to the cable's line of pull, with the toes lined up with the base of the column of the cable machine. The weight to be lifted should be suspended off the rest of the stack; reposition the feet farther away from the cable column as needed.
- Hold the handle directly in front of the chest with the elbows fully extended and the palms facing down (a).

Movement Phases

1. Allow the cable to pull the hands across the body (to lower the weight lifted to the rest of the stack) while stabilizing the lower body and pelvis (b).
2. Once the cable has pulled the hands fully across the body, rotate the torso to pull the handle back across the body at chest height until the right hand is in front of (or slightly past) the left shoulder (or vice versa) (c).
3. At the end of the set, repeat the movement on the other side.

Exercise Modifications and Variations

Half-Kneeling Cable Chop

Set up in a half-kneeling position with the inside knee (the knee closest to the cable machine) on the floor.

Split-Stance Cable Chop

Set up in a split-stance position, with the inside leg closest to the cable machine.

Downward Chop

Set the pulley slightly above shoulder height, and pull the handle down across the body from one shoulder to the opposite hip.

Coaching Tips

- The athlete should allow for thoracic rotation during this exercise by turning the shoulders toward the cable machine during the loading phase.
- When setting up, cue the athlete to imagine a line drawn between the toes and make sure that line is pointed directly toward the cable machine or pulley.

Figure 8.11 Cable chop: *(a)* beginning position; *(b)* rotate toward the machine; *(c)* rotate away from the machine.

CABLE LIFT

Primary Muscles Trained

Transversus abdominis, external and internal obliques, rectus abdominis, pectoralis major

Beginning Position

- Attach a rope or straight bar handle to a cable machine, and set the pulley at roughly knee height. An elastic band can also be used in lieu of a cable machine.

- Assume an athletic stance facing 90 degrees away from the cable machine, perpendicular to the cable's line of pull, with the toes lined up with the base of the column of the cable machine. The weight to be lifted should be suspended off the rest of the stack; reposition the feet farther away from the cable column as needed.
- Hold the handle at a 45-degree angle in front of the body with the elbows fully extended and the palms facing down (a).

Movement Phases

1. Allow the cable to pull the hands down and across the body (to lower the weight lifted to the rest of the stack) while stabilizing the lower body and pelvis (b).

Figure 8.12 Cable lift: (a) beginning position; (b) rotate toward the machine; (c) rotate away from the machine.

2. Once the arms have reached fully across the body, pull the handle back across the body with the cable at a 45-degree angle until the right hand is in front of—or slightly past and above—the left shoulder (or vice versa) *(c)*.

3. At the end of the set, repeat the movement on the other side.

Exercise Modifications and Variations

Half-Kneeling Cable Lift

Set up in a half-kneeling position with the inside knee (closest to the cable machine) on the floor.

Split-Stance Cable Lift

Set up in a split-stance position with the back leg closest to the cable machine.

Coaching Tips

- The athlete should allow for thoracic rotation during this exercise by turning the shoulders toward the cable machine during the loading phase.
- When setting up, cue the athlete to imagine a line drawn between the toes and make sure that line is pointed directly toward the cable machine or pulley.

MEDICINE BALL CHOP CIRCUIT

Primary Muscles Trained

Transversus abdominis, external and internal obliques, rectus abdominis

Beginning Position

- Stand in an athletic position with the hips and knees slightly flexed and the feet pointed straight ahead or slightly out.
- Hold the medicine ball straight out in front of the sternum with the elbows extended and the arms parallel to the floor with the hands on either side of the medicine ball *(a)*.

Movement Phases

1. Keeping the elbows extended, rapidly move the ball from side to side while stabilizing the lower body and core, not allowing any additional hip flexion, knee flexion, pelvic rotation, or torso rotation *(b and c)*.

2. Rapidly move the ball diagonally from one shoulder to the opposite hip (alternating directions with each repetition) while stabilizing the lower body and core, not allowing any additional hip flexion, knee flexion, pelvic rotation, or torso rotation (not shown).

Coaching Tips

- Cue the athlete to achieve the biggest range of motion possible with the medicine ball, absent any movement below the shoulders. Ideally, the ball should move back and forth repeatedly as fast as possible.
- If the athlete is unable to stabilize his or her lower body during this exercise, use a lighter ball or have the athlete use smaller movements.

Figure 8.13 Medicine ball chop circuit: *(a)* beginning position; *(b)* rotate to the right; *(c)* rotate to the left.

- Cue the athlete to keep the shoulders in front of the knees to promote a good hinge position.
- Use medicine balls between 2 and 6 pounds (about 1 to 3 kg).

MEDICINE BALL CHOP AND REBOUND

Primary Muscles Trained

Transversus abdominis, external and internal obliques, rectus abdominis, gluteus maximus, gluteus medius, gluteus minimus, adductor longus, adductor brevis

Beginning Position

- Stand in an athletic position with the medicine ball held directly in front of the chest with both hands.
- Begin with the elbows extended and the arms held directly out in front between sternum and shoulder height *(a)*.

Movement Phases

1. Initiate the movement by shifting weight to one foot and rotating the torso and pelvis toward that foot, allowing the opposite foot to lift onto the toe and rotate *(b)*.
2. After reaching full hip internal rotation and thoracic rotation, pull the heel of the opposite foot into the floor and shift weight back into that foot *(c)*.
3. Once the opposite leg is weight bearing, powerfully uncoil the pelvis and torso and use the arms to chop the ball across the body.
4. Firmly decelerate the pelvis and torso, causing the arms and medicine ball to rebound back to the other side of the body *(d)*.

5. At the end of the set, repeat the movement by rotating and chopping the ball to the other side first.

Breathing Guidelines

Attempt to force air out against a closed mouth during the deceleration to increase intra-thoracic pressure, which will aid in stabilizing the core.

Coaching Tip

Cue the athlete to keep the knees stable during the chop motion. Any knee flexion beyond a normal athletic stance should be discouraged.

Figure 8.14 Medicine ball chop and rebound: *(a)* beginning position; *(b)* rotate to the right; *(c)* shift weight back; *(d)* chop the ball across the body to the left.

MEDICINE BALL CATCH AND DECELERATION

Primary Muscles Trained

Transversus abdominis, external and internal obliques, rectus abdominis

Beginning Position

- Assume an athletic stance with the feet roughly shoulder-width apart and the knees and hips slightly flexed. Stand facing 90 degrees from a partner, who will be throwing the medicine ball (a).

Movement Phases

1. Catch the medicine ball with the elbows extended and quickly decelerate the ball by stabilizing the pelvis, torso, and arms (b).
2. Toss the ball back using a side or scoop toss (c) and prepare to catch the next throw.

Exercise Modifications and Variations

Half-Kneeling Medicine Ball Catch and Deceleration

Set up in a half-kneeling position with the inside knee (the knee closest to the partner) down on the floor.

Split-Stance Medicine Ball Catch and Deceleration

Set up in a split-stance position with one foot back in a quarter-lunge position.

Breathing Guidelines

Attempt to force air out against a closed mouth during the deceleration to increase intra-thoracic pressure, which will aid in stabilizing the core.

Coaching Tip

Vary the angle at which the medicine ball is delivered to build stability over a wide range of force vectors.

Figure 8.15 Medicine ball catch and deceleration: *(a)* beginning position; *(b)* catch the ball; *(c)* toss the ball back.

MEDICINE BALL CHOP TOSS

Primary Muscles Trained

Transversus abdominis, external and internal obliques, rectus abdominis, latissimus dorsi

Beginning Position

- Start with the feet, pelvis, and torso oriented 90 degrees from the target, with the medicine ball held in front of the face.
- Assume an athletic stance with the knees and hips slightly flexed and the weight on the midfoot (a).

Movement Phases

1. Lift the front foot and stride toward the target while coiling the pelvis and torso.
2. While striding toward the target, allow the pelvis to rotate open while holding the shoulders and torso closed to create hip–shoulder separation (b).

igure 8.16   Medicine ball chop toss: (a) beginning position; (b) create hip–shoulder separa-on; (c) accelerate the torso; (d) whip the ball forward.

3. Firmly plant the front foot pointed toward the target or slightly pointed in, with the pelvis oriented toward the target and the shoulders and torso beginning to rotate toward the target.

4. Fully rotate the pelvis, culminating in internal rotation of the lead hip, and then decelerate the pelvis firmly while accelerating torso rotation (c).

5. Once the torso has reached peak rotational velocity, use the arms to whip the ball forward as powerfully as possible toward the target (d).

Breathing Guidelines

Exhale forcefully at the point of ball release to produce the highest possible ball velocity.

Exercise Modifications and Variations

Turn and Burn

Begin by standing in an athletic position with the body oriented 180 degrees from the target, then backpedal toward the target to build momentum before turning and throwing the ball.

Drop Step

Begin by standing in an athletic position with the body oriented 180 degrees from the target, then quickly rotate the lower body toward the target by performing a drop step before rotating the upper body and throwing the ball.

Shuffle Step

Begin in an athletic position with the feet, pelvis, and torso oriented 90 degrees from the target, then perform a lateral shuffle step to build momentum before rotating and throwing the ball.

Coaching Tips

- Vary target positions to build explosiveness across a range of ball trajectories (e.g., high, low, chest height, or slightly to the right or left of the center of the athlete's body). Tape can be used on a wall to provide these different targets.

- The athlete should focus on generating power from the lower body and core, not just throwing the ball with the arms. If the exercise is done correctly, the athlete should feel the lead leg's glutes and hamstrings working to stabilize the front leg after the front foot landing.

- Cue athletes to use a two-handed karate chop movement to throw the ball.

- Use light medicine balls between 2 and 4 pounds (about 1 to 2 kg).

MEDICINE BALL SLAM

Primary Muscles Trained

Transversus abdominis, external and internal obliques, rectus abdominis, latissimus dorsi

Beginning Position

- Start in an athletic stance with the medicine ball held directly in front of the chest with both hands.
- Begin with the elbows flexed and the ball above the elbows *(a)*.

Movement Phases

1. Extend the knees and hips, and plantar flex the ankles while reaching overhead with the medicine ball and rising up onto the balls of the feet *(b)*.
2. Once a full overhead reach has been achieved, begin the slam by bringing the heels back to the floor.
3. Stabilize the knees and initiate a hinge movement at the hips by driving the chest toward the floor.
4. Once the chest has started to drive toward the floor, aggressively slam the ball on the floor *(c)*.

Breathing Guidelines

Exhale forcefully at the point of ball release to produce the highest possible ball velocity.

Figure 8.17 Medicine ball slam: *(a)* beginning position; *(b)* full overhead reach; *(c)* slam.

Exercise Modifications and Variations

Jump Slam

Begin by standing in an athletic position with the elbows flexed and the ball held at chest height. Perform a countermovement jump by dropping into a quarter squat, then jumping straight up and raising the ball overhead. Upon landing, stabilize the knees while driving the chest toward the floor and using the arms to slam the ball into the floor.

Single-Leg Slam

Start with both feet on the floor, then raise the medicine ball overhead and perform a single-leg hinge to slam the ball into the floor, finishing with the opposite leg off the floor.

Coaching Tips

- Cue the athlete to finish the slam with the hips high in a hinge position rather than dropping into a squat.
- Make sure the athlete reaches the ball straight overhead with the arms fully extended rather than flexing the elbows and pulling the ball behind the head.
- Use medicine balls between 6 and 10 pounds (about 3 to 5 kg).

MEDICINE BALL SHOT PUT

Primary Muscles Trained

Transversus abdominis, external and internal obliques, rectus abdominis, pectoralis major

Beginning Position

- Start with the feet, pelvis, and torso oriented 90 degrees from the target, with the medicine ball held in the center of the chest.
- Assume an athletic stance with the knees and hips slightly flexed and the weight on the midfoot (a).

Movement Phases

1. Lift the front foot and stride toward the target while coiling the pelvis and torso.
2. While striding toward the target, allow the pelvis to rotate open while holding the shoulders and torso closed to create hip–shoulder separation (b).
3. Firmly plant the front foot pointed toward the target or slightly pointed in, with the pelvis oriented toward the target and the shoulders and torso beginning to rotate toward the target.
4. Fully rotate the pelvis, culminating in internal rotation of the lead hip, then decelerate the pelvis firmly while accelerating torso rotation (c).
5. Once the torso has reached peak rotational velocity, use the back arm to accelerate the ball as powerfully as possible toward the target in a shot put motion (d).

Breathing Guidelines

Exhale forcefully at the point of ball release to produce the highest possible ball velocity.

Figure 8.18   Medicine ball shot put: *(a)* beginning position; *(b)* create hip–shoulder separation; *(c)* accelerate the torso; *(d)* shot put the ball forward.

Exercise Modifications and Variations

Turn and Burn

Begin by standing in an athletic position with the body oriented 180 degrees from the target, then backpedal toward the target to build momentum before turning and throwing the ball.

Drop Step

Begin by standing in an athletic position with the body oriented 180 degrees from the target, then quickly rotate the lower body toward the target by performing a drop step before rotating the upper body and throwing the ball.

Shuffle Step

Begin in an athletic position with the feet, pelvis, and torso oriented 90 degrees from the target, then perform a lateral shuffle step to build momentum before rotating and throwing the ball.

Coaching Tips

- Vary target positions to build explosiveness across a range of ball trajectories (e.g., high, low, chest height, or slightly to the right or left of the center of the athlete's body). Tape can be used on a wall to provide these different targets.
- The athlete should focus on generating power from the lower body and core, not just throwing the ball with the arms. If the exercise is done correctly, the athlete should feel the lead leg's glutes and hamstrings working to stabilize the front leg after the front foot landing.
- Cue athletes to use a punching motion with the back arm rather than a throwing motion.
- Use medicine balls between 4 and 8 pounds (about 2 to 4 kg).

LANDMINE ROTATIONS

Primary Muscles Trained

Transversus abdominis, external and internal obliques, rectus abdominis

Beginning Position

- Start in an athletic stance with the end of the barbell held in both hands in line with the middle of the body (the elbows will be somewhat flexed to hold the bar in position).
- Stand close enough to the base of the landmine that the hands are above head height (a).

Movement Phases

1. Begin by shifting the weight laterally into one foot, and rotate the pelvis and shoulders toward that foot. Allow the opposite foot to rotate (pivot) on the ball of the foot with the heel lifted off the floor.
2. Allow the hands to drop to just above knee height and hinge into the working hip, maintaining a firm, stable knee. Load the working hip by coiling the body around the fixed femur (b).
3. Once the pelvis and torso have fully rotated and the hands have reached knee height, shift the weight back into the opposite foot and pull the heel back to the floor. Then pull back on the hip and knee to rotate the pelvis and begin to uncoil the body.
4. Fully rotate the pelvis, culminating in internal rotation of the lead hip, and then decelerate the pelvis firmly while accelerating the torso and shoulders.
5. Once the torso has reached peak rotational velocity, use the arms to whip the barbell back up to the beginning position (i.e., back to a).
6. Follow the same guidelines to rotate the body to move the barbell to the opposite side (c).

Exercise Modifications and Variations

Stationary Landmine Rotation

Keep both feet firmly planted during the loading phase and only rotate from the thoracic spine, as opposed to coiling the entire body.

Coaching Tips

- Cue the athlete to generate power with the lower body and core and let the arms be along for the ride until the last moment when the arms whip the barbell into the finish position.
- When appropriate, progress the exercise by cueing the athlete to not "squish the bug" with the opposite foot by keeping both feet planted while shifting the weight to create maximal hip–shoulder separation.

Figure 8.19 Landmine rotations: (a) beginning position; (b) rotate to one side; (c) rotate to the other side.

MEDICINE BALL SIDE TOSS

Primary Muscles Trained

Transversus abdominis, external and internal obliques, rectus abdominis

Beginning Position

- Start in an athletic stance with the medicine ball held in front of the chest with both hands.
- Begin with the elbows extended and the ball between sternum and belly button height.

Movement Phases

1. Lift the front foot and coil the pelvis and torso by bringing the front leg toward the back leg and turning slightly away from the target.
2. While striding toward the target, allow the pelvis to rotate open while holding the shoulders and torso closed to create hip–shoulder separation.
3. Firmly plant the front foot pointed toward the target or slightly pointed in, with the pelvis oriented toward the target and the shoulders and torso beginning to rotate toward the target.
4. Fully rotate the pelvis, culminating in internal rotation of the lead hip, and then decelerate the pelvis firmly while accelerating the torso and shoulders.
5. Once the torso has reached peak rotational velocity, use the arms to throw the ball as powerfully as possible toward the target.

Breathing Guidelines

Exhale forcefully at the point of ball release to produce the highest possible ball velocity.

Exercise Modifications and Variations

Turn and Burn

Begin by standing in an athletic position with the body oriented 180 degrees from the target, then backpedal toward the target to build momentum before turning and throwing the ball.

Drop Step

Begin by standing in an athletic position with the body oriented 180 degrees from the target, then quickly rotate the lower body toward the target by performing a drop step before rotating the upper body and throwing the ball.

Shuffle Step

Begin in an athletic position with the feet, pelvis, and torso oriented 90 degrees from the target, then perform a lateral shuffle step to build momentum before rotating and throwing the ball.

Coaching Tips

- Cue the athlete to generate power with the lower body and core and let the arms be along for the ride until the final phase of the throw.
- The athlete should finish in a stacked position over the front leg. If the athlete's head ends up out in front of the front leg, cue him or her to keep the head over the belly button.
- Use medicine balls between 4 and 8 pounds (about 2 to 4 kg).

PROGRAM DESIGN GUIDELINES AND SAMPLE PROGRAMS

9

OFF-SEASON PROGRAMMING

DRAZEN GLISIC (HIGH SCHOOL), TRACY ZIMMER (COLLEGE WOMEN), DAVID EUGENIO MANNING (COLLEGE MEN), AND JOEL RAETHER (PROFESSIONAL)

The off-season program for the high school lacrosse athlete is primarily geared toward developing a strong foundation of learning proper exercise technique and building a base of muscular strength and aerobic endurance. The college lacrosse athlete will use the off-season to gain proficiency in major movement (exercise) patterns and adaptational resilience to reduce injury risk during the long college lacrosse season. Professional lacrosse athletes have a less structured off-season; attention is given to addressing each athlete's need for recovery and goal setting for the upcoming season.

GOALS AND OBJECTIVES

For these three levels of play, the goals and objectives for a lacrosse athlete can vary. The details that are specific to high school, college (women and men), and professional athletes are described in the following sections.

High School

At the high school level, the strength and conditioning professional is responsible for preparing lacrosse athletes for their high school season and developing a strong foundation for those who aspire to play at the collegiate level. Another crucial responsibility, which is equally if not more important, is fostering a passion for an active and healthy lifestyle, because many athletes may not have the opportunity to play lacrosse in college. While chapters 9-12 will primarily focus on preparing athletes for their competitive season and continued pursuit of lacrosse, creating positive training environments and lifelong habits should not be overlooked.

When working with high school athletes, the off-season should be used to establish strong training techniques. It is a time when the demands of the sport are reduced, providing an extended opportunity to practice exercises and establish proper technique in primary movement patterns. Along with building a strong foundation from a movement perspective, the off-season period should be viewed as an opportunity to develop overall strength.

College

The goals and objectives during the college off-season will differ by the mesocycle. Mesocycle 1 is used to progressively accumulate stress so that the athletes are ready for the rigors of a college sport practice that will be introduced in week 3 or 4 of the fall semester. Mesocycle 2 coincides with the college teams' *fall ball* or *fall ball season*, as it is often referred to in the lacrosse community, and its primary objectives are to manage athlete fatigue and health while the team practices every day and to teach the primary exercises that athletes will use in mesocycles 3 or 4. The last one to two mesocycles are when physiological adaptations can be pursued in the weight room and workouts will start to include more position-specific exercises, if developmentally appropriate.

Professional

At the professional level, the off-season tends to be somewhat fluid, because many professional-level athletes play in one or more professional leagues. These include the National Lacrosse League (NLL, indoor) and the Premier Lacrosse League (PLL, outdoor) as well as the Major Series Lacrosse (MSL, Senior A, indoor), originating in Ontario, and the Western Lacrosse Association (WLA, Senior A, indoor) of British Columbia, with an end-of-season title championship between the MSL and WLA at the end of August or in early September. The NLL season runs approximately from November until May and the PLL, MSL, and WLA from approximately June to September, with some athletes participating concurrently in three of these leagues yearly but most athletes participating in two. Athletes who choose not to participate in or are not part of multiple professional leagues would follow a more traditional off-season training program, but these cases are typically the minority in the current landscape. Due to the nature of this landscape, off-season programming can be challenging and very individual.

LENGTH, STRUCTURE, AND ORGANIZATION

There are some notable differences in the length, structure, and organization of off-season resistance training programs for high school, college, and professional lacrosse athletes. For high school and college athletes, a primary influencing factor is the school year.

High School

High school lacrosse athletes typically start their off-season at the beginning of the school year, which can range from mid-August to early September, depending on their location. If a strength and conditioning professional has access to athletes outside of regular school hours and dates, the off-season program can start earlier in the summer. In this situation, the exact start date will depend on the athletes' schedules and whether they continued playing lacrosse into the summer after the school season ended.

The high school off-season period can last anywhere from 16 to 20 weeks before a transition is made to preseason programming. The winter school holidays or the end of the first semester can be considered a natural end to the off-season, with lacrosse athletes starting their preseason training period once they return from the holidays or start their second semester. In the off-season period, the first and second weeks should be used to conduct baseline fitness testing for the athletes. After this, the off-season can be broken down into two eight-week phases (mesocycles), focusing on strength-endurance and basic strength. For athletes who are younger in training, chronological, or developmental age, the strength-endurance phase can be extended to allow for more time to solidify training technique. As a result, the basic-strength phase would be reduced.

College

The off-season coincides with the start of the fall semester for college lacrosse programs. The incoming freshman class will make up approximately one-fourth of a team, along with the rest of the 45 to 50 or more members who make up a typical college men's lacrosse team and the 25 to 35 members of a typical college women's lacrosse team.

The structure of each team's fall semester varies based on National Collegiate Athletics Association (NCAA) restrictions by division and the sport coach's preference; however, most programs will allow a few weeks prior to the start of fall ball for progressive development of the muscle and ligament tissues. This design should eliminate drastic increases in workload, which in turn should reduce the likelihood of injury. During this time, skill work is also done on the field. For Division I programs, the off-season schedule begins with 8 hours for sport activity as dictated by the NCAA, which must be broken up between on-field work with a sport coach and the work that occurs with a strength and conditioning professional. At the Division III level, all workouts with a strength and conditioning professional are voluntary and do not have a limit on associated hours. All skill work is also done at the discretion of the athlete and cannot be done with a coach. It is important to note this work being done, because it relates to the total workload and how an athlete may recover.

Generally, two or three resistance training workouts a week will be performed during this season. After the athletes perform a barbell complex warm-up that is used to pattern essential movements for the upcoming workout, they will do a series of plyometric drills (the plane of movement changes with each session). These extensive plyometrics are the only exercises where sets will increase week by week, and this is done so the athletes can progressively accumulate floor contacts before the start of sport practices.

This ramp-up period leads into fall ball and is essentially a mini-season of 20 hours per week for about four to five weeks of sport practice, with three scrimmages or competition weekends toward the middle or end of the season. This provides the strength and conditioning professional an opportunity to prepare for the in-season resistance training the lacrosse athletes will do come spring. It also provides student-athletes the opportunity to learn how to manage time in order to balance academic demands with training and game schedules while focusing on recovery and nutrition to perform at a high level. The exercises may be slightly different or further progressed during the in-season cycles, but the goals and principles will be the same when creating these programs. Because teams will likely practice four or five days each week with a scrimmage at the end of the week, maintenance of the training volume while minimizing fatigue is the most important objective. Talking with athletes and getting feedback on soreness and fatigue are important, and the athletes' health and wellness should be prioritized over pushing neural or muscular adaptations. Two or three full-body workouts per week will be used in this cycle. Intensity will remain low, because the priority is managing soreness and fatigue associated with practices and mastering the primary exercises athletes will use in subsequent cycles.

Once fall ball is over, strength and conditioning professionals will have anywhere from four to eight weeks where physical preparation is prioritized. The coaches will only work with the athletes during individual skills sessions 1 to 2 hours a week. This last portion of the off-season is when physiological adaptations can really be chased, and workouts will move to three full-body days, which often fall on Monday, Wednesday, and Friday. The previous six to eight weeks should have allowed ample time to teach the primary exercises that will be used to drive these adaptations. Lacrosse has not been as extensively researched as other sports with regard to game demands, and not every lacrosse team will have the ability to use GPS to gain insight on the stress athletes will experience during sport practice and games. One study on the Japanese men's national team does provide such values and details, and while it needs to be interpreted with the international match rules used in mind, the findings can still provide insight on the differences between positions. The most notable differences between positions were the high number of low- to mid-intensity accelerations and decelerations by attack and defense positions and the relative high-speed volume that midfielders experienced compared to the other positions (1). Based on these findings, it behooves the strength and conditioning professional to prepare offensive and defensive athletes for the number of floor contacts and forces associated with accelerative and decelerative movements and to expose the midfielders to exercises and preventive care measures that transfer better to sprinting. With those considerations in mind, along with the need to improve rotational velocity and health in offensive athletes and the ability to manage contact and not lose key athletic positions when maneuvering and leveraging opposing athletes for defenders, specific exercises and protocols can be programmed for each position to improve those qualities.

Although the program design variables of a resistance training program apply equally to men and women, it is essential to consider several unique physiological and biomechanical differences between men and women that may affect programming. Women may need heightened focus on building lower body strength (5), enhancing neuromuscular control and stability at the knee joints to reduce risk of anterior cruciate ligament injury (5), and raising awareness of potential hormonal influences on performance and recovery (3).

Professional

Due to the yearly schedule at the professional level, the off-season often consists of a very condensed 8- to 10-week period when the athletes are not playing in a competitive season, which is typically in the months of September and October. This period usually consists of three or four training sessions a week that focus on addressing injuries, recovery, and general strength during the early stages in the first two to four weeks and then progress into more specific strength, power, and explosiveness as the upcoming indoor (NLL) season nears. Additionally, the emphasis on addressing injuries and recovery in the form of mobility work, low-level aerobic activity, and working in conjunction with the sports medicine staff becomes paramount to getting athletes ready to embark upon another intense season.

RECOMMENDED EXERCISES

Often, differences in the exercises that are recommended for the three levels of play are rooted in the differences in skill and experience needed to perform resistance training exercises. For any lacrosse athlete, the priority is learning proper technique before applying repetition maximum (RM) loading schemes.

High School

During the strength-endurance phase of the high school off-season period, the focus is on ingraining the athletes' technique in simple variations of movement patterns that will be used throughout the year. The goal is to establish a strong foundation in the athletes' technique so that when it comes time to learn more complex variations, they have a solid base upon which to build. The primary exercises for this phase are bilateral, compound (multijoint) exercises, such as goblet squats, hex or trap bar deadlifts, Romanian deadlifts, reverse lunges, push-ups, inverted rows, dumbbell bench press, bent-over rows, and chin-ups. As the athlete progresses to the basic strength phase, alternative-stance (e.g., staggered, split) and unilateral versions of the movement patterns should be used more frequently if the athlete is ready for them. These can include split-stance squats, staggered-stance Romanian deadlifts, single-leg deadlifts and squats, step-ups, single-arm bench press, and one-arm bent-over rows. This is also a great time to introduce and practice proper technique for exercises aimed at improving power, such as cleans, snatches, and swings.

It is important to make sex-based adjustments in programming, since there are differences in the rules and regulations for girls and boys playing lacrosse in high school. Shoulder injuries are more common among boys, and there needs to be an emphasis on including exercises that strengthen the shoulder girdle and rotator cuff muscles and improve mobility and control (2). Examples of these exercises include banded internal and external shoulder rotation, thoracic spine mobility, and variations of I's, Y's, T's, and W's.

In both boys' and girls' high school lacrosse, the most common injuries include those to the head (concussions); lower leg, foot, and ankle; knee; thigh; groin; and shoulder (particularly among boys) (2, 6). Along with the exercises mentioned previously, exercises that strengthen these areas, such as the Nordic curl, single-leg squat, and Copenhagen plank, should be included, along with exercises that improve control and mobility of the ankles, hips, and shoulders.

College Women

The first phase of the off-season period for women's college lacrosse will consist of two days of full-body resistance training. As the athletes transition from the postseason, two days will allow sufficient recovery for the desired strength adaptations to occur, considering novice athletes may have little training experience and returning athletes may have focused on regeneration and may return in a detrained state. Each exercise will begin with prehab and activation for the upper body, lower body, or both.

Day 1 will focus on squat patterns, beginning with the overhead (OH) squat, which can reveal movement incompetencies that need to be addressed before getting further into the exercises, and front squats, which will help develop lower body strength and reinforce the rack position for hang cleans and clean variations. The kettlebell (KB) swings and RDL shrug will serve as power and hinge patterns that will aid in explosive ability. Programming bodyweight upper body pull exercises, such as inverted rows, is a great way to gauge progress because these relate to relative strength, which can be significant for female athletes. The military press rounds out day 1 as the primary resisted movement for developing shoulder strength and stability.

Day 2 of the first phase will introduce unilateral work with single-leg (SL) squats to box that are superset with single-effort vertical jumps. This will challenge the athletes' balance and stability while exposing them to producing and absorbing force in a controlled environment. The hang clean is the most technical exercise in this phase and will be a constant in the annual training plan. The push-pull variation for day 2 will allow athletes to challenge themselves by progressively adding weight to their dumbbell (DB) bench and plate (or DB) pullovers over the course of the training cycle.

It is important to establish competency in foundational strength exercises before introducing and loading more complex movements. As the phases progress, the degree of difficulty increases and new movements, such as neck work, are added to the training plan. Once the athletes have consistently trained twice a week, the strength and conditioning professional will have the ability to add a third resistance training day and incorporate new movements requiring a greater degree of coordination.

College Men

In mesocycle 1 for men's college lacrosse, the primary exercises are regressed to their most basic variations, and a variety of accessory (assistance) exercises are included that work the muscles and joints through the full range of motion in all movement planes. Additional accessory movements are chosen based on the athlete's position and are included to begin to accumulate volume in movements that will occur repeatedly in practice. Building up rotational volume for offensive positions is important, and work on bracing and contact preparation is key for defensive positions.

Mesocycle 2 coincides with the fall ball season and is when foundational exercises will be introduced and mastered. The hang clean and push jerk are the main power exercises that will be used throughout the preseason and in-season. The RDL is the main hinge pattern and will be done bilaterally and unilaterally. Back squats and split squats will encompass the squat patterns in this phase. The main upper body movements that will be taught and used in this cycle are the barbell bench press, shoulder press, barbell bent-over row, and chin-up.

Mesocycles 3 and 4 are when true off-season strength and conditioning can be developed. Exercises that are specific to positional demands and goals can be prioritized in these cycles. Rotational medicine ball throws, such as the shot put toss, side toss, and chop toss, are incorporated into the programming of attack and offensive midfielder positions. Force production from a static, set position is prioritized for goalkeepers. For defense positions, more training sets of hang cleans and push jerks will be performed along with depth drops to enhance athletes' ability to manage external forces in different postures and positions.

Professional

Typically during the professional off-season, with the aforementioned landscape in mind, it is important for the strength and conditioning professional to begin by focusing on communication with athletes and understanding what each individual athlete's current status is when coming off the competitive season. Does the athlete have any lingering soft-tissue injuries? How does he or she feel overall physically? Does he or she need some rest before starting any off-season training? The wear and tear of a season often is synonymous with central nervous system fatigue, local muscular fatigue, and the overarching effect of joint stress due to the rigors of competition.

INTENSITY

Resistance training intensity is commonly assigned as a certain percentage of the 1-repetition maximum (1RM) (8) or a category (or *rate* or *rating*) of perceived exertion (RPE) (9).

High School

The intensity of the off-season training for high school should be adjusted according to the prescribed volume. When the volume is high, the intensity should be low to moderate (50%-75% 1RM) (4, 8). As the volume decreases, the intensity should increase (80%-95% 1RM). The intensity should also be progressively increased for a given exercise to allow athletes to adapt, especially those who are new to the program. For example, an athlete can use a load that is closer to 65% to 70% of the 1RM for 10 repetitions of the dumbbell bench press, instead of 75% of the 1RM (8).

College Women

The intensity for women's college lacrosse athletes is individualized based on factors such as athlete history, training age, and movement proficiency. Athletes may work off of a 1RM, estimated 1RM, or estimated multiple RM for barbell movements such as the front squat, military (shoulder) press, and hang clean during phase 1. For all resisted assistance work, athletes should be coached to increase the load while maintaining quality technique. This may be done using an RPE scale (figure 9.1) or by progressively increasing weight from one week to the next, especially if repetitions decrease—for example, the hang clean repetitions decrease from 3 in phase 2 to 2 in phase 3.

Rating	Description of perceived exertion
10	Maximum effort
9.5	No further repetitions but could increase load
9	1 repetition remaining
8.5	1 or 2 repetitions remaining
8	2 repetitions remaining
7.5	2 or 3 repetitions remaining
7	3 repetitions remaining
5-6	4-6 repetitions remaining
3-4	Light effort
1-2	Little to no effort

Figure 9.1   Resistance training–specific rating of perceived exertion.

Reprinted by permission from M.C. Zourdos, A. Klemp, C. Dolan, et al., "Novel Resistance Training-Specific Rating of Perceived Exertion Scale Measuring Repetitions in Reserve, "*Journal of Strength and Conditioning Research* 30, no. 1 (2016): 267-275.

College Men

For a men's college lacrosse program, intensity is purposefully constrained in mesocycles 1 and 2 to properly ramp up athletes at the beginning of the semester and to allow for technical mastery of foundational exercise patterns while managing the stress the athletes face with the reintroduction of sport practices. An RPE is assigned to the core exercises during these cycles to make sure the athletes are staying in proper training zones before any testing or intensification can take place with the new team. Intensities will naturally increase as repetition ranges are lowered from 15 to 20 in week 1 to 12 to 15 in week 2. If there is a third week of ramp-up leading into the program's fall season, a third week is provided with lower ranges of 8 to 12 repetitions. Mesocycle 2 incorporates a more traditional 3 × 5 work set protocol but with an assigned RPE of 6 to 7 so that the intensities stay low while the athletes are practicing every day and still learning the basic foundational exercises of the year. Work sets are performed in a step-loading protocol, where the weight is increased with each set to work up to a heavy top set for the exercise. The first two weeks of mesocycle 2 have work sets of 5 repetitions for the strength exercises. The weight will presumably increase each week as the repetitions are lowered to a 3 × 4 scheme in week 3 and 3 × 3 in week 4, all with an assigned RPE of 6 to 7.

Mesocycle 3 is when intensification of the primary exercises will occur, and specific exercises and methods will be incorporated based on positional goals. Week 4 will serve as a testing week for the primary exercises and the last set will be used to calculate an estimated 1RM for the primary exercises that will be used in future cycles to program intensity.

Week 1 of mesocycle 4 serves as a deload week with work set ranges capped at no higher than 80% of the 1RM. Weeks 2 to 4 will use a plateau protocol for work sets instead of the step-loading protocol used in the previous two cycles. This method has all work sets performed either at the same weight or in the same prescribed range of percentages of the 1RM. Week 2 will start with work sets performed in a range of 80% to 85% of the exercise's 1RM, and with each subsequent week, the range will increase by 2.5%, so that week 4 work sets should consist of 3 repetitions in a range of 85% to 90% of the estimated 1RM. (*Note*: This level of detail is not reflected in the sample programs.)

Day 3 for mesocycles 3 and 4 incorporates the tempo method, which is designed to maintain constant tension on the muscles throughout the working sets. The eccentric and concentric portions of each repetition are performed with a 3-second tempo, whereas the isometric and rest in between repetitions are eliminated so that the muscles are constantly under tension. Thus, "[3030]" corresponds to the tempo used for all repetitions; in other words, the first "3" designates the time spent on the eccentric potion of the exercise, the first "0" designates the time spent on the isometric portion of the exercise, the second "3" designates the time spent on the concentric portion of the exercise, and the second "0" designates the time spent resting in between repetitions. The assigned tempo will force athletes to use lighter weights (50%-65% 1RM) and will encourage them to concentrate on executing the proper movement in a slow, controlled pattern to really feel the targeted muscle groups. This is a great method to improve exercise technique by slowing down the movement.

Professional

For professional lacrosse athletes, the off-season period intensity, albeit short, will focus on low to moderate intensities to reintroduce the body to some regular density of training that typically has been moderate to high at certain points throughout the in-season period. The focus is to gradually progress during the first four to six weeks from lower intensity to moderate intensity through the first phase of the off-season.

VOLUME

Resistance training volume varies inversely with intensity and often changes across the mesocycles within off-season resistance training programs.

High School

During the high school off-season period, the training volume is high during the strength-endurance phase and then shifts to moderate to high volume during the basic strength phase (8). The number of repetitions can range from 8 to 20 during the strength-endurance phase and should be reduced to 2 to 6 as the focus shifts to strength development. Athletes should aim to train three or four times per week during this period, depending on their schedules (8). While it is important to have a high volume during the first four to eight weeks of the off-season period, this should be progressively built up, especially for younger athletes, by gradually increasing the number of repetitions or sets performed or by adjusting the intensity as previously mentioned.

When working with high school athletes, it is important to be mindful of the other demands that athletes might be facing during the off-season. Some athletes may still be playing club lacrosse in the fall, while others might be competing in other school sports. Additionally, athletes may be under academic and social pressures and still learning how to manage their time effectively. Therefore, strength and conditioning professionals need to ensure that they are not overburdening the athletes and consider these factors when designing their training program.

College Women

During the women's college lacrosse off-season, strength is the primary focus. While the off-season is also the time to focus on hypertrophy, the volume will remain relatively low compared to the men's college lacrosse off-season. Women typically have less muscle mass, and keeping the repetitions lower will allow them to successfully complete their repetitions, maintain their technique, and progressively load each movement. Female athletes with a lower training age will typically see hypertrophy in addition to strength gains, even with lower repetition ranges. All exercises during phase 1 call for 2 to 5 sets of 2 to 6 repetitions, with the exception of pulling movements (e.g., inverted rows, plate pullovers). In phases 2 to 3, some movements are programmed for 6 sets while the number of repetitions remains low (2-3) for athletes to increase intensity.

College Men

In mesocycle 1 during the men's college lacrosse off-season, volume is intentionally constrained to 1 set of each exercise to expose the athletes to a variety of movement patterns during the workout session. Repetition ranges are lowered week to week from 15 to 20 repetitions of each set in week 1 to 12 to 15 in week 2. If there is an additional week of ramp-up leading into the program's fall season, a range of 8 to 12 repetitions would be used for week 3.

The first week of mesocycle 2 starts with only 2 sets of each exercise as the new primary exercises are being introduced, increasing to a total of 3 work sets for all exercises throughout the cycle. Each work set will consist of 5 repetitions for the primary exercises.

Mesocycles 3 and 4 contain the highest total training volume of the cycles in the off-season. These are the weeks where physical adaptations can be prioritized, and the athletes will need to progressively accumulate enough specific stress for the body to adapt.

Days 1 and 2 use lower ranges of repetitions for the primary power and strength exercises to preferentially recruit and fatigue type II muscles fibers, while higher volumes of sets with greater time under tension are performed on day 3 of both mesocycles to target type I fibers (7).

Professional

For professional lacrosse athletes, volume during the off-season period will be moderate to high (8-12 repetitions) for 3 or 4 sets, trending inversely with sets and repetitions over the first phase. The intent is to begin the process of the general adaptation phase, (GPP) as mentioned in previous chapters. This will help prepare the tissues for higher intensities, build strength, and prepare for power and dynamic exercises that will be introduced during the preseason period.

CONCLUSION

At the high school level, the off-season program should focus on creating a strong foundation in all lacrosse athletes. It is a great opportunity for strength and conditioning professionals to teach and refine movement technique as well as develop a strong baseline of muscular strength and aerobic endurance. Taking the time to do this will allow lacrosse athletes to handle the demands of the preseason and in-season programming.

At the college level, the off-season program is meant to at first indoctrinate new team members into a college strength and conditioning system and get them technically proficient in the major movement patterns they will use the rest of the year. Once the exercises are mastered and off-season sport practices have concluded, the resistance training program can start to intensify and drive physiological adaptations. These periods are critical times to help reduce the risk of injury while preparing tissues to endure a full college lacrosse season.

Due to the nature of the landscape for professional athletes, the off-season period is typically a very fluid time of year where the strength and conditioning professional should be sensitive to the current status of each athlete, adjusting the off-season accordingly to ensure that programming matches the needs of athletes so that they have time to recover from the preceding season and begin training for the impending season.

Warm-Ups: Dynamic and Mobility Series

DYNAMIC WARM-UP SERIES

- Jog down and backpedal back (10 yards or meters each)
- Side shuffle down and side shuffle back (10 yards or meters each)
- Walking knee hugs down and lateral lunge back (10 yards or meters each)
- Walking quad pull down and inchworm jog back (10 yards or meters each)
- Walking leg cradle down and reverse lunge back (10 yards or meters each)
- A-skip forward down and A-skip backward back (10 yards or meters each)
- Lateral A-skip right down and lateral A-skip left back (10 yards or meters each)
- Power skip (2 × 20 yards or meters)
- Straight-leg run (2 × 20 yards or meters)

MOBILITY SERIES

- 90/90 hold + back heel lift + back leg lift (5 × 10 seconds each)
- Hip series (× as needed)
- Supine knee hug with ankle circle (× 3 each way)
- Floor slide with breathing (× 10)
- Cat–cow (× 10 each)
- Side-lying floor sweep (× 10 each)
- Quadruped and reach (× 10 each)

Interpreting the Sample Program Tables

+ = *Do the two exercises back-to-back*

[3030] = Tempo method for all repetitions (i.e., three seconds for the eccentric potion, no pause between movement phases, three seconds for the concentric portion, and no pause in between repetitions)

Abd = Abduction

Add = Adduction

Alt = Alternated

AMAP = As many as possible (but quality repetitions)

BB = Barbell

BW = Body weight

Bwd = Backward

CMJ = Countermovement jump

Diag = Diagonal

DB = Dumbbell

DL = Double leg

DWU = Dynamic warm-up

Ea = Each side (arm or leg), direction, or exercise

E:I:C = Eccentric:Isometric:Concentric

Ext = External

Fwd = Forward

GH = Glue-ham

GHR = Glute-ham raise

Goblet = Holding DB or KB with both hands below the chin and elbows pointed out to the side in the midline of the body

ISO = Isometric

KB = Kettlebell

Lat = Lateral

LM = Landmine

MB = Medicine ball

OH = Overhead

Order = Performing one set of each exercise (1a, 1b, 1c) in the group one after the other. After the first set is completed, go back to the first exercise in the group and do the second set of each exercise. If certain exercises call for fewer sets than others in the group, perform those sets on the back end of the grouping. For example, if exercise 1a calls for 4 sets and exercise 1b calls for 3 sets, perform exercise 1b during sets 2 through 4 of exercises 1a.

RDL = Romanian deadlift

RFE = Rear foot elevated

RM = Repetition maximum

Rot = Rotation

RPE = Rating of perceived exertion (intensity based on level of perceived difficulty)

SA = Single arm

SB = Stability ball

Scap = Scapula

(continued)

Interpreting the Sample Program Tables *(continued)*

SL = Single leg

TKE = Terminal knee extension

T-spine = Thoracic spine

Tempo = The time, in seconds, for each phase or portion of the exercise, written as "eccentric phase: top (or bottom) position: concentric phase" (King, I., How to write strength training programs. In *Speed of Movement*, p. 123, 1998.). For example, a tempo of "1:5:1" for the back squat means 1 second to lower, 5 seconds held at the bottom position, and 1 second to stand back up.

WU = Warm-up

yd = yard (*Note:* distance is approximate, so meters can be used instead of yards)

SAMPLE PROGRAMS

Tables 9.1 through 9.4 provide examples of off-season programs for high school lacrosse athletes, tables 9.5 through 9.7 provide examples for college women, tables 9.8 through 9.27 provide examples for college men, and tables 9.28 and 9.29 provide examples for professional athletes.

Table 9.1   High School Lacrosse: Off-Season Mesocycle, Strength-Endurance, Weeks 1 to 4

Monday: Lower Body (Push Emphasis)

Order	Exercise	Sets × reps (% 1RM) or time	Sets × reps (% 1RM) or time	Sets × reps (% 1RM) or time	Sets × reps (% 1RM) or time
		Week 1	Week 2	Week 3	Week 4
1a	Goblet squat (DB)	3 × 8 (75%)	3 × 8 (75%)	3 × 10 (75%)	4 × 10 (75%)
1b	90/90 hold	3 × 20 s	3 × 20 s	3 × 20 s	4 × 20 s
2a	Split squat (DB)	3 × 8 (75%)	3 × 8 (75%)	3 × 10 (75%)	4 × 10 (75%)
2b	Hurdle step-over	3 × 10 ea	3 × 10 ea	3 × 10 ea	4 × 10 ea
3a	Reverse lunge	3 × 10 ea (70%)	3 × 10 ea (70%)	3 × 10 ea (75%)	4 × 10 ea (75%)
3b	Front plank	3 × 45 s	3 × 45 s	3 × 45 s	4 × 45 s
4a	Lateral lunge	3 × 10 ea (70%)	3 × 10 ea (70%)	3 × 10 ea (75%)	4 × 10 ea (75%)
4b	Pallof press	3 × 15 ea	3 × 15 ea	3 × 15 ea	4 × 15 ea
5a	Copenhagen plank	3 × 15 s	3 × 15 s	3 × 15 s	3 × 15 s
5b	Calf raise (DB)	3 × 12 (65%)	3 × 12 (65%)	3 × 12 (65%)	3 × 12 (65%)

Tuesday: Upper Body (Push Emphasis)

Order	Exercise	Sets × reps (% 1RM)	Sets × reps (% 1RM)	Sets × reps (% 1RM)	Sets × reps (% 1RM)
		Week 1	Week 2	Week 3	Week 4
1a	Bench press (DB)	3 × 8 (75%)	3 × 8 (75%)	3 × 10 (75%)	4 × 10 (75%)
1b	Quadruped and roll	3 × 10 ea	3 × 10 ea	3 × 10 ea	4 × 10 ea
2a	Seated shoulder press (DB)	3 × 8 (75%)	3 × 8 (75%)	3 × 10 (75%)	4 × 10 (75%)

Order	Exercise	Sets × reps (% 1RM)	Sets × reps (% 1RM)	Sets × reps (% 1RM)	Sets × reps (% 1RM)
		Week 1	Week 2	Week 3	Week 4
2b	Seated T-spine rot	3 × 6 ea	3 × 6 ea	3 × 6 ea	4 × 6 ea
3a	Bench row (BB)	3 × 8 (75%)	3 × 8 (75%)	3 × 10 (75%)	4 × 10 (75%)
3b	Supine leg raise	3 × 12	3 × 12	3 × 12	4 × 12
4a	Chest press standing (cable)	3 × 10 (70%)	3 × 10 (70%)	3 × 10 (75%)	4 × 10 (75%)
4b	Pallof press	3 × 15	3 × 15	3 × 15	4 × 15
5a	Push-up	3 × 8	3 × 8	3 × 10	3 × 10
5b	3-way shoulder raise	3 × 8 ea (75%)	3 × 8 ea (75%)	3 × 8 ea (80%)	3 × 8 ea (80%)

Thursday: Lower Body (Pull Emphasis)

Order	Exercise	Sets × reps (% 1RM) or time	Sets × reps (% 1RM) or time	Sets × reps (% 1RM) or time	Sets × reps (% 1RM) or time
		Week 1	Week 2	Week 3	Week 4
1a	Trap bar deadlift	3 × 8 (75%)	3 × 8 (75%)	3 × 10 (75%)	4 × 10 (75%)
1b	90/90, alt	3 × 20 s ea	3 × 20 s ea	3 × 20 s ea	3 × 20 s ea
2a	RDL (DB)	3 × 8 ea (75%)	3 × 8 ea (75%)	3 × 10 ea (75%)	4 × 10 ea (75%)
2b	Hurdle step-over	3 × 10 ea	3 × 10 ea	3 × 10 ea	3 × 10 ea
3a	Glute bridge (DB)	3 × 12 ea (60%)	3 × 12 ea (60%)	3 × 12 ea (65%)	3 × 12 ea (65%)
3b	Side plank	3 × 15 s	3 × 15 s	3 × 20 s	3 × 20 s
4a	Lateral step-up (DB)	3 × 10 ea (70%)	3 × 10 ea (70%)	3 × 10 ea (75%)	4 × 10 ea (75%)
4b	McGill crunch	3 × 10 ea	3 × 10 ea	3 × 15 ea	4 × 15 ea
5a	Nordic curl	3 × 15 s ea	3 × 15 s ea	3 × 20 s ea	3 × 20 s ea
5b	Hip adduction (cable)	3 × 10 ea (75%)	3 × 10 ea (75%)	3 × 10 ea (75%)	3 × 10 ea (75%)

Friday: Upper Body (Pull Emphasis)

Order	Exercise	Sets × reps (% 1RM)	Sets × reps (% 1RM)	Sets × reps (% 1RM)	Sets × reps (% 1RM)
		Week 1	Week 2	Week 3	Week 4
1a	Bent-over row (DB)	3 × 8 (75%)	3 × 8 (75%)	3 × 10 (75%)	4 × 10 (75%)
1b	Quadruped and reach	3 × 10 ea	3 × 10 ea	3 × 10 ea	4 × 10 ea
2a	Pull-up	3 × 8 (75%)	3 × 8 (75%)	3 × 10 (75%)	4 × 10 (75%)
2b	Floor slide	3 × 6 ea	3 × 6 ea	3 × 6 ea	4 × 6 ea
3a	Push press	3 × 8 (75%)	3 × 8 (75%)	3 × 10 (75%)	4 × 10 (75%)
3b	Supine leg raise	3 × 12	3 × 12	3 × 12	4 × 12
4a	Pullover (DB)	3 × 10 (70%)	3 × 10 (70%)	3 × 10 (75%)	4 × 10 (75%)
4b	Oblique twist (LM)	3 × 8 ea	3 × 8 ea	3 × 10 ea	4 × 10 ea
5a	Inverted row	3 × 8 (75%)	3 × 8 (75%)	3 × 10 (75%)	3 × 10 (75%)
5b	Prone I's, Y's, T's, W's	3 × 8 (75%)	3 × 8 (75%)	3 × 8 (75%)	3 × 10 (75%)

Table 9.2 High School Lacrosse: Off-Season Mesocycle, Strength-Endurance, Weeks 5 to 8

Monday: Lower Body (Push Emphasis)

Order	Exercise	Sets × reps (% 1RM) or time	Sets × reps (% 1RM) or time	Sets × reps (% 1RM) or time	Sets × reps (% 1RM) or time
		Week 5	Week 6	Week 7	Week 8
1a	Front squat (BB)	4 × 10 (75%)	4 × 10 (75%)	4 × 10 (75%)	4 × 10 (75%)
1b	90/90, alt	4 × 10 ea	4 × 10 ea	4 × 10 ea	4 × 10 ea
2a	Split squat (DB)	4 × 10 ea (75%)	4 × 10 ea (75%)	4 × 10 ea (75%)	4 × 10 ea (75%)
2b	T-spine thread the needle	4 × 10 ea	4 × 10 ea	4 × 10 ea	4 × 10 ea
3	Lateral lunge (DB)	4 × 10 ea (75%)	4 × 10 ea (75%)	4 × 10 ea (75%)	4 × 10 ea (75%)
4a	Rear lunge to step-up	3 × 8 ea (75%)	3 × 8 ea (75%)	3 × 10 ea (75%)	3 × 10 ea (75%)
4b	Front plank	4 × 60 s	4 × 60 s	4 × 75 s	4 × 75 s
5a	Copenhagen plank	4 × 20 s ea	4 × 20 s ea	4 × 20 s ea	4 × 20 s ea
5b	Pallof press	4 × 20 ea	4 × 20 ea	4 × 20 ea	4 × 20 ea

Tuesday: Upper Body (Push Emphasis)

Order	Exercise	Sets × reps (% 1RM)	Sets × reps (% 1RM)	Sets × reps (% 1RM)	Sets × reps (% 1RM)
		Week 5	Week 6	Week 7	Week 8
1a	Bench press (BB)	4 × 10 (75%)	4 × 10 (75%)	4 × 10 (75%)	4 × 10 (75%)
1b	Quadruped and roll	4 × 10 ea	4 × 10 ea	4 × 10 ea	4 × 10 ea
2a	Shoulder press, SA (LM)	4 × 8 ea (80%)	4 × 8 ea (80%)	4 × 10 ea (75%)	4 × 10 ea (75%)
2b	Wall slide	4 × 10	4 × 10	4 × 10	4 × 10
3a	Chin-up, neutral grip	4 × 8 (80%)	4 × 8 (80%)	4 × 10 (75%)	4 × 10 (75%)
3b	Supine leg raise	4 × 15	4 × 15	4 × 15	4 × 15
4a	Standing shoulder press (DB)	4 × 10 (75%)	4 × 10 (75%)	4 × 10 (75%)	4 × 10 (75%)
4b	Oblique twist (LM)	4 × 8 ea	4 × 8 ea	4 × 8 ea	4 × 8 ea
5a	Cuban press	3 × 12 (65%)	3 × 12 (65%)	3 × 12 (65%)	3 × 12 (65%)
5b	Prone I's, Y's, T's, W's	3 × 8 ea (80%)	3 × 8 ea (80%)	3 × 8 ea (80%)	3 × 8 ea (80%)

Thursday: Lower Body (Pull Emphasis)

Order	Exercise	Sets × reps (% 1RM) or time	Sets × reps (% 1RM) or time	Sets × reps (% 1RM) or time	Sets × reps (% 1RM) or time
		Week 5	Week 6	Week 7	Week 8
1a	Trap bar deadlift	4 × 10 (75%)	4 × 10 (75%)	4 × 10 (75%)	4 × 10 (75%)
1b	Shin box hold	4 × 20 s ea	4 × 20 s ea	4 × 20 s ea	4 × 20 s ea
2a	RDL, staggered stance (DB)	4 × 10 ea (75%)	4 × 10 ea (75%)	4 × 10 ea (75%)	4 × 10 ea (75%)
2b	Quadruped reach	3 × 10 ea	3 × 10 ea	3 × 10 ea	3 × 10 ea
3a	Multidirectional lunge (3-way)	4 × 4 ea (65%)	4 × 4 ea (65%)	4 × 5 ea (65%)	4 × 5 ea (65%)

Order	Exercise	Sets × reps (% 1RM) or time	Sets × reps (% 1RM) or time	Sets × reps (% 1RM) or time	Sets × reps (% 1RM) or time
		Week 5	Week 6	Week 7	Week 8
3b	Side plank	4 × 30 s	4 × 30 s	4 × 30 s	4 × 30 s
4a	Hamstring curl, SL (SB)	4 × 10 ea	4 × 10 ea	4 × 12 ea	4 × 12 ea
4b	McGill crunch	4 × 15 ea	4 × 15 ea	4 × 15 ea	4 × 15 ea
5a	Nordic curl	3 × 8	3 × 8	3 × 8	3 × 8
5b	Reverse hyper	3 × 10	3 × 10	3 × 10	3 × 10

Friday: Upper Body (Pull Emphasis)

Order	Exercise	Sets × reps (% 1RM)	Sets × reps (% 1RM)	Sets × reps (% 1RM)	Sets × reps (% 1RM)
		Week 5	Week 6	Week 7	Week 8
1a	Pull-up	4 × 10 (75%)	4 × 10 (75%)	4 × 10 (75%)	4 × 10 (75%)
1b	Side-lying floor sweep	4 × 10 ea	4 × 10 ea	4 × 10 ea	4 × 10 ea
2a	Row (LM)	4 × 8 ea (80%)	4 × 8 ea (80%)	4 × 8 ea (80%)	4 × 8 ea (80%)
2b	Half-kneeling wall circle	4 × 6 ea	4 × 6 ea	4 × 6 ea	4 × 6 ea
3a	Bench press, alt (DB)	4 × 8 ea (80%)	4 × 8 ea (80%)	4 × 10 ea (80%)	4 × 10 ea (75%)
3b	Supine leg raise	4 × 15	4 × 15	4 × 15	4 × 15
4a	Lat pulldown	4 × 10 (75%)	4 × 10 (75%)	4 × 10 (75%)	4 × 10 (75%)
4b	Oblique twist (LM)	4 × 10 ea	4 × 10 ea	4 × 10 ea	4 × 10 ea
5a	Biceps curl (DB)	3 × 10 (75%)	3 × 10 (75%)	3 × 12 (75%)	3 × 12 (75%)
5b	Overhead triceps extension	3 × 10 (75%)	3 × 10 (75%)	3 × 12 (75%)	3 × 12 (75%)

Table 9.3 High School Lacrosse: Off-Season Mesocycle, Basic Strength, Weeks 9 to 12

Monday: Lower Body (Push Emphasis)

Order	Exercise	Sets × reps (% 1RM) or time	Sets × reps (% 1RM) or time	Sets × reps (% 1RM) or time	Sets × reps (% 1RM) or time
		Week 9	Week 10	Week 11	Week 12
1	Front squat (BB)	4 × 6 (80%)	4 × 6 (80%)	4 × 6 (85%)	4 × 6 (85%)
2	Walking lunge (DB)	4 × 6 (80%)	4 × 6 (80%)	4 × 6 (85%)	4 × 6 (85%)
3a	Lateral lunge (DB)	3 × 8 ea (80%)	3 × 8 ea (80%)	4 × 8 ea (80%)	4 × 8 ea (80%)
3b	Child's pose	3 × 30 s	3 × 30 s	4 × 30 s	4 × 30 s
4a	Squat, SL	3 × 8 ea (80%)	3 × 8 ea (80%)	4 × 8 ea (80%)	4 × 8 ea (80%)
4b	Half-kneeling ankle mobility	3 × 20 s ea	3 × 20 s ea	4 × 20 s ea	4 × 20 s ea
5a	Hip abduction (cable)	3 × 12 ea (65%)	3 × 12 ea (65%)	3 × 12 ea (65%)	3 × 12 ea (65%)

(continued)

Table 9.3 High School Lacrosse: Off-Season Mesocycle, Basic Strength, Weeks 9 to 12 *(continued)*

Monday: Lower Body (Push Emphasis) *(continued)*

Order	Exercise	Sets × reps (% 1RM) or time	Sets × reps (% 1RM) or time	Sets × reps (% 1RM) or time	Sets × reps (% 1RM) or time
		Week 9	Week 10	Week 11	Week 12
5b	Hip adduction (cable)	3 × 12 ea (65%)	3 × 12 ea (65%)	3 × 12 ea (65%)	3 × 12 ea (65%)
6a	Ab wheel rollout	2 × 8	2 × 8	3 × 8	3 × 8
6b	V-sit with Russian twist	2 × 10 ea	2 × 10 ea	3 × 12 ea	3 × 12 ea
6c	GHR back extension hold	2 × 30 s	2 × 30 s	3 × 45 s	3 × 45 s

Tuesday: Upper Body (Push Emphasis)

Order	Exercise	Sets × reps (% 1RM) or time	Sets × reps (% 1RM) or time	Sets × reps (% 1RM) or time	Sets × reps (% 1RM) or time
		Week 9	Week 10	Week 11	Week 12
1	Bench press (BB)	4 × 6 (80%)	4 × 6 (80%)	4 × 6 (85%)	4 × 6 (85%)
2	Shoulder press, SA (LM)	4 × 6 ea (80%)	4 × 6 ea (80%)	4 × 6 ea (85%)	4 × 6 ea (85%)
3a	Chin-up, neutral grip	4 × 8 (80%)	4 × 8 (80%)	4 × 8 (80%)	4 × 8 (80%)
3b	Side-lying floor sweep	4 × 10 ea	4 × 10 ea	4 × 10 ea	4 × 10 ea
4a	Half-kneeling shoulder press, SA (DB)	4 × 8 ea (80%)	4 × 8 ea (80%)	4 × 8 ea (80%)	4 × 8 ea (80%)
4b	Hurdle step-over	4 × 8 ea	4 × 8 ea	4 × 8 ea	4 × 8 ea
5a	Cuban press	3 × 10 (75%)	3 × 10 (75%)	3 × 10 (75%)	3 × 10 (75%)
5b	Prone I's, Y's, T's, W's	3 × 8 ea	3 × 8 ea	3 × 8 ea	3 × 8 ea
6a	Oblique twist (LM)	3 × 8 ea	3 × 8 ea	3 × 8 ea	3 × 8 ea
6b	Side plank	3 × 25 s ea	3 × 25 s ea	3 × 25 s ea	3 × 25 s ea
6c	McGill crunch	3 × 15 ea	3 × 15 ea	3 × 15 ea	3 × 15 ea

Thursday: Lower Body (Pull Emphasis)

Order	Exercise	Sets × reps (% 1RM)	Sets × reps (% 1RM)	Sets × reps (% 1RM)	Sets × reps (% 1RM)
		Week 9	Week 10	Week 11	Week 12
1	Deadlift	4 × 6 ea (80%)	4 × 6 ea (80%)	4 × 6 ea (85%)	4 × 6 ea (85%)
2	RDL, staggered stance (DB)	4 × 6 ea (80%)	4 × 6 ea (80%)	4 × 6 ea (85%)	4 × 6 ea (85%)
3a	Lateral squat (DB)	4 × 8 ea (80%)	4 × 8 ea (80%)	4 × 8 ea (80%)	4 × 8 ea (80%)
3b	90/90, alt	3 × 10 ea	3 × 10 ea	3 × 10 ea	3 × 10 ea
4a	Glute bridge, SL (DB)	4 × 10 ea (75%)	4 × 10 ea (75%)	4 × 10 ea (75%)	4 × 10 ea (75%)
4b	Hurdle step-over	4 × 8 ea	4 × 8 ea	4 × 8 ea	4 × 8 ea

Order	Exercise	Sets × reps (% 1RM) Week 9	Sets × reps (% 1RM) Week 10	Sets × reps (% 1RM) Week 11	Sets × reps (% 1RM) Week 12
5a	Hamstring curl, SL (SB)	4 × 10 ea	4 × 10 ea	4 × 10 ea	4 × 10 ea
5b	McGill crunch	4 × 15 ea	4 × 15 ea	4 × 15 ea	4 × 15 ea
6a	Hamstring slide	3 × 10	3 × 10	3 × 10	3 × 10
6b	Copenhagen hip raise	3 × 8 ea	3 × 8 ea	3 × 10 ea	3 × 10 ea

Friday: Upper Body (Pull Emphasis)

Order	Exercise	Sets × reps (% 1RM) Week 9	Sets × reps (% 1RM) Week 10	Sets × reps (% 1RM) Week 11	Sets × reps (% 1RM) Week 12
1	Pull-up, weighted (if able)	4 × 6 (80%)	4 × 6 (80%)	4 × 6 (85%)	4 × 6 (85%)
2	SA row, hand supported (DB)	4 × 6 ea (80%)	4 × 6 ea (80%)	4 × 6 ea (85%)	4 × 6 ea (85%)
3a	Incline bench press (DB)	4 × 8 (80%)	4 × 8 (80%)	4 × 8 (80%)	4 × 8 (80%)
3b	Quadruped and reach	4 × 12 ea	4 × 12 ea	4 × 12 ea	4 × 12 ea
4a	Lat pulldown, SA	4 × 8 ea (80%)	4 × 8 ea (80%)	4 × 8 ea (80%)	4 × 8 ea (80%)
4b	Quadruped and roll	4 × 15	4 × 15	4 × 15	4 × 15
5a	Banded I's, Y's, T's, W's	4 × 8 ea (80%)	4 × 8 ea (80%)	4 × 8 ea (80%)	4 × 10 ea (75%)
5b	Straight-arm row (cable)	4 × 12 (65%)	4 × 12 (65%)	4 × 12 (65%)	4 × 12 (65%)
6a	Plank shoulder tap	3 × 10 ea	3 × 10 ea	3 × 10 ea	3 × 10 ea
6b	Supine leg raise	3 × 12	3 × 12	3 × 12	3 × 12

Table 9.4 High School Lacrosse: Off-Season Mesocycle, Basic Strength, Weeks 13 to 16

Monday: Lower Body (Push Emphasis)

Order	Exercise	Sets × reps (% 1RM) or time Week 13	Sets × reps (% 1RM) or time Week 14	Sets × reps (% 1RM) or time Week 15	Sets × reps (% 1RM) or time Week 16
1	Hang high pull	4 × 4 (75%)	4 × 4 (75%)	5 × 4 (80%)	5 × 4 (80%)
2	Front squat (BB)	4 × 6 (85%)	4 × 6 (85%)	5 × 6 (85%)	5 × 6 (85%)
3	Lateral lunge (DB)	4 × 6 ea (85%)	4 × 6 ea (85%)	5 × 6 (85%)	5 × 6 (85%)
4a	Split squat (DB)	4 × 6 ea (85%)	4 × 6 ea (85%)	4 × 6 ea (85%)	4 × 6 ea (85%)
4b	90/90, alt	4 × 30 s	4 × 30 s	4 × 30 s	4 × 30 s
5a	Squat, SL (DB)	4 × 6 ea (85%)	4 × 6 ea (85%)	4 × 6 ea (85%)	4 × 6 ea (85%)
5b	Hurdle step-over, lat	4 × 8 ea	4 × 8 ea	4 × 8 ea	4 × 8 ea
6a	Ab wheel rollout	2 × 8	2 × 8	3 × 8	3 × 8
6b	GH back extension hold	2 × 30 s	2 × 30 s	3 × 45 s	3 × 45 s

(continued)

Table 9.4   High School Lacrosse: Off-Season Mesocycle, Basic Strength, Weeks 13 to 16   *(continued)*

Tuesday: Upper Body (Push Emphasis)

Order	Exercise	Sets × reps (% 1RM) or time	Sets × reps (% 1RM) or time	Sets × reps (% 1RM) or time	Sets × reps (% 1RM) or time
		Week 13	Week 14	Week 15	Week 16
1	Push jerk (DB)	4 × 4 (75%)	4 × 4 (75%)	5 × 4 (80%)	5 × 4 (80%)
2	Bench press (BB)	4 × 6 (85%)	4 × 6 (85%)	5 × 6 (85%)	5 × 6 (85%)
3	Row, SA, hand supported (DB)	4 × 6 ea (85%)	4 × 6 ea (85%)	5 × 6 ea (85%)	5 × 6 ea (85%)
4a	Standing shoulder press, SA (DB)	4 × 6 ea (85%)	4 × 6 ea (85%)	4 × 6 ea (85%)	4 × 6 ea (85%)
4b	Seated thoracic rot	4 × 15 s ea	4 × 15 s ea	4 × 15 s ea	4 × 15 s ea
5a	Incline bench press, SA (DB)	4 × 6 ea (85%)	4 × 6 ea (85%)	4 × 6 ea (85%)	4 × 6 ea (85%)
5b	Half-kneeling wall circle	4 × 8 ea	4 × 8 ea	4 × 8 ea	4 × 8 ea
6a	Oblique twist (LM)	3 × 8 ea	3 × 8 ea	3 × 8 ea	3 × 8 ea
6b	Side plank	3 × 25 s ea	3 × 25 s ea	3 × 25 s ea	3 × 25 s ea

Thursday: Lower Body (Pull Emphasis)

Order	Exercise	Sets × reps (% 1RM) or time	Sets × reps (% 1RM) or time	Sets × reps (% 1RM) or time	Sets × reps (% 1RM) or time
		Week 13	Week 14	Week 15	Week 16
1	Hang clean	4 × 4 (75%)	4 × 4 (75%)	5 × 4 (80%)	5 × 4 (80%)
2	Trap bar deadlift	4 × 6 (85%)	4 × 6 (85%)	5 × 6 (85%)	5 × 6 (85%)
3	RDL, SL (DB)	4 × 6 ea (85%)	4 × 6 ea (85%)	5 × 6 ea (85%)	5 × 6 ea (85%)
4a	Glute bridge, SL (DB)	4 × 6 ea (85%)	4 × 6 ea (85%)	4 × 6 ea (85%)	4 × 6 ea (85%)
4b	90/90, alt	4 × 10 ea	4 × 10 ea	4 × 10 ea	4 × 10 ea
5a	Hamstring curl, SL (SB)	4 × 10 ea	4 × 10 ea	4 × 10 ea	4 × 10 ea
5b	Half-kneeling ankle mobility	4 × 30 s ea	4 × 30 s ea	4 × 30 s ea	4 × 30 s ea
6a	Copenhagen plank	2 × 20 s ea	2 × 20 s ea	3 × 25 s ea	3 × 25 s ea
6b	Russian twist	2 × 15 ea	2 × 15 ea	3 × 15 ea	3 × 15 ea

Friday: Upper Body (Pull Emphasis)

Order	Exercise	Sets × reps (% 1RM)	Sets × reps (% 1RM)	Sets × reps (% 1RM)	Sets × reps (% 1RM)
		Week 13	Week 14	Week 15	Week 16
1	Snatch, SA (DB)	4 × 2 ea (75%)	4 × 2 ea (75%)	5 × 2 ea (80%)	5 × 2 ea (80%)
2	Pull-up, weighted if able	4 × 6 (85%)	4 × 6 (85%)	5 × 6 (85%)	5 × 6 (85%)
3	Seated row	4 × 6 (85%)	4 × 6 (85%)	5 × 6 (85%)	5 × 6 (85%)
4a	Press (LM)	4 × 8 ea (80%)	4 × 8 ea (80%)	4 × 8 ea (80%)	4 × 8 ea (80%)
4b	Quadruped and reach	4 × 12 ea	4 × 12 ea	4 × 12 ea	4 × 12 ea

Order	Exercise	Sets × reps (% 1RM)	Sets × reps (% 1RM)	Sets × reps (% 1RM)	Sets × reps (% 1RM)
		Week 13	Week 14	Week 15	Week 16
5a	Lat pulldown, SA	4 × 8 ea (80%)	4 × 8 ea (80%)	4 × 8 ea (80%)	4 × 8 ea (80%)
5b	Quadruped and roll	4 × 10 ea	4 × 10 ea	4 × 10 ea	4 × 10 ea
6a	Plank shoulder tap	2 × 10 ea	2 × 10 ea	3 × 12 ea	3 × 12 ea
6b	Supine leg raise	2 × 12	2 × 12	3 × 15	3 × 15

Table 9.5 College Women's Lacrosse: Off-Season, Phase 1

Day 1: Total-Body Focus

Order	Exercise	Tempo (E:I:C)	Intensity	Sets	Reps	Rest
1	Shoulder care—prone I's, Y's, T's, A's	—	2.5 lb (~1 kg)	1	10 ea	—
2	Activation (scap push-up)	—	BW	1	10	—
3	OH squat	2:0:1	—	5	2	2 min
4	Swing (KB)	—	—	3	6	1 min
5	Front squat	1:0:1	—	4	5	2 min
6	RDL shrug	2:0:1	—	4	5	1 min
7	Inverted row	1:0:1	—	3	6-10	1 min
8	Shoulder press	1:2:1	—	4	5	1-2 min

Day 2: Total-Body Focus

Order	Exercise	Tempo (E:I:C)	Intensity	Sets	Reps	Rest
1	Lower limb care—Peterson step-down	—	BW	2	10/leg	—
2	Activation—glute bridge	0:10:0	BW or mini band	3	—	—
3	Hurdle mobility at rack	—	—	—	5/leg	—
4a	Squat to box, SL	1:1:1	—	3	5/leg	1 min
4b	Vertical jump (with reset)	—	—	3	3	1 min
5	Hang clean	—	—	5	3	2 min
6	DB bench press	1:1:1	—	4	5	2 min
7	Plate pullover	1:1:1	—	3	8	1 min
8	Nordic curl	5+:0:0	—	2	3	2 min

Table 9.6 College Women's Lacrosse: Off-Season, Phase 2

Day 1: Total-Body Focus

Order	Exercise	Tempo (E:I:C)	Intensity	Sets	Reps	Rest
1	Shoulder care—prone I's, Y's, T's, A's	—	2.5 lb (~1 kg)	1	10 ea	—
2	Activation—scap push-up	—	BW	1	10	—
3a	OH squat	2:0:1	—	5	3	2 min

(continued)

Table 9.6 College Women's Lacrosse: Off-Season, Phase 2 *(continued)*

Day 1: Total-Body Focus *(continued)*

Order	Exercise	Tempo (E:I:C)	Intensity	Sets	Reps	Rest
3b	Hurdle hop and stick, SL	—	—	3	5/leg	1 min
4	Hang clean	—	—	6	3	2 min
5	Squat	1:0:1	—	6	3	2 min
6	Bent-over row	1:0:1	—	4	5	1 min
7	Push press	—	—	6	3	2 min
8	Plank (optional)	—	—	—	—	—

Day 2: Total-Body Focus

Order	Exercise	Tempo (E:I:C)	Intensity	Sets	Reps or distance	Rest
1	Lower limb care—Peterson step-down	—	BW	2	10/leg	—
2	Activation—glute bridge	0:10:0	BW or mini band	3	—	—
3	Hurdle mobility at rack	—	—	5/leg	—	—
4	Swing (KB)	—	—	4	6	1 min
5	Lateral hop-and-stick landing	—	—	3	3/leg	1-2 min
6a	Sumo deadlift	1:0:1	—	5	3	2 min
6b	Banded shuffle	—	—	4	10 yd, left and right	2 min
7a	Push-up	1:0:1	—	3	AMAP	2 min
7b	Inverted row or pull-up	1:0:1	—	3	AMAP	2 min
8	Nordic curl	5+:0:0	—	2	3	2 min
9	LM rot	—	—	3	5	1 min

Day 3: Total-Body Focus

Order	Exercise	Tempo (E:I:C)	Intensity	Sets	Reps or distance	Rest
WU	DWU series					
1	Snatch transfer series*	—	—	1	3	—
2	Box jump	—	—	5	3	1 min
3	Bent-over row	1:0:1	—	4	6	1 min
4	Bench press (BB)	1:0:1	—	6	3	2 min
5	Walking lunge (DB)	—	—	4	15 yd	1 min
6	Slam (MB)	—	—	3	8	1 min
7	Neck—BB or DB shrug	—	—	3	10	1 min

*Snatch transfer series: 3 OH squats + 3 pressing snatch balance + 3 snatch balance

Table 9.7   College Women's Lacrosse: Off-Season, Phase 3

Day 1: Total-Body Focus

Order	Exercise	Tempo (E:I:C)	Intensity	Sets	Reps	Rest
1	Shoulder care—prone I's, Y's, T's, A's	—	2.5 lb (~1 kg)	1	10 ea	—
2	Activation—scap push-up	—	BW	1	10	—
3a	OH squat	2:0:1	—	5	3	2 min
3b	Hurdle hop, SL (rapid fire)	—	—	4	3/leg	<1 min
4	Hang clean	—	—	6	2	2 min
5	Squat (front or back)	1:0:1	—	6	2	2 min
6	Bench press (BB)	1:0:1	—	5	4	2 min
7	Plank (optional)	—	—	—	—	—

Day 2: Total-Body Focus

Order	Exercise	Tempo (E:I:C)	Intensity	Sets	Reps	Rest
1	Lower limb care—Peterson step-down	—	BW	2	10/leg	—
2	Activation—glute bridge	0:10:0	BW or mini band	3	—	—
3	Hurdle mobility at rack	—	—	5/leg	—	—
4	Swing (KB)	—	—	3	8	1 min
5	Trap bar deadlift	1:1:1	—	5	4	2 min
6	DB bench press	1:2:1	—	5	4	2 min
7	Nordic curl	5+:0:0	—	2	3	2 min

Day 3: Total-Body Focus

Order	Exercise	Tempo (E:I:C)	Intensity	Sets	Reps or distance	Rest
WU	DWU series					
1	Snatch transfer series*	—	—	1	3	—
2	Complex: RDL shrug + hang clean + front squat	—	—	4	3	2 min
3	RFE split squat	1:0:1	—	4	4/leg	2 min
4	BB incline bench press	1:0:1	—	6	3	2 min
5	Farmer's walk	—	—	4	30 yd	1-2 min
6	Neck—BB or DB shrug	—	—	4	8	1 min

*Snatch transfer series: 3 OH squats + 3 pressing snatch balance + 3 snatch balance

Table 9.8 College Men's Lacrosse: Off-Season, Mesocycle 1

Day 1

Order	Exercise	Sets × reps, time, or distance	Sets × reps, time, or distance	Sets × reps, time, or distance
		Week 1	**Week 2**	**Week 3**
WU	BB complex: RDL + clean pull + muscle clean + hang clean	2 × 5 ea	2 × 5 ea	2 × 5 ea
1a	Linear box jump	2 × 4	3 × 4	4 × 4
1b	Linear hurdle hop	2 × 4 ea	3 × 4 ea	4 × 4 ea
1c	Forward and backward line hop	2 × 10 s ea foot	3 × 10 s ea foot	4 × 10 s ea foot
2a	Push-up	1 × 15-20 RPE 6-7	1 × 12-15 RPE 6-7	1 × 8-12 RPE 6-7
2b	Lat pulldown	1 × 15-20 or AMAP RPE 6-7	1 × 12-15 RPE 6-7	1 × 8-12 RPE 6-7
2c	Goblet squat	1 × 15-20 RPE 6-7	1 × 12-15 RPE 6-7	1 × 8-12 RPE 6-7
2d	**Goalies, defenders, and long-stick midfielders:** Half-kneeling lift	1 × 8 ea RPE 6-7	1 × 10 ea RPE 6-7	1 × 12 ea RPE 6-7
2d	**Attackers and midfielders:** Half-kneeling chop	1 × 8 ea RPE 6-7	1 × 10 ea RPE 6-7	1 × 12 ea RPE 6-7
3a	Floor-seated shoulder press (DB)	1 × 15-20 RPE 6-7	1 × 12-15 RPE 6-7	1 × 8-12 RPE 6-7
3b	Inverted row	1 × 15-20 RPE 6-7	1 × 12-15 RPE 6-7	1 × 8-12 RPE 6-7
3c	Hip bridge, SL	1 × 8 ea RPE 6-7	1 × 10 ea RPE 6-7	1 × 12 ea RPE 6-7
3d	**Goalies and defenders:** Push-up position pull-through (sandbag or KB)	1 × 8 ea RPE 6-7	1 × 10 ea RPE 6-7	1 × 12 ea RPE 6-7
3d	**Attackers and midfielders:** Side toss (MB)	1 × 8 ea RPE 6-7	1 × 10 ea RPE 6-7	1 × 12 ea RPE 6-7
4a	Hammer curl (DB)	1 × 15-20 RPE 6-7	1 × 12-15 RPE 6-7	1 × 8-12 RPE 6-7
4b	Overhead triceps extension (DB)	1 × 15-20 RPE 6-7	1 × 12-15 RPE 6-7	1 × 8-12 RPE 6-7
4c	5-way lunge complex: Fwd + diag + lat + rotational + reverse	1 × 2 ea	1 × 3 ea	1 × 4 ea
4d	Overhead carry, SA	1 × 20 yd ea	1 × 30 yd ea	1 × 40 yd ea

Day 2

Order	Exercise	Sets × reps, time, or distance	Sets × reps, time, or distance	Sets × reps, time, or distance
		Week 1	**Week 2**	**Week 3**
WU	BB complex: Front squat + shoulder press + push press	2 × 5 ea Bar only	2 × 5 ea Bar only	1 × 5 ea Bar only

Order	Exercise	Sets × reps, time, or distance	Sets × reps, time, or distance	Sets × reps, time, or distance
		Week 1	**Week 2**	**Week 3**
1a	Lateral box jump	2 × 4	3 × 4	4 × 4
1b	Lateral or medial hurdle hop	2 × 4 ea	3 × 4 ea	4 × 4 ea
1c	Side-to-side line hop	2 × 10 s ea foot	3 × 10 s ea foot	4 × 10 s ea foot
2a	Bench press (DB)	1 × 15-20 RPE 6-7	1 × 12-15 RPE 6-7	1 × 8-12 RPE 6-7
2b	Pullover (DB)	1 × 15-20 or AMAP	1 × 12-15 RPE 6-7	1 × 8-12 RPE 6-7
2c	RDL with 2 DBs	1 × 15-20 RPE 6-7	1 × 12-15 RPE 6-7	1 × 8-12 RPE 6-7
2d	**Goalies, defenders, and long-stick midfielders:** Standing lift	1 × 8 ea RPE 6-7	1 × 10 ea RPE 6-7	1 × 12 ea RPE 6-7
2d	**Attackers and midfielders:** Standing chop	1 × 8 ea RPE 6-7	1 × 10 ea RPE 6-7	1 × 12 ea RPE 6-7
3a	Seated Arnold press (DB)	1 × 15-20 RPE 6-7	1 × 12-15 RPE 6-7	1 × 8-12 RPE 6-7
3b	Chest-supported incline row (DB)	1 × 15-20 RPE 6-7	1 × 12-15 RPE 6-7	1 × 8-12 RPE 6-7
3c	Goblet split squat	1 × 15-20 RPE 6-7	1 × 12-15 RPE 6-7	1 × 8-12 RPE 6-7
3d	**Defenders:** Push-up position pull-through (sandbag or KB)	1 × 8 ea RPE 6-7	1 × 10 ea RPE 6-7	1 × 12 ea RPE 6-7
3d	**All other positions:** Chop toss (MB)	1 × 8 ea RPE 6-7	1 × 10 ea RPE 6-7	1 × 12 ea RPE 6-7
4a	Palms-up biceps curl (DB)	1 × 15-20 RPE 6-7	1 × 12-15 RPE 6-7	1 × 8-12 RPE 6-7
4b	Skull crusher (DB)	1 × 15-20 RPE 6-7	1 × 12-15 RPE 6-7	1 × 8-12 RPE 6-7
4c	5-way lunge complex: Fwd + diag + lat + rotational + reverse	1 × 2 ea	1 × 3 ea	1 × 4 ea
4d	Farmer's carry, SA	1 × 20 yd ea	1 × 30 yd ea	1 × 40 yd ea

Day 3

Order	Exercise	Sets × reps, time, or distance	Sets × reps, time, or distance	Sets × reps, time, or distance
		Week 1	**Week 2**	**Week 3**
WU	BB complex: RDL + bent-over row + front squat + shoulder press	2 × 5 ea Bar only	2 × 5 ea Bar only	1 × 5 ea Bar only
1a	Broad jump	2 × 4	3 × 4	4 × 4
1b	Ice skater bound	2 × 4 ea	3 × 4 ea	4 × 4 ea
1c	Forward and backward line jump	2 × 10 s	3 × 10 s	4 × 10 s
1d	Side-to-side line jump	2 × 10 s	3 × 10 s	4 × 10 s
2a	Half-kneeling landmine press	1 × 10-12 ea RPE 6-7	1 × 8-10 ea RPE 6-7	1 × 6-8 ea RPE 6-7

(continued)

Table 9.8 College Men's Lacrosse: Off-Season, Mesocycle 1 *(continued)*

Day 3 *(continued)*

Order	Exercise	Sets × reps, time, or distance	Sets × reps, time, or distance	Sets × reps, time, or distance
		Week 1	**Week 2**	**Week 3**
2b	Row, SA (DB)	1 × 10-12 ea RPE 6-7	1 × 8-10 ea RPE 6-7	1 × 6-8 ea RPE 6-7
2c	Cossack squat	1 × 10-12 ea RPE 6-7	1 × 8-10 ea RPE 6-7	1 × 6-8 ea RPE 6-7
2d	**Goalies, defenders, and long-stick midfielders:** Split-stance lift	1 × 8 ea RPE 6-7	1 × 10 ea RPE 6-7	1 × 12 ea RPE 6-7
2d	**Attackers and midfielders:** Split-stance chop	1 × 8 ea RPE 6-7	1 × 10 ea RPE 6-7	1 × 12 ea RPE 6-7
3a	3-way shoulder raise	1 × 15-20 RPE 6-7	1 × 12-15 RPE 6-7	1 × 8-12 RPE 6-7
3b	Shrug (DB)	1 × 15-20 RPE 6-7	1 × 12-15 RPE 6-7	1 × 8-12 RPE 6-7
3c	Hamstring curl (SB)	1 × 8 ea RPE 6-7	1 × 10 ea RPE 6-7	1 × 12 ea RPE 6-7
3d	**Goalies and defenders:** Push-up position pull-through (sandbag or KB)	1 × 8 ea RPE 6-7	1 × 10 ea RPE 6-7	1 × 12 ea RPE 6-7
3d	**Attackers and midfielders:** Shot put toss (MB)	1 × 8 ea RPE 6-7	1 × 10 ea RPE 6-7	1 × 12 ea RPE 6-7
4a	Reverse-grip curl (DB)	1 × 15-20 RPE 6-7	1 × 12-15 RPE 6-7	1 × 8-12 RPE 6-7
4b	Close-grip bench press	1 × 15-20 RPE 6-7	1 × 12-15 RPE 6-7	1 × 8-12 RPE 6-7
4c	5-way lunge complex: Fwd + diag + lat + rotational + reverse	1 × 2 ea	1 × 3 ea	1 × 4 ea
4d	Belly-up waiter's carry, SA (KB)	1 × 20 yd ea	1 × 30 yd ea	1 × 40 yd ea

Table 9.9 College Men's Lacrosse: Off-Season, Mesocycle 2 (Fall Ball)

Day 1

Order	Exercise	Sets × reps or time	Sets × reps or time	Sets × reps or time	Sets × reps or time
		Week 1	**Week 2**	**Week 3**	**Week 4**
WU	Mobility series	× 1	× 1	× 1	× 1
WU	BB complex: RDL + clean pull + muscle clean + hang clean	1 × 5 ea	1 × 5 ea	1 × 5 ea	1 × 5 ea
WU	Banded shoulder I's, Y's, T's, W's	1 × 8 ea	1 × 8 ea	1 × 8 ea	1 × 8 ea
WU	Peterson step-down	1 × 5 ea	1 × 5 ea	1 × 5 ea	1 × 5 ea
1a	Hang clean	2 × 5	3 × 4	3 × 3	3 × 2

Order	Exercise	Sets × reps or time	Sets × reps or time	Sets × reps or time	Sets × reps or time
		Week 1	**Week 2**	**Week 3**	**Week 4**
1b	Broad jump	2 × 5	3 × 3	3 × 3	3 × 3
1c	Slam (MB)	2 × 5	3 × 5	3 × 5	3 × 5
1d	Deadbug	2 × 5 ea	3 × 5 ea	3 × 5 ea	3 × 5 ea
2a	RDL (BB)	2 × 5 RPE 6-7	3 × 5 RPE 6-7	3 × 4 RPE 6-7	3 × 3 RPE 6-7
2b	Shoulder press (BB)	2 × 5 RPE 6-7	3 × 5 RPE 6-7	3 × 4 RPE 6-7	3 × 3 RPE 6-7
2c	**Goalies and defenders:** Side toss (MB)	2 × 5 ea	3 × 5 ea	3 × 5 ea	3 × 5 ea
2c	**Attackers and midfielders:** Split-stance Pallof hold	2 × 10 s ea	3 × 10 s ea	3 × 10 s ea	3 × 10 s ea
3a	Split squat with 2 DBs	2 × 8 ea	3 × 8 ea	3 × 8 ea	3 × 8 ea
3b	Chin-up	2 × 5	3 × 5	3 × 5	3 × 5
3c	**Goalies and defenders:** Split-stance chop	2 × 8 ea	3 × 8 ea	3 × 10 ea	3 × 12 ea
3c	**Attackers and midfielders:** Split-stance lift	2 × 8 ea	3 × 8 ea	3 × 10 ea	3 × 12 ea

Day 2

Order	Exercise	Sets × reps or time	Sets × reps or time	Sets × reps or time	Sets × reps or time
		Week 1	**Week 2**	**Week 3**	**Week 4**
WU	Mobility series	× 1	× 1	× 1	× 1
WU	BB complex: RDL + clean pull + muscle clean + hang clean	1 × 5 ea	1 × 5 ea	1 × 5 ea	1 × 5 ea
WU	Banded shoulder I's, Y's, T's, W's	1 × 8 ea	1 × 8 ea	1 × 8 ea	1 × 8 ea
WU	Peterson step-down	1 × 5 ea	1 × 5 ea	1 × 5 ea	1 × 5 ea
1a	Push jerk (BB)	2 × 5	3 × 4	3 × 3	3 × 2
1b	Box jump	2 × 5	3 × 3	3 × 3	3 × 3
1c	Chest toss (MB)	2 × 5	3 × 5	3 × 5	3 × 5
1d	Deadbug	2 × 5 ea	3 × 5 ea	3 × 5 ea	3 × 5 ea
2a	Back squat (BB)	2 × 5 RPE 6-7	3 × 5 RPE 6-7	3 × 4 RPE 6-7	3 × 3 RPE 6-7
2b	Bench press (BB)	2 × 5 RPE 6-7	3 × 5 RPE 6-7	3 × 4 RPE 6-7	3 × 3 RPE 6-7
2c	**Goalies and defenders:** Shot put toss (MB)	2 × 5 ea	3 × 5 ea	3 × 5 ea	3 × 5 ea
2c	**Attackers and midfielders:** Push-up position sandbag or KB drag-through	2 × 8 ea	3 × 8 ea	3 × 10 ea	3 × 12 ea
3a	RDL, SL with 2 DBs	2 × 8 ea	3 × 8 ea	3 × 8 ea	3 × 8 ea
3b	BB bent-over row	2 × 5	3 × 5	3 × 5	3 × 5
3c	Copenhagen plank	2 × 20 s ea	3 × 20 s ea	3 × 25 s ea	3 × 30 s ea

Table 9.10 College Men's Lacrosse: Off-Season, Mesocycle 3

Day 1 (Attackers)

See table 9.20 for day 2 and table 9.26 for day 3.

Order	Exercise	Sets × reps or time	Sets × reps or time	Sets × reps or time	Sets × reps or time
		Week 1	Week 2	Week 3	Week 4
1a	Shot put toss (MB)	2 × 5 ea	3 × 5 ea	3 × 5 ea	3 × 5 ea
1b	Chop toss (MB)	2 × 5 ea	3 × 5 ea	3 × 5 ea	3 × 5 ea
2a	Hang clean	2 × 5	3 × 5	3 × 5	3 × 5
2b	Short-lever deadbug with DB pullover	2 × 5 ea	3 × 5 ea	3 × 5 ea	3 × 5 ea
3a	Lateral lunge (LM)	2 × 5 ea	3 × 5 ea	3 × 5 ea	3 × 5 ea
3b	Weighted chin-up	2 × 5	3 × 5	3 × 5	3 × 5
3c	Side plank	2 × 20 s	3 × 25 s	3 × 30 s	3 × 35 s
4a	Hamstring curl, SL	2 × 8 ea	3 × 8 ea	3 × 8 ea	3 × 8 ea
4b	Half-kneeling shoulder press, SA (LM)	2 × 8 ea	3 × 8 ea	3 × 8 ea	3 × 8 ea
4c	Half-kneeling chop	2 × 8 ea	3 × 8 ea	3 × 10 ea	3 × 12 ea

Table 9.11 College Men's Lacrosse: Off-Season, Mesocycle 4

Day 1 (Attackers)

See table 9.21 for day 2 and table 9.27 for day 3.

Order	Exercise	Sets × reps or time	Sets × reps or time	Sets × reps or time	Sets × reps or time
		Week 1	Week 2	Week 3	Week 4
1a	Shot put toss (MB), drop-set method	3 × 2/2/2 ea	3 × 2/2/2 ea	3 × 2/2/2 ea	3 × 2/2/2 ea
1b	Chop toss (MB), drop-set method	3 × 2/2/2 ea	3 × 2/2/2 ea	3 × 2/2/2 ea	3 × 2/2/2 ea
2a	Hang clean	3 × 5	3 × 4	3 × 3	3 × 2
2b	Broad jump	3 × 3	3 × 3	3 × 3	3 × 3
2c	Long-lever deadbug with DB pullover	3 × 5 ea	3 × 5 ea	3 × 5 ea	3 × 5 ea
3a	Lateral lunge (LM)	3 × 4 ea	3 × 3 ea	3 × 2 ea	3 × 2 ea
3b	Weighted chin-up	3 × 5/3/1	3 × 5/3/1	3 × 5/3/1	3 × 5/3/1
3c	Side plank with top leg raise	3 × 20 s	3 × 25 s	3 × 30 s	3 × 35 s
4a	Hamstring curl, SL	2 × 8 ea	3 × 8 ea	3 × 8 ea	3 × 8 ea
4b	Split-stance shoulder press, SA (LM)	3 × 5 ea	3 × 4 ea	3 × 3 ea	3 × 3 ea
4c	Split-stance chop	3 × 8 ea	3 × 8 ea	3 × 10 ea	3 × 12 ea

Table 9.12 College Men's Lacrosse: Off-Season, Mesocycle 3

Day 1 (Defenders)
See table 9.22 for day 2 and table 9.26 for day 3.

Order	Exercise	Sets × reps	Sets × reps	Sets × reps	Sets × reps
		Week 1	**Week 2**	**Week 3**	**Week 4**
1	Depth drop, DL landing	2 × 4	3 × 4	3 × 4	3 × 4
2a	Hang clean	3 × 5	4 × 4	4 × 5	4 × 5
2b	Short-lever deadbug with DB pullover	2 × 5 ea	3 × 5 ea	3 × 5 ea	3 × 5 ea
3a	Reverse lunge (BB)	2 × 5 ea	3 × 5 ea	3 × 5 ea	3 × 5 ea
3b	Weighted chin-up	2 × 5	3 × 5	3 × 5	3 × 5
3c	Half-kneeling lift	2 × 8 ea	3 × 8 ea	3 × 8 ea	3 × 8 ea
4a	Hamstring curl, SL	2 × 8 ea	3 × 8 ea	3 × 8 ea	3 × 8 ea
4b	Shoulder press (BB)	2 × 5	3 × 5	3 × 5	3 × 5
4c	LM rot from athletic stance	2 × 5 ea	3 × 5 ea	3 × 5 ea	3 × 5 ea

Table 9.13 College Men's Lacrosse: Off-Season, Mesocycle 4

Day 1 (Defenders)
See table 9.23 for day 2 and table 9.27 for day 3.

Order	Exercise	Sets × reps	Sets × reps	Sets × reps	Sets × reps
		Week 1	**Week 2**	**Week 3**	**Week 4 (optional)**
1	Depth drop jump	3 × 4	3 × 4	3 × 4	3 × 4
2a	Hang clean	4 × 3	4 × 3	4 × 3	4 × 3
2b	Long-lever deadbug with DB pullover	3 × 5 ea	3 × 5 ea	3 × 5 ea	3 × 5 ea
3a	Reverse lunge (BB)	3 × 4 ea	3 × 3 ea	3 × 2 ea	3 × 2 ea
3b	Weighted chin-up	3 × 5/3/1	3 × 5/3/1	3 × 5/3/1	3 × 5/3/1
3c	Split-stance lift	3 × 8 ea	3 × 8 ea	3 × 8 ea	3 × 8 ea
4a	Hamstring curl, SL	3 × 5 ea	3 × 5 ea	3 × 5 ea	3 × 5 ea
4b	Standing shoulder press (BB)	3 × 5	3 × 4	3 × 3	3 × 2
4c	Split-stance catch and deceleration (MB)	3 × 5 ea	3 × 5 ea	3 × 5 ea	3 × 5 ea

Table 9.14 College Men's Lacrosse: Off-Season, Mesocycle 3

Day 1 (Midfielders)
See table 9.18 for day 2 and table 9.26 for day 3.

Order	Exercise	Sets × reps or time	Sets × reps or time	Sets × reps or time	Sets × reps or time
		Week 1	**Week 2**	**Week 3**	**Week 4**
1a	Shot put toss (MB)	2 × 5 ea	3 × 5 ea	3 × 5 ea	3 × 5 ea
1b	Chop toss (MB)	2 × 5 ea	3 × 5 ea	3 × 5 ea	3 × 5 ea
2a	Hang clean	2 × 5	3 × 4	3 × 3	3 × 2
2b	Short-lever deadbug with DB pullover	2 × 5 ea	3 × 5 ea	3 × 5 ea	3 × 5 ea
3a	Reverse lunge (BB)	2 × 5 ea	3 × 5 ea	3 × 5 ea	3 × 5 ea

(continued)

Table 9.14 College Men's Lacrosse: Off-Season, Mesocycle 3 *(continued)*

Day 1 (Midfielders) *(continued)*
See table 9.18 for day 2 and table 9.26 for day 3.

Order	Exercise	Sets × reps or time	Sets × reps or time	Sets × reps or time	Sets × reps or time
		Week 1	Week 2	Week 3	Week 4
3b	Weighted chin-up	2 × 5	3 × 5	3 × 5	3 × 5
3c	Side plank	3 × 20 s	3 × 25 s	3 × 30 s	3 × 35 s
4a	Hamstring curl, SL	2 × 8 ea	3 × 8 ea	3 × 8 ea	3 × 8 ea
4b	Half-kneeling shoulder press, SA (LM)	2 × 8 ea	3 × 8 ea	3 × 8 ea	3 × 8 ea
4c	Half-kneeling chop	2 × 8 ea	3 × 8 ea	3 × 10 ea	3 × 12 ea

Table 9.15 College Men's Lacrosse: Off-Season, Mesocycle 4

Day 1 (Midfielders)
See table 9.19 for day 2 and table 9.27 for day 3.

Order	Exercise	Sets × reps or time	Sets × reps or time	Sets × reps or time	Sets × reps or time
		Week 1	Week 2	Week 3	Week 4
1a	Shot put toss (MB), drop-set method	3 × 2/2/2 ea	3 × 2/2/2 ea	3 × 2/2/2 ea	3 × 2/2/2 ea
1b	Chop toss (MB), drop-set method	3 × 2/2/2 ea	3 × 2/2/2 ea	3 × 2/2/2 ea	3 × 2/2/2 ea
2a	Hang clean	3 × 4	3 × 4	3 × 3	3 × 2
2b	Broad jump	3 × 3	3 × 3	3 × 3	3 × 3
2c	Long-lever deadbug with DB pullover	2 × 5 ea	3 × 5 ea	3 × 5 ea	3 × 5 ea
3a	Reverse lunge (BB)	3 × 5 ea	3 × 5 ea	3 × 4 ea	3 × 3 ea
3b	Weighted chin-up	3 × 5/3/1	3 × 5/3/1	3 × 5/3/1	3 × 5/3/1
3c	Side plank with top leg raise	3 × 20 s	3 × 25 s	3 × 30 s	3 × 35 s
4a	Hamstring curl, SL	3 × 5 ea	3 × 5 ea	3 × 5 ea	3 × 5 ea
4b	Split-stance shoulder press, SA (LM)	3 × 5 ea	3 × 4 ea	3 × 3 ea	3 × 3 ea
4c	Split-stance chop	2 × 8 ea	3 × 8 ea	3 × 10 ea	3 × 12 ea

Table 9.16 College Men's Lacrosse: Off-Season, Mesocycle 3

Day 1 (Goalies)
See table 9.24 for day 2 and table 9.26 for day 3.

Order	Exercise	Sets × reps or time	Sets × reps or time	Sets × reps or time	Sets × reps or time
		Week 1	Week 2	Week 3	Week 4
1	Static vertical jump	2 × 4	3 × 4	3 × 4	3 × 4
2a	Hang clean	3 × 5	4 × 4	4 × 3	4 × 2
2b	Short-lever deadbug with DB pullover	2 × 5 ea	3 × 5 ea	3 × 5 ea	3 × 5 ea
3a	Front squat with 5 s ISO hold (BB)	2 × 5	3 × 5	3 × 4	3 × 3

Order	Exercise	Sets × reps or time	Sets × reps or time	Sets × reps or time	Sets × reps or time
		Week 1	Week 2	Week 3	Week 4
3b	Weighted chin-up	2 × 5	3 × 5	3 × 4	3 × 3
3c	Split-stance lift	2 × 8 ea	3 × 8 ea	3 × 8 ea	3 × 8 ea
4a	Hamstring curl, SL	2 × 8 ea	3 × 8 ea	3 × 8 ea	3 × 8 ea
4b	Floor press (BB)	2 × 5	3 × 5	3 × 4	3 × 3
4c	Tall-kneeling Pallof hold	2 × 10 s	3 × 10 s	3 × 15 s	3 × 20 s

Table 9.17 College Men's Lacrosse: Off-Season, Mesocycle 4

Day 1 (Goalies)
See table 9.25 for day 2 and table 9.27 for day 3.

Order	Exercise	Sets × reps or time	Sets × reps or time	Sets × reps or time	Sets × reps or time
		Week 1	Week 2	Week 3	Week 4
1a	Hang clean	3 × 5	4 × 4	4 × 3	4 × 2
1b	Static vertical jump	3 × 3	3 × 3	3 × 3	3 × 3
1c	Long-lever deadbug with DB pullover	3 × 5 ea	3 × 5 ea	3 × 5 ea	3 × 5 ea
2a	Quarter front squat with 5 s ISO hold (BB)	3 × 5	3 × 5	3 × 4	3 × 3
2b	Weighted chin-up	3 × 5/3/1	3 × 5/3/1	3 × 5/3/1	3 × 5/3/1
2c	Athletic stance lift	3 × 8 ea	3 × 8 ea	3 × 8 ea	3 × 8 ea
3a	Hamstring curl, SL	3 × 5 ea	3 × 5 ea	3 × 5 ea	3 × 5 ea
3b	Floor press with 5 s pause on the floor (BB)	3 × 5	3 × 5	3 × 4	3 × 3
3c	Athletic stance Pallof hold	3 × 10 s	3 × 10 s	3 × 15 s	3 × 20 s

Table 9.18 College Men's Lacrosse: Off-Season, Mesocycle 3

Day 2 (Midfielders)

Order	Exercise	Sets × reps or distance	Sets × reps or distance	Sets × reps or distance	Sets × reps or distance
		Week 1	Week 2	Week 3	Week 4
1a	Side toss (MB)	2 × 5 ea	3 × 5 ea	3 × 5 ea	3 × 5 ea
1b	Slam (MB)	2 × 5	3 × 5	3 × 5	3 × 5
2a	Push jerk	2 × 5	3 × 5	3 × 5	3 × 5
2b	Short-lever deadbug with DB pullover	2 × 5 ea	3 × 5 ea	3 × 5 ea	3 × 5 ea
3a	RDL, SL (BB)	2 × 5 ea	3 × 5 ea	3 × 5 ea	3 × 5 ea
3b	Bent-over row (BB)	2 × 5	3 × 5	3 × 5	3 × 5
3c	Half-kneeling Pallof press	2 × 8 ea	3 × 8 ea	3 × 8 ea	3 × 8 ea
4a	Goblet lat squat (DB)	2 × 8 ea	3 × 8 ea	3 × 8 ea	3 × 8 ea
4b	Bench press (BB)	2 × 5	3 × 5	3 × 5	3 × 5
4c	Overhead carry, SA (KB)	2 × 20 yd ea	3 × 20 yd ea	3 × 20 yd ea	3 × 20 yd ea

Table 9.19 College Men's Lacrosse: Off-Season, Mesocycle 4

Day 2 (Midfielders)

Order	Exercise	Sets × reps or distance	Sets × reps or distance	Sets × reps or distance	Sets × reps or distance
		Week 1	Week 2	Week 3	Week 4
1a	Side toss (MB), drop-set method	3 × 2/2/2 ea	3 × 2/2/2 ea	3 × 2/2/2 ea	3 × 2/2/2 ea
1b	Slam (MB), drop-set method	3 × 2/2/2	3 × 2/2/2	3 × 2/2/2	3 × 2/2/2
2a	Push jerk	3 × 4	3 × 4	3 × 3	3 × 2
2b	Maximum vertical jump	3 × 3	3 × 3	3 × 3	3 × 3
2c	Long-lever deadbug with DB pullover	2 × 5 ea	3 × 5 ea	3 × 5 ea	3 × 5 ea
3a	RDL, SL (BB)	3 × 4 ea	3 × 3 ea	3 × 2 ea	3 × 2 ea
3b	Bent-over row (BB)	3 × 5	3 × 5	3 × 4	3 × 3
3c	Split-stance Pallof press	3 × 8 ea	3 × 8 ea	3 × 8 ea	3 × 8 ea
4a	Lateral squat (LM)	3 × 5 ea	3 × 5 ea	3 × 5 ea	3 × 5 ea
4b	Bench press (BB)	3 × 5	3 × 4	3 × 3	3 × 2
4c	Belly-up waiter's carry, SA (KB)	3 × 20 yd ea	3 × 20 yd ea	3 × 20 yd ea	3 × 20 yd ea

Table 9.20 College Men's Lacrosse: Off-Season, Mesocycle 3

Day 2 (Attackers)

Order	Exercise	Sets × reps or distance	Sets × reps or distance	Sets × reps or distance	Sets × reps or distance
		Week 1	Week 2	Week 3	Week 4
1a	Side toss (MB)	2 × 5 ea	3 × 5 ea	3 × 5 ea	3 × 5 ea
1b	Slam (MB)	2 × 5	3 × 5	3 × 5	3 × 5
2a	Push jerk (BB)	2 × 5	3 × 4	3 × 3	3 × 2
2b	Short-lever deadbug with DB pullover	2 × 5 ea	3 × 5 ea	3 × 5 ea	3 × 5 ea
3a	RDL, SL (BB)	2 × 5 ea	3 × 5 ea	3 × 5 ea	3 × 5 ea
3b	Bent-over row (BB)	2 × 5	3 × 5	3 × 5	3 × 5
3c	Half-kneeling Pallof press	2 × 8 ea	3 × 8 ea	3 × 8 ea	3 × 8 ea
4a	RFE split squat	2 × 8 ea	3 × 8 ea	3 × 8 ea	3 × 8 ea
4b	Bench press (BB)	2 × 5	3 × 5	3 × 5	3 × 5
4c	Overhead carry, SA (KB)	2 × 20 yd ea	3 × 20 yd ea	3 × 20 yd ea	3 × 20 yd ea

Table 9.21   College Men's Lacrosse: Off-Season, Mesocycle 4

Day 2 (Attackers)

Order	Exercise	Sets × reps or distance	Sets × reps or distance	Sets × reps or distance	Sets × reps or distance
		Week 1	Week 2	Week 3	Week 4
1a	Side toss (MB), drop-set method	3 × 2/2/2 ea	3 × 2/2/2 ea	3 × 2/2/2 ea	3 × 2/2/2 ea
1b	Slam (MB), drop-set method	3 × 2/2/2	3 × 2/2/2	3 × 2/2/2	3 × 2/2/2
2a	Push jerk	3 × 4	3 × 4	3 × 3	3 × 2
2b	Maximum vertical jump	3 × 3	3 × 3	3 × 3	3 × 3
2c	Long-lever deadbug with DB pullover	2 × 5 ea	3 × 5 ea	3 × 5 ea	3 × 5 ea
3a	RDL, SL (BB)	3 × 4 ea	3 × 3 ea	3 × 2 ea	3 × 2 ea
3b	Bent-over row (BB)	3 × 5	3 × 5	3 × 4	3 × 3
3c	Split-stance Pallof press	3 × 8 ea	3 × 8 ea	3 × 8 ea	3 × 8 ea
4a	RFE split squat	3 × 5 ea	3 × 5 ea	3 × 5 ea	3 × 5 ea
4b	Bench press (BB)	3 × 5	3 × 4	3 × 3	3 × 2
4c	Belly-up waiter's carry, SA (KB)	3 × 20 yd ea	3 × 20 yd ea	3 × 20 yd ea	3 × 20 yd ea

Table 9.22   College Men's Lacrosse: Off-Season, Mesocycle 3

Day 2 (Defenders)

Order	Exercise	Sets × reps or distance	Sets × reps or distance	Sets × reps or distance	Sets × reps or distance
		Week 1	Week 2	Week 3	Week 4
1	Depth drop, DL landing	2 × 4	3 × 4	3 × 4	3 × 4
2a	Push jerk	3 × 5	4 × 4	4 × 3	4 × 2
2b	Short-lever deadbug with DB pullover	2 × 5 ea	3 × 5 ea	3 × 5 ea	3 × 5 ea
3a	Lateral lunge (LM)	2 × 5 ea	3 × 5 ea	3 × 5 ea	3 × 5 ea
3b	Bent-over row (BB)	2 × 5	3 × 5	3 × 4	3 × 3
3c	Push-up position KB or sandbag drag-through	2 × 8 ea	3 × 8 ea	3 × 8 ea	3 × 8 ea
4a	RDL, SL, with 2 DBs	2 × 8 ea	3 × 8 ea	3 × 8 ea	3 × 8 ea
4b	Bench press (BB)	2 × 5	3 × 5	3 × 4	3 × 3
4c	Farmer's carry with 2 DBs	2 × 20 yd	3 × 20 yd	3 × 20 yd	3 × 20 yd

Table 9.23   College Men's Lacrosse: Off-Season, Mesocycle 4

Day 2 (Defenders)

Order	Exercise	Sets × reps or distance	Sets × reps or distance	Sets × reps or distance	Sets × reps or distance
		Week 1	Week 2	Week 3	Week 4 (optional)
1	Depth drop jump	3 × 4	3 × 4	3 × 4	3 × 4
2a	Push jerk	4 × 3	4 × 3	4 × 3	4 × 3
2b	Long-lever deadbug with DB pullover	3 × 5 ea	3 × 5 ea	3 × 5 ea	3 × 5 ea
3a	Lateral lunge (LM)	3 × 4 ea	3 × 3 ea	3 × 2 ea	3 × 2 ea
3b	Bent-over row (BB)	3 × 5	3 × 5	3 × 4	3 × 3
3c	Split-stance lift	3 × 8 ea	3 × 8 ea	3 × 8 ea	3 × 8 ea
4a	RDL, SL, with 2 DBs	3 × 5 ea	3 × 5 ea	3 × 5 ea	3 × 5 ea
4b	Bench press (BB)	3 × 5	3 × 4	3 × 3	3 × 2
4c	Farmer's carry with 1 DB	3 × 20 yd ea	3 × 20 yd ea	3 × 20 yd ea	3 × 20 yd ea

Table 9.24   College Men's Lacrosse: Off-Season, Mesocycle 3

Day 2 (Goalies)

Order	Exercise	Sets × reps or distance	Sets × reps or distance	Sets × reps or distance	Sets × reps or distance
		Week 1	Week 2	Week 3	Week 4
1	Ice skater bound	2 × 4 ea	3 × 4 ea	3 × 4 ea	3 × 4 ea
2a	Push jerk	3 × 5	4 × 4	4 × 3	4 × 2
2b	Short-lever deadbug with DB pullover	2 × 5 ea	3 × 5 ea	3 × 5 ea	3 × 5 ea
3a	Lateral lunge (LM)	2 × 5 ea	3 × 5 ea	3 × 5 ea	3 × 5 ea
3b	Bent-over row (BB)	2 × 5	3 × 5	3 × 5	3 × 5
3c	Standing 4-way hip machine	2 × 8 ea	3 × 8 ea	3 × 8 ea	3 × 8 ea
4a	RDL, SL with 2 DBs	2 × 8 ea	3 × 8 ea	3 × 8 ea	3 × 8 ea
4b	Incline bench press (DB)	2 × 5	3 × 5	3 × 4	3 × 3
4c	Farmer's carry with 2 DBs	2 × 20 yd	3 × 20 yd	3 × 20 yd	3 × 20 yd

Table 9.25   College Men's Lacrosse: Off-Season, Mesocycle 4

Day 2 (Goalies)

Order	Exercise	Sets × reps or distance	Sets × reps or distance	Sets × reps or distance	Sets × reps or distance
		Week 1	Week 2	Week 3	Week 4
1a	Push jerk	3 × 5	4 × 4	4 × 3	4 × 2
1b	Static vertical jump	3 × 3	3 × 3	3 × 3	3 × 3
1c	Long-lever deadbug with DB pullover	3 × 5 ea	3 × 5 ea	3 × 5 ea	3 × 5 ea
2a	Lateral lunge (LM)	3 × 5	3 × 5	3 × 4	3 × 3
2b	Ice skater bound	3 × 3 ea	3 × 3 ea	3 × 3 ea	3 × 3 ea

Order	Exercise	Sets × reps or distance	Sets × reps or distance	Sets × reps or distance	Sets × reps or distance
		Week 1	Week 2	Week 3	Week 4
2c	Bent-over row (BB)	3 × 5	3 × 5	3 × 4	3 × 3
2d	Banded walk forward, backward, side to side	3 × 10 yd ea	3 × 10 yd ea	3 × 10 yd ea	3 × 10 yd ea
3a	RDL, SL with 2 DBs	3 × 5 ea	3 × 5 ea	3 × 5 ea	3 × 5 ea
3b	Incline bench press (DB)	3 × 5	3 × 5	3 × 4	3 × 3
3c	Farmer's carry with 1 DB	3 × 20 yd ea	3 × 20 yd ea	3 × 20 yd ea	3 × 20 yd ea

Table 9.26   College Men's Lacrosse: Off-Season, Mesocycle 3

Day 3 (All Positions)

Order	Exercise	Sets × reps	Sets × reps	Sets × reps	Sets × reps
		Week 1	Week 2	Week 3	Week 4
1	RDL (tempo method)	3 × 8 [3030]	3 × 9 [3030]	3 × 10 [3030]	4 × 8 [3030]
Two rounds each: Front plank × 30 s, side plank × 30 s ea, reverse plank × 30 s					
2	Bench press (tempo method)	3 × 8 [3030]	3 × 9 [3030]	3 × 10 [3030]	4 × 8 [3030]
Two rounds each: Front plank × 30 s, side plank × 30 s ea, reverse plank × 30 s					
3	Squat (tempo method)	3 × 8 [3030]	3 × 9 [3030]	3 × 10 [3030]	4 × 8 [3030]
Two rounds each: Front plank × 30 s, side plank × 30 s ea, reverse plank × 30 s					
4	Incline row (tempo method)	3 × 8 [3030]	3 × 9 [3030]	3 × 10 [3030]	4 × 8 [3030]

Table 9.27   College Men's Lacrosse: Off-Season, Mesocycle 4

Day 3 (All Positions)

Order	Exercise	Sets × reps	Sets × reps	Sets × reps	Sets × reps
		Week 1	Week 2	Week 3	Week 4
1	RDL (tempo method)	4 × 9 [3030]	4 × 10 [3030]	4 × 10 [3030]	4 × 10 [3030]
Two rounds each: Front plank × 30 s, side plank × 30 s ea, reverse plank × 30 s					
2	Bench press (tempo method)	4 × 9 [3030]	4 × 10 [3030]	4 × 10 [3030]	4 × 10 [3030]
Two rounds each: Front plank × 30 s, side plank × 30 s ea, reverse plank × 30 s					
3	Squat (tempo method)	4 × 9 [3030]	4 × 10 [3030]	4 × 10 [3030]	4 × 10 [3030]
Two rounds each: Front plank × 30 s, side plank × 30 s ea, reverse plank × 30 s					
4	Incline row (tempo method)	4 × 9 [3030]	4 × 10 [3030]	4 × 10 [3030]	4 × 10 [3030]

Table 9.28   Professional Lacrosse: Off-Season, Mesocycle 1

Day 1

Order	Exercise	Sets × reps, time, or distance	Sets × reps, time, or distance	Sets × reps, time, or distance	Sets × reps, time, or distance
		Week 1	Week 2	Week 3	Week 4
WU	Hip series + 90-90 hip mobility + foam roll	10 min	10 min	10 min	10 min
1a	Goblet squat	3 × 10	3 × 10	3 × 10	3 × 8

(continued)

Table 9.28 Professional Lacrosse: Off-Season, Mesocycle 1 *(continued)*

Day 1 *(continued)*

Order	Exercise	Sets × reps, time, or distance	Sets × reps, time, or distance	Sets × reps, time, or distance	Sets × reps, time, or distance
		Week 1	**Week 2**	**Week 3**	**Week 4**
1b	Jump squat (DB)	3 × 6	3 × 6	3 × 6	3 × 4
1c	Granny toss (MB)	3 × 6	3 × 6	3 × 6	3 × 4
2a	Lateral step-up (DB)	3 × 8 ea	3 × 8 ea	3 × 8 ea	3 × 6 ea
2b	Lat hop and hold, SL	3 × 5 ea	3 × 5 ea	3 × 5 ea	3 × 4 ea
2c	Lateral throw (MB)	3 × 5 ea	3 × 5 ea	3 × 5 ea	3 × 3 ea
2d	**Goalies, defenders, and long-stick midfielders:** Half-kneeling lift with cable	1 × 8 ea	1 × 10 ea	1 × 12 ea	1 × 8 ea
2d	**Attackers and midfielders:** Half-kneeling chop with cable	1 × 8 ea	1 × 10 ea	1 × 12 ea	1 × 8 ea
3a	RDL (DB)	3 × 10	3 × 10	3 × 10	3 × 8
3b	Swing (KB)	3 × 10	3 × 10	3 × 10	3 × 8
3c	Copenhagen plank	3 × 10 s ea	3 × 10 s ea	3 × 10 s ea	3 × 8 s ea
3d	**Goalies and defenders:** Push-up position pull-through (sandbag or KB)	2 × 6 ea	2 × 6 ea	3 × 6 ea	3 × 6 ea
3d	**Attackers and midfielders:** Windmill throw down (MB)	1 × 6 ea	1 × 6 ea	1 × 6 ea	1 × 5 ea
4a	Banded I's, Y's, T's, W's	3 × 8 ea	3 × 8 ea	3 × 8 ea	3 × 6 ea
4b	Rear delt ISO hold	3 × 10 s	3 × 10 s	3 × 10 s	3 × 8 s
5	Dead farmer's carry	3 × 20 yd	3 × 20 yd	3 × 20 yd	—

Day 2

Order	Exercise	Sets × reps or time	Sets × reps or time	Sets × reps or time	Sets × reps or time
		Week 1	**Week 2**	**Week 3**	**Week 4**
WU	Wall slide + cat–cow + peanut mobility	2 × 5 ea	2 × 5 ea	2 × 5 ea	2 × 5 ea
1a	Bench press (DB)	3 × 10	3 × 10	3 × 10	3 × 8
1b	Bent-over row (DB)	3 × 10	3 × 10	3 × 10	3 × 8
1c	Jammer press with rot	3 × 8 ea	3 × 8 ea	3 × 8 ea	3 × 6 ea
2a	Shoulder press (DB)	3 × 10	3 × 10	3 × 10	3 × 8
2b	Suspension face pull	3 × 12	3 × 12	3 × 12	3 × 10
2c	Slam (MB)	3 × 10	3 × 10	3 × 10	3 × 8
2d	**Goalies, defenders, and long-stick midfielders:** Pallof hold	3 × 10 s ea	3 × 10 s ea	3 × 10 s ea	3 × 8 s ea
2d	**Attackers and midfielders:** Chop toss (MB)	3 × 8 ea	3 × 8 ea	3 × 8 ea	3 × 6 ea

Order	Exercise	Sets × reps or time	Sets × reps or time	Sets × reps or time	Sets × reps or time
		Week 1	**Week 2**	**Week 3**	**Week 4**
3a	Shoulder front and side raise (DB)	3 × 8 ea	3 × 8 ea	3 × 8 ea	3 × 6 ea
3b	Lawn mower row from lunge position (DB)	3 × 8 ea	3 × 8 ea	3 × 8 ea	3 × 6 ea
3c	4-way neck ISO bench hold	3 × 10 s ea	3 × 10 s ea	3 × 10 s ea	—
4a	Rollout (SB)	2 × 10	2 × 10	2 × 10	1 × 10
4b	Stir the pot (MB)	2 × 5 ea	2 × 5 ea	2 × 5 ea	1 × 5 ea
4c	Palms-up biceps curl (DB)	1 × 15-20	1 × 12-15	1 × 8-12	2 × 10
4d	Skull crusher (DB)	1 × 15-20	1 × 12-15	1 × 8-12	2 × 10

Day 3

Order	Exercise	Sets × reps, time, or distance	Sets × reps, time, or distance	Sets × reps, time, or distance	Sets × reps, time, or distance
		Week 1	**Week 2**	**Week 3**	**Week 4**
WU	Hip series + leg swing + toe touch progression	2 × 5 ea	2 × 5 ea	2 × 5 ea	2 × 5 ea
1a	Snatch (DB)	3 × 6	3 × 6	3 × 6	3 × 5
1b	Vertical jump	3 × 6	3 × 6	3 × 6	3 × 5
1c	Box jump (16-24 in. [41-61 cm])	3 × 6	3 × 6	3 × 6	3 × 5
1d	RKC plank	3 × 10 s ea	3 × 10 s ea	3 × 10 s ea	2 × 10 s ea
2a	Step-up (DB)	3 × 8 ea	3 × 8 ea	3 × 8 ea	3 × 6 ea
2b	Box power skip	3 × 6 ea	3 × 6 ea	3 × 6 ea	3 × 5 ea
2c	Glute bridge, SL	3 × 10 s ea	3 × 10 s ea	3 × 10 s ea	2 × 10 s ea
2d	**Goalies, defenders, and long-stick midfielders:** Split-stance lift	1 × 8 ea	1 × 10 ea	1 × 12 ea	1 × 8 ea
2d	**Attackers and midfielders:** Split-stance chop	1 × 8 ea	1 × 10 ea	1 × 12 ea	1 × 8 ea
3a	Split-stance deceleration (MB)	3 × 8 ea	3 × 8 ea	3 × 8 ea	3 × 6 ea
3b	Lateral Japanese stick	3 × 8 ea	3 × 8 ea	3 × 8 ea	3 × 6 ea
3c	Grip work/sticks	3 × 10 ea	3 × 10 ea	3 × 10 ea	—
4a	Back extension with rear delt raise	3 × 10	3 × 10	3 × 10	3 × 8
4b	Uneven carry	3 × 20 yd ea	3 × 20 yd ea	3 × 20 yd ea	—
4c	Peterson step-down	3 × 6 ea	3 × 6 ea	3 × 6 ea	3 × 6 ea

Table 9.29 Professional Lacrosse: Off-Season, Mesocycle 2

Day 1

Order	Exercise	Sets × reps or time	Sets × reps or time	Sets × reps or time	Sets × reps or time
		Week 1	Week 2	Week 3	Week 4
WU	Hurdle step-over	6 ea	6 ea	6 ea	6 ea
WU	Stretch strap series + toe-touch progression	10 min	10 min	10 min	10 min
WU	Banded shoulder I's, Y's, T's, W's	1 × 8 ea	1 × 8 ea	1 × 8 ea	1 × 8 ea
WU	90/90 hip rockers	6 ea	6 ea	6 ea	6 ea
1a	Bulgarian split squat	4 × 8 ea	4 × 8 ea	4 × 6 ea	4 × 6 ea
1b	Split jump	4 × 3 ea	4 × 3 ea	4 × 4 ea	4 × 4 ea
1c	Side throw with split stance (MB)	4 × 3 ea	4 × 3 ea	4 × 5 ea	4 × 5 ea
1d	Cable chop (speed)	4 × 6 ea	4 × 6 ea	4 × 5 ea	4 × 5 ea
2a	Push jerk (DB)	4 × 5	4 × 5	4 × 4	4 × 4
2b	Pullover (DB)	4 × 8	4 × 8	4 × 6	4 × 6
2c	**Goalies and defenders:** Positional Pallof hold	2 × 10 s ea	2 × 10 s ea	3 × 10 s ea	3 × 10 s ea
2c	**Attackers and midfielders:** Split-stance cable rot	2 × 10 s ea	3 × 10 s ea	3 × 10 s ea	3 × 10 s ea
3a	Heel walkout	2 × 8 ea	3 × 8 ea	3 × 8 ea	3 × 8 ea
3b	Reverse hyper	2 × 8	3 × 8	3 × 8	3 × 8
3c	**Goalies and defenders:** LM rot	2 × 8 ea	3 × 8 ea	3 × 10 ea	3 × 12 ea
3c	**Attackers and midfielders:** Chop circuit (MB)	2 × 8 ea	3 × 8 ea	3 × 10 ea	3 × 12 ea

Day 2

Order	Exercise	Sets × reps or time	Sets × reps or time	Sets × reps or time	Sets × reps or time
		Week 1	Week 2	Week 3	Week 4
WU	Floor slide	8	8	8	8
WU	Cat–cow + peanut mobility + quadruped and reach	1 × 5 ea	1 × 5 ea	1 × 5 ea	1 × 5 ea
1a	Snatch, SA and SL (opposite) (DB)	3 × 5 ea	3 × 5 ea	4 × 4 ea	4 × 4 ea
1b	Half-kneeling broad jump to bilateral landing	3 × 5 ea	3 × 5 ea	4 × 4 ea	4 × 4 ea
1c	Hurdle hop multiple response, SL	3 × 5 ea	3 × 5 ea	4 × 4 ea	4 × 4 ea
1d	RDL ISO hold, SL	3 × 10 s ea	3 × 10 s ea	4 × 8 s ea	4 × 8 s ea
2a	Bench press (BB)	4 × 8	4 × 8	4 × 6	4 × 6
2b	Chin-up	4 × 8	4 × 8	4 × 6 with weight	4 × 6 with weight
2c	**Goalies and defenders:** Shot put toss (MB)	3 × 5 ea	3 × 5 ea	4 × 4 ea	4 × 4 ea

Order	Exercise	Sets × reps or time	Sets × reps or time	Sets × reps or time	Sets × reps or time
		Week 1	Week 2	Week 3	Week 4
2c	**Attackers and midfielders:** Banded skaters	3 × 5 ea	3 × 5 ea	4 × 4 ea	4 × 4 ea
3a	Cuban press	4 × 8	4 × 8	4 × 6	4 × 6
3b	Row (LM)	4 × 8 ea	4 × 8 ea	4 × 6 ea	4 × 6 ea
3c	Prone toe tap (opposite hand to foot)	2 × 6 ea	2 × 6 ea	2 × 6 ea	2 × 6 ea

Day 3

Order	Exercise	Sets × reps or time	Sets × reps or time	Sets × reps or time	Sets × reps or time
		Week 1	Week 2	Week 3	Week 4
1a	Shot put toss (MB)	2 × 5 ea	3 × 5 ea	3 × 5 ea	3 × 5 ea
1b	Chop toss (MB)	2 × 5 ea	3 × 5 ea	3 × 5 ea	3 × 5 ea
2a	Hang clean	2 × 5	3 × 5	3 × 5	3 × 5
2b	Short-lever deadbug with DB pullover	2 × 5 ea	3 × 5 ea	3 × 5 ea	3 × 5 ea
3a	Lateral lunge (LM)	2 × 5 ea	3 × 5 ea	3 × 5 ea	3 × 5 ea
3b	Weighted chin-up	2 × 5	3 × 5	3 × 5	3 × 5
3c	Side plank	2 × 20 s	3 × 25 s	3 × 30 s	3 × 35 s
4a	Hamstring curl, SL	2 × 8 ea	3 × 8 ea	3 × 8 ea	3 × 8 ea
4b	Half-kneeling shoulder press, SA (LM)	2 × 8 ea	3 × 8 ea	3 × 8 ea	3 × 8 ea
4c	Half-kneeling chop	2 × 8 ea	3 × 8 ea	3 × 10 ea	3 × 12 ea

Day 4

Order	Exercise	Sets × reps or time	Sets × reps or time	Sets × reps or time	Sets × reps or time
		Week 1	Week 2	Week 3	Week 4
1a	Shot put toss (MB), drop-set method	3 × 2/2/2 ea	3 × 2/2/2 ea	3 × 2/2/2 ea	3 × 2/2/2 ea
1b	Chop toss (MB), drop-set method	3 × 2/2/2 ea	3 × 2/2/2 ea	3 × 2/2/2 ea	3 × 2/2/2 ea
2a	Hang clean	3 × 5	3 × 4	3 × 3	3 × 2
2b	Broad jump	3 × 3	3 × 3	3 × 3	3 × 3
2c	Long-lever deadbug with DB pullover	3 × 5 ea	3 × 5 ea	3 × 5 ea	3 × 5 ea
3a	Lateral lunge (LM)	3 × 4 ea	3 × 3 ea	3 × 2 ea	3 × 2 ea
3b	Weighted chin-up	3 × 5/3/1	3 × 5/3/1	3 × 5/3/1	3 × 5/3/1
3c	Side plank with top leg raise	3 × 20 s	3 × 25 s	3 × 30 s	3 × 35 s
4a	Hamstring curl, SL	2 × 8 ea	3 × 8 ea	3 × 8 ea	3 × 8 ea
4b	Split-stance shoulder press, SA (LM)	3 × 5 ea	3 × 4 ea	3 × 3 ea	3 × 3 ea
4c	Split-stance chop	3 × 8 ea	3 × 8 ea	3 × 10 ea	3 × 12 ea

10

PRESEASON PROGRAMMING

DRAZEN GLISIC (HIGH SCHOOL), TRACY ZIMMER (COLLEGE WOMEN), DAVID EUGENIO MANNING (COLLEGE MEN), AND JOEL RAETHER (PROFESSIONAL)

The purpose of the preseason resistance training program for high school lacrosse athletes is to prepare them for the start of their season. For college lacrosse athletes, the goal of the preseason resistance program is to emphasize position-specific physiological adaptations. Professional lacrosse athletes need preseason, athlete-specific programming that is similar to their off-season programming to manage physical qualities, fatigue, and injury prevention.

GOALS AND OBJECTIVES

The aims and targets for a lacrosse athlete can differ across the three tiers of competition. The distinct objectives tailored for high school, for collegiate women and men, and for athletes competing at the professional level will be outlined in the subsequent sections.

High School

After high school lacrosse athletes have established a solid strength foundation and improved their technique, the strength and conditioning professional can begin to build upon this foundation by placing more emphasis on maximum strength and power production. However, during the preseason period, it is important for the strength and conditioning professional to align his or her training with the coach's plans for the upcoming season. This requires collaboration and communication between the two to ensure that the resistance training is complementary and will help the lacrosse athletes achieve their performance goals on the field.

College

The preseason is the final piece of preparation for college lacrosse athletes before they begin their competitive season. During this time, greater emphasis is placed on sport readiness. The preseason goals are to finish preparing the athletes to handle the game demands of their positions and to teach the primary exercises that will be used in-season to help manage stress and maintain strength and power outputs.

The workouts will be a continuation or progression of the previous mesocycle from the off-season phase to avoid introducing new exercises while the athletes are at home. When the athletes return to campus in early January, the primary exercises of the in-season will be introduced (see chapter 11), and intensity in the weight room will decrease because resistance training goes back to twice a week as the athletes start practices and have scrimmages on the weekends.

Professional

The professional preseason can range from one to four weeks, depending on the league in which an athlete is participating. The National Lacrosse League (NLL) includes four weeks of training camp, the Premier Lacrosse League (PLL) includes a one-week intensive training camp, and Major Series Lacrosse (MSL) and the Western Lacrosse Association (WLA) typically do not have any preseason period, because athletes usually transition directly from an NLL season into their respective league. The preseason goal is to enhance strength and power parameters while increasing metabolic readiness in preparation for the respective training camp or in-season period.

LENGTH, STRUCTURE, AND ORGANIZATION

Variations in the duration, format, and arrangement of preseason resistance training regimens are evident among high school athletes, college women's and men's teams, and professional athletes. In the case of high school and collegiate lacrosse athletes, one key determinant is the academic calendar.

High School

The preseason period for high school lacrosse usually starts in January, after athletes return from the school holidays. With the season typically starting in mid-March to late March, this allows for an 8- to 10-week preseason period. During this time, athletes should be resistance training three or four times per week, either with a two-day upper and lower body split (e.g., Monday and Thursday, lower body and Tuesday and Friday, upper body) or one upper body day, one lower body day, and a whole-body day (e.g., Monday, lower body; Wednesday, upper body; and Friday, whole body), depending on the team's practice schedule.

The last week of the preseason period is meant to have a lighter volume and intensity and to be used as a recovery week before the start of the season. In an eight-week preseason, the first three weeks should focus on maximal strength, with power exercises still being included. The following four weeks should then shift the focus to power production, with the final week being a low-volume, low-intensity week. It is important to ensure that the training plan aligns with what the coach has planned for the team.

College

Preseason programming for college lacrosse begins once the athletes finish final exams and head home for the winter break. Length can range from a couple of weeks to a couple of months, based on the semester cycles. While the athletes are home, the first cycle of workouts will be a continuation of the previous mesocycle from the off-season. Three or four workouts will be performed each week for all positions. Workouts will generally start with intensive plyometrics followed by a power exercise or contrast pairing set and will end with either upper or lower limb care exercises and then a circuit of extensive plyometrics. The extensive plyometrics are used to accumulate substantial volumes of floor contacts to prepare the athletes for what they will experience when they start practices and games.

The start of preseason practices and competitions is when the highest incidence of injury occurs (2). Concussions, ankle sprains, and hamstring tears are the three injuries collegiate lacrosse athletes experience the most (2). Therefore, while physiological adaptations are still being pushed during this cycle, the second half of each workout is meant to address and help mitigate these injuries.

Mesocycle 2 of the men's preseason training program is an example of how in-season exercises will be introduced if athletes return to campus in early January (see chapter 11). Intensity in the weight room will decrease slightly in the first week as the athletes start practices with the coaching staff. This phase will usually have a duration of three to four weeks, with scrimmages against other schools in the last one to two weekends before the regular season begins. The four weeks of fall ball are great preparation for this phase. Management of stress and fatigue from sporting practice and teaching the primary exercises are the two priorities, very similar to what occurred in mesocycle 2 of the off-season. Workouts will go back to twice a week and will start with a power complex followed by technical practice of the new primary exercises that focus on concentric output and restrict eccentric stress.

Professional

For professional lacrosse athletes, due to the condensed and narrow windows of preparation, it is key that the preseason, albeit short, is centered around a continuation of the off-season period and extends the window of preparation as much as possible, with an emphasis on specific strength exercises, power training, and dynamic-effort exercises. The preseason also has a minor emphasis on metabolic demands, because the length of competitive seasons requires extended windows of high metabolic output. The PLL, MSL, and WLA have such a short turnaround leading up to the NLL season that there is minimal attenuation of metabolic qualities, compared with the longer window from the subsequent summer seasons. Athletes who solely play in the PLL can afford a more traditional preseason period, where four to eight weeks can be designated to prepare for the upcoming season. Training during the preseason period typically encompasses a four-day training cycle. The training structure during this period will consist of maximizing strength gains, increasing explosive power in the form of Olympic lift–based exercises and plyometrics, and metabolic training in the form of sprint repeats of various lengths, along with some aerobic work to improve recovery and aerobic endurance.

RECOMMENDED EXERCISES

Variances in suggested exercises for the three tiers of play often stem from discrepancies in skill levels and familiarity with resistance training. Additionally, some of the exercises incorporated into the regimen will introduce those that will be performed during the in-season. Correspondingly, there is a trend toward incorporating exercises tailored to the specific demands of the sport and individual athlete positions, aiming to better equip lacrosse athletes for their forthcoming season.

High School

During the preseason phase for high school lacrosse athletes, the exercises used in the programming will be similar to those introduced in the off-season program. However, exercises should be more sport-specific and position-specific to better prepare the athletes for their lacrosse season. To improve the ability to accelerate and move laterally and linearly, all lacrosse athletes will benefit from exercises such as multidirectional lunges, single-leg squats, single-leg Romanian deadlifts (RDLs), and lateral squats during the basic strength phase. In the power phase, exercises such as cleans, snatches, high pulls, kettlebell swings, and dumbbell and barbell jerk variations will be used. It is important to maintain proper technique during these exercises, and strength and conditioning professionals must be prepared to provide regressions of exercises if the athletes are not yet ready to perform them.

College Women

The preseason mesocycle for women's college lacrosse lasts from four to six weeks. The primary focus on athlete health, strength, and readiness is ultimately preparing each individual to practice, compete in games, and display skills at the highest level. This is the last training cycle in which athletes will have the ability to consistently train three or four days per week. After this cycle, training days will be reduced or eliminated for travel and competition. Several movements can be seen as a continuation of the off-season period: kettlebell swings, hang cleans, hinge patterns, squat variations, and pressing variations. Each exercise will continue to focus on training the total body while also giving athletes the autonomy to choose exercises: inverted rows or pull-ups and variations of deadlifts, squats, and dumbbell presses.

College Men

For men's college lacrosse athletes, mesocycle 1 is a progression of the off-season's mesocycle 4, and the primary and specialty exercises remain the same. A series of upper and lower limb care exercises and extensive plyometrics is added to the ends of the workouts in mesocycle 1. During winter break, some of the athletes may be in situations where they do not have regular access to indoor turf facilities to do change-of-direction and sprint work. In these cases, intensive and extensive plyometrics can be helpful for progressively accumulating floor contacts throughout the break to prepare the connective tissues of the lower extremities for the number of changes of direction and sprints that will occur in-season. Attack and defense athletes will do more forward and backward and side-to-side (lateral) line hops; midfielders will also do intensive linear bounds and hops, since their position demands slightly more sprinting ability compared with attack and defense positions. Goalies will do extensive lateral skater bounds to build up resilience in the frontal plane.

In-season exercises will be taught in mesocycle 2 (again, in preparation for the in-season; see chapter 11). These exercises will place constraints on the eccentric portion of the primary lifting patterns. RDL rack pulls, pin bench presses, barbell pin squats, and bent-over rows from the floor all restrict and limit the stress of the eccentric portion of the exercises. This allows athletes who are experiencing high workloads from playing time in games and practices to maintain strength and power outputs without unnecessary fatigue.

Professional

The season a professional lacrosse athlete has just completed will determine where the strength and conditioning professional should start. In the case of the NLL, anywhere from four to eight weeks of preparation are typically allotted before the in-season period. PLL athletes, depending on their prior season involvement, may have only a week or two, but in some cases, athletes who do not participate in the NLL season will have a more traditional preseason period to prepare for the upcoming competitive season. For athletes who transition into the MSL or WLA, there is little to no time off, because preseason practices typically begin before the finish of the NLL season. The program in any of these cases must be sensitive to the athletes' current status. Programming should also be flexible to allow for progressing into the preseason gradually, where permitted, and potentially allow for some unloading if there is not much time granted to transition directly into another competitive season.

INTENSITY

There is an inverse relationship between volume and intensity during the preseason, and it may differ between upper and lower body movements. Regardless, intensity remains high for all power-themed exercises that require a rapid rate of force production.

High School

The training intensity during the preseason period for high school lacrosse athletes will vary depending on the goal of the exercise. For exercises that focus on developing strength, such as the front squat, deadlift, bench press, and bent-over row, the training intensity should be within the range of 87% to 95% of the 1-repetition maximum (1RM) (5). On the other hand, exercises that aim to improve power will require lower intensities of 30% to 85% of the 1RM, depending on the specific exercise (5). For instance, exercises such as bench press throws or trap bar jumps are better suited for intensities of 30% to 50% of the 1RM. For clean, snatch, and jerk variations, the load used should be within the range of 70% to 85% of the 1RM to improve power development. In the last week of the preseason period, the training load and volume should be reduced while continuing to perform the same movement patterns.

College

The college preseason program maintains a high intensity for power-based movements such as plyometrics and hang cleans. The intensity for the lower body may fluctuate depending on the sport demands and the volume of running as practice duration increases. Since athletes can select exercises, the intensity for the front squat may differ from that for the back squat and so on. Upper body intensity also may fluctuate but can remain relatively high during the preseason.

In the preseason training program for college men, intensity will remain high for mesocycle 1 while the athletes are home for winter break and the main source of physical stress can still come from the strength and conditioning plan. This cycle features a contrast pairing between strength and dynamic exercises (3). This set is immediately followed by a similar movement pattern that is performed much more dynamically and explosively. The dynamic exercises will either be a bodyweight jump or will use a lightly resisted implement, such as a medicine ball or band, to perform the task.

Intensity will have to be managed in mesocycle 2 as the athletes return to campus and start practice with the coaches. Weeks 1 and 2 are a great time to reduce intensity in the weight room and focus on teaching and refining the primary exercises the athletes will use at the start of the season. A rating of perceived exertion (RPE) of 6 to 7 (see figure 9.1 on page 171) is assigned to the primary exercises during this cycle, and intensity is slowly increased after week 2 as the number of work set repetitions decreases by one (similar to off-season mesocycle 1). Weeks 1 and 2 will restrict maximum work sets to 70% to 75% of each exercise's 1RM. An additional 5% of the 1RM will be added to the intensity range each week so that by week 4, the athletes are performing a final set of 3 repetitions of a primary exercise in a range of 80% to 85% of the 1RM. (*Note*: This level of detail is not reflected in the sample programs.)

Professional

As stated previously, the intensity for professional lacrosse athletes will depend on the individual case. For example, a PLL athlete who did not participate in an NLL season will be afforded the ability to follow a progression from a traditional off-season period into the preseason, during which the intensity will gradually increase. The intensity may range from 75% to 95% of the 1RM as the in-season period approaches. For NLL athletes transitioning to MSL or PLL seasons, the intensity will need to be lowered, because the cumulative fatigue from the previous season will have a negative effect on the small window to transition directly into another competitive season. The intensity in these cases may range from 50% to 75% of the 1RM, respectively.

VOLUME

Although volume decreases as intensity increases, there are qualifiers based on the level of play and programmatic priorities within preseason resistance training programs.

High School

As the demands from the sport increase during the preseason period, the volume of a high school lacrosse athlete's training sessions should decrease. The number of sets will range from 2 to 5, and the number of repetitions should also be in the 2 to 5 range for the primary exercises (4). As with the intensity, the volume should also be reduced during the last week of the preseason phase in preparation for the upcoming season. This can be done by reducing the number of sets and repetitions performed for each exercise.

College Women

During the college women's lacrosse preseason, the volume may remain the same as during the off-season, since the athletes are adapted to that level of training, or it may be reduced so that it does not affect the athletes' ability to recover and play lacrosse. Volume must be manipulated so athletes can remain strong and continue developing strength in areas such as balance and stability without making inroads into their recovery. It is important that athletes continue getting exposure to full-body resistance training.

College Men

The volume of the main exercises should remain high for mesocycle 1 of the college men's lacrosse program, because physiological adaptations continue to be the priority. Volume is immediately reduced once sport practice starts and the in-season exercises are introduced to the athletes in week 1 of mesocycle 2. Repetitions for the primary exercises are reduced by 1 repetition each week after week 2, because they coincide with a progressive increase in intensity as the exercises are mastered.

Regarding plyometric programming in mesocycle 2, volume becomes especially important. Research performed on male lacrosse athletes shows a high number of accelerations and decelerations and a large number of floor contacts during the game for every position except the goalkeeper (1). The best way to prepare the tendons and joints for this stress is to progressively expose athletes to the number of contacts they will potentially experience. Most accelerations and decelerations are performed at less than 4.5 mph (7.2 km/h), so a tolerance for these sporting actions can be built upon an accumulation of extensive repetitions of plyometrics in various planes of motion (1).

Professional

A traditional PLL athlete can follow a continuum where the volume will be inverse to the intensity generated as the off-season and preseason periods commence. Volume considerations for traditional PLL athletes will range from 4 to 6 sets with the number of repetitions typically between 4 and 8. For NLL athletes, these ranges will differ due to the minimal downtime between seasons. The volume for NLL athletes is typically between 3 and 4 sets with the number of repetitions ranging from 6 to 10, with lower intensities as previously stated.

CONCLUSION

Preseason programming for high school lacrosse athletes should focus on preparing them for the start of their competitive season. As the focus shifts to power, the volume is tapered, as is the amount of time spent in the gym. Collaboration between the strength and conditioning professional and the coach is crucial to align training with the athletes' performance goals and ensure they are not overwhelmed.

The preseason resistance program for college lacrosse athletes provides workouts for them to do at home while on winter break, with the goal of continuing to drive position-specific physiological adaptations. Once athletes return to campus, the strength and conditioning professional shifts the resistance training program goals to managing fatigue and implementing the exercises and protocols that will be used once the season starts.

Within the professional level, communication and understanding the landscape are critical for the strength and conditioning professional, because each athlete most likely will present a unique challenge when appropriately designing and implementing successful seasonal programs. Management of physical qualities, cumulative fatigue, and injury prevention are paramount to maintaining optimal performance.

Warm-Ups: Dynamic and Mobility Series

DYNAMIC WARM-UP SERIES

- Jog down and backpedal back (10 yards or meters each)
- Side shuffle down and side shuffle back (10 yards or meters each)
- Walking knee hugs down and lateral lunge back (10 yards or meters each)
- Walking quad pull down and inchworm jog back (10 yards or meters each)
- Walking leg cradle down and reverse lunge back (10 yards or meters each)
- A-skip forward down and A-skip backward back (10 yards or meters each)
- Lateral A-skip right down and lateral A-skip left back (10 yards or meters each)
- Power skip (2 × 20 yards or meters)
- Straight-leg run (2 × 20 yards or meters)

(continued)

Warm-Ups: Dynamic and Mobility Series *(continued)*

MOBILITY SERIES

- 90/90 hold + back heel lift + back leg lift (5 × 10 seconds each)
- Hip series (× as needed)
- Supine knee hug with ankle circle (× 3 each way)
- Floor slide with breathing (× 10)
- Cat–cow (× 10 each)
- Side-lying floor sweep (× 10 each)
- Quadruped and reach (× 10 each)

Interpreting the Sample Program Tables

+ = *Do the two exercises back-to-back*

Abd = Abduction

Add = Adduction

Alt = Alternated

AMAP = As many as possible (but quality repetitions)

BB = Barbell

BW = Body weight

Bwd = Backward

CMJ = Countermovement jump

Diag = Diagonal

DB = Dumbbell

DL = Double leg

DWU = Dynamic warm-up

Ea = Each side (arm or leg), direction, or exercise

E:I:C = Eccentric:Isometric:Concentric

Ext = External

Fwd = Forward

GH = Glute-ham

GHR = Glute-ham raise

Goblet = Holding DB or KB with both hands below the chin and elbows pointed out to the side in the midline of the body

ISO = Isometric

KB = Kettlebell

Lat = Lateral

LM = Landmine

MB = Medicine ball

OH = Overhead

Order = Performing one set of each exercise (1a, 1b, 1c) in the group one after the other. After the first set is completed, go back to the first exercise in the group and do the second set of each exercise. If certain exercises call for fewer sets than others in the group, perform those sets on the back end of the grouping. For example, if exercise 1a calls for 4 sets and exercise 1b calls for 3 sets, perform exercise 1b during sets 2 through 4 of exercises 1a.

RDL = Romanian deadlift

RFE = Rear foot elevated

RM = Repetition maximum

Rot = Rotation

RPE = Rating of perceived exertion (intensity based on level of perceived difficulty)

SA = Single arm

SB = Stability ball

Scap = Scapula

SL = Single leg

TKE = Terminal knee extension

T-spine = Thoracic spine

Tempo = The time, in seconds, for each phase or portion of the exercise, written as "eccentric phase: top (or bottom) position: concentric phase" (King, I., How to write strength training programs. In *Speed of Movement*, p. 123, 1998.). For example, a tempo of "1:5:1" for the back squat means 1 second to lower, 5 seconds held at the bottom position, and 1 second to stand back up.

WU = Warm-up

yd = yard (*Note*: distance is approximate, so meters can be used instead of yards)

SAMPLE PROGRAMS

Tables 10.1 through 10.3 provide examples of preseason programs for high school lacrosse athletes, table 10.4 provides an example for college women, tables 10.5 through 10.9 provide examples for college men, and table 10.10 provides an example for professional athletes.

Table 10.1   High School Lacrosse: Preseason Mesocycle, Basic Strength, Weeks 1 to 3

Monday: Lower Body

Order	Exercise	Sets × reps (% 1RM) or time	Sets × reps (% 1RM) or time	Sets × reps (% 1RM) or time
		Week 1	Week 2	Week 3
1	Hang high pull	4 × 4 (75%)	5 × 3 (75%)	5 × 3 (80%)
2	Back squat (BB)	4 × 4 (93%)	5 × 3 (93%)	5 × 3 (93%)
3	RDL, SL (DB)	4 × 4 ea (93%)	5 × 3 ea (93%)	5 × 3 ea (93%)
4a	Lat lunge (DB)	4 × 6 ea (85%)	4 × 4 ea (90%)	4 × 4 ea (90%)
4b	GH back extension hold	2 × 30 s	2 × 30 s	3 × 45 s
5a	Squat, SL (DB)	4 × 6 ea (85%)	4 × 4 ea (90%)	4 × 4 ea (90%)
5b	Ab wheel rollout	4 × 8	4 × 8	4 × 8

(continued)

Table 10.1 High School Lacrosse: Preseason Mesocycle, Basic Strength, Weeks 1 to 3 *(continued)*

Tuesday: Upper Body

Order	Exercise	Sets × reps (% 1RM), time, or distance	Sets × reps (% 1RM), time, or distance	Sets × reps (% 1RM), time, or distance
		Week 1	Week 2	Week 3
1	Push jerk, SA (DB)	4 × 2 ea (75%)	5 × 2 ea (75%)	5 × 2 ea (75%)
2	Bench press (BB)	4 × 4 (93%)	5 × 3 (93%)	5 × 3 (93%)
3	Split-stance row, SA (DB)	4 × 4 ea (93%)	5 × 3 ea (93%)	5 × 3 ea (93%)
4a	Standing shoulder press, SA (DB)	4 × 6 ea (85%)	4 × 4 ea (90%)	4 × 4 ea (90%)
4b	Farmer's carry	4 × 20 yd	4 × 20 yd	4 × 20 yd
5a	Chin-up (neutral grip)	4 × 6 ea (85%)	4 × 4 ea (90%)	4 × 4 ea (90%)
5b	Side plank	3 × 25 s ea	3 × 25 s ea	3 × 25 s ea

Thursday: Lower Body

Order	Exercise	Sets × reps (% 1RM)	Sets × reps (% 1RM)	Sets × reps (% 1RM)
		Week 1	Week 2	Week 3
1	Hang clean	4 × 4 (75%)	5 × 4 (75%)	5 × 4 (80%)
2	RDL	4 × 4 (93%)	5 × 3 (93%)	5 × 3 (93%)
3	RFE split squat (DB)	4 × 4 ea (93%)	5 × 3 ea (93%)	5 × 3 ea (93%)
4a	Glute bridge, SL (DB)	4 × 6 ea (85%)	4 × 4 ea (90%)	4 × 4 ea (90%)
4b	Russian twist	4 × 15 ea	4 × 15 ea	4 × 15 ea
5a	Lat step-up (DB)	4 × 6 ea (85%)	4 × 4 ea (90%)	4 × 4 ea (90%)
5b	Oblique twist (LM)	3 × 8 ea	3 × 8 ea	3 × 8 ea

Friday: Upper Body

Order	Exercise	Sets × reps (% 1RM)	Sets × reps (% 1RM)	Sets × reps (% 1RM)
		Week 1	Week 2	Week 3
1	Snatch, SA (DB)	4 × 2 ea (75%)	5 × 2 ea (75%)	5 × 2 ea (75%)
2	Weighted pull-up	4 × 4 (93%)	5 × 3 (93%)	5 × 3 (93%)
3	Shoulder press, SA (LM)	4 × 4 ea (93%)	5 × 3 ea (93%)	5 × 3 ea (93%)
4a	Bench press, SA (DB)	4 × 6 ea (85%)	4 × 4 ea (90%)	4 × 4 ea (90%)
4b	Plank shoulder tap	4 × 12 ea	4 × 12 ea	4 × 15 ea
5a	Weighted inverted row	4 × 6 ea (85%)	4 × 4 ea (90%)	4 × 4 ea (90%)
5b	Quadruped opposites (bird dog)	4 × 15 ea	4 × 15 ea	4 × 20 ea

Table 10.2 High School Lacrosse: Preseason Mesocycle, Power, Weeks 4 to 7

Monday: Lower Body

Order	Exercise	Sets × reps (% 1RM)	Sets × reps (% 1RM)	Sets × reps (% 1RM)	Sets × reps (% 1RM)
		Week 4	Week 5	Week 6	Week 7
1	Hang high pull	5 × 3 (80%)	5 × 3 (80%)	5 × 2 (80%)	5 × 2 (80%)
2	Trap bar jump	4 × 4 (30%)	4 × 4 (30%)	5 × 3 (30%)	5 × 3 (30%)

Order	Exercise	Sets × reps (% 1RM)	Sets × reps (% 1RM)	Sets × reps (% 1RM)	Sets × reps (% 1RM)
		Week 4	**Week 5**	**Week 6**	**Week 7**
3	Squat, SL (DB)	4 × 4 ea (93%)	5 × 3 ea (93%)	5 × 3 ea (93%)	5 × 3 ea (93%)
4	Lat lunge (DB)	4 × 5 ea (87%)	4 × 4 ea (90%)	4 × 4 ea (90%)	4 × 4 ea (90%)
5	RDL, SL	4 × 5 ea (87%)	4 × 4 ea (90%)	4 × 4 ea (90%)	4 × 4 ea (90%)

Tuesday: Upper Body

Order	Exercise	Sets × reps (% 1RM)	Sets × reps (% 1RM)	Sets × reps (% 1RM)	Sets × reps (% 1RM)
		Week 4	**Week 5**	**Week 6**	**Week 7**
1	Shot throw (MB)	4 × 3 ea	4 × 3 ea	4 × 3 ea	4 × 3 ea
2	Push jerk, SA (DB)	4 × 2 ea (75%)	5 × 2 ea (75%)	5 × 2 ea (75%)	5 × 2 ea (75%)
3	Rotational press (LM)	4 × 4 ea (93%)	5 × 3 ea (93%)	5 × 3 ea (93%)	5 × 3 ea (93%)
4	Split-stance row, SA (DB)	4 × 4 ea (93%)	5 × 3 ea (93%)	5 × 3 ea (93%)	5 × 3 ea (93%)
5	Push press, SA (DB)	4 × 4 ea (85%)	4 × 4 ea (90%)	4 × 4 ea (90%)	4 × 4 ea (90%)
6	Chin-up (neutral grip)	4 × 4 (90%)	4 × 4 (90%)	4 × 4 (90%)	4 × 4 (90%)

Thursday: Lower Body

Order	Exercise	Sets × reps (% 1RM)	Sets × reps (% 1RM)	Sets × reps (% 1RM)	Sets × reps (% 1RM)
		Week 4	**Week 5**	**Week 6**	**Week 7**
1	Rotational throw (MB)	4 × 3 ea	4 × 3 ea	4 × 3 ea	4 × 3 ea
2	Power clean	4 × 3 (75%)	4 × 3 (75%)	5 × 3 (80%)	5 × 3 (80%)
3	RDL	4 × 4 (93%)	5 × 3 (93%)	5 × 3 (93%)	5 × 3 (93%)
4	RFE split squat (BB)	4 × 4 ea (93%)	5 × 3 ea (93%)	5 × 3 ea (93%)	5 × 3 ea (93%)
5	Glute bridge, SL (DB)	4 × 5 ea (87%)	4 × 4 ea (90%)	4 × 4 ea (90%)	4 × 4 ea (90%)
6	Lat step-up (DB)	4 × 5 ea (87%)	4 × 4 ea (90%)	4 × 4 ea (90%)	4 × 4 ea (90%)

Friday: Upper Body

Order	Exercise	Sets × reps (% 1RM) or distance	Sets × reps (% 1RM) or distance	Sets × reps (% 1RM) or distance	Sets × reps (% 1RM) or distance
		Week 4	**Week 5**	**Week 6**	**Week 7**
1	Chest pass, SA (MB)	4 × 2 ea	4 × 2 ea	4 × 2 ea	4 × 2 ea
2	Snatch, SA (DB)	4 × 2 ea (75%)	5 × 2 ea (75%)	5 × 2 ea (75%)	5 × 2 ea (75%)
3	Sled row, SA (explosive)	4 × 4 ea (75%)	4 × 4 ea (75%)	5 × 3 ea (80%)	5 × 3 ea (80%)
4	Row to press (LM)	4 × 4 ea (90%)	5 × 3 ea (90%)	5 × 3 ea (90%)	5 × 3 ea (90%)
5a	Bench press, SA (DB)	4 × 5 ea (87%)	4 × 4 ea (90%)	4 × 4 ea (90%)	4 × 4 ea (90%)

(continued)

Table 10.2   High School Lacrosse: Preseason Mesocycle, Power, Weeks 4 to 7   *(continued)*

Friday: Upper Body *(continued)*

Order	Exercise	Sets × reps (% 1RM) or distance	Sets × reps (% 1RM) or distance	Sets × reps (% 1RM) or distance	Sets × reps (% 1RM) or distance
		Week 4	Week 5	Week 6	Week 7
5b	Farmer's carry, SA	4 × 20 yd ea	4 × 20 yd ea	4 × 20 yd ea	4 × 20 yd ea
6a	Inverted row, weighted	4 × 6 ea (85%)	4 × 4 ea (90%)	4 × 4 ea (90%)	4 × 4 ea (90%)
6b	Quadruped opposites (bird dog)	4 × 15 ea	4 × 15 ea	4 × 20 ea	4 × 20 ea

Table 10.3   High School Lacrosse: Preseason Mesocycle, Deload, Week 8

Monday: Lower Body

Order	Exercise	Sets × reps (% 1RM)
		Week 8
1	Rotational throw (MB)	2 × 3 ea
2	Hang clean	3 × 2 (80%)
3	Squat, SL (DB)	2 × 3 ea (87%)
4	Lat lunge (DB)	2 × 4 ea (85%)
5	RDL, SL	2 × 4 ea (85%)

Tuesday: Upper Body

Order	Exercise	Sets × reps (% 1RM)
		Week 8
1	Shot throw (MB)	2 × 3 ea
2	Push jerk, SA (DB)	3 × 2 ea (75%)
3	Rotational press (LM)	3 × 3 ea (85%)
4	Split-stance row, SA (DB)	3 × 3 ea (85%)
5	Bench press, SA (DB)	3 × 3 ea (85%)

Thursday: Whole Body

Order	Exercise	Sets × reps (% 1RM) or distance
		Week 8
1	Swing (KB)	3 × 3 (65%)
2	Sled row, SA (explosive)	3 × 3 ea (70%)
3	RFE split squat (BB)	3 × 3 ea (85%)
4	Lat step-up (DB)	3 × 3 ea (85%)
5a	Push press, SA (DB)	2 × 3 ea (85%)
5b	Farmer's carry, SA	2 × 10 yd ea

Table 10.4 College Women's Lacrosse: Preseason, Phase 1

Day 1: Total-Body Focus

Order	Exercise	Tempo (E:I:C)	Intensity	Sets	Reps	Rest
1	Shoulder care—prone I's, Y's, T's, A's	—	2.5 lb (~1 kg)	1	10 ea	—
2	Activation: scap push-up	—	BW	1	10	—
3	Snatch transfer series*	—	—	1	3	—
4	Complex: RDL shrug + hang clean + front squat	—	—	6	2	1 min
5	Reverse lunge (BB)	1:0:1	—	4	4/leg	2 min
6a	Inverted row with pull-up	1:0:1	—	3	AMAP	2 min
6b	Push-up	1:0:1	—	3	AMAP	2 min
7	Rot (LM)	—	—	3	5	<1 min

*Snatch transfer series: 3 OH squats + 3 pressing snatch balance + 3 snatch balance

Day 2: Total-Body Focus

Order	Exercise	Tempo (E:I:C)	Intensity	Sets	Reps or distance	Rest
1	Lower limb care—Peterson step down	—	BW	2	10/leg	—
2	Activation—glute bridge	0:10:0	BW or mini band	3	—	—
3a	OH squat	2:0:1	—	5	3	1 min
3b	Hurdle hop, SL	—	—	4	3/leg	<1 min
4	Quarter-squat jump, rapid fire (BB)	—	—	5	3	2 min
5	Deadlift (trap bar or sumo)	1:1:1	—	5	3	2 min
6	Push press	—	—	5	3	2 min
7	Farmer's carry	—	—	4	30 yd	<1 min
8	Neck—shrug (BB or DB)	—	—	3	8	1 min

Day 3: Total-Body Focus

Order	Exercise	Tempo (E:I:C)	Intensity	Sets	Reps	Rest
WU	DWU series					
1	Snatch transfer series*	—	—	1	3	—
2	Hang clean	—	—	6	3	2 min
3	Squat (front and back)	1:0:1	—	6	3	2 min
4	Nordic curl	5+:0:0	—	2	3	2 min
5	Incline bench press (BB)	2:0:1	—	4	6	2 min
6	Slam (MB)	—	—	4	6	<1 min

*Snatch transfer series: 3 OH squats + 3 pressing snatch balance + 3 snatch balance

(continued)

Table 10.4   College Women's Lacrosse: Preseason, Phase 1   *(continued)*

Day 4: Total-Body Focus (Optional)

Order	Exercise	Tempo (E:I:C)	Intensity	Sets	Reps or distance	Rest
1	Hurdle mobility at rack	—	—	5/leg	—	—
2	KB swing	—	—	3	8	1 min
3	Walking lunge (DB)	—	—	3	20 yd	1 min
4	Press or bench press (DB)	1:0:1	—	3	12	1 min
5	Pallof hold	2:5:2	—	2	5	<1 min

Table 10.5   College Men's Lacrosse: Preseason, Mesocycle 1

Day 1 (Attackers)

Order	Exercise	Sets × reps, time, or distance	Sets × reps, time, or distance	Sets × reps, time, or distance
		Week 1	**Week 2**	**Week 3**
1a	Hang clean	3 × 4	3 × 5	3 × 6
1b	Repeat broad jump	3 × 4	3 × 4	3 × 4
1c	Short-lever deadbug with 2 DBs and mini-band around feet	3 × 5 ea	3 × 5 ea	3 × 5 ea
2a	Jammer or LM press with rot	3 × 3 ea	3 × 3 ea	3 × 3 ea
2b	Shot put toss (MB)	3 × 8 ea	3 × 10 ea	3 × 12 ea
2c	Incline row, alt arm (DB)	3 × 5 ea	3 × 5 ea	3 × 5 ea
2d	Hamstring curl, alt leg (explosive)	3 × 4 ea	3 × 5 ea	3 × 6 ea
3a	Shoulder scarecrow	2 × 8	2 × 10	2 × 12
3b	Neck 4-way seated contraction	2 × 5 ea	2 × 5 ea	2 × 5 ea
3c	4-way ankle series	2 × 5 ea	2 × 5 ea	2 × 5 ea
3d	Overhead carry, SA (KB or DB)	2 × 20 yd ea	2 × 20 yd ea	2 × 20 yd ea
4a	Line hop fwd and bwd	3 × 10 s ea	4 × 10 s ea	5 × 10 s ea
4b	Line hop side to side	3 × 10 s ea	4 × 10 s ea	5 × 10 s ea

Day 2 (Attackers)

Order	Exercise	Sets × reps or time	Sets × reps or time	Sets × reps or time
		Week 1	**Week 2**	**Week 3**
1a	Push jerk	3 × 4	3 × 5	3 × 6
1b	Repeat vertical jump	3 × 4	3 × 4	3 × 4
1c	Ab rollout	3 × 4	3 × 6	3 × 8
2a	Lateral squat (LM)	3 × 3 ea	3 × 3 ea	3 × 3 ea
2b	Side toss (MB)	3 × 8 ea	3 × 10 ea	3 × 12 ea
2c	Banded or cable push–pull combo in split stance	3 × 5 ea	3 × 5 ea	3 × 5 ea
3a	Banded I's, Y's, T's, W's	2 × 5 ea	2 × 5 ea	2 × 5 ea

Order	Exercise	Sets × reps or time	Sets × reps or time	Sets × reps or time
		Week 1	**Week 2**	**Week 3**
3b	Shrug, SA (DB)	2 × 8 ea	2 × 10 ea	2 × 12 ea
3c	Peterson step-down	2 × 5 ea	2 × 5 ea	2 × 5 ea
3d	Prone pull-through (sandbag or KB)	2 × 5 ea	2 × 6 ea	2 × 7 ea
4a	Line hop fwd and bwd	3 × 10 s ea	4 × 10 s ea	5 × 10 s ea
4b	Line hop side to side	3 × 10 s ea	4 × 10 s ea	5 × 10 s ea

Day 3 (Attackers)

Order	Exercise	Sets × reps or time	Sets × reps or time	Sets × reps or time
		Week 1	**Week 2**	**Week 3**
1a	Explosive lat lunge	3 × 3 ea	3 × 3 ea	3 × 3 ea
1b	Banded ice skater bound	3 × 3 ea	3 × 3 ea	3 × 3 ea
1c	Maximum ice skater bound	3 × 3 ea	3 × 3 ea	3 × 3 ea
2a	Incline bench press, alt (DB)	3 × 5 ea	3 × 5 ea	3 × 5 ea
2b	Pullover (DB)	3 × 5	3 × 5	3 × 5
2c	Slam (MB)	3 × 8	3 × 10	2 × 12
2d	Reverse lunge to step-up (DB)	3 × 5 ea	3 × 5 ea	3 × 5 ea
3a	Suspension Y row with 3-s ISO hold at top	2 × 5 ea	2 × 5 ea	2 × 5 ea
3b	4-way neck ISO contraction	2 × 10 s ea	2 × 15 s ea	2 × 20 s ea
3c	Hamstring curl, SL	2 × 5 ea	2 × 6 ea	2 × 7 ea
3d	Copenhagen plank	2 × 30 s	2 × 35 s	2 × 40 s
4a	Line hop fwd and bwd	3 × 10 s ea	4 × 10 s ea	5 × 10 s ea
4b	Line hop side to side	3 × 10 s ea	4 × 10 s ea	5 × 10 s ea

Table 10.6 College Men's Lacrosse: Preseason, Mesocycle 1

Day 1 (Defenders)

Order	Exercise	Sets × reps, time, or distance	Sets × reps, time, or distance	Sets × reps, time, or distance
		Week 1	**Week 2**	**Week 3**
1a	Hang clean + push jerk combo	3 × 3	3 × 3	3 × 3
1b	Depth drop jump	3 × 4	3 × 4	3 × 4
1c	Short-lever deadbug with 2 DBs and mini-band around feet	3 × 5 ea	3 × 5 ea	3 × 5 ea
2a	Bench press (BB)	3 × 3	3 × 3	3 × 3
2b	Partner drop and chest toss (MB)	3 × 5	3 × 5	3 × 5

(continued)

Table 10.6 College Men's Lacrosse: Preseason, Mesocycle 1 *(continued)*

Day 1 (Defenders) *(continued)*

Order	Exercise	Sets × reps, time, or distance	Sets × reps, time, or distance	Sets × reps, time, or distance
		Week 1	**Week 2**	**Week 3**
2c	Hamstring curl, alt leg (explosive)	3 × 4 ea	3 × 5 ea	3 × 6 ea
2d	Push-up position row (DB)	3 × 5 ea	3 × 5 ea	3 × 5 ea
3a	Shoulder scarecrow	2 × 8	2 × 10	2 × 12
3b	Neck 4-way seated contraction	2 × 5 ea	2 × 5 ea	2 × 5 ea
3c	4-way ankle series	2 × 5 ea	2 × 5 ea	2 × 5 ea
3d	Overhead carry, SA (KB or DB)	2 × 20 yd ea	2 × 20 yd ea	2 × 20 yd ea
4a	Line hop fwd and bwd	3 × 10 s ea	4 × 10 s ea	5 × 10 s ea
4b	Line hop side to side	3 × 10 s ea	4 × 10 s ea	5 × 10 s ea

Day 2 (Defenders)

Order	Exercise	Sets × reps or time	Sets × reps or time	Sets × reps or time
		Week 1	**Week 2**	**Week 3**
1a	Hang clean + push jerk combo	3 × 4	3 × 5	3 × 6
1b	Vertical jump to broad jump	3 × 3	3 × 3	3 × 3
1c	Ab rollouts	3 × 4	3 × 6	3 × 8
2a	Weighted chin-up	3 × 3	3 × 3	3 × 3
2b	Slam (MB)	3 × 8	3 × 10	3 × 12
2c	Incline bench press, half-rep, full-rep method (DB)	3 × 5 ea	3 × 4 ea	3 × 3 ea
2d	3-way lunge (fwd, lat, rotational)	3 × 3 ea	3 × 3 ea	3 × 3 ea
3a	Banded I's, Y's, T's, W's	2 × 5 ea	2 × 5 ea	2 × 5 ea
3b	Shrug, SA (DB)	2 × 8 ea	2 × 10 ea	2 × 12 ea
3c	Peterson step-down	2 × 5 ea	2 × 5 ea	2 × 5 ea
3d	PVC C-R-C	2 × 10 s	2 × 10 s	2 × 10 s
4a	Line hop fwd and bwd	3 × 10 s ea	4 × 10 s ea	5 × 10 s ea
4b	Line hop side to side	3 × 10 s ea	4 × 10 s ea	5 × 10 s ea

Day 3 (Defenders)

Order	Exercise	Sets × reps or time	Sets × reps or time	Sets × reps or time
		Week 1	**Week 2**	**Week 3**
1a	Lat lunge (LM)	3 × 5 ea	3 × 5 ea	3 × 5 ea
1b	Banded ice skater bound	3 × 4 ea	3 × 4 ea	3 × 4 ea
1c	Maximum ice skater bound	3 × 3 ea	3 × 3 ea	3 × 3 ea
2a	Tall-kneeling press (LM)	3 × 5 ea	3 × 5 ea	3 × 5 ea
2b	Meadow row (LM)	3 × 5 ea	3 × 5 ea	3 × 5 ea

Order	Exercise	Sets × reps or time	Sets × reps or time	Sets × reps or time
		Week 1	**Week 2**	**Week 3**
2c	Reverse lunge to step-up (DB)	3 × 5 ea	3 × 6 ea	3 × 7 ea
3a	Suspension Y row with 3-s ISO hold at top	2 × 5 ea	2 × 5 ea	2 × 5 ea
3b	4-way neck ISO contraction	2 × 10 s ea	2 × 15 s ea	2 × 20 s ea
3c	Hamstring curl, SL	2 × 5 ea	2 × 6 ea	2 × 7 ea
3d	Copenhagen plank	2 × 30 s	2 × 35 s	2 × 40 s
4a	Line hop fwd and bwd	3 × 10 s ea	4 × 10 s ea	5 × 10 s ea
4b	Line hop side to side	3 × 10 s ea	4 × 10 s ea	5 × 10 s ea

Table 10.7 College Men's Lacrosse: Preseason, Mesocycle 1

Day 1 (Midfielders)

Order	Exercise	Sets × reps, time, or distance	Sets × reps, time, or distance	Sets × reps, time, or distance
		Week 1	**Week 2**	**Week 3**
1a	Hang clean	3 × 4	3 × 5	3 × 6
1b	Repeat broad jump	3 × 4	3 × 5	3 × 6
1c	Short-lever deadbug with 2 DBs and mini-band around feet	3 × 5 ea	3 × 5 ea	3 × 5 ea
2a	Jammer or LM press with rot	3 × 3 ea	3 × 3 ea	3 × 3 ea
2b	Shot put toss (MB)	3 × 8 ea	3 × 10 ea	3 × 12 ea
2c	Incline row, alt arm (DB)	3 × 5 ea	3 × 5 ea	3 × 5 ea
2d	Hamstring curl, alt leg (explosive)	3 × 4 ea	3 × 5 ea	3 × 6 ea
3a	Shoulder scarecrow	2 × 8	2 × 10	2 × 12
3b	Neck 4-way seated contraction	2 × 5 ea	2 × 5 ea	2 × 5 ea
3c	4-way ankle series	2 × 5 ea	2 × 5 ea	2 × 5 ea
3d	Overhead carry, SA (KB or DB)	2 × 20 yd ea	2 × 20 yd ea	2 × 20 yd ea
4a	Line hop fwd and bwd	1 × 10 s ea	2 × 10 s ea	2 × 10 s ea
4b	Line hop side to side	1 × 10 s ea	2 × 10 s ea	2 × 10 s ea
4c	Hurdle hop	2 × 6 ea	2 × 6 ea	3 × 6 ea

Day 2 (Midfielders)

Order	Exercise	Sets × reps or time	Sets × reps or time	Sets × reps or time
		Week 1	**Week 2**	**Week 3**
1a	Push jerk	3 × 4	3 × 5	3 × 6
1b	Repeat vertical jump	3 × 4	3 × 5	3 × 6
1c	Ab rollouts	3 × 4	3 × 6	3 × 8
2a	Lat squat (LM)	3 × 3 ea	3 × 3 ea	3 × 3 ea
2b	Side toss (MB)	3 × 8 ea	3 × 10 ea	3 × 12 ea
2c	Push–pull combo (banded or cable) in split stance	3 × 5 ea	3 × 5 ea	3 × 5 ea

(continued)

Table 10.7 College Men's Lacrosse: Preseason, Mesocycle 1 *(continued)*

Day 2 (Midfielders) *(continued)*

Order	Exercise	Sets × reps or time	Sets × reps or time	Sets × reps or time
		Week 1	**Week 2**	**Week 3**
3a	Banded I's, Y's, T's, W's	2 × 5 ea	2 × 5 ea	2 × 5 ea
3b	Shrug, SA (DB)	2 × 8 ea	2 × 10 ea	2 × 12 ea
3c	Hamstring curl, SL	2 × 5 ea	2 × 6 ea	2 × 7 ea
3d	Prone pull-through (sandbag or KB)	2 × 5 ea	2 × 6 ea	2 × 7 ea
4a	Line hop fwd and bwd	1 × 10 s ea	2 × 10 s ea	2 × 10 s ea
4b	Line hop side to side	1 × 10 s ea	2 × 10 s ea	2 × 10 s ea
4c	Hurdle hop	2 × 6 ea	2 × 6 ea	3 × 6 ea

Day 3 (Midfielders)

Order	Exercise	Sets × reps, time, or distance	Sets × reps, time, or distance	Sets × reps, time, or distance
		Week 1	**Week 2**	**Week 3**
1a	Reverse lunge to step-up on 12-in. (31 cm) box (BB)	3 × 3 ea	3 × 3 ea	3 × 3 ea
1b	Sprinter bound	3 × 20 yd	3 × 20 yd	3 × 20 yd
1c	Intensive linear hurdle hop	3 × 6 ea	3 × 6 ea	3 × 6 ea
2a	Incline bench press, alt (DB)	3 × 5 ea	3 × 5 ea	3 × 5 ea
2b	Pullover (DB)	3 × 5	3 × 5	3 × 5
2c	Slam (MB)	3 × 8	3 × 10	2 × 12
2d	Curtsy to diag lunge (DB)	3 × 5 ea	3 × 5 ea	3 × 5 ea
3a	Suspension Y row with 3-s ISO hold at top	2 × 5 ea	2 × 5 ea	2 × 5 ea
3b	4-way neck ISO contraction	2 × 10 s ea	2 × 15 s ea	2 × 20 s ea
3c	Peterson step-down	2 × 5 ea	2 × 5 ea	2 × 5 ea
3d	Copenhagen plank	2 × 30 s	2 × 35 s	2 × 40 s
4a	Line hop fwd and bwd	3 × 10 s ea	4 × 10 s ea	5 × 10 s ea
4b	Line hop side to side	3 × 10 s ea	4 × 10 s ea	5 × 10 s ea

Table 10.8 College Men's Lacrosse: Preseason, Mesocycle 1

Day 1 (Goalies)

Order	Exercise	Sets × reps, time, or distance	Sets × reps, time, or distance	Sets × reps, time, or distance
		Week 1	**Week 2**	**Week 3**
1a	Hang clean (3-s pause at midthigh before pull)	3 × 3	3 × 3	3 × 3
1b	Static vertical jump	3 × 3	3 × 3	3 × 3
1c	Short-lever deadbug with 2 DBs and mini-band around feet	3 × 5 ea	3 × 5 ea	3 × 5 ea

Order	Exercise	Sets × reps, time, or distance	Sets × reps, time, or distance	Sets × reps, time, or distance
		Week 1	Week 2	Week 3
2a	Front quarter squat with 5-s ISO hold (BB)	3 × 3	3 × 3	3 × 3
2b	Repeat vertical jump	3 × 3	3 × 4	3 × 5
2c	Weighted chin-up	3 × 5/3/1	3 × 5/3/1	3 × 5/3/1
2d	Bilateral chop circuit (MB)	3 × 5 ea	3 × 5 ea	3 × 5 ea
3a	Shoulder scarecrow	2 × 8	2 × 10	2 × 12
3b	Neck 4-way seated contraction	2 × 5 ea	2 × 5 ea	2 × 5 ea
3c	4-way banded walk	2 × 10 yd ea	2 × 10 yd ea	2 × 10 yd ea
3d	Overhead carry, SA (KB or DB)	2 × 20 yd ea	2 × 20 yd ea	2 × 20 yd ea
4	Continuous extensive ice skater	1 × 15 s	4 × 15 s	6 × 15 s

Day 2 (Goalies)

Order	Exercise	Sets × reps or time	Sets × reps or time	Sets × reps or time
		Week 1	Week 2	Week 3
1a	Push jerk (3-s pause on dip before push-off)	3 × 3	3 × 3	3 × 3
1b	Static vertical jump	3 × 3	3 × 3	3 × 3
1c	Ab rollouts	3 × 4	3 × 6	3 × 8
2a	RDL with 5-s ISO hold at bottom (BB)	3 × 3	3 × 3	3 × 3
2b	Repeat broad jump or KB swing	3 × 3	3 × 4	3 × 5
2c	Push–pull combo in split stance (banded or cable)	3 × 5 ea	3 × 5 ea	3 × 5 ea
2d	Athletic stance Pallof press	3 × 8 ea	3 × 10 ea	3 × 12 ea
3a	Banded I's, Y's, T's, W's	2 × 5 ea	2 × 5 ea	2 × 5 ea
3b	Shrug, SA (DB)	2 × 8 ea	2 × 10 ea	2 × 12 ea
3c	Standing 4-way hip machine	2 × 5 ea	2 × 6 ea	2 × 7 ea
3d	Prone pull-through (sandbag or KB)	2 × 5 ea	2 × 6 ea	2 × 7 ea
4	Continuous extensive ice skater	2 × 15 s	5 × 15 s	6 × 15 s

Day 3 (Goalies)

Order	Exercise	Sets × reps or time	Sets × reps or time	Sets × reps or time
		Week 1	Week 2	Week 3
1a	Explosive lat lunge	3 × 3 ea	3 × 3 ea	3 × 3 ea
1b	Banded ice skater bound	3 × 3 ea	3 × 3 ea	3 × 3 ea
1c	Maximum ice skater bound	3 × 3 ea	3 × 3 ea	3 × 3 ea
2a	Floor press with 5-s pause on the floor (BB)	3 × 3	3 × 3	3 × 3

(continued)

Table 10.8   College Men's Lacrosse: Preseason, Mesocycle 1   *(continued)*

Day 3 (Goalies) *(continued)*

Order	Exercise	Sets × reps or time	Sets × reps or time	Sets × reps or time
		Week 1	Week 2	Week 3
2b	Supine chest toss (MB)	3 × 4	3 × 5	3 × 6
2c	Bent-over row (BB)	3 × 5	3 × 5	3 × 5
2d	Split-stance lift	3 × 8 ea	3 × 10 ea	3 × 12 ea
3a	Suspension Y row with 3-s ISO hold at top	2 × 5 ea	2 × 5 ea	2 × 5 ea
3b	4-way neck ISO contraction	2 × 10 s ea	2 × 15 s ea	2 × 20 s ea
3c	Peterson step-down	2 × 5 ea	2 × 5 ea	2 × 5 ea
3d	Copenhagen plank	2 × 30 s	2 × 35 s	2 × 40 s
4	Continuous extensive ice skater	3 × 15 s	6 × 15 s	6 × 15 s

Table 10.9   College Men's Lacrosse: Preseason, Mesocycle 2

Day 1

Order	Exercise	Sets × reps or distance	Sets × reps or distance	Sets × reps or distance	Sets × reps or distance
		Week 1	Week 2	Week 3	Week 4
WU	BB complex: RDL + clean pull + muscle clean + hang clean	1 × 5 ea	1 × 5 ea	1 × 5 ea	1 × 5 ea
WU	Banded shoulder I's, Y's, T's, W's	1 × 8 ea	1 × 8 ea	1 × 8 ea	1 × 8 ea
WU	Peterson step-down	1 × 5 ea	1 × 5 ea	1 × 5 ea	1 × 5 ea
1a	Hang clean	2 × 3	3 × 3	3 × 3	3 × 3
1b	Slam (MB)	2 × 5	3 × 5	3 × 5	3 × 5
1c	Short-lever deadbug with mini-band around feet	2 × 5 ea	3 × 5 ea	3 × 5 ea	3 × 5 ea
2a	RDL rack pull (BB)	2 × 5 RPE 6-7	3 × 5 RPE 6-7	3 × 4 RPE 6-7	3 × 3 RPE 6-7
2b	Half-kneeling shoulder press, SA (LM)	2 × 8 ea	3 × 8 ea	3 × 8 ea	3 × 8 ea
2c	**Goalies and defenders:** Half-kneeling chop	2 × 8 ea	3 × 8 ea	3 × 10 ea	3 × 12 ea
2c	**Attackers and midfielders:** Half-kneeling lifts	2 × 8 ea	3 × 8 ea	3 × 10 ea	3 × 12 ea
3a	Bent-over row (Pendlay row) (BB)—pull from ground ea rep	2 × 5 RPE 6-7	3 × 5 RPE 6-7	3 × 4 RPE 6-7	3 × 3 RPE 6-7
3b	Squat off box, SL	2 × 5 ea	3 × 5 ea	3 × 5 ea	3 × 5 ea
3c	4-way bear crawl (fwd, bwd, side to side)	2 × 5 yd ea	3 × 5 yd ea	3 × 5 yd ea	3 × 5 yd ea

Day 2

Order	Exercise	Sets × reps, time, or distance	Sets × reps, time, or distance	Sets × reps, time, or distance	Sets × reps, time, or distance
		Week 1	Week 2	Week 3	Week 4
WU	BB complex: front squat + shoulder press + push press	1 × 5 ea	1 × 5 ea	1 × 5 ea	1 × 5 ea
WU	Banded shoulder I's, Y's, T's, W's	1 × 8 ea	1 × 8 ea	1 × 8 ea	1 × 8 ea
WU	Peterson step-down	1 × 5 ea	1 × 5 ea	1 × 5 ea	1 × 5 ea
1a	Push jerk (BB)	2 × 5	3 × 4	3 × 3	3 × 2
1b	Supine chest toss (MB)	2 × 5	3 × 5	3 × 5	3 × 5
1c	Hanging knee raise with MB between knees	2 × 10	3 × 10	3 × 10	3 × 10
2a	Back pin squats (BB)	2 × 5 RPE 6-7	3 × 5 RPE 6-7	3 × 4 RPE 6-7	3 × 3 RPE 6-7
2b	Mixed-grip chin-up	2 × 3-5 ea	3 × 3-5 ea	3 × 3-5 ea	3 × 3-5 ea
2c	**Goalies:** 4-way banded walk	2 × 5 yd ea	3 × 5 yd ea	3 × 5 yd ea	3 × 5 yd ea
2c	**Defenders:** LM rot	2 × 5 ea	3 × 5 ea	3 × 5 ea	3 × 5 ea
2c	**Attackers and midfielders:** Belly-up waiter's carry, SA (KB)	2 × 20 yd ea	3 × 20 yd ea	3 × 20 yd ea	3 × 20 yd ea
3a	Pin bench press (BB)	2 × 5 RPE 6-7	3 × 5 RPE 6-7	3 × 4 RPE 6-7	3 × 3 RPE 6-7
3b	Hamstring curl, SL	2 × 5 ea	3 × 5 ea	3 × 5 ea	3 × 5 ea
3c	Copenhagen plank	2 × 20 s ea	3 × 20 s ea	3 × 25 s ea	3 × 30 s ea

Table 10.10   Professional Lacrosse: Preseason, Mesocycle 1

Day 1

Order	Exercise	Sets × reps or time	Sets × reps or time	Sets × reps or time	Sets × reps or time
		Week 1	Week 2	Week 3	Week 4
WU	Hip series + foam roll + dynamic warm-up	10 min	10 min	10 min	10 min
1a	Split squat	4 × 5	4 × 5	5 × 5	5 × 5
1b	Split-stance vertical jump	4 × 3 ea	4 × 3 ea	5 × 4 ea multiple response	5 × 4 ea multiple response
1c	Hurdle hop (12 in. [31 cm]), SL	4 × 5 ea	4 × 5 ea	5 × 5 ea	5 × 5 ea
2a	Lat DB step-up (power)	3 × 6 ea	3 × 6 ea	4 × 5 ea	4 × 5 ea
2b	Lat box power skip	3 × 6 ea	3 × 6 ea	4 × 5 ea	4 × 5 ea
2c	Kneeling lat start	3 × 2 ea	3 × 2 ea	4 × 2 ea	4 × 2 ea
2d	Copenhagen plank	3 × 10 s ea	3 × 10 s ea	4 × 10 s ea	4 × 10 s ea

(continued)

Table 10.10 Professional Lacrosse: Preseason, Mesocycle 1 *(continued)*

Day 1 *(continued)*

Order	Exercise	Sets × reps or time	Sets × reps or time	Sets × reps or time	Sets × reps or time
		Week 1	**Week 2**	**Week 3**	**Week 4**
3a	Push jerk (DB)	3 × 4	3 × 4	4 × 4	4 × 4
3b	Windmill slam (MB)	3 × 4 ea	3 × 4 ea	4 × 4 ea	4 × 4 ea
3c	Rot (LM)	3 × 4 ea	3 × 4 ea	4 × 4 ea	4 × 4 ea
4a	Rollout (SB)	2 × 10	2 × 10	3 × 10	3 × 10
4b	Pike-up (SB)	2 × 10	2 × 10	3 × 10	3 × 10
5	Full-body stretch	10 min	10 min	10 min	10 min

Day 2

Order	Exercise	Sets × reps, time, or distance	Sets × reps, time, or distance	Sets × reps, time, or distance	Sets × reps, time, or distance
		Week 1	**Week 2**	**Week 3**	**Week 4**
WU	Cat–cow + quadruped reach back + Bretzel + seated T-spine rot	8-10 ea	8-10 ea	8-10 ea	8-10 ea
1a	Incline bench press (DB)	4 × 6 ea	4 × 6 ea	5 × 5 ea	5 × 5 ea
1b	Row, SA, lunge position (DB)	4 × 6 ea	4 × 6 ea	5 × 5 ea	5 × 5 ea
1c	Shot put (MB)	4 × 5 ea	4 × 5 ea	5 × 4 ea	5 × 4 ea
2a	Shoulder press, alt arm (DB)	3 × 6 ea	3 × 6 ea	4 × 5 ea	4 × 5 ea
2b	Pulldown, alt arm (cable)	3 × 6 ea	3 × 6 ea	4 × 5 ea	4 × 5 ea
2c	Sandbag pull-through	3 × 6 ea	3 × 6 ea	4 × 5 ea	4 × 5 ea
3a	Prone I's, Y's, T's, W's	3 × 8 ea	3 × 8 ea	3 × 8 ea	3 × 8 ea
3b	Rear delt raise	3 × 8	3 × 8	3 × 8	3 × 8
3c	Bear crawl (opposites)	5 yd fwd/bwd	5 yd fwd/bwd	5 yd fwd/bwd	5 yd fwd/bwd
3d	4-way neck (seated)	3 × 10 ea	3 × 10 ea	3 × 10 ea	3 × 10 ea
4a	Prone plank with march	3 × 8 ea	3 × 8 ea	3 × 8 ea	3 × 8 ea
4b	Side plank	3 × 10 s ea	3 × 10 s ea	3 × 10 s ea	3 × 10 s ea

Day 3

Order	Exercise	Sets × reps, time, or distance	Sets × reps, time, or distance	Sets × reps, time, or distance	Sets × reps, time, or distance
		Week 1	**Week 2**	**Week 3**	**Week 4**
WU	90/90 hip rocker + leg swing + toe touch progression + foam roll	10 min	10 min	10 min	10 min
1a	Snatch, SA and SL (opposites) (DB)	4 × 4 ea	4 × 4 ea	4 × 3 ea	4 × 3 ea
1b	Jump to box, SL (land on 2 feet)	4 × 4 ea	4 × 4 ea	4 × 3 ea	4 × 3 ea

Order	Exercise	Sets × reps, time, or distance	Sets × reps, time, or distance	Sets × reps, time, or distance	Sets × reps, time, or distance
		Week 1	Week 2	Week 3	Week 4
1c	Hop, SL	4 × 4 ea	4 × 4 ea	4 × 3 ea	4 × 3 ea
2a	Swing (KB)	3 × 6	3 × 6 ea	4 × 5 ea	4 × 5 ea
2b	Broad jump	3 × 6	3 × 6	4 × 5	4 × 5
2c	Thrust to sprint, 5 yd (MB)	3 × 3	3 × 3	4 × 3	4 × 3
2d	Slider mountain climber	3 × 8 ea	3 × 8 ea	4 × 8 ea	4 × 8 ea
3a	Cable chop, split stance (speed)	3 × 8 ea	3 × 8 ea	4 × 6 ea	4 × 6 ea
3b	Cable lift, split stance	3 × 8 ea	3 × 8 ea	4 × 6 ea	4 × 6 ea
3c	Catch, decel, and throw, split stance (MB)	3 × 8 ea	3 × 8 ea	4 × 6 ea	4 × 6 ea
3d	Band scarecrow	3 × 10	3 × 10	4 × 8	4 × 8
4a	Half-kneeling Pallof press	3 × 8 ea	3 × 8 ea	4 × 8 ea	4 × 8 ea
4b	Farmer's carry or waiter's walk	3 × 20 yd ea	3 × 20 yd ea	4 × 20 yd ea	4 × 20 yd ea
5	Full-body stretch	10 min	10 min	10 min	10 min

Day 4

Order	Exercise	Sets × reps or time	Sets × reps or time	Sets × reps or time	Sets × reps or time
		Week 1	Week 2	Week 3	Week 4
WU	Half-kneeling wall circle + side-lying floor sweep + 4-way ankle series + stretch strap series	10 min	10 min	10 min	10 min
1a	Lunge with curl and press (DB)	4 × 6 ea	4 × 6 ea	4 × 5 ea	4 × 5 ea
1b	Inverted row with pause hold	4 × 6	4 × 6	4 × 6	4 × 6
1c	RDL, SL (DB)	4 × 6	4 × 6	4 × 5	4 × 5
2a	Suspension row series— row, face pull, Y row	4 × 6 ea	4 × 6 ea	4 × 5 ea	4 × 5 ea
2b	Partner drop and chest toss (MB)	4 × 6	4 × 6	4 × 5	4 × 5
2c	Back extension with rot	4 × 4 ea	4 × 4 ea	4 × 5 ea	4 × 5 ea
3a	Renegade row (DB)	4 × 5 ea	4 × 5 ea	4 × 4 ea	4 × 4 ea
3b	3-way shoulder raise	4 × 5 ea	4 × 5 ea	4 × 5 ea	4 × 5 ea
4a	Grip work and wrist roll	3 × 10	3 × 10	3 × 10	3 × 10
4b	Biceps curl	3 × 10	3 × 10	4 × 8	4 × 8
4c	Triceps pushdown	3 × 10	3 × 10	4 × 8	4 × 8
5a	RKC plank	3 × 20 s	3 × 20 s	3 × 30 s	3 × 30 s
5b	Cable Pallof walkout (8-count hold)	3 × 8 s	3 × 8 s	3 × 10 s	3 × 10 s

IN-SEASON PROGRAMMING

DRAZEN GLISIC (HIGH SCHOOL), TRACY ZIMMER (COLLEGE WOMEN), DAVID EUGENIO MANNING (COLLEGE MEN), AND JOEL RAETHER (PROFESSIONAL)

Throughout the in-season period for high school lacrosse athletes, the main focus is on maintaining strength and power levels while managing the intense demands of the sport, including both games and practices. Collegiate lacrosse athletes require flexible in-season programming, empowering them to modify their regimen based on their daily condition. Given their extensive competitive schedule, maintaining robust health and strength throughout these months is crucial for teams eyeing success in postseason competitions. Throughout the in-season phase for professional lacrosse athletes, the aim is to build upon the groundwork laid during the off-season and preseason. For athletes at all levels of play, it is important that the strength and conditioning professional monitors and communicates with athletes regarding their readiness to train, especially during the in-season.

GOALS AND OBJECTIVES

The goals and objectives for lacrosse athletes vary depending on the level of competition. The following sections will present the specific aims tailored for high school athletes, collegiate women and men, and professional athletes.

High School

During the high school lacrosse in-season period, the primary goal is to maintain strength and power while accommodating the high demands of the sport, including games and practices. It is important to strike a balance between providing enough training stimulus to maintain the goals established during the off-season and managing the fatigue associated with regular practices and games (3, 8). The strength and conditioning professional must design training sessions that do not induce excessive fatigue in lacrosse athletes, which could adversely affect their performance in games.

College

For starters and athletes who play many minutes in a game, the in-season goals will be to manage fatigue and recovery between games and to maintain the mobility, strength, and power qualities that were developed in the off-season. Starters and high-minute athletes will make up only half the roster, so the other 20 to 30 athletes who are not experiencing that same level of game-day stress can still be trained over the course of the season. They will be able to handle more stress in the weight room, and physical development can still be pursued.

Professional

The professional in-season period typically begins in late May (Premier Lacrosse League [PLL], Major Series Lacrosse [MSL], or Western Lacrosse Association [WLA]) or in December (National Lacrosse League [NLL]), depending on the respective athletes and their contracted league or team. The PLL typically consists of one contest per week for 11 games until late September, with a three-game, single-elimination championship format. The MSL and WLA consist of two or three games per week for approximately 18 games, leading up to a championship playoff in which teams play a best-of-seven-games series for potentially four rounds, with teams playing every other day until a winner is determined. The finals feature the respective winners of the WLA and MSL. The NLL consists of one game per week for 18 games, with a playoff format that has a single-elimination round and two rounds of a best-of-three series covering a five-week period to crown a champion.

Based on the fact that most PLL and NLL athletes travel each week to play because they live full-time in many different locations, practice for both of these leagues is minimal and usually consists of a short practice the night before contests and a shorter game-day shoot around on the day of competitions. Athletes in the MSL and WLA are primarily in market (i.e., live in the location of their team); however, based on the game frequency, teams in these leagues also only practice once or twice weekly at a maximum.

The goal during any professional league's in-season period is to maintain strength, power, and metabolic qualities (i.e., sport-specific conditioning). Due to the low number of practices, the strength and conditioning professional needs to continually incorporate conditioning activities into the training program to maintain metabolic qualities in the form of sprint work and aerobic training. This will enhance and assist in maintaining conditioning demands throughout the in-season period.

LENGTH, STRUCTURE, AND ORGANIZATION

Differences in the length, structure, and organization of off-season resistance training programs are apparent across high school athletes, college women and men, and professional athletes. At all levels of play, postseason games and tournaments can further extend the in-season.

High School

In high school, the in-season period for lacrosse typically spans from the middle or end of March until the end of May or early June, depending on the playoffs and conference schedule. The duration of the in-season period is usually 8 to 10 weeks, during which the athletes will have one to three games per week and three or four practices. The number of training sessions will vary based on the game and practice schedule. Coaches must adjust the timing and intensity of training sessions based on the weekly game schedule. For instance, if a team plays on Wednesday and Saturday, a lower body session can be scheduled for Monday and an upper body session for Tuesday, followed by a rest day on Thursday and a whole-body session on Friday. The intensity of the Monday session can be moderate, while Tuesday and Friday sessions can be low intensity. During the in-season period, coaches must be flexible and adjust training sessions if athletes are not responding as expected to the training stimuli.

College

College lacrosse teams usually open their season within the first two weeks of February, with the regular season concluding by the end of April. The length of in-season programming can range from 13 to 17 weeks, depending on postseason participation, and teams will typically play 14 to 20 games—one to three games per week—during that time frame. (Postseason games can extend the season by one week for conference tournaments and an additional three weeks leading up to the Final Four and championship series on Memorial Day weekend at the end of May.)

Teams will lift weights twice a week, either on Mondays and Wednesdays or Tuesdays and Thursdays. There can be midweek games that break up this split, but typically, teams have a week of preparation leading into games. Athletes should begin each workout with a mobility series, a barbell movement complex, and an assessment of each athlete's readiness to train via a maximal countermovement (vertical) jump (CMJ) test (4, 9, 10), a wellness questionnaire (7), or both. The CMJ test can serve as an assessment of neuromuscular fatigue and readiness to train (4, 10), but if this is not a feasible protocol, a simple wellness check of each athlete on a scale of 1 to 10 can be used (7). If CMJ test scores are down by approximately 8% (10) or if an athlete's wellness score is low (7), the intensity of each work set should be performed at the low end of the range prescribed. A fluid model of periodization can be used to make daily load and volume adjustments to optimize training in accordance with the athletes' readiness levels (6).

Looking at the men's in-season training program, both workout days in-season consist of three **bisets** or **trisets** (a set of two [bi] or three [tri] exercises performed one after the other before a rest period) of exercises to deliver the optimal training response. The first biset or triset incorporates the primary power-based exercise of the day. The second and third bisets or trisets incorporate the primary and accessory (assistance) exercises. All three in-season mesocycles follow this workout template.

Mesocycle 1 covers the first four to five weeks of the season and will lead into the team's spring break. Starters and high-minute athletes should be managed during this cycle as they adapt to the stress of playing in games again. Athletes who are not playing very many minutes on the field can still be pushed in the weight room and will self-select higher training volumes and intensities. The primary exercises in this cycle are all variations of foundational exercises that have been programmed and mastered since the beginning of the off-season, but they are performed in a manner that reduces the eccentric portion of each repetition to limit muscle soreness. These exercise variations can be used throughout the season to help manage fatigue and recovery, even when full-range-of-motion exercises return in mesocycle 2. The volume and intensity of the work sets will be self-selected by the athletes according to how well they jump or how they self-report readiness to train at the end of the warm-ups. Based on their scores, athletes can choose to perform primary exercises at the low or high end of weight and repetition ranges.

The start of mesocycle 2 should coincide with spring break for the athletes and will be a time to restore full range of motion to the primary strength exercises. Mesocycle 3 will cover the rest of the regular season and into postseason competition.

It is important to note here that women lacrosse athletes may experience fluctuations in hormone levels during their menstrual cycle, which can affect energy levels and recovery (1). Individual responses vary, and some women may not experience significant differences (5).

This is important to understand throughout the entire training year but even more so during the in-season phase to place the athletes in the most optimal situation to be healthy and injury free. The assessments (e.g., vertical jump testing and wellness questionnaires), along with sport practice workload management strategies, will provide valuable information; however, creating lines of communication and talking with athletes will solidify the strength and conditioning professional's knowledge of each athlete's daily readiness.

Professional

Both the PLL and NLL in-season periods rely heavily on weekly resistance training and metabolic conditioning to ensure physical readiness, enhance performance, and mitigate the rigors of a season. In the MSL and WLA, strength and conditioning focuses largely on programs with low frequency and moderate to low volume that are centered on strength maintenance and power and have low metabolic demands due to game frequency. Typically, training during the in-season period will consist of one to two sessions, depending on the upcoming game and travel schedule. The training session farthest out from the upcoming game will have a higher density of training, where intensity is higher and full-body movements are the focus. If the schedule permits, a second training session will be included to concentrate on and promote recovery.

RECOMMENDED EXERCISES

Similar to the preseason exercises, recommended exercises for the three levels of play in lacrosse often differ due to variations in skill levels and experience with resistance training. Nevertheless, across all levels, it is generally not advised to introduce unfamiliar exercises during the in-season phase.

High School

During the high school in-season period, the strength and conditioning professional's programming should use primary exercises that athletes are comfortable with and can competently perform. Exercises used in the off-season and preseason periods can continue to be implemented during the in-season period. Keeping athletes healthy and managing injuries are priorities during the in-season period. Exercises to improve ankle, hip, and shoulder control and mobility and to strengthen the hamstrings, groin, shoulders, and neck need to be implemented as well. Strengthening exercises can include hamstring curls; Copenhagen planks; prone I's, Y's, T's, and W's; and four-way iso bench holds.

To avoid unwanted fatigue and soreness, introducing new exercises is not usually recommended during the in-season period. However, strength and conditioning professionals need to pay attention to how their team reacts to the training program, and if needed, they should introduce variety and new exercises to keep engagement, effort, and focus high. If new exercises are introduced, volume and intensity should be kept low at the start to allow the lacrosse athletes to adapt to the new stimuli while minimizing the risk of injury or overfatigue.

College Women

During the in-season period for women's college lacrosse, no new resistance training exercises are introduced. It is important that all movements in the training plan have been done in the off-season or preseason so that the athletes have mastered the technique and developed strength through a full range of motion. Power movements, squatting, hip hinging, and pressing are still the foundation of the in-season training plan. As training frequency decreases, it is the strength and conditioning professional's responsibility to select exercises that will yield the best results given a limited amount of time in the weight room.

College Men

Mesocycle 1 of the in-season program for a college men's lacrosse team includes a mobility series that is added to the warm-up, with exercises focusing on the ankle, hip, shoulder, and thoracic spine to offset the repeated stress each athlete experiences while playing his position. Offensive athletes will perform more exercises to work on bracing and anti-rotation of the torso, while defensive athletes will perform more torso rotational movements.

The resistance training exercises are mostly the same as in mesocycle 2 of the preseason; notably, they are exercises that restrict the stress of the eccentric portion of primary movements. In mesocycle 2, the primary exercises return to being performed over a full range of motion, although starters and high-minute athletes can still self-select variations with reduced range of motion during this cycle if preferred.

In mesocycle 3, unilateral exercises start to become primary exercises again. As the season approaches its last month, athletes have grown accustomed to the routine and stressors of the competitive schedule; compensation patterns may have started to occur throughout the season, and these can start to be addressed during this cycle.

Professional

During the professional lacrosse in-season period, the goal is largely to maintain strength and power and mitigate injury potential. With games typically on the weekends in the PLL, athletes will focus training on one or two days, with a possible third day consisting of regeneration and preparation for the upcoming game. This is also the case with NLL games. Conversely, in the MSL, game schedules are more dense, and the number of games may range up to 30 per season, with games happening midweek and also on weekends. This makes the in-season training slightly more fluid, and athletes must find one or two days within the schedule to train.

INTENSITY

The level of intensity prescribed for a lacrosse athlete's in-season resistance training regimen is contingent upon various factors, including the upcoming game schedule for the week and the amount of time the athlete spent playing in the most recent game. These considerations help tailor the training program to ensure optimal performance while managing fatigue and recovery effectively.

High School

During the high school in-season period, training intensities will vary from low to high depending on the weekly game schedule and exercises used. Exercises focusing on basic strength should use higher intensities, ranging from 80% to 93% of the 1-repetition maximum (1RM), while those focusing on power development should use lower intensities, ranging from 30% to 80% of the 1RM (3). The intensities used for a given day will likely be influenced by the game schedule for that week. To ensure that athletes are feeling recovered and fresh for games, training intensities may need to be reduced if training the day before a game or during a busy stretch in the season.

College Women

The college women's lacrosse in-season program is characterized by having no general intensity across the program, because intensity assignments will vary greatly based on minutes played per game. Specific exercises, such as the hang clean, squat and deadlift variations, and push press, may use a percentage of the 1RM, estimated 1RM, or estimated multiple-repetition maximum, commonly with intensity between 65% and 85%. All accessory movements should be done using a moderate load, which can be prescribed using a rating of perceived exertion (RPE) (see figure 9.1 on page 171). The Nordic curl is the one exercise where maximum effort is expected in order to assess and develop eccentric hamstring strength.

College Men

Similar to the women's program, intensity assignments for a college men's lacrosse in-season program are managed on an exercise-by-exercise basis for each athlete, either based on a vertical jump assessment at the end of the warm-up or via a subjective wellness score.

The eccentric portion of the repetitions for main exercises is restricted until approximately spring break to accommodate the stress of games in-season. By spring break, teams are usually already five games into the season and have had at least one midweek contest, so during that time, stress management in the weight room is at an all-time high. Strength will be maintained as much as possible with low repetitions at weight ranges from 80% to 90% of the primary exercise's 1RM. Mesocycle 2 starts at the onset of spring break, when athletes can enjoy some time off from school and just focus on lacrosse and training. Full range of motion for the primary exercises will be restored during this week, and work sets will progress in the same manner as in the previous cycle.

For mesocycles 1 and 2, all work sets will be performed in a step-loading protocol, where the weight is increased for each set. Ranges for the percentage of the 1RM and RPE are assigned to the primary exercises used in-season to allow the athletes to autoregulate stress in the weight room and have more autonomy in their plan (2). Work set 1 is performed at an intensity between 70% and 75% of the exercises' 1RM, work set 2 at 75% to 80%, and work set 3 at 80% to 85%. Starters and high-minute athletes can keep the ranges from week 1 throughout the mesocycles. For athletes who do not have much playing time and can tolerate more intense training, after week 2 of each cycle, the ranges of the 1RM can be increased by 2.5% for all work sets, so that by week 4, work set 3 is being performed with 85% to 90% of the 1RM. This system allows the strength and conditioning professional to manage athletes with a lot of playing time and to keep progressively overloading the other athletes when they have the energy. (*Note*: This level of detail is not reflected in the sample programs.)

Mesocycle 3 incorporates more unilateral exercises and will have a reduction in volume and/or intensity in week 1 of the cycle, but it otherwise follows the same work set protocols as the previous two phases.

Professional

The intensity during the in-season period for all professional lacrosse levels will focus on a progression of moderate to high intensity, with the goal of peaking near the playoffs in each respective season. Often, the goal is to achieve a higher-intensity day that is the farthest out from a competition, comprising more major full-body exercises, followed by a lower-intensity day as the week progresses that is centered around auxiliary exercises and general strength.

VOLUME

Reducing the volume of a lacrosse athlete's resistance training program during the in-season is common practice. However, like they did for intensity, strength and conditioning professionals should base their decisions about volume on factors such as the frequency and timing of games during the week and the amount of playing time each athlete has had in recent games.

High School

In high school lacrosse, the in-season period is a time when less is more. The volume of training should be kept at a low to moderate level, with repetitions ranging from 3 to 6 and sets kept to 2 to 5. As with training intensity, the volume may also need to be reduced based on the game schedule. If athletes are training before or after a game, a lower volume should be used to ensure they are feeling fresh and recovered for competition.

College Women

During the college women's lacrosse in-season, volume will be lowest, especially for athletes with many minutes of per-game play. Power and strength movements will be performed with repetitions in ranges of 2 to 4. Sets for all movements will range from 2 to 6, with greater volume for upper body exercises compared to lower body exercises. The strength and conditioning professional should strive to answer this question in-season: What is the least amount of work that can be prescribed to yield the desired training benefits?

College Men

In the college men's lacrosse in-season program, primary and accessory (assistance) exercises are kept at 3 sets per exercise. In the first week of mesocycles 2 and 3, volume is reduced to 2 sets of all exercises to manage stress as new exercises are introduced to the athletes. Because mesocycle 1 is a continuation of preseason mesocycle 2, no reduction in volume is needed at the start.

Primary exercises will be performed with repetitions in ranges of 2 to 5, with an assigned RPE of 8 (see figure 9.1 on page 171). Readiness to train will be assessed during warm-ups; if athletes feel good, they can perform their final work set at a higher-percentage intensity and for more repetitions, keeping in mind that an assigned RPE of 8 means the athlete should have 2 repetitions in reserve at the end of the set. If an athlete's jump or readiness scores are low, intensity and volume can be reduced.

Professional

Volume in the early part of the in-season period typically will be moderate (6-8 repetitions), and as the season evolves and the playoffs approach, volume will regress into lower ranges of repetitions (4-6). It is important that auxiliary exercises during the in-season period maintain priority as well. These include exercises that target the shoulder girdle (rotator cuff) and hips (gluteus maximus and gluteus medius) for maintenance. These exercises can be done with resistance bands and are performed with moderate to higher numbers of repetitions (8-12) for injury-prevention reasons.

CONCLUSION

During high school lacrosse athletes' in-season period, the primary objective is to sustain strength and power levels while accommodating the rigorous demands of the sport, which include games and practices. Striking a balance is crucial to maintain training goals from the off-season while managing fatigue associated with regular activities. Training should align with the game schedule, and intensity must be managed to ensure athletes' readiness and recovery.

In-season programming for collegiate lacrosse athletes needs to be adaptable and allow the athletes autonomy to adjust their plan based on how they are feeling each day. These athletes play a long, competitive schedule; staying healthy and strong during these months is paramount for teams looking to compete in postseason events.

The mission during the professional lacrosse athletes' in-season period is to focus on continuation of the work established from the off-season and preseason periods. As the season progresses, it is critical for the program to progress in intensity while keeping volume lower in an effort to ramp up the nervous system and attempt to maximize power output as the playoff period approaches. Achieving peak performance at the most critical time of the year also requires the strength and conditioning professional to continually monitor and communicate with athletes regarding their readiness. Using readiness scales to poll athletes can be advantageous when determining how the in-season program should be adjusted to routinely stave off overtraining, cumulative fatigue, and staleness.

Warm-Ups: Dynamic and Mobility Series

DYNAMIC WARM-UP SERIES

- Jog down and backpedal back (10 yards or meters each)
- Side shuffle down and side shuffle back (10 yards or meters each)
- Walking knee hugs down and lateral lunge back (10 yards or meters each)
- Walking quad pull down and inchworm jog back (10 yards or meters each)
- Walking leg cradle down and reverse lunge back (10 yards or meters each)
- A-skip forward down and A-skip backward back (10 yards or meters each)
- Lateral A-skip right down and lateral A-skip left back (10 yards or meters each)
- Power skip (2 × 20 yards or meters)
- Straight-leg run (2 × 20 yards or meters)

MOBILITY SERIES

- 90/90 hold + back heel lift + back leg lift (5 × 10 seconds each)
- Hip series (× as needed)
- Supine knee hug with ankle circle (× 3 each way)
- Floor slide with breathing (× 10)
- Cat–cow (× 10 each)
- Side-lying floor sweep (× 10 each)
- Quadruped and reach (× 10 each)

Interpreting the Sample Program Tables

+ = *Do the two exercises back-to-back*

Abd = Abduction

Add = Adduction

Alt = Alternated

AMAP = As many as possible (but quality repetitions)

BB = Barbell

BW = Body weight

Bwd = Backward

CMJ = Countermovement jump

Diag = Diagonal

DB = Dumbbell

DL = Double leg

DWU = Dynamic warm-up

Ea = Each side (arm or leg), direction, or exercise

E:I:C = Eccentric:Isometric:Concentric

Ext = External

Fwd = Forward

GH = Glue-ham

GHR = Glute-ham raise

Goblet = Holding DB or KB with both hands below the chin and elbows pointed out to the side in the midline of the body

ISO = Isometric

KB = Kettlebell

Lat = Lateral

LM = Landmine

MB = Medicine ball

OH = Overhead

Order = Performing one set of each exercise (1a, 1b, 1c) in the group one after the other. After the first set is completed, go back to the first exercise in the group and do the second set of each exercise. If certain exercises call for fewer sets than others in the group, perform those sets on the back end of the grouping. For example, if exercise 1a calls for 4 sets and exercise 1b calls for 3 sets, perform exercise 1b during sets 2 through 4 of exercises 1a.

RDL = Romanian deadlift

RFE = Rear foot elevated

RM = Repetition maximum

Rot = Rotation

RPE = Rating of perceived exertion (intensity based on level of perceived difficulty)

SA = Single arm

(continued)

Interpreting the Sample Program Tables *(continued)*

SB = Stability ball

Scap = Scapula

SL = Single leg

TKE = Terminal knee extension

T-spine = Thoracic spine

Tempo = The time, in seconds, for each phase or portion of the exercise, written as "eccentric phase: top (or bottom) position: concentric phase" (King, I., How to write strength training programs. In *Speed of Movement*, p. 123, 1998.). For example, a tempo of "1:5:1" for the back squat means 1 second to lower, 5 seconds held at the bottom position, and 1 second to stand back up.

WU = Warm-up

yd = yard (*Note*: distance is approximate, so meters can be used instead of yards)

SAMPLE PROGRAMS

Table 11.1 provides an example of an in-season program for high school lacrosse athletes, table 11.2 provides an example for college women, tables 11.3 through 11.5 provide examples for college men, and tables 11.6 through 11.8 provide examples for professional athletes.

Table 11.1 High School Lacrosse: Attackers: In-Season Mesocycle, Weeks 1 to 8

Monday: Lower Body

Order	Exercise	Sets × reps (% 1RM) or time	Sets × reps (% 1RM) or time	Sets × reps (% 1RM) or time	Sets × reps (% 1RM) or time
		Week 1, Week 5	Week 2, Week 6	Week 3, Week 7	Week 4, Week 8
1	High pull (BB)	3 × 4 (80%)	3 × 4 (80%)	3 × 3 (85%)	3 × 3 (85%)
2	RDL, SL (BB)	4 × 4 ea (80%)	4 × 4 ea (80%)	3 × 3 ea (85%)	3 × 3 ea (85%)
3a	Lat step-up (DB)	4 × 4 ea (80%)	4 × 4 ea (80%)	3 × 3 ea (85%)	3 × 3 ea (85%)
3b	Hurdle step-over	4 × 8 ea	4 × 8 ea	3 × 8 ea	3 × 8 ea
4a	RFE split squat (DB)	4 × 4 ea (80%)	3 × 4 ea (80%)	3 × 4 ea (80%)	3 × 4 ea (80%)
4b	Anti-rot hold	4 × 20 s ea	3 × 20 s ea	3 × 20 s ea	3 × 20 s ea
5a	Copenhagen plank	2 × 20 s	2 × 20 s	2 × 25 s	2 × 25 s
5b	Hamstring curl, SL (SB)	2 × 15 ea	2 × 15 ea	2 × 15 ea	2 × 15 ea

Tuesday: Upper Body

Order	Exercise	Sets × reps (% 1RM) or time	Sets × reps (% 1RM) or time	Sets × reps (% 1RM) or time	Sets × reps (% 1RM) or time
		Week 1, Week 5	**Week 2, Week 6**	**Week 3, Week 7**	**Week 4, Week 8**
1	Chest pass, SL (MB)	3 × 2 ea	3 × 2 ea	3 × 2 ea	3 × 2 ea
2	Push jerk, SA (DB)	4 × 4 ea (80%)	4 × 4 ea (80%)	3 × 3 ea (85%)	3 × 3 ea (85%)
3	Rotational press (LM)	4 × 4 ea (80%)	4 × 4 ea (80%)	3 × 3 ea (85%)	3 × 3 ea (85%)
4a	SA row, hand supported (DB)	4 × 4 ea (80%)	4 × 4 ea (80%)	3 × 3 ea (85%)	3 × 3 ea (85%)
4b	Wall slide	4 × 8	4 × 8	3 × 8	3 × 8
5a	Bench press, SA (DB)	4 × 4 ea (80%)	3 × 4 ea (80%)	3 × 4 ea (80%)	3 × 4 ea (80%)
5b	Suspension superman	4 × 20 s ea	3 × 20 s ea	3 × 20 s ea	3 × 20 s ea
6	Prone I's, Y's, T's, W's	2 × 8 ea	2 × 8 ea	2 × 8 ea	2 × 8 ea

Thursday: Whole Body

Order	Exercise	Sets × reps (% 1RM) or distance	Sets × reps (% 1RM) or distance	Sets × reps (% 1RM) or distance	Sets × reps (% 1RM) or distance
		Week 1, Week 5	**Week 2, Week 6**	**Week 3, Week 7**	**Week 4, Week 8**
1	Swing (KB)	3 × 2 ea	3 × 2 ea	3 × 2 ea	3 × 2 ea
2a	Sled row, SA (explosive)	4 × 4 ea (70%)	4 × 4 ea (70%)	3 × 3 ea (75%)	3 × 3 ea (75%)
2b	90/90 alternating hip rot	4 × 10 ea	4 × 10 ea	3 × 10 ea	3 × 10 ea
3	RFE split squat (BB)	4 × 4 ea (80%)	4 × 4 ea (80%)	3 × 3 ea (85%)	3 × 3 ea (85%)
4	Push press, SA (DB)	4 × 4 ea (80%)	4 × 4 ea (80%)	3 × 3 ea (85%)	3 × 3 ea (85%)
5a	Lat lunge	4 × 4 ea (80%)	3 × 4 ea (80%)	3 × 4 ea (80%)	3 × 4 ea (80%)
5b	Farmer's carry, SA	4 × 20 yd	3 × 20 yd	3 × 20 yd	3 × 20 yd
6	4-way ISO bench hold	2 × 3 ea	2 × 3 ea	2 × 3 ea	2 × 3 ea

Table 11.2   College Women's Lacrosse: In-Season

Day 1: Total-Body Focus

Order	Exercise	Tempo (E:I:C)	Intensity	Sets	Reps	Rest
1	Shoulder care—prone I's, Y's, T's, A's	—	2.5 lb (1.1 kg)	1	10 ea	—
2	Activation—scap push-up	—	BW	1	10	—
3	Snatch transfer series*	—	—	1	3	—

(continued)

Table 11.2 College Women's Lacrosse: In-Season *(continued)*

Day 1: Total-Body Focus *(continued)*

Order	Exercise	Tempo (E:I:C)	Intensity	Sets	Reps	Rest
4	Throw (MB)	—	—	3-6	2-3	<1 min
5	Hang clean or clean pull	—	—	4-6	1-3	1-2 min
6	Front-back squat or trap bar deadlift	1:0:1	—	3-4	4	1-2 min
7	Inverted row or pull-up	1:0:1	—	2-3	AMAP	2 min
8	Push press	—	—	4-6	2-3	2 min

*Snatch transfer series: 3 OH squats + 3 pressing snatch balance + 3 snatch balance

Day 2: Total-Body Focus

Order	Exercise	Tempo (E:I:C)	Intensity	Sets	Reps or distance	Rest
1	Lower limb care—Peterson step-down	—	BW	2	10/leg	—
2	Activation—glute bridge	0:10:0	BW or mini-band	3	—	—
3	OH squat	1:0:1	—	1-5	2-3	1 min
4	Box jump + KB swing	—	—	3-6 / 3-4	2-3 / 6-8	1 min
5	Nordic curl	5+:0:0	—	3	3	2 min
6	Half-kneeling press (LM)	0:1:1	—	5	3/arm	2 min
7	Farmer's carry	—	—	4	30 yd	<1 min
8	Shrug (BB or DB)	—	—	3	6	<1 min

Table 11.3 College Men's Lacrosse: In-Season, Mesocycle 1

Day 1

Order	Exercise	Sets × reps or distance Week 1	Sets × reps or distance Week 2	Sets × reps or distance Week 3	Sets × reps or distance Week 4
WU	Mobility series	× 1	× 1	× 1	× 1
WU	BB complex: RDL + clean pull + muscle clean + hang clean	1 × 5 ea	1 × 5 ea	1 × 5 ea	1 × 5 ea
WU	Banded shoulder I's, Y's, T's, W's	1 × 8 ea	1 × 8 ea	1 × 8 ea	1 × 8 ea
WU	Peterson step-down	1 × 5 ea	1 × 5 ea	1 × 5 ea	1 × 5 ea
WU	CMJ assessment (hands on hips) or wellness check	2-3 attempts	2-3 attempts	2-3 attempts	2-3 attempts
1a	Hang clean	3 × 2-5	3 × 2-5	3 × 2-5	3 × 2-5
1b	Slam (MB)	3 × 5	3 × 5	3 × 5	3 × 5
1c	Short-lever deadbug with mini-band around feet	3 × 5 ea	3 × 5 ea	3 × 5 ea	3 × 5 ea

Order	Exercise	Sets × reps or distance	Sets × reps or distance	Sets × reps or distance	Sets × reps or distance
		Week 1	Week 2	Week 3	Week 4
2a	RDL rack pull (BB)	3 × 2-5 RPE 8	3 × 2-5 RPE 8	3 × 2-5 RPE 8	3 × 2-5 RPE 8
2b	Half-kneeling shoulder press, SA (LM)	3 × 5-8 ea RPE 8	3 × 5-8 ea RPE 8	3 × 5-8 ea RPE 8	3 × 5-8 ea RPE 8
2c	**Goalies and defenders:** Split-stance chop	3 × 8 ea	3 × 8 ea	3 × 10 ea	3 × 12 ea
2c	**Attackers and midfielders:** Split-stance lift	3 × 8 ea	3 × 8 ea	3 × 10 ea	3 × 12 ea
3a	Bent-over row (BB)—pull from the ground for each rep	3 × 2-5 RPE 8	3 × 2-5 RPE 8	3 × 2-5 RPE 8	3 × 2-5 RPE 8
3b	Step-up (DB)	3 × 5-8 ea RPE 8	3 × 5-8 ea RPE 8	3 × 5-8 ea RPE 8	3 × 5-8 ea RPE 8
3c	4-way bear crawl (fwd, bwd, side to side)	3 × 5 yd ea	3 × 5 yd ea	3 × 5 yd ea	3 × 5 yd ea

Day 2

Order	Exercise	Sets × reps, time, or distance	Sets × reps, time, or distance	Sets × reps, time, or distance	Sets × reps, time, or distance
		Week 1	Week 2	Week 3	Week 4
WU	Mobility series	× 1	× 1	× 1	× 1
WU	BB complex: front squat + shoulder press + push press	1 × 5 ea	1 × 5 ea	1 × 5 ea	1 × 5 ea
WU	Banded shoulder I's, Y's, T's, W's	1 × 8 ea	1 × 8 ea	1 × 8 ea	1 × 8 ea
WU	Peterson step-down	1 × 5 ea	1 × 5 ea	1 × 5 ea	1 × 5 ea
WU	CMJ assessment (hands on hips) or wellness check	2-3 attempts	2-3 attempts	2-3 attempts	2-3 attempts
1a	Push jerk (BB)	3 × 2-5	3 × 2-5	3 × 2-5	3 × 2-5
1b	Supine chest toss (MB)	3 × 5	3 × 5	3 × 5	3 × 5
1c	Hanging knee raise with MB between knees	3 × 10	3 × 10	3 × 10	3 × 10
2a	Back pin squat (BB)	3 × 2-5 RPE 8	3 × 2-5 RPE 8	3 × 2-5 RPE 8	3 × 2-5 RPE 8
2b	Mixed-grip chin-up	3 × 5-8 ea	3 × 5-8 ea	3 × 5-8 ea	3 × 5-8 ea
2c	**Goalies:** 4-way banded walk	3 × 5 yd ea	3 × 5 yd ea	3 × 5 yd ea	3 × 5 yd ea
2c	**Defenders:** Prone pull-through (sandbag or KB)	3 × 5 ea	3 × 5 ea	3 × 5 ea	3 × 5 ea
2c	**Attackers and midfielders:** Overhead carry, SA (KB)	3 × 20 yd ea	3 × 20 yd ea	3 × 20 yd ea	3 × 20 yd ea

(continued)

Table 11.3 College Men's Lacrosse: In-Season, Mesocycle 1 *(continued)*

Day 2 *(continued)*

Order	Exercise	Sets × reps, time, or distance	Sets × reps, time, or distance	Sets × reps, time, or distance	Sets × reps, time, or distance
		Week 1	Week 2	Week 3	Week 4
3a	Pin bench press (BB)	3 × 2-5 RPE 8	3 × 2-5 RPE 8	3 × 2-5 RPE 8	3 × 2-5 RPE 8
3b	Hamstring curl, SL (concentric phase only)	3 × 5 ea	3 × 5 ea	3 × 5 ea	3 × 5 ea
3c	Copenhagen plank with top arm holding KB or DB	3 × 15 s ea	3 × 20 s ea	3 × 25 s ea	3 × 30 s ea

Table 11.4 College Men's Lacrosse: In-Season, Mesocycle 2

Day 1

Order	Exercise	Sets × reps or distance	Sets × reps or distance	Sets × reps or distance	Sets × reps or distance
		Week 1	Week 2	Week 3	Week 4
WU	Mobility series	× 1	× 1	× 1	× 1
WU	BB complex: RDL + clean pull + muscle clean + hang clean	1 × 5 ea	1 × 5 ea	1 × 5 ea	1 × 5 ea
WU	Banded shoulder I's, Y's, T's, W's	1 × 8 ea	1 × 8 ea	1 × 8 ea	1 × 8 ea
WU	Peterson step-down	1 × 5 ea	1 × 5 ea	1 × 5 ea	1 × 5 ea
WU	CMJ assessment (hands on hips) or wellness check	2-3 attempts	2-3 attempts	2-3 attempts	2-3 attempts
1a	Hang clean	2 × 2-5	3 × 2-5	3 × 2-5	3 × 2-5
1b	Slam (MB)	2 × 5	3 × 5	3 × 5	3 × 5
1c	Short-lever deadbug with mini-band around feet	2 × 5 ea	3 × 5 ea	3 × 5 ea	3 × 5 ea
2a	RDL (BB)	2 × 2-5 RPE 8	3 × 2-5 RPE 8	3 × 2-5 RPE 8	3 × 2-5 RPE 8
2b	Half-kneeling shoulder press, SA (KB)	2 × 5-8 ea RPE 8	3 × 5-8 ea RPE 8	3 × 5-8 ea RPE 8	3 × 5-8 ea RPE 8
2c	**Goalies and defenders:** Athletic-stance chop	2 × 8 ea	3 × 8 ea	3 × 10 ea	3 × 12 ea
2c	**Attackers and midfielders:** Athletic-stance lift	2 × 8 ea	3 × 8 ea	3 × 10 ea	3 × 12 ea
3a	Chest-supported incline row (DB)	2 × 5-8 ea RPE 8	3 × 5-8 ea RPE 8	3 × 5-8 ea RPE 8	3 × 5-8 ea RPE 8
3b	Squat off box, SL	2 × 5-8 ea RPE 8	3 × 5-8 ea RPE 8	3 × 5-8 ea RPE 8	3 × 5-8 ea RPE 8
3c	4-way bear crawl (fwd, bwd, side to side)	2 × 5 yd ea	3 × 5 yd ea	3 × 5 yd ea	3 × 5 yd ea

Day 2

Order	Exercise	Sets × reps or distance	Sets × reps or distance	Sets × reps or distance	Sets × reps or distance
		Week 1	**Week 2**	**Week 3**	**Week 4**
WU	Mobility series	× 1	× 1	× 1	× 1
WU	BB complex: front squat + shoulder press + push press	1 × 5 ea	1 × 5 ea	1 × 5 ea	1 × 5 ea
WU	Banded shoulder I's, Y's, T's, W's	1 × 8 ea	1 × 8 ea	1 × 8 ea	1 × 8 ea
WU	Peterson step-down	1 × 5 ea	1 × 5 ea	1 × 5 ea	1 × 5 ea
WU	CMJ assessment (hands on hips) or wellness check	2-3 attempts	2-3 attempts	2-3 attempts	2-3 attempts
1a	Push jerk (BB)	2 × 2-5	3 × 2-5	3 × 2-5	3 × 2-5
1b	Supine chest toss (MB)	2 × 5	3 × 5	3 × 5	3 × 5
1c	Hanging knee raise with MB between knees	2 × 10	3 × 10	3 × 10	3 × 10
2a	Back squat (BB)	2 × 2-5 RPE 8	3 × 2-5 RPE 8	3 × 2-5 RPE 8	3 × 2-5 RPE 8
2b	Mixed-grip chin-up	2 × 3-5 ea	3 × 3-5 ea	3 × 3-5 ea	3 × 3-5 ea
2c	**Goalies:** 4-way banded walk	2 × 5 yd ea	3 × 5 yd ea	3 × 5 yd ea	3 × 5 yd ea
2c	**Defenders:** Prone pull-through (sandbag or KB)	2 × 5 ea	3 × 5 ea	3 × 5 ea	3 × 5 ea
2c	**Attackers and midfielders:** Overhead carry, SA (KB)	2 × 20 yd ea	3 × 20 yd ea	3 × 20 yd ea	3 × 20 yd ea
3a	Bench press (BB)	2 × 2-5 RPE 8	3 × 2-5 RPE 8	3 × 2-5 RPE 8	3 × 2-5 RPE 8
3b	Hamstring curl, DL (SB)	2 × 5-8	3 × 5-8	3 × 5-8	3 × 5-8
3c	Copenhagen plank with top arm banded row	2 × 8 ea	3 × 8 ea	3 × 10 ea	3 × 12 ea

Table 11.5 College Men's Lacrosse: In-Season, Mesocycle 3

Day 1

Order	Exercise	Sets × reps or distance	Sets × reps or distance	Sets × reps or distance	Sets × reps or distance
		Week 1	**Week 2**	**Week 3**	**Week 4**
WU	Mobility series	× 1	× 1	× 1	× 1
WU	BB complex: RDL + clean pull + muscle clean + hang clean	1 × 5 ea	1 × 5 ea	1 × 5 ea	1 × 5 ea
WU	Banded shoulder I's, Y's, T's, W's	1 × 8 ea	1 × 8 ea	1 × 8 ea	1 × 8 ea
WU	Peterson step-down	1 × 5 ea	1 × 5 ea	1 × 5 ea	1 × 5 ea
WU	CMJ assessment (hands on hips) or wellness check	2-3 attempts	2-3 attempts	2-3 attempts	2-3 attempts

(continued)

Table 11.5 College Men's Lacrosse: In-Season, Mesocycle 3 *(continued)*

Day 1 *(continued)*

Order	Exercise	Sets × reps or distance	Sets × reps or distance	Sets × reps or distance	Sets × reps or distance
		Week 1	Week 2	Week 3	Week 4
1a	Hang clean	3 × 2-5	3 × 2-5	3 × 2-5	3 × 2-5
1b	Slam (MB)	3 × 5	3 × 5	3 × 5	3 × 5
1c	Short-lever deadbug with mini-band around feet	3 × 5 ea	3 × 5 ea	3 × 5 ea	3 × 5 ea
2a	RDL, SL with 2 DBs	2 × 2-5 ea RPE 8	3 × 2-5 ea RPE 8	3 × 2-5 ea RPE 8	3 × 2-5 ea RPE 8
2b	Half-kneeling shoulder press, SA (KB)	2 × 5-8 ea RPE 8	3 × 5-8 ea RPE 8	3 × 5-8 ea RPE 8	3 × 5-8 ea RPE 8
2c	**Goalies and defenders:** Half-kneeling chop	2 × 8 ea	3 × 8 ea	3 × 10 ea	3 × 12 ea
2c	**Attackers and midfielders:** Half-kneeling lift	2 × 8 ea	3 × 8 ea	3 × 10 ea	3 × 12 ea
3a	Bent-over row, SA (DB)	2 × 5-8 ea RPE 8	3 × 5-8 ea RPE 8	3 × 5-8 ea RPE 8	3 × 5-8 ea RPE 8
3b	Squat off box, SL	2 × 5-8 ea RPE 8	3 × 5-8 ea RPE 8	3 × 5-8 ea RPE 8	3 × 5-8 ea RPE 8
3c	4-way bear crawl (fwd, bwd, side to side)	2 × 5 yd ea	3 × 5 yd ea	3 × 5 yd ea	3 × 5 yd ea

Day 2

Order	Exercise	Sets × reps or distance	Sets × reps or distance	Sets × reps or distance	Sets × reps or distance
		Week 1	Week 2	Week 3	Week 4
WU	Mobility series	× 1	× 1	× 1	× 1
WU	BB complex: front squat + shoulder press + push press	1 × 5 ea	1 × 5 ea	1 × 5 ea	1 × 5 ea
WU	Banded shoulder I's, Y's, T's, W's	1 × 8 ea	1 × 8 ea	1 × 8 ea	1 × 8 ea
WU	Peterson step-down	1 × 5 ea	1 × 5 ea	1 × 5 ea	1 × 5 ea
WU	CMJ assessment (hands on hips) or wellness check	2-3 attempts	2-3 attempts	2-3 attempts	2-3 attempts
1a	Push jerk (BB)	3 × 2-5	3 × 2-5	3 × 2-5	3 × 2-5
1b	Supine chest toss (MB)	3 × 5	3 × 5	3 × 5	3 × 5
1c	Hanging knee raise with MB between knees	3 × 10	3 × 10	3 × 10	3 × 10
2a	Split squat (DB)	2 × 2-5 ea RPE 8	3 × 2-5 ea RPE 8	3 × 2-5 ea RPE 8	3 × 2-5 ea RPE 8
2b	Mixed-grip chin-up	2 × 3-5 ea	3 × 3-5 ea	3 × 3-5 ea	3 × 3-5 ea
2c	**Goalies:** 4-way banded walk	2 × 5 yd ea	3 × 5 yd ea	3 × 5 yd ea	3 × 5 yd ea

Order	Exercise	Sets × reps or distance	Sets × reps or distance	Sets × reps or distance	Sets × reps or distance
		Week 1	Week 2	Week 3	Week 4
2c	**Defenders:** Prone pull-through (sandbag or KB)	2 × 5 ea	3 × 5 ea	3 × 5 ea	3 × 5 ea
2c	**Attackers and midfielders:** Overhead carry, SA (KB)	2 × 20 yd ea	3 × 20 yd ea	3 × 20 yd ea	3 × 20 yd ea
3a	Flat bench press with 2 DBs	2 × 5-8 RPE 8	3 × 5-8 RPE 8	3 × 5-8 RPE 8	3 × 5-8 RPE 8
3b	Goblet lat squat	2 × 5 ea	3 × 5 ea	3 × 5 ea	3 × 5 ea
3c	Hamstring curl, SL (SB)	2 × 3-5 ea	3 × 3-5 ea	3 × 3-5 ea	3 × 3-5 ea

Table 11.6   Professional Lacrosse: In-Season, Mesocycle 1

Day 1

Order	Exercise	Sets × reps or time	Sets × reps or time	Sets × reps or time	Sets × reps or time
		Week 1	Week 2	Week 3	Week 4
WU	Foam roll + hip series + 4-way ankle series + hurdle step-over	10 min	10 min	10 min	10 min
WU	Banded shoulder I's, Y's, T's, W's	1 × 8 ea	1 × 8 ea	1 × 8 ea	1 × 8 ea
1a	Single-side loaded Bulgarian split squat (KB)	3 × 5 ea	3 × 5 ea	4 × 4 ea	4 × 4 ea
1b	6-in. (15 cm) hurdle hop, SL (single response)	3 × 5 ea	3 × 5 ea	4 × 4 ea	4 × 4 ea
2a	Elevated glute driver, SL	3 × 6 ea	3 × 6 ea	4 × 5 ea	4 × 5 ea
2b	Split-stance jerk, SA (LM)	3 × 5 ea	3 × 5 ea	4 × 4 ea	4 × 4 ea
3a	Rotational row, SA (cable)	3 × 6 ea	3 × 6 ea	4 × 5 ea	4 × 5 ea
3b	Split-stance side throw (MB)	3 × 5 ea	3 × 5 ea	4 × 4 ea	4 × 4 ea
4a	Front and side shoulder raise, alt	3 × 4 ea	3 × 4 ea	4 × 3 ea	4 × 3 ea
4b	Banded face pull	3 × 8	3 × 8	4 × 6	4 × 6
5a	Rollout (SB)	2 × 10	2 × 10	3 × 8	3 × 8
5b	Russian twist (MB)	2 × 5 ea	2 × 5 ea	3 × 5 ea	3 × 5 ea

Day 2

Order	Exercise	Sets × reps, time, or distance	Sets × reps, time, or distance	Sets × reps, time, or distance	Sets × reps, time, or distance
		Week 1	Week 2	Week 3	Week 4
WU	Cat–cow mobility + T-spine rot + side-lying floor sweep + DWU series	10 min	10 min	10 min	10 min

(continued)

Table 11.6   Professional Lacrosse: In-Season, Mesocycle 1   *(continued)*

Day 2 *(continued)*

Order	Exercise	Sets × reps, time, or distance	Sets × reps, time, or distance	Sets × reps, time, or distance	Sets × reps, time, or distance
		Week 1	Week 2	Week 3	Week 4
1a	Glute bridge chest press	3 × 6	3 × 6	4 × 5	4 × 5
1b	Supine chest drop (MB)	3 × 6	3 × 6	4 × 5	4 × 5
1c	Pull-up	3 × 6	3 × 6	4 × 5	4 × 5
1d	Slam (MB)	3 × 6	3 × 6	4 × 5	4 × 5
2a	Leg up (on bench) curl and press (DB)	3 × 6 ea	3 × 6 ea	4 × 5 ea	4 × 5 ea
2b	Cable drop step to chop	3 × 6 ea	3 × 6 ea	4 × 5 ea	4 × 5 ea
2c	Crow hop and throw (MB)	3 × 5 ea	3 × 5 ea	4 × 4 ea	4 × 4 ea
3a	Hamstring curl (SB)	3 × 6	3 × 6	4 × 5	4 × 5
3b	Straight-arm row (cable)	3 × 8	3 × 8	4 × 6	4 × 6
3c	Suitcase carry, SA	3 × 20 yd	3 × 20 yd	2 × 30 yd	2 × 30 yd
3d	Revolving Pallof hold (split stance)	× 3 ea	× 3 ea	× 4 ea	× 4 ea

Table 11.7   Professional Lacrosse: In-Season, Mesocycle 2

Day 1

Order	Exercise	Sets × reps or time	Sets × reps or time	Sets × reps or time	Sets × reps or time
		Week 1	Week 2	Week 3	Week 4
WU	90/90 hip rocker + stretch strap series + leg swing + hurdle step-over	10 min	10 min	10 min	10 min
1a	Snatch (DB)	4 × 4	4 × 4	5 × 3	5 × 3
1b	Jump squat (DB)	4 × 4	4 × 4	5 × 3	5 × 3
1c	Granny toss (MB)	4 × 4	4 × 4	5 × 3	5 × 3
2a	Lunge to row, SA (cable)	3 × 5 ea	3 × 5 ea	4 × 4 ea	4 × 4 ea
2b	Half-kneeling shoulder press, bottoms up, SA (KB)	3 × 5 ea	3 × 5 ea	4 × 4 ea	4 × 4 ea
2c	Step and chop, speed (cable)	3 × 5 ea	3 × 5 ea	4 × 4 ea	4 × 4 ea
3a	Back extension with Y-lift	3 × 8	3 × 8	4 × 6	4 × 6
3b	Cable drop step and lift	3 × 5 ea	3 × 5 ea	4 × 6 ea	4 × 6 ea
3c	Plank with opposite arm and leg reach (raise)	3 × 5 ea	3 × 5 ea	4 × 5 ea	4 × 5 ea

Day 2

Order	Exercise	Sets × reps, time, or distance	Sets × reps, time, or distance	Sets × reps, time, or distance	Sets × reps, time, or distance
		Week 1	Week 2	Week 3	Week 4
WU	Foam roll + peanut mobility + Bretzel + half-kneeling wall circle	10 min	10 min	10 min	10 min
WU	Banded shoulder I's, Y's, T's, W's	1 × 8 ea	1 × 8 ea	1 × 8 ea	1 × 8 ea
1a	Half-supported bench press (DB)	4 × 4 ea	4 × 4 ea	5 × 3 ea	5 × 3 ea
1b	Bird dog row, opposites (DB)	4 × 4 ea	4 × 4 ea	5 × 4 ea	5 × 4 ea
1c	Row to shoulder press, SA (LM)	4 × 4 ea	4 × 4 ea	5 × 3 ea	5 × 3 ea
2a	Side-plank row, top arm (cable)	4 × 5 ea	4 × 5 ea	4 × 6 ea	4 × 6 ea
2b	Lat lunge with front shoulder raise (DB)	4 × 5 ea	4 × 5 ea	5 × 3 ea	5 × 3 ea
2c	Shoulder press, SA and SL opposites (DB)	4 × 5 ea	4 × 5 ea	5 × 3 ea	5 × 3 ea
3a	Jammer press with rot	4 × 5 ea	4 × 5 ea	5 × 3 ea	5 × 3 ea
3b	Shot put, SA, lat (MB)	4 × 5 ea	4 × 5 ea	5 × 3 ea	5 × 3 ea
3c	Bear crawl, opposites, side to side	2 × 5 yd ea	2 × 5 yd ea	2 × 5 yd ea	2 × 5 yd ea

Table 11.8 Professional Lacrosse: In-Season, Mesocycle 3

Day 1

Order	Exercise	Sets × reps or time	Sets × reps or time	Sets × reps or time	Sets × reps or time
		Week 1	Week 2	Week 3	Week 4
WU	Hip kick stand + 4-way ankle series + 90/90 hip rocker + foam roll	10 min	10 min	10 min	10 min
WU	Banded shoulder I's, Y's, T's, W's	1 × 8 ea	1 × 8 ea	1 × 8 ea	1 × 8 ea
1a	Front rack squat to overhead press (DB)	3 × 5	3 × 5	4 × 4	4 × 4
1b	Two-hand shot push to sprint, 5 yd (MB)	3 × 5	3 × 5	4 × 4	4 × 4
1c	Hurdle hop, 12 in. (31 cm), multiple response	3 × 5	3 × 5	4 × 4	4 × 4
2a	Inverted row, chin-up grip	3 × 6	3 × 6	4 × 5	4 × 5
2b	Incline bench press, SA (DB)	3 × 6 ea	3 × 6 ea	4 × 5 ea	4 × 5 ea
2c	Rot (LM)	3 × 5 ea	3 × 5 ea	4 × 5 ea	4 × 5 ea

(continued)

Table 11.8 Professional Lacrosse: In-Season, Mesocycle 3 *(continued)*

Day 1 *(continued)*

Order	Exercise	Sets × reps or time	Sets × reps or time	Sets × reps or time	Sets × reps or time
		Week 1	Week 2	Week 3	Week 4
2d	Windmill throw down, speed (MB)	3 × 5 ea	3 × 5 ea	4 × 4 ea	4 × 4 ea
3a	Lat hop lunge (sandbag)	3 × 5 ea	3 × 5 ea	4 × 4 ea	4 × 4 ea
3b	Lat hurdle hop, SL with 5-yd sprint	3 × 5 ea	3 × 5 ea	4 × 4 ea	4 × 4 ea
3c	Slam to side throw (MB)	3 × 3 ea	3 × 3 ea	4 × 3 ea	4 × 3 ea
4	Full-body stretch	10 min	10 min	10 min	10 min

Day 2

Order	Exercise	Sets × reps or time	Sets × reps or time	Sets × reps or time	Sets × reps or time
		Week 1	Week 2	Week 3	Week 4
WU	Quadruped and reach + seated T-spine rot + floor slide + toe-touch progression	10 min	10 min	10 min	10 min
1a	RDL to snatch, SA and SL (DB)	3 × 3 ea	3 × 3 ea	4 × 2 ea	4 × 2 ea
1b	Front rack crossover step-up (KB)	3 × 5 ea	3 × 5 ea	4 × 4 ea	4 × 4 ea
1c	Skater hop, multiple response	3 × 3 ea	3 × 3 ea	4 × 3 ea	4 × 3 ea
2a	Shoulder press to push (DB)	3 × 3 ea	3 × 3 ea	4 × 3 ea	4 × 3 ea
2b	Pull-down from squat position, alternating arm (cable)	3 × 5 ea	3 × 5 ea	4 × 4 ea	4 × 4 ea
2c	Hip toss, alternating, speed (MB)	3 × 5 ea	3 × 5 ea	4 × 4 ea	4 × 4 ea
3a	Glute bridge chest press, SA and SL (DB)	3 × 5 ea	3 × 5 ea	4 × 4 ea	4 × 4 ea
3b	Press and pull, split stance (cable)	3 × 5 ea	3 × 5 ea	4 × 4 ea (speed)	4 × 4 ea (speed)
3c	Hamstring curl, SL (SB)	2 × 3-5 ea	3 × 3-5 ea	3 × 3-5 ea	3 × 3-5 ea
4	Full-body stretch + foam roll	10 min	10 min	10 min	10 min

POSTSEASON PROGRAMMING

DRAZEN GLISIC (HIGH SCHOOL), TRACY ZIMMER (COLLEGE WOMEN), DAVID EUGENIO MANNING (COLLEGE MEN), AND JOEL RAETHER (PROFESSIONAL)

The postseason serves as a vital period for lacrosse athletes to recuperate physically and mentally after the demanding in-season, offering a chance for strength and conditioning professionals to review and strategize for the upcoming off-season. As athletes progress through the postseason, they gradually ramp up training intensity, emphasizing technique and mobility. During this break, programs are tailored to accommodate diverse athlete schedules, acknowledging individuals' training needs as they prepare for the next season. It is crucial to assess athletes' physical and psychological readiness before transitioning into postseason training, ensuring they are fully prepared for the challenges ahead.

GOALS AND OBJECTIVES

The main objectives of the postseason are rest and recovery to prepare the athlete for the next season. The extent that a lacrosse athlete will resistance train depends on a variety of factors.

High School

The postseason is a crucial time for high school lacrosse athletes to recover and rest both physically and mentally after the intense in-season period. It is also a great time for strength and conditioning professionals to evaluate the season and determine any changes needed for the upcoming off-season. Athletes can start with one or two training sessions per week, working with low volumes and intensities at first and then gradually increasing the workload. This allows coaches to focus on specific areas, such as mobility, flexibility, and technique, for individual athletes or groups. At the end of the postseason program, athletes should be prepared to handle the high volume and intensity of the upcoming off-season program.

College

The goals for the college lacrosse postseason are twofold. First, directly after the competitive season, the athletes need to recover from injuries sustained over the course of the competitive season and take a much-needed break from the sport (and even from training, for some individuals). This period may be only a week for some athletes, while others may need longer to rehabilitate and recover. This is often a time when athletes may be training on their own or with a general plan provided by the strength and conditioning professional. The second objective of the postseason is to get the athletes prepared for the off-season, as described in chapter 9. Because the strength and conditioning professional has minimal ramp-up time to get athletes ready for fall practice, the athletes need to start building their foundation over summer break.

Professional

Like the in-season resistance training programming, postseason training for professional lacrosse athletes varies drastically depending on the league or leagues in which they are involved. For those who compete in the Premier Lacrosse League (PLL) only, the postseason period begins in September. Athletes who transition from the PLL, Major Series Lacrosse (MSL), or Western Lacrosse Association (WLA) to a National Lacrosse League (NLL) season typically do not have much of an off-season, because the NLL training camps will be underway in November, which only leaves about 8 to 10 weeks. During this period, most likely will take one to four weeks off, training on their own or using a less specific training plan provided by their strength and conditioning professional.

LENGTH, STRUCTURE, AND ORGANIZATION

The length of the postseason depends on the extent of the end-of-season tournaments, but once those are finished, the postseason can begin. Typically, the initial few weeks are dedicated to engaging in active rest activities, which are not sport-specific and are characterized by low intensity.

High School

The high school lacrosse season typically ends in late May or early June, but many athletes may continue playing lacrosse with a club team through June or July. In Canada, boys and girls may play box lacrosse, which has seasons that finish at the end of August. Regardless of the start date of the postseason program, it is recommended to avoid structured resistance training for the first one to two weeks. Athletes can stay active by participating in other sports, such as volleyball, basketball, baseball, and swimming. After a break to recover mentally and physically, the postseason period can be used to prepare for the upcoming off-season period. Athletes can begin with two training sessions during the third week and gradually increase to four resistance training sessions the week leading into the off-season period. Options include a whole-body circuit training program or a traditional resistance training program.

College

The length of the postseason will be affected by conference and National Collegiate Athletics Association (NCAA) tournament play, but it will extend to include the rest of the athletes' summer break until they get back to campus. During this time, athletes train wherever they can, which could include a local gym, a home gym, or a college athletic weight room, or they could have little to no equipment available.

   In this chapter, there are three types of microcycles that athletes can choose to follow once summer begins.

   1. The first type of microcycle (table 12.3) is regenerative (i.e., for athletes who sustained injuries or still feel beat up from the season).

2. The second type of microcycle (table 12.4) is composed of an **accumulation block**, in which each microcycle builds on the previous one to gradually strengthen the muscles with exercises performed through a full range of motion in all planes.

3. The third type of microcycle (table 12.5) allows athletes to choose their exercises based on the movement pattern prescribed. This will help athletes who may not have certain pieces of equipment available to still train the movement pattern, ultimately keeping them engaged in training without frustration due to not having access to their normally available equipment.

The length of each microcycle can be adjusted to fit any length of postseason. If the program plays far into May, the athletes may only have about 10 to 12 weeks until they report back to campus. If this is the case, one to two weeks can be spent on microcycle 0 and three weeks on each microcycle option from 1 through 3, and then the final two weeks of summer can use microcycle option 4. If the postseason is longer, each microcycle can be performed for three to four weeks before progressing. There is also no expectation that these microcycles be performed immediately back-to-back. Summer break is when these athletes need to have downtime and decompress, so cycles can be broken up and scheduled around vacations and other life events.

Professional

During the professional lacrosse postseason, the emphasis is not focused on lacrosse skills. It is important for strength and conditioning professionals to give athletes freedom to take time off to recover, rest, and get their nervous and musculoskeletal systems back to neutral as well as to reinvigorate them to reengage in normal training activities. This transition period, when athletes are not following a structured plan, may last one to four weeks.

Where allowed based on the upcoming season, it is recommended for athletes to take one to two weeks to recuperate with rest, whether that be active, low-level, nonstructured training or completely passive rest, to allow time to recover from the previous season before transitioning back into training.

When the postseason training begins, the training goal in the early weeks will be to emphasize general physical preparation (GPP), where sets and repetitions are set at low and moderate schemes, respectively (i.e., 3-4 sets × 8-10 repetitions). After the GPP phase is established, the program will progress toward developing strength leading up to the preseason period. These set and repetition schemes are reflected in the sample programs.

RECOMMENDED EXERCISES

For the postseason, a common thread across all levels of competition is the selection of basic versions of exercises that involve primary movements with full range of motion to improve mobility, address any injuries, and promote limb care.

High School

During the high school postseason, exercises should focus on reinforcing the primary movement patterns used in the annual program but with minimal external load. Bodyweight squats, glute bridges, push-ups, inverted rows, and lunges are great exercises with which to start. To improve training technique, more complex movements can be used, such as clean, snatch, and jerk variations using PVC pipes or training bars, as well as exercises that focus on improving joint range of motion and overall mobility, such as overhead squats, hip airplanes, and thoracic rotations. (*Note:* The sample programs do not include all of these exercises.)

College

Similar to microcycle 1 in the off-season, primary exercises in the college postseason are regressed to their more basic variations through full ranges of motion in all movement planes. The regeneration microcycle incorporates upper and lower limb care exercises included in microcycle 2 of the preseason. Plyometrics are reincorporated into microcycles 1 through 3 and are separated into linear and lateral series in days 1 and 2, with the extensive line hops that were a part of the preseason microcycle 1 added to day 3 of these cycles. From a movement-pattern perspective (microcycle option 4), the major patterns of total body explosive, lower body push, lower body pull (or hinge), upper body push, upper body pull, and brace or carry exercises should be completed three times a week.

Professional

With the rigors of a long competition period, the professional postseason period should focus on reintroducing athletes to a more routine schedule of training. This typically will start with three or four days of training intended to establish a training base, where general adaptation will be the focus; addressing any injuries that may have accumulated throughout the previous season will also be emphasized. In addition, a sound integration of mobility work (e.g., hips, shoulder girdle, and thoracic spine) is a common area of focus early in the postseason program.

INTENSITY

It is common to assign low-intensity levels to training and to active-rest types of activities, at least in the initial portion of the postseason. Later, as the athletes recover from the in-season, the intensity can increase as training moves toward the off-season.

High School

For high school lacrosse athletes, the intensity used during the off-season will start low and gradually increase to moderate (50%-75% of the 1-repetition maximum [1RM]). Body weight and lightly resisted exercises should be used at the start of the cycle, followed by a transition to resistance using dumbbells and barbells.

College

After the regeneration microcycle, an extensive-to-intensive progression is used to reintroduce college athletes to organized and more demanding training. For returning athletes who have tested their 1RMs, the intensity can range from 50% to 65% in microcycle 1, 60% to 75% in microcycle 2, and 65% to 80% in microcycle 3. (*Note:* This level of detail is not reflected in the sample programs.) In the movement-pattern microcycle example, repetitions can also vary at lower ranges (2-6) with a repetition-intensity goal that uses a repetitions in reserve (RIR) model (e.g., an RIR of 2 indicates that 2 extra repetitions could have been performed at the selected intensity, but they were not completed; i.e., the athlete stopped 2 repetitions short of a repetition-maximum effort) (1).

The plyometrics performed at the beginning of days 1 and 2 will follow an extensive-to-intensive approach throughout each cycle. Week 1 is used to adapt to the increased hurdle height and will be performed at a low to moderate intensity; in week 2, the hops and jumps should be performed slightly faster with more force being directed into the floor; and in weeks 3 to 4, they should be executed as intensely as possible while maintaining proper technique and posture.

Professional

For professional athletes, intensity during the postseason period will typically range between 50% and 75% of the 1RM or can be assigned based on a rating of perceived exertion (RPE) between 5 and 7 (on a scale of 1-10; see figure 9.1 on page 171). Assigning RPE values is a helpful strategy when 1RMs are unknown or because the strength and conditioning professional does not have daily contact with the athletes to fully guide their training sessions.

VOLUME

Similar to intensity assignments, volume is low at the beginning of the postseason, but then it is increased as athletes gradually return to more demanding training.

High School

During the off-season, high school lacrosse athletes should aim for 6 to 15 repetitions per set while keeping sets to 2 to 4.

College

Volume starts low for the college lacrosse athletes who choose the regeneration microcycle first. In this cycle, exercises are restricted to 1-3 sets each with repetitions in the range of 10 to 15 for bilateral exercises and 5 to 8 for unilateral exercises.

Microcycle 1 has the highest volume in regard to the primary exercises, with the 3 work sets of each exercise performed in a traditional pyramid protocol of 15, 12, and 10 repetitions per set. As the primary exercises are intensified over the cycle, the repetitions are reduced to 12, 10, and 8 and then to 10, 8, and 6 for microcycles 2 and 3, respectively.

Plyometric volume on day 3 exercises will be increased progressively throughout the cycles to prepare the athletes for the high numbers of floor contacts that they will experience when practice begins in the fall.

Using the exercise selection microcycle allows for variable volume. Due to the nature of the postseason, when recovery is a major focus at the risk of causing detraining, athletes have the ability to select their volume based on how they are feeling. This methodology is used more often with athletes who have been participating in a resistance training program for a couple of years and understand what their body may need at this time.

Professional

Throughout the postseason period for professional lacrosse athletes, the volume will be moderate and will gradually increase in an attempt to reacclimatize athletes into the density and frequency of training that is typically lost throughout the competitive season.

CONCLUSION

The postseason should act as a time for lacrosse athletes to recover and recharge both physically and mentally following the intense in-season. It is also an opportune time for strength and conditioning professionals to assess their programming for the year and plan for the upcoming off-season. As the postseason progresses, lacrosse athletes need to gradually begin increasing their workload while having a stronger focus on technique and mobility.

The postseason is a time for athletes to relax and heal after a long competitive season and to begin the process of reintensifying training. Programs are adaptable to the vastly different schedules athletes will have during this break, and some athletes may want or need to get more training in during this time than others. This disparity in training should be considered and evaluated during week 1 of the off-season when athletes report back for team training.

The postseason period is a critical time for getting athletes to reset and for reintroducing them into training that will set the stage for preseason training. It is important to evaluate where athletes are both physically and psychologically (readiness to train) before instituting the postseason training program. Because of the length of time that athletes spend during the in-season period, it is paramount that rest, recovery, and readiness are established before off-season training begins so that athletes can fully prepare for the rigors of another season.

Warm-Ups: Dynamic and Mobility Series

DYNAMIC WARM-UP SERIES

- Jog down and backpedal back (10 yards or meters each)
- Side shuffle down and side shuffle back (10 yards or meters each)
- Walking knee hugs down and lateral lunge back (10 yards or meters each)
- Walking quad pull down and inchworm jog back (10 yards or meters each)
- Walking leg cradle down and reverse lunge back (10 yards or meters each)
- A-skip forward down and A-skip backward back (10 yards or meters each)
- Lateral A-skip right down and lateral A-skip left back (10 yards or meters each)
- Power skip (2 × 20 yards or meters)
- Straight-leg run (2 × 20 yards or meters)

MOBILITY SERIES

- 90/90 hold + back heel lift + back leg lift (5 × 10 seconds each)
- Hip series (× as needed)
- Supine knee hug with ankle circle (× 3 each way)
- Floor slide with breathing (× 10)
- Cat–cow (× 10 each)
- Side-lying floor sweep (× 10 each)
- Quadruped and reach (× 10 each)

Interpreting the Sample Program Tables

+ = *Do the two exercises back-to-back*

Abd = Abduction

Add = Adduction

Alt = Alternated

AMAP = As many as possible (but quality repetitions)

BB = Barbell

BW = Body weight

Bwd = Backward

CMJ = Countermovement jump

Diag = Diagonal

DB = Dumbbell

DL = Double leg

DWU = Dynamic warm-up

Ea = Each side (arm or leg), direction, or exercise

E:I:C = Eccentric:Isometric:Concentric

Ext = External

Fwd = Forward

GH = Glue-ham

GHR = Glute-ham raise

Goblet = Holding DB or KB with both hands below the chin and elbows pointed out to the side in the midline of the body

ISO = Isometric

KB = Kettlebell

Lat = Lateral

LM = Landmine

MB = Medicine ball

OH = Overhead

Order = Performing one set of each exercise (1a, 1b, 1c) in the group one after the other. After the first set is completed, go back to the first exercise in the group and do the second set of each exercise. If certain exercises call for fewer sets than others in the group, perform those sets on the back end of the grouping. For example, if exercise 1a calls for 4 sets and exercise 1b calls for 3 sets, perform exercise 1b during sets 2 through 4 of exercises 1a.

RDL = Romanian deadlift

RFE = Rear foot elevated

RM = Repetition maximum

Rot = Rotation

RPE = Rating of perceived exertion (intensity based on level of perceived difficulty)

SA = Single arm

SB = Stability ball

(continued)

Interpreting the Sample Program Tables *(continued)*

Scap = Scapula

SL = Single leg

TKE = Terminal knee extension

T-spine = Thoracic spine

Tempo = The time, in seconds, for each phase or portion of the exercise, written as "eccentric phase: top (or bottom) position: concentric phase" (King, I., How to write strength training programs. In *Speed of Movement*, p. 123, 1998.). For example, a tempo of "1:5:1" for the back squat means 1 second to lower, 5 seconds held at the bottom position, and 1 second to stand back up.

WU = Warm-up

yd = yard (*Note*: distance is approximate, so meters can be used instead of yards)

SAMPLE PROGRAMS

Tables 12.1 and 12.2 provide an example of a postseason program for high school lacrosse athletes, tables 12.3 through 12.5 provide examples for college women and men, and table 12.6 provides an example for professional athletes.

Table 12.1 High School Lacrosse: Attackers: Postseason Mesocycle, Whole-Body Circuit (Weeks 1-4)

Order	Exercise	Sets* × reps or time	Sets* × reps or time	Sets* × reps or time	Sets* × reps or time
		Week 1	Week 2	Week 3	Week 4
1	Goblet squat (DB or BW)	3 × 10	3 × 10	4 × 10	4 × 10
2	Push-up	3 × 10	3 × 10	4 × 10	4 × 10
3	Glute bridge (DB or BW)	3 × 10	3 × 10	4 × 10	4 × 10
4	Inverted row	3 × 10	3 × 10	4 × 10	4 × 10
5	Front plank	3 × 30 s	3 × 30 s	4 × 30 s	4 × 30 s
6	Reverse lunge (DB or BW)	3 × 10 ea	3 × 10 ea	4 × 10 ea	4 × 10 ea
7	Biceps curl	3 × 10	3 × 10	4 × 10	4 × 10
8	Triceps extension (cable)	3 × 10	3 × 10	4 × 10	4 × 10
9	Side plank	3 × 20 s	3 × 20 s	4 × 20 s	4 × 20 s

*Perform 1 set of each exercise (moving down the list of exercises) and repeat 2 more circuits for a total of 3 sets (circuits).

Table 12.2 High School Lacrosse: Attackers: Postseason Mesocycle, Whole-Body Resistance Training (Weeks 1-4)

Order	Exercise	Sets × reps (% 1RM) or time	Sets × reps (% 1RM) or time	Sets × reps (% 1RM) or time	Sets × reps (% 1RM) or time
		Week 1	Week 2	Week 3	Week 4
1a	Goblet squat (DB)	3 × 10 (70%)	3 × 10 (70%)	3 × 12 (65%)	3 × 12 (65%)
1b	Bench press (DB)	3 × 10 (70%)	3 × 10 (70%)	3 × 12 (65%)	3 × 12 (65%)
2a	RDL (DB)	3 × 10 (70%)	3 × 10 (70%)	3 × 12 (65%)	3 × 12 (65%)

Order	Exercise	Sets × reps (% 1RM) or time	Sets × reps (% 1RM) or time	Sets × reps (% 1RM) or time	Sets × reps (% 1RM) or time
		Week 1	**Week 2**	**Week 3**	**Week 4**
2b	Inverted row	3 × 10 (70%)	3 × 10 (70%)	3 × 12 (65%)	3 × 12 (65%)
3a	Reverse lunge	3 × 10 (70%)	3 × 10 (70%)	3 × 12 (65%)	3 × 12 (65%)
3b	Hamstring curl (SB)	3 × 12	3 × 12	3 × 15	3 × 15
4a	Half-kneeling shoulder press (DB)	3 × 10 ea (70%)	3 × 10 ea (70%)	3 × 10 ea (75%)	3 × 10 ea (75%)
4b	Face pull	3 × 15 ea	3 × 15 ea	3 × 15 ea	3 × 15 ea
5a	Front plank	2 × 45 s	2 × 45 s	2 × 60 s	2 × 60 s
5b	Side plank	2 × 20 s ea	2 × 20 s ea	2 × 25 s ea	2 × 25 s ea
5c	Prone back extension hold	2 × 45 s	2 × 45 s	2 × 60 s	2 × 60 s

Table 12.3   College Lacrosse: Postseason, Microcycle 0 (Regeneration)

Day 1

Order	Exercise	Sets × reps or time
1a	Bench press (DB)	1-3 × 10-15
1b	Face pull	1-3 × 10-15
1c	Supine heel walk-out	1-3 × 3-5 down and back
1d	RKC plank	1-3 × 30 s
2a	Lat pulldown	1-3 × 10-15
2b	Standing Cuban press (DB)	1-3 × 8-12
2c	BW 5-way lunge (fwd, diag, lat, rot, curtsy)	1-3 × 2-4 ea
2d	Side plank	1-3 × 15 s
3	Banded I's, Y's, T's, W's	1 × 5-8 ea
4	TKE	1 × 10-15 ea
5	4-way seated neck contraction	1 × 5-8 ea
6	Peterson step-down	1 × 5-8 ea
7	4-way ankle series	1 × 5-8 ea
8	Bar shrug	1 × 10-15

Day 2

Order	Exercise	Sets × reps
1a	Incline bench press (DB)	1-3 × 10-15
1b	Incline row (DB)	1-3 × 10-15
1c	Hip bridge, DL, with upper back elevated on bench	1-3 × 10-15
1d	Half-kneeling chop	1-3 × 8-12 ea
2a	Biceps curl with full twist (DB)	1-3 × 10-15
2b	Triceps pushdown	1-3 × 10-15
2c	Goblet squat	1-3 × 10-15
2d	Half-kneeling lift	1-3 × 8-12 ea
3	Banded I's, Y's, T's, W's	1 × 5-8 ea
4	TKE	1 × 10-15 ea

(continued)

Table 12.3 College Lacrosse: Postseason, Microcycle 0 (Regeneration) *(continued)*

Day 2 *(continued)*

Order	Exercise	Sets × reps
5	4-way seated neck contraction	1 × 5-8 ea
6	Peterson step-down	1 × 5-8 ea
7	4-way ankle series	1 × 5-8 ea
8	Bar shrug	1 × 10-15

Table 12.4 College Lacrosse: Postseason, Microcycle Options 1 to 3

Day 1

Order	Exercise	Microcycle 1 sets × reps or time	Microcycle 2 sets × reps or time	Microcycle 3 sets × reps or time
WU	DWU series	× 1	× 1	× 1
1	Linear hurdle hop	3 × 6 ea with 10-in. (25 cm) hurdle	3 × 6 ea with 12-in. (31 cm) hurdle	3 × 6 ea with 14-16-in. (36-41 cm) hurdle
2	Linear hurdle jump	3 × 6 with 16-in. (41 cm) hurdle	3 × 6 with 20-in. (51 cm) hurdle	3 × 6 with 24-in. (61 cm) hurdle
WU	BB complex: RDL + bent-over row + front squat + shoulder press	2 × 5 ea	2 × 5 ea	2 × 5 ea
3a	Swing (KB)	3 × 8	3 × 5	3 × 5/4/3
3b	Slam (MB)	3 × 10	3 × 8	3 × 6
4a	Flat bench press with full twist (DB)	3 × 15/12/10	3 × 12/10/8	3 × 10/8/6
4b	Bent-over row, SA (DB)	3 × 15/12/10 ea	3 × 12/10/8 ea	3 × 10/8/6 ea
4c	RDL with 2 DBs	3 × 15/12/10	3 × 12/10/8	3 × 10/8/6
4d	Half-kneeling chop	3 × 8 ea	3 × 10 ea	3 × 12 ea
5a	Hammer curl (DB)	3 × 15/12/10	3 × 12/10/8	3 × 10/8/6
5b	Front and side shoulder raise	3 × 15/12/10 ea	3 × 12/10/8 ea	3 × 10/8/6 ea
5c	Lunge complex	3-way lunge: 3 × 2 ea	4-way lunge: 3 × 2 ea	5-way lunge: 3 × 2 ea
5d	Front plank	3 × 30 s	3 × 45 s	3 × 1 min

Day 2

Order	Exercise	Microcycle 1 sets × reps	Microcycle 2 sets × reps	Microcycle 3 sets × reps
WU	DWU series	× 1	× 1	× 1
1	Lat hurdle hop	3 × 6 ea with 10-in. (25 cm) hurdle	3 × 6 ea with 12-in. (31 cm) hurdle	3 × 6 ea with 14-16-in. (36-41 cm) hurdle
2	Lat hurdle jump	3 × 3 ea with 16-in. (41 cm) hurdle	3 × 3 ea with 20-in. (51 cm) hurdle	3 × 3 ea with 24-in. (61 cm) hurdle
WU	BB complex: RDL + bent-over row + front squat + shoulder press	2 × 5 ea	2 × 5 ea	2 × 5 ea

Order	Exercise	Microcycle 1 sets × reps	Microcycle 2 sets × reps	Microcycle 3 sets × reps
3a	Squat jump (DB)	3 × 6	3 × 4	3 × 5/4/3
3b	Supine chest toss (MB)	3 × 10	3 × 8	3 × 6
4a	Incline bench press (DB)	3 × 15/12/10	3 × 12/10/8	3 × 10/8/6
4b	Incline row (DB)	3 × 15/12/10	3 × 12/10/8	3 × 10/8/6
4c	Lat squat	3 × 8 ea	3 × 6 ea	3 × 5 ea
4d	Half-kneeling lift	3 × 8 ea	3 × 10 ea	3 × 12 ea
5a	Triceps extension	3 × 15/12/10	3 × 12/10/8	3 × 10/8/6
5b	Curl with full twist (DB)	3 × 15/12/10	3 × 12/10/8	3 × 10/8/6
5c	Shrug (DB)	3 × 15/12/10	3 × 12/10/8	3 × 10/8/6
5d	Push-up position alt hip tap	3 × 8 ea	3 × 10 ea	3 × 12 ea

Day 3

Order	Exercise	Microcycle 1 sets × reps, time, or distance	Microcycle 2 sets × reps, time, or distance	Microcycle 3 sets × reps, time, or distance
WU	DWU series	× 1	× 1	× 1
1	Line hop fwd and bwd	3 × 10 s ea	4 × 10 s ea	5 × 10 s ea
2	Line hop side to side	3 × 10 s ea	4 × 10 s ea	5 × 10 s ea
WU	BB complex: RDL + bent-over row + front squat + shoulder press	2 × 5 ea	2 × 5 ea	2 × 5 ea
3a	Seated Arnold press	3 × 15/12/10	3 × 12/10/8	3 × 10/8/6
3b	Lat pulldown	3 × 15/12/10	3 × 12/10/8	3 × 10/8/6
3c	Goblet squat	3 × 15/12/10	3 × 12/10/8	3 × 10/8/6
3d	Weighted crunch	3 × 15/12/10	3 × 12/10/8	3 × 10/8/6
4a	Close-grip bench press	3 × 15/12/10	3 × 12/10/8	3 × 10/8/6
4b	Reverse grip curl (BB)	3 × 15/12/10	3 × 12/10/8	3 × 10/8/6
4c	Hamstring curl, DL	3 × 8	3 × 10	3 × 12
4d	Farmer's carry variation	2 DB 3 × 20 yd	1 DB 3 × 20 yd ea	1 KB overhead 3 × 20 yd ea
5	Banded I's, Y's, T's, W's	1 × 5-8 ea	1 × 5-8 ea	1 × 5-8 ea
6	TKE	1 × 10-15 ea	1 × 10-15 ea	1 × 10-15 ea
7	4-way seated neck contraction	1 × 5-8 ea	1 × 5-8 ea	1 × 5-8 ea
8	Peterson step-down	1 × 5-8 ea	1 × 5-8 ea	1 × 5-8 ea
9	4-way ankle series	1 × 5-8 ea	1 × 5-8 ea	1 × 5-8 ea
10	Bar shrug	1 × 10-15	1 × 10-15	1 × 10-15

Table 12.5 College Lacrosse: Postseason, Microcycle Option 4

Days 1-3: Total-Body Focus

Order	Exercise type or movement pattern	Tempo (E:I:C)	Intensity	Sets	Reps or distance	Rest
1	WU	—	—	1-2	2-3	<1 min
2	Total-body explosive	—	—	4-6	3-5	2 min
3	Lower body push–pull (or hinge)	1:0:1	—	3-6	2-6	2 min
4	Upper body push–pull	1:0:1	—	3-6	2-6	2 min
5	Brace or carry	—	—	2-5	2-5 / 15-30 yd	2 min

Table 12.6 Professional Lacrosse: Postseason, Mesocycle 1

Day 1

Order	Exercise	Sets × reps, time, or distance	Sets × reps, time, or distance	Sets × reps, time, or distance
		Week 1	Week 2	Week 3
WU	Foam roll + hip series + 4-way ankle series + hip kickstand + 90/90 hip rocker	15 min	15 min	15 min
WU	Mini-band hip series (lat, fwd, 45-degree split stance)	5 yd ea	5 yd ea	5 yd ea
1a	Goblet squat	2 × 10 RPE 5	2 × 12 RPE 5	2 × 10-12 RPE 6
1b	Bench press (DB)	2 × 10 RPE 5	2 × 12 RPE 5	2 × 10-12 RPE 6
1c	Supine deadbug	2 × 5 ea	2 × 5 ea	2 × 6 ea
2a	Glute bridge march	2 × 8 ea	2 × 8 ea	2 × 10 ea
2b	Side plank hold	2 × 10 s ea	2 × 10 s ea	2 × 15 s ea
2c	Pull-through (sandbag)	2 × 5 ea	2 × 5 ea	2 × 6 ea
3a	Shoulder press (DB)	2 × 10 RPE 5	2 × 10 RPE 5	2 × 10-12 RPE 6
3b	Bent-over row (DB)	2 × 10 RPE 5	2 × 12 RPE 5	2 × 10-12 RPE 6
4a	Biceps curl	2 × 12	2 × 12	2 × 15
4b	Triceps extension	2 × 12	2 × 12	2 × 15
5	Plank hold	2 × 20 s	2 × 20 s	2 × 30 s
6	Recovery bike ride	10 min	12 min	15 min
7	Full-body stretch	10 min	10 min	10 min

Day 2

Order	Exercise	Sets × reps, time, or distance	Sets × reps, time, or distance	Sets × reps, time, or distance
		Week 1	Week 2	Week 3
WU	Wall slide + band TKE × 10 ea + band I's, Y's, T's, W's × 10 ea + side-lying floor sweep + T-spine rot	10 min	10 min	10 min
1a	Suspension strap row	2 × 10 RPE 6	2 × 10 RPE 6	2 × 12 RPE 7
1b	Suspension strap face pull	2 × 10 RPE 6	2 × 10 RPE 6	2 × 12 RPE 7
1c	Supine heel walk-out	2 × 5	2 × 5	2 × 5
2a	ISO hold lunge	2 × 10 s ea	2 × 10 s ea	2 × 10 s ea
2b	Half-kneeling cable chop	2 × 8 ea	2 × 8 ea	2 × 10 ea
2c	Half-kneeling cable lift	2 × 8 ea	2 × 8 ea	2 × 10 ea
3a	Incline bench press (DB)	2 × 10	2 × 10	2 × 12
3b	3-way shoulder series	2 × 5 ea	2 × 5 ea	2 × 5 ea
3c	Inverted row (high bar position)	2 × 10 RPE 6	2 × 10 RPE 6	2 × 12 RPE 7
4	Bear crawl series (contralateral, ipsilateral, lat)	1 × 5 yd ea	1 × 5 yd ea	2 × 5 yd ea
5	Supine hollow hold	2 × 10 s	2 × 10 s	2 × 10 s
6	Side plank	2 × 10 s ea	2 × 10 s ea	2 × 10 s ea
7	Foam roll	10 min	10 min	10 min

Day 3

Order	Exercise	Time	Time	Time
		Week 1	Week 2	Week 3
WU	Hip series + cat–cow + seated T-spine rot + quadruped and roll + toe-touch progression	10 min	10 min	10 min
WU	DWU series	10 min	10 min	10 min
1a	Push-up	15 s	20 s	30 s
1b	BW lat lunge	15 s	20 s	30 s
1c	Line hop fwd and bwd	15 s	20 s	30 s
1d	Glute bridge march	15 s	20 s	30 s
1e	Band pull apart	15 s	20 s	30 s
1f	Copenhagen plank	15 s	20 s	30 s
1g	Band biceps curl	15 s	20 s	30 s
1h	Band triceps extension	15 s	20 s	30 s
1i	Rollout (SB)	15 s	20 s	30 s
1j	Half-kneeling Pallof hold	15 s	20 s	30 s
2a	Recovery bike ride	10 min	12 min	15 min
2b	Foam roll	10 min	10 min	10 min

REFERENCES

Introduction

1. World Lacrosse. History. https://worldlacrosse.sport/the-game/origin-history. Accessed March 10, 2024.

Chapter 1

1. Alvehus, M, Boman, N, Söderlund, K, Svensson, MB, and Burén J. Metabolic adaptations in skeletal muscle, adipose tissue, and whole-body oxidative capacity in response to resistance training. *Eur J Appl Physiol* 114:1463-1471, 2014.

2. Angeli, A, Minetto, M, Dovio, A, and Paccotti, P. The overtraining syndrome in athletes: a stress-related disorder. *J Endocrinol Invest* 27:603-612, 2004.

3. Barnes, KR, and Kilding, AE. Running economy: measurement, norms, and determining factors. *Sports Med Open*, 2015. [e-pub ahead of print].

4. Burgomaster, KA, Heigenhauser, GJF, and Gibala MJ. Effect of short-term sprint interval training on human skeletal muscle carbohydrate metabolism during exercise and time-trial performance. *J Appl Physiol* 100:2041-2047, 2006.

5. Carroll, TJ, Riek, S, and Carson, RG. Neural adaptations to resistance training: implications for movement control. *Sports Med* 31:829-840, 2001.

6. Chesley, A, MacDougall, JD, Tarnopolsky, MA, Atkinson, SA, and Smith, K. Changes in human muscle protein synthesis after resistance exercise. *J Appl Physiol (1985)* 73:1383-1388, 1992.

7. Fahey, TD, Rolph, R, Moungmee, P, Nagel, J, and Mortara, S. Serum testosterone, body composition, and strength of young adults. *Med Sci Sports Exerc* 8:31-34, 1976.

8. Ghosh, AK. Anaerobic threshold: its concept and role in endurance sport. *Malays J Med Sci* 11:24-36, 2004.

9. Gibala, MJ, Little, JP, Van Essen, M, Wilkin, GP, Burgomaster, KA, Safdar, A, Raha, S, and Tarnopolsky, MA. Short-term sprint interval versus traditional endurance training: similar initial adaptations in human skeletal muscle and exercise performance. *J Physiol* 575:901-911, 2006.

10. Gilchrist, J, Mandelbaum, BR, Melancon, H, Ryan, GW, Silvers, HJ, Griffin, LY, Watanabe, DS, Dick, RW, and Dvorak, J. A randomized controlled trial to prevent noncontact anterior cruciate ligament injury in female collegiate soccer players. *Am J Sports Med* 36:1476-1483, 2008.

11. Haff, GG. Periodization. In *Essentials of Strength Training and Conditioning*. 4th ed. Haff, GG, and Triplett, NT, eds. Champaign, IL: Human Kinetics, 583-604, 2016.

12. Handelsman, DJ, Hirschberg, AL, and Bermon, S. Circulating testosterone as the hormonal basis of sex differences in athletic performance. *Endocr Rev* 39:803-829, 2018.

13. Haugen, T, Seiler, S, Sandbakk, Ø, and Tønnessen, E. The training and development of elite sprint performance: an integration of scientific and best practice literature. *Sports Med Open* 5(1):44, 2019.

14. Hewett, TE. Neuromuscular and hormonal factors associated with knee injuries in female athletes: strategies for intervention. *Sports Med* 29:313-327, 2000.

15. Hunter, GR, Bamman, MM, Larson-Meyer, DE, Joanisse, DR, McCarthy, JP, Blaudeau, TE, and Newcomer, BR. Inverse relationship between exercise economy and oxidative capacity in muscle. *Eur J Appl Physiol* 94:558-568, 2005.

16. Keiner, M, Sander, A, Wirth, K, and Schmidtbleicher, D. Long-term strength training effects on change-of-direction sprint performance. *J Strength Cond Res* 28:223-231, 2014.

17. Koopman, R, Manders, RJ, Zorenc, AH, Hul, GB, Kuipers, H, Keizer, HA, and van Loon, LJ. A single session of resistance exercise enhances insulin sensitivity for at least 24 h in healthy men. *Eur J Appl Physiol* 94:180-187, 2005.

18. Kraemer, WJ, Fry, AC, Frykman, PN, Conroy, B, and Hoffman, J. Resistance training and youth. *Pediatr Exerc Sci* 1:336-350, 1989.

19. Kraemer, WJ, Fry, AC, Warren BJ, Stone, MH, Fleck, SJ, Kearney, JT, Conroy, BP, Maresh, CM, Weseman, CA, Triplett, NT, and Gordon, SE. Acute hormonal responses in elite junior weightlifters. *Int J Sports Med* 13:103-109, 1992.

20. Kuipers, H, and Keizer, HA. Overtraining in elite athletes: review and directions for the future. *Sports Med* 6:79-92, 1988.

21. McBride, JM. Biomechanics of resistance exercise. In *Essentials of Strength Training and Conditioning.* 4th ed. Haff, GG, and Triplett, NT, eds. Champaign, IL: Human Kinetics, 19-42, 2016.

22. McGuigan, MR, Egan, AD, and Foster, C. Salivary cortisol responses and perceived exertion during high intensity and low intensity bouts of resistance exercise. *J Sports Sci Med* 3:8-15, 2004.

23. Mendiguchia, J, Ford, KR, Quatman, CE, Alentorn-Geli, E, and Hewett, TE. Sex differences in proximal control of the knee joint. *Sports Med* 41:541-557, 2011.

24. Nguyen, A-D, Boling, MC, Levine, B, and Shultz, SJ. Relationships between lower extremity alignment and the quadriceps angle. *Clin J Sport Med* 19:201-206, 2009.

25. Powers, S, and Howley, E. Common measurements in exercise physiology. In Powers, S, and Howley, E, eds. *Exercise Physiology: Theory and Application to Fitness and Performance.* 10th ed. New York, NY: McGraw Hill, 16-37, 2018.

26. Pullinen, T, Mero, A, MacDonald, E, Pakarinen, A, and Komi, PV. Plasma catecholamine and serum testosterone responses to four units of resistance exercise in young and adult male athletes. *Eur J Appl Physiol Occup Physiol* 77(5):413-420, 1998.

27. Sonchan, W, Moungmee, P, and Sootmongkol, A. The effects of a circuit training program on muscle strength agility anaerobic performance and cardiovascular endurance. *Int J Sport Health Sci* 11:176-179, 2017.

28. Suchomel, TJ, Nimphius, S, and Stone, MH. The importance of muscular strength in athletic performance. *Sports Med* 46:1419-1449, 2016.

29. Tesch, PA. Skeletal muscle adaptations consequent to long-term heavy resistance exercise. *Med Sci Sports Exerc* 20:S132-S134, 1988.

30. Waldén, M, Hägglund, M, Werner, J, and Ekstrand, J. The epidemiology of anterior cruciate ligament injury in football (soccer): a review of the literature from a gender-related perspective. *Knee Surg Sports Traumatol Arthrosc* 19(1):3-10, 2011.

31. Wilk, KE, Voight, ML, Keirns, MA, Gambetta, V, Andrews, JR, and Dillman, C. Stretch-shortening drills for the upper extremities: theory and clinical application. *J Orthop Sports Phys Ther* 17:225-239, 1993.

Chapter 2

1. Akiyama, K, Sasaki, T, and Masahiro, M. Elite male lacrosse players' match activity profile. *J Sports Sci Med* 18:290-294, 2019.

2. Bynum, L, Snarr, RL, Myers, BJ, and Bunn, JA. Assessment of relationships between external load metrics and game performance in women's lacrosse. *Int J Exerc Sci* 15:488-497, 2022.

3. Calder, AR, Duthie, GM, Johnston, RD, and Engle, HD. Physical demands of female collegiate lacrosse competition: whole-match and peak periods analysis. *Sport Sci Hlth* 17:103-109, 2021.

4. Collins, SM, Silberlicht, M, Perzinski, C, Smith, SP, and Davidson, PW. The relationship between body composition and preseason performance tests of collegiate male lacrosse players. *J Strength Cond Res* 28:2673-2679, 2014.

5. Devine, NF, Hegedus, EJ, Nguyen, A, Ford, KR, and Taylor, JB. External match load in women's collegiate lacrosse. *J Strength Cond Res* 36:503-507, 2022.

6. Dominey, S. *The Influence of Pocket Characteristics on Shot Performance During a Men's Overhand Lacrosse Shot.* Doctoral dissertation. University of Toronto, 2022.

7. Enemark-Miller, EA, Seegmiller, JG, and Rana, SR. Physiological profile of women's lacrosse players. *J Strength Cond Res* 23:39-43, 2009.

8. Fields, JB, Jones, MT, Feit, MK, and Jagim, AR. Athlete external loads across a collegiate men's lacrosse season. *J Strength Cond Res* 37:e455-e461, 2023.

9. Fortney, C, Kilian, J, Schaefer, A, and Glauser, J. Association of fitness testing, external load metrics, and hard endpoints in NCAA Division I women's lacrosse. *J Strength Cond Res* 35:e364, 2021.

10. Gutowski, AE, and Rosene, JM. Preseason performance testing battery for men's lacrosse. *Strength Cond J* 33:16-22, 2011.

11. Hamlet, MD, Frick, MD, and Bunn, JA. High-speed running density in collegiate women's lacrosse. *Res Sports Med* 29:386-394, 2021.

12. Hirao, T, and Masaki, H. The effects of computer-based and motor-imagery training on scoring ability in lacrosse. *Front Psych* 11:1-12, 2020.

13. Hoffman, JR, Ratamess, NA, Neese, KL, Ross, RE, Kang, J, Magrelli, JF, and Faigenbaum, AD. Physical performance characteristics in National Collegiate Athletic Association Division III champion female lacrosse athletes. *J Strength Cond Res* 23:1524-1529, 2009.

14. Howley, T. *Complete Conditioning for Lacrosse*. Champaign, IL: Human Kinetics, 2016.

15. Kaley, J, and Donovan, R. *Lacrosse Essentials*. Champaign, IL: Human Kinetics, 13-27, 2015.

16. Kilian, J, Cochrane-Snyman, K, and Miyashita, T. Comparison of in-game external load metrics among positions and between halves for Division I collegiate women's lacrosse athletes. *Int J Strength Cond* 2:1-8, 2022.

17. Klemz, BL. Lacrosse: Biomechanics, Injuries, Prevention and Rehabilitation (Order No. 3619649). Available from ProQuest Central; ProQuest Dissertations & Theses Global, (1535735428). Florida Gulf Coast University, 2014.

18. Macaulay, CA, Katz, L, Stergiou, P, Stefanyshyn, D, and Tomaghelli, L. Kinematic and kinetic analysis of overhand, side-arm and underhand lacrosse shot techniques. *J Sports Sci* 35:2350-2356, 2017.

19. Marsh, DW, Richard, LA, Verre, AB, and Myers, J. Relationships among balance, visual search, and lacrosse-shot accuracy. *J Strength Cond Res* 24:1507-1514, 2010.

20. Mcclain, M. *Physiological and Fitness Profile of Female Lacrosse Athletes*. Dissertation. Durham University, 2022.

21. Mercer, JA, and Nielson, JH. Description of phases and discrete events of the lacrosse shot. *Sport J* 16:1, 2013.

22. Millard, BM, and Mercer, JA. Lower extremity muscle activity during a women's overhand lacrosse shot. *J Hum Kinet* 41:15-22, 2014.

23. Plummer, HA, and Oliver, GD. Quantitative analysis of the kinematics of the overhand lacrosse shot in youth. *Int Biomech* 2:29-35, 2015.

24. Polley, CS, Cormack, SJ, Gabbett, TJ, and Polglaze, T. Activity profile of high-level Australian lacrosse players. *J Strength Cond Res* 29:126-136, 2015.

25. Rooney, RC, Bottoni, CR, and Snider, D. The power behind the time and room shot. *Am J Biomed Sci Res* 2:152-154, 2019.

26. Rosenberg, RC, Myers, BJ, and Bunn, JA. Sprint and distance zone analysis by position of Division I women's lacrosse. *JSHP* 9:51-57, 2021.

27. Sell, KM, Prendergast, JM, Ghigiarelli, JJ, Gonzalez, AM, Biscardi, LM, Jajtner, AR, and Rothstein, AS. Comparison of physical fitness parameters for starters vs. non-starters in an NCAA Division I men's lacrosse team. *J Strength Cond Res* 32:3160-3168, 2018.

28. Talpey, SW, Axtell, R, Gardner, E, and James, L. Changes in lower body muscular performance following a season of NCAA Division I men's lacrosse. *Sports* 7:1-12, 2019.

29. Van Dyke, M. JOP matrix—application to lacrosse. *NSCA Coach* 4:28, January 16, 2017.

30. Vescovi, JD, Brown, TD, and Murray, TM. Descriptive characteristics of NCAA Division I women lacrosse players. *J Sci Med Sport* 10:334-340, 2007.

31. Vincent, HK, Chen, C, Zdziarski, LA, Montes, J, and Vincent, KR. Shooting motion in high school, collegiate, and professional men's lacrosse players. *Sports Biomech* 14:448-458, 2015.

32. Wasser, JG, Chen, C, and Vincent, HK. Kinematics of shooting in high school and collegiate lacrosse players with and without low back pain. *Ortho J Sports Med* 4:2325967116657535, 2016.

33. Zabriskie, HA, Dobrosielski, DA, Leppert, KM, Droege, AJ, Knuth, ND, and Lisman, PJ. Positional analysis of body composition using dual-energy X-ray absorptiometry in National Collegiate Athletic Association Division I football and men's lacrosse. *J Strength Cond Res* 36:1699-1707, 2022.

Chapter 3

1. Baker, DG, and Newton, RU. An analysis of the ratio and relationship between upper body pressing and pulling strength. *J Strength Cond Res* 18:594-598, 1982.

2. Bishop, C, Turner, A, Jordan, M, Harry, J, Loturco, I, Lake, J, and Comfort, P. A framework to guide practitioners for selecting metrics during the countermovement and drop jump tests. *Strength Cond J* 44:95-103, 2022.

3. Buckthorpe, M, Morris, J, and Folland, JP. Validity of vertical jump measurement devices. *J Sports Sci* 30:63-69, 2012.

4. Cronin, J, Lawton, T, Harris, N, Kilding, A, and McMaster, DT. A brief review of handgrip strength and sport performance. *J Strength Cond Res* 31:3187-3217, 2017.

5. Cronin, JB, and Hansen, KT. Strength and power predictors of sports speed. *J Strength Cond Res* 2005 19:349-357, 2005.

6. González-Badillo, JJ, and Sánchez-Medina, L. Movement velocity as a measure of loading intensity in resistance training. *Int J Sports Med* 23:347-52, 2010.

7. Izquierdo, M, González-Badillo, JJ, Häkkinen, K, Ibanez, J, Kraemer, WJ, Altadill, A, Eslava, J, and Gorostiaga, E. Effect of loading on unintentional lifting velocity declines during single sets of repetitions to failure during upper and lower extremity muscle actions. *Int J Sports Med* 27:718-24, 2006.

8. Kraemer, WJ, and Fleck, SJ. *Optimizing Strength Training: Designing Nonlinear Periodization Workouts.* Champaign, IL: Human Kinetics, 110, 2007.

9. Lake, J. The "ODS system": a guide to selecting your force-time metrics. Hawkin Dynamics. March 16, 2020. www.hawkindynamics.com/blog/select-your-force-time-metrics-with-this-simple-system.

10. Lockie, RG, Birmingham-Babauta, SA, Stokes, JJ, Liu, TM, Risso, FG, Lazar, A, Giuliano, DV, Orjalo, AJ, Moreno, MR, Stage, AA, and Davis, DL. An analysis of collegiate club-sport female lacrosse players: sport-specific field test performance and the influence of lacrosse stick carrying. *Int J Exerc Sci* 11:269-280, 2018.

11. Martin, G, and Kraemer, WJ. *300 Conditioning.* (nda).

12. Mirifar, A, Luan, M, and Ehrlenspiel, F. Effects of unilateral dynamic handgrip on reaction time and error rate. *Cognitive Processing* 23:169-178, 2022.

13. Newton, RU, and Kraemer, WJ. Developing explosive muscular power: implications for a mixed methods training strategy. *Strength Cond J* 16:20-31, 1994.

14. Poliquin, C, and McDermott, A. Applied strongman training for sport: theory and technical. Nevada City, CA: Ironmind Enterprises, Inc., 2005.

15. Prue, P, McGuigan, MR, and Newton, RU. Influence of strength on magnitude and mechanisms of adaptation to power training. *Med Sci Sports Exerc* 42:1566-1581, 2010.

16. Sayers, SP, Harackiewicz, DV, Harman, EA, Frykman, PN, and Rosenstein, MT. Cross-validation of three jump power equations. *Med Sci Sports Exerc* 31:572-577, 1999.

17. Sell, KM, Prendergast, JM, Ghigiarelli, JJ, Gonzalez, AM, Biscardi, LM, Jajtner, AR, and Rothstein, AS. Comparison of physical fitness parameters for starters vs. nonstarters in an NCAA Division I men's lacrosse team. *J Strength Cond Res* 32:3160-3168, 2018.

18. Shay, A. Personal communication. May 7, 2024.

19. Talpey, SW. Personal communication. April 15, 2024.

20. Talpey, SW, Axtell, R, Gardner, E, and James, L. Changes in lower body muscular performance following a season of NCAA Division I men's lacrosse. *Sports* 7:1-12, 2019.

21. Thomas, C, Mather, D, and Comfort, P. Changes in sprint, change of direction and jump performance during a competitive season in male lacrosse players. *J Athl Enhance* 3, 2014.

22. Viana, RB, de Lira, CA, Naves, JP, Coswig, VS, Del Vecchio, FB, and Gentil, P. Tabata protocol: a review of its application, variations and outcomes. *Clin Physiol Funct Imag* 39:1-8, 2019.

23. Zaragoza, JA, Johnson, QR, Lawson, DJ, Alfaro, EL, Dawes, JJ, and Smith, DB. Relationships between lower-body power, sprint and change of direction speed among collegiate basketball players by sex. *Int J Exerc Sci* 15:974, 2022.

Chapter 4

1. Akiyama, K, Sasaki, T, and Mashiko, M. Elite male lacrosse players' match activity profile. *J Sports Sci Med* 18:290-294, 2019.

2. Caterisano, A, Decker, D, Snyder, B, Feigenbaum, M, Glass, R, House, P, Sharp, C, Waller, M, and Witherspoon, Z. CSCCa and NSCA joint consensus guidelines for transition periods: safe return to training following inactivity. *Strength Cond J* 41:1-23, 2019.

3. Chorney, EMK, and Simonson, SR. Comprehensive needs analysis for women's collegiate lacrosse. *Strength Cond J* 44:1-9, 2022.

4. Comfort, P, Haff, GG, Suchomel, TJ, Soriano, M, Pierce, KC, Hornsby, WG, Haff, EE, Sommerfield, LM, Chavda, S, Morris, SJ, Fry, AC, and Stone, MH. National Strength and Conditioning Association position statement on weightlifting for sports performance. *J Strength Cond Res* 37:1163-1190, 2023.

5. Haff, GG. Periodization and programming for individual sports. In *NSCA's Essentials of Sport Science.* French, D, and Torres Ronda, L, eds. Champaign, IL: Human Kinetics, 27-41, 2022.

6. Kiely, J. Periodization theory: confronting an inconvenient truth. *Sports Med* 48:753-764, 2018.

7. Kraemer, WJ, and Ratamess, NA. Fundamentals of resistance training: progression and exercise prescription. *Med Sci Sports Exerc* 36:674-688, 2004.

8. Mackey, ER, and Riemann, BL. Biomechanical differences between the Bulgarian split-squat and back squat. *Int J Exerc Sci* 14:533-543, 2021.

9. Mann, JB, Thyfault, JP, Ivey, PA, and Sayers, SP. The effect of autoregulatory progressive resistance exercise vs. linear periodization on strength improvement in college athletes. *J Strength Cond Res* 24:1718-1723, 2010.

10. McBride, JM. Biomechanics of resistance exercises. In *Essentials of Strength Training and Conditioning,* 4th ed. Haff, GG, and Triplett, NT, eds. Champaign, IL: Human Kinetics, 19-42, 2016.

11. Schumann, M, Feuerbacher, JF, Sünkeler, M, Freitag, N, Rønnestad, BR, Doma, K, and Lundberg, TR. Compatibility of concurrent aerobic and strength training for skeletal muscle size and function: an updated systematic review and meta-analysis. *Sports Med* 52:601-612, 2022.

12. Sforzo, GA, and Touey, PR. Manipulating exercise order affects muscular performance during a resistance exercise training session. *J Strength Cond Res* 10:20-24, 1996.

13. Sheppard, JM, and Triplett, NT. Program design for resistance training. In *Essentials of Strength Training and Conditioning*, 4th ed. Haff, GG, and Triplett, NT, eds. Champaign, IL: Human Kinetics, 439-469, 2016.

14. Suchomel, T, Comfort, P, and Lake, J. Enhancing the force–velocity profile of athletes using weightlifting derivatives. *Strength Cond J* 39:10-20, 2017.

15. Stone, M, Hornsby, G, Suarez, D, Duca, M, and Pierce, K. Training specificity for athletes: emphasis on strength-power training: a narrative review. *J Funct Morphol Kinesiol* 7:102, 2022.

16. Wilson, GJ, Newton, RU, Murphy, AJ, and Humphries, BJ. The optimal training load for the development of dynamic athletic performance. *Med Sci Sports Exerc* 25:1279-86, 1993.

Chapter 5

1. Siff, MC. *Supertraining*. Denver, CO: Supertraining International, 2000.

Chapter 6

1. National Strength and Conditioning Association. *Exercise Technique Manual for Resistance Training*. 4th ed. Champaign, IL: Human Kinetics, 2021.

2. Suchomel, TJ, Nimphius, S, and Stone, MH. The importance of muscular strength in athletic performance. *Sports Med* 46:1419-4149, 2016.

Chapter 7

1. Collins, CL, Fletcher, EN, Fields, SK, Kluchurosky, L, Rohrkemper, MK, Comstock, RD, and Cantu, RC. Neck strength: a protective factor reducing risk for concussion in high school sports. *J Prim Prev* 35:309-319, 2014.

2. National Strength and Conditioning Association. *Exercise Technique Manual for Resistance Training*. 4th ed. Champaign, IL: Human Kinetics, 2021.

3. Taylor, R. Coaching neck training. https://smarterteamtraining.com/coaching-neck-training/. Accessed December 13, 2023.

4. Taylor, R. Manual resistance neck flexion strength training. https://smarterteamtraining.com/manual-resistance-neck-flexion-strength-training/. Accessed December 13, 2023.

Chapter 8

1. Behm, DG, Drinkwater, EJ, Willardson, JM, and Cowley, PM. Canadian Society for Exercise Physiology position stand: the use of instability to train the core in athletic and nonathletic conditioning. *Appl Physiol Nutr Metab* 35:109-112, 2010.

2. Behm, DG, Drinkwater, EJ, Willardson, JM, and Cowley, PM. The use of instability to train the core musculature. *Appl Physiol Nutr Metab* 35:91-108, 2010.

3. Bullock, GS, Strahm, J, Hulburt, TC, Beck, EC, Waterman, BR, and Nicholson, KF. The relationship of range of motion, hip shoulder separation, and pitching kinematics. *Int J Sports Phys Ther* 15:1119-1128, 2020.

4. Fleisig, GS, Hsu, WK, and Fortenbaugh, D. Trunk axial rotation in baseball pitching and batting. *Sports Biomech* 12:324-333, 2013.

5. Myers, J, Lephart, S, Tsai, YS, Sell, T, Smoliga, J, and Jolly, J. The role of upper torso and pelvis rotation in driving performance during the golf swing. *J Sports Sci* 26:181-188, 2008.

6. Oliver, GD. Relationship between gluteal muscle activation and upper extremity kinematics and kinetics in softball position players. *Med Biol Eng Comput* 52:265-270, 2014.

7. Vincent, HK, Chen, C, Zdziarski, LA, Montes, J, and Vincent, KR. Shooting motion in high school, collegiate, and professional men's lacrosse players. *Sports Biomech* 14:448-458, 2015.

Chapter 9

1. Akiyama, K, Sasaki, T, and Mashiko, M. Elite male lacrosse players' match activity profile. *J Sports Sci Med* 18:290-294, 2019.

2. D'Alonzo, BA, Bretzin, AC, Chandran, A, Boltz, AJ, Robison, HJ, Collins, CL, and Morris, SN. Epidemiology of injuries in National Collegiate Athletic Association men's lacrosse: 2014-2015 through 2018-2019. *J Athl Train* 56:758-765, 2021.

3. Hackney, AC, Kallman, AL, and Ağgön, E. Female sex hormones and the recovery from exercise: menstrual cycle phase affects responses. *Biomed Hum Kinet* 11:87-89, 2019.

4. Haff, GG. Periodization. In *Essentials of Strength Training and Conditioning*. 4th ed. Haff, GG, and Triplett, NT, eds. Champaign, IL: Human Kinetics, 583-604, 2016.

5. Henry, JC, and Kaeding, C. Neuromuscular differences between male and female athletes. *Curr Womens Health Rep* 1:241-244, 2001.
6. Pierpoint, LA, Lincoln, AE, Walker, N, Caswell, SV, Currie, DW, Knowles, SB, Wasserman, EB, Dompier, TP, Comstock, RD, Marshall, SW, and Kerr, ZY. The first decade of web-based sports injury surveillance: descriptive epidemiology of injuries in US high school boys' lacrosse (2008-2009 through 2013-2014) and National Collegiate Athletic Association men's lacrosse (2004-2005 through 2013-2014). *J Athl Train* 54:30-41, 2019.
7. Schoenfeld, BJ, Grgic, J, Van Every, DW, and Plotkin, DL. Loading recommendations for muscle strength, hypertrophy, and local endurance: a re-examination of the repetition continuum. *Sports (Basel)* 9:32, 2021.
8. Sheppard, JM, and Triplett, NT. Program design for resistance training. In *Essentials of Strength Training and Conditioning*. 4th ed. Haff, GG, and Triplett, NT, eds. Champaign, IL: Human Kinetics, 439-469, 2016.
9. Zourdos, MC, Klemp, A, Dolan, C, Quiles, JM, Schau, KA, Jo, E, Helms, E, Esgro, B, Duncan, S, Merino, SG, and Blanco, R. Novel resistance training–specific rating of perceived exertion scale measuring repetitions in reserve. *J Strength Cond Res* 30:267-275, 2016.

Chapter 10

1. Akiyama, K, Sasaki, T, and Mashiko, M. Elite male lacrosse players' match activity profile. *J Sports Sci Med* 18:290-294, 2019.
2. D'Alonzo, BA, Bretzin, AC, Chandran, A, Boltz, AJ, Robison, HJ, Collins, CL, and Morris, SN. Epidemiology of injuries in National Collegiate Athletic Association men's lacrosse: 2014-2015 through 2018-2019. *J Athl Train* 56:758-765, 2021.
3. Garbisu-Hualde, A, and Santos-Concejero, J. Post-activation potentiation in strength training: a systematic review of the scientific literature. *J Hum Kinet* 78:141-50, 2021.
4. Haff, GG. Periodization. In *Essentials of Strength Training and Conditioning*. 4th ed. Haff, GG, and Triplett, NT, eds. Champaign, IL: Human Kinetics, 583-604, 2016.
5. Sheppard, JM, and Triplett, NT. Program design for resistance training. In *Essentials of Strength Training and Conditioning*. 4th ed. Haff, GG, and Triplett, NT, eds. Champaign, IL: Human Kinetics, 439-469, 2016.

Chapter 11

1. Antero, J, Golovkine, S, Niffoi, L, Meignié, A, Chassard, T, Delarochelambert, Q, Duclos, M, Maitre, C, Maciejewski, H, Diry, A, and Toussaint, JF. Menstrual cycle and hormonal contraceptive phases' effect on elite rowers' training, performance and wellness. *Front Physiol* 14:1110526, 2023.
2. Emanuel, A, Har-Nir, I, Rozen Smukas, II, and Halperin, I. The effect of self-selecting the number of repetitions on motor performance and psychological outcomes. *Psychol Res* 85:2398-2407, 2021.
3. Haff, GG. Periodization. In *Essentials of Strength Training and Conditioning*. 4th ed. Haff, GG, and Triplett, NT, eds. Champaign, IL: Human Kinetics, 583-604, 2016.
4. Heishman, AD, Curtis, MA, Saliba, E, Hornett, RJ, Malin, SK, and Weltman, AL. Noninvasive assessment of internal and external player load: implications for optimizing athletic performance. *J Strength Cond Res* 32:1280-1287, 2018.
5. Meignié, A, Duclos, M, Carling, C, Orhant, E, and Antero, J. The effects of menstrual cycle phase on elite athlete performance: a critical and systematic review. *Front Physiol* 12:654585, 2021.
6. Morris, CW. *The Effect of Fluid Periodization on Athletic Performance Outcomes in American Football Players*. Dissertation. University of Kentucky, 2015. www.proquest.com/docview/1749037908. Accessed March 14, 2024.
7. Saw, AE, Main, LC, and Gastin, PB. Monitoring the athlete training response: subjective self-reported measures trump commonly used objective measures: a systematic review. *Br J Sports Med* 50:281-291, 2016.
8. Sheppard, JM, and Triplett, NT. Program design for resistance training. In *Essentials of Strength Training and Conditioning*. 4th ed. Haff, GG, and Triplett, NT, eds. Champaign, IL: Human Kinetics, 439-469, 2016.
9. Watkins, CM, Barillas, SR, Wong, MA, Archer, DC, Dobbs, IJ, Lockie, RG, Coburn, JW, Tran, TT, and Brown, LE. Determination of vertical jump as a measure of neuromuscular readiness and fatigue. *J Strength Cond Res* 31:3305-3310, 2017.
10. Wiewelhove, T, Raeder, C, Meyer, T, Kellmann, M, Pfeiffer, M, and Ferrauti, A. Markers for routine assessment of fatigue and recovery in male and female team sport athletes during high-intensity interval training. *PloS One* 2015 Oct 7;10:e0139801, 2015.

Chapter 12

1. Lovegrove, S, Hughes, LJ, Mansfield, SK, Read, PJ, Price, P, and Patterson, SD. Repetitions in reserve is a reliable tool for prescribing resistance training load. *J Strength Cond Res* 36:2696-2700, 2022.

INDEX

Note: The italicized *f* and *t* following page numbers refer to figures and tables, respectively.

A

acceleration 7, 19, 134
accessory exercises
    lower body 90-96
    total body 63-64, 70-75
    upper body 107, 121-125
accumulation block 249
adenosine triphosphate (ATP) 3
agility
    assessment of 22
    importance of 17
    improvements in 6-8
    tests of 28, 36-39, 38*t*
alarm phase 47
altitude drop 52
anaerobic training 3
anatomical core exercises 133-134. *See also* bracing exercises;
    movement exercises
Andy Shay's box passing drill 43-44
ankle–foot complex 53
anterior cruciate ligament (ACL) injuries 8, 9*f*, 10
anti-rotation single-arm kettlebell swing 75-76, 76*f*
approach phase, of shooting 11-12
assault bike Tabata protocol 40-42
assistance exercises 46
attackers
    aerobic fitness of 20
    agility test scores for 16
    description of 14
    exercise selection for 50-51
    in-season programming for 236*t*-237*t*, 239*t*, 240*t*-241*t*
    off-season programming for 186*t*-188*t*, 189*t*, 190*t*, 194*t*,
        195*t*, 198*t*-199*t*, 200*t*-201*t*
    positional demands of 18-21, 50-51
    preseason programming for 216*t*-217*t*, 222*t*-223*t*
    shooting by 18
    technical abilities of 19
    in women's lacrosse 20
autoregulating progressive resistance exercise (APRE) 57
axial skeleton 133

B

band exercises
    iron cross triceps extension 122-123, 122*f*
    maximum-sprint posture march 99-100, 99*f*
    tantrum kick 101-102, 102*f*
    T-spine rotational row 125, 125*f*
barbell exercises
    back squat 29-30, 52
    bench press (BBBP) 31-32, 108-109, 108*f*
    bent-over row (BBBOR) 112-113, 112*f*
    clean (BBC) 66

hang clean (BBHC) 64-66, 65*f*
hang high pull 66
hang high pull (with snatch grip) 68
hang power clean 66
hang power snatch (BBHPS) 66-68, 67*f*
hang snatch (BBHS) 68
high pull 66
overhead press (BBOHP) 110-111, 110*f*
push jerk (BBPJ) 111
push press (BBPP) 111
snatch 68
split jerk 111
bench press
    barbell (BBBP) 31-32, 108-109, 108*f*
    dumbbell (DBBP) 109
    offset-load 129-130, 129*f*
biceps drop catch 125-126, 126*f*
biomechanical analysis 11-13
bisets 229
body checks 13
body composition 16
bounds 102-103
box lacrosse 15
bracing exercises
    farmer's carry 140-141, 140*f*, 141*f*
    list of 134-135
    overview of 134-135
    Pallof hold 138-139, 138*f*
    prone pull-through 137-138, 137*f*
    RKC plank 136-137
    rollout 139-140, 139*f*
    suitcase carry 142-143, 142*f*
    waiter's carry 143-144, 143*f*

C

cable exercises
    chop 147, 148*f*
    dipping bird 100-101, 101*f*
    lift 148-150, 149*f*
    straight-arm row 115
checking 13
chin lift 132
chin-up 32-33, 114
circuits/circuit training 17, 54-55
college athletes
    in-season programming for 227-233, 237*t*-238*t*,
        238*t*-240*t*, 240*t*-241*t*, 241*t*-243*t*
    off-season programming for 166-173, 183*t*, 183*t*-184*t*,
        185*t*, 186*t*-188*t*, 188*t*-189*t*, 190*t*, 191*t*, 191*t*-192*t*,
        192*t*-193*t*, 194*t*, 195*t*, 196*t*, 196*t*-197*t*
    postseason programming for 247-251, 255*t*-256*t*,
        256*t*-258*t*

preseason programming for 203-208, 215t-216t, 216t-217t, 217t-219t

Collegiate Strength and Conditioning Coaches Association (CSCCa) 48

competition phase 58, 60t

compound set 54

concentric muscle action 5

conditioning endurance tests 29

contralateral exercises 51-52

Copenhagen plank 91-92, 91f

core exercises 46

crank-back phase, of shooting 12

crease 24

crossover step-up 95, 96f

cycles, training 59, 60t

D

deceleration 7-8, 19, 134

defenders

    body composition of 23

    description of 15

    exercise selection for 52

    in-season programming for 239t, 240t-241t

    off-season programming for 186t-188t, 189t, 191t, 195t, 196t, 198t-199t, 200t

    positional demands of 23-24

    preseason programming for 217t-219t, 222t-223t

    strength and power tests for 16

depth drop 103

downward chop 147

draw specialists 53

drivers 27

dumbbell exercises

    bench press (DBBP) 109

    contralateral kickstand RDL 87-88, 88f

    half-kneeling overhead press 119, 119f

    heel-floating split squat 85-86, 85f

    incline bench press 109

    overhead press 111

    pullover 115

    single-arm snatch 68

    suitcase shrug 121, 121f

dumbbell single-arm bent-over row (DBSAR) 113

dynamic warm-ups

    description of 17-18

    in in-season programming 234

    in off-season programming 174

    in postseason programming 252

    in preseason programming 209

dynamometers 33

E

eccentric muscle action 5

elevated push-up position single-arm row 70-71, 70f

emphasis training model 59

estimated 1-repetition maximum (e1RM) 55, 57

exercise(s). *See also specific exercises*

    for attackers 50-51

    for defenders 52

    for goalies 52-53

    intensity of 55-57, 57t

    for midfielders 51-52

    order of 54-55

F

face off, get off (FOGO) 15, 63

face-off specialists 15, 53

farmer's carry

    handle suitcase 72-73, 72f

    loaded 33-34

    technique for 140-141, 140f

    uneven 141-142, 141f

fast-twitch muscle fibers 6, 16-17

female athletes. *See also* women's lacrosse

    anaerobic and aerobic capacity of 20

    attackers 20

    midfielders 22-23

    peak power in 36t

    resistance training for 9

    stick checks by 13

    testosterone production by 3

floating heel 53

floor press 109

follow-through phase, of shooting 12

force transfer 105

force–velocity (F-V) curve 6f, 55

force-yielding exercises 51-52, 63

four-way short-lever bench neck holds 132

frequency, intensity, and time (FIT) guidelines 48

frontal plane 46-47

G

general adaptation syndrome (GAS) 47, 48f

general physical preparation (GPP)

    description of 45, 49, 53, 58

    focus of 63

    lower body exercises for 84

    total body exercises for 64-69

    upper body exercises for 106, 108-115

glute bridge press 109

glycolytic pathway 3, 17

goalies

    in crease 24-25

    description of 15

    exercise selection for 52-53

goalies *(continued)*
    in-season programming for 239*t*, 240*t*-241*t*
    off-season programming for 186*t*-188*t*, 189*t*, 192*t*-193*t*, 193*t*, 196*t*-197*t*, 198*t*-199*t*, 200*t*
    positional demands of 24-25
    preseason programming for 220*t*-222*t*, 222*t*-223*t*
grip strength 33
ground balls 13
growth hormone 4

H
half-kneeling exercises
    cable chop 147
    cable lift 150
    medicine ball catch and deceleration 153
heavy reverse sled drag 94-95, 94*f*
high acceleration force (HAF) sled march 89, 89*f*
high school athletes
    in-season programming for 227-233, 236*t*-237*t*
    off-season programming for 165-173, 176*t*-177*t*, 178*t*-179*t*, 179*t*-181*t*, 181*t*-183*t*
    postseason programming for 247-251, 254*t*, 255*t*-256*t*
    preseason programming for 203-208, 211*t*-212*t*, 212*t*-214*t*, 214*t*
high-velocity 300-yard (274 m) shuttle 42-43
hip abduction 53
hip–shoulder separation 133-134
hops 102-103
horizontal pull exercises 112-113, 112*f*
horizontal push exercises 106, 108-109

I
Illinois Agility Test 20
injuries 8, 45
in-season programming
    for college athletes 227-233, 237*t*-238*t*, 238*t*-240*t*, 240*t*-241*t*, 241*t*-243*t*
    dynamic warm-ups in 234
    exercises in 230-231
    goals and objectives of 227-228
    for high school athletes 227-233, 236*t*-237*t*
    intensity of 231-233
    length of 228-230
    mobility series in 234
    organization of 228-230
    for professional athletes 228, 230-233, 243*t*-244*t*, 244*t*-245*t*, 245*t*-246*t*
    sample programs in 236-246
    structure of 228-230
    volume of 233
insulin-like growth factor 1 (IGF-1) 4
inverted row 113
isometric muscle action 5

J
jumps 102-103
jump slam 158

K
kettlebell exercises
    anti-rotation single-arm 75-76, 76*f*
    swing 68-69, 69*f*
    technique for 68-69, 69*f*
    windmill 78, 79*f*
kickstand row (with contralateral load) 115-116, 116*f*
kinetic sequencing 133

king deadlift 88-89, 88*f*

L
landings 102-103
landmine exercises
    lateral acceleration single-leg squat 96-98, 97*f*
    rotational press 111
    rotations 160-161, 161*f*
    row 113
    row to press 74-75, 74*f*
    single-arm press 111
    single-arm push press 117-119, 118*f*
    sway squat 92-93, 93*f*
lateral bound into rotational shot-put throw 76-78, 77*f*
lat pulldown 114
lawn mower row 113
LAX lunge 86-87, 86*f*
Leydig cells 3
linear periodization 58
line of movement 47
loaded farmer's carry 33-34
long-lever three-way isometric neck falls 132
long-stick midfielders (LSMs) 15, 24, 186*t*-188*t*, 198*t*-199*t*
lower body exercises
    accessory 90-96
    banded maximum-sprint posture march 99-100, 99*f*
    band tantrum kick 101-102, 102*f*
    cable dipping bird 100-101, 101*f*
    Copenhagen plank 91-92, 91*f*
    crossover step-up 95, 96*f*
    dumbbell contralateral kickstand RDL 87-88, 88*f*
    dumbbell heel-floating split squat 85-86, 85*f*
    for general physical preparation 84
    heavy reverse sled drag 94-95, 94*f*
    high acceleration force sled march 89, 89*f*
    in in-season programming 236*t*
    king deadlift 88-89, 88*f*
    landmine lateral acceleration single-leg squat 96-98, 97*f*
    landmine sway squat 92-93, 93*f*
    LAX lunge 86-87, 86*f*
    in off-season programming 176*t*-177*t*, 178*t*, 179*t*-181*t*, 181*t*-182*t*
    overview of 83-84
    plyometric 102-103
    in preseason programming 211*t*-212*t*, 212*t*-213*t*, 214*t*
    single-leg hip thrust drop 98-99, 98*f*
    single-leg squat with slider 90-91, 90*f*
    specialized 96-102
    for specific physical preparation 83-102
low-volume, high-intensity resistance training 57

M
macrocycles 58-59, 60*t*
Matveyev, Leo 5
maximum velocity 7
meadow row 113
medicine ball exercises
    altitude drop, catch, and throw 127, 128*f*
    catch and deceleration 153, 154*f*
    chop and rebound 151-152, 152*f*
    chop circuit 150-151, 151*f*
    chop toss 155-156, 155*f*
    shot put 158-160, 159*f*
    side toss 162
    single-leg snap down 79-80, 80*f*

slam 156-158, 157*f*
squat to vertical throw 73-74, 73*f*
mesocycles
description of 58-59, 60*t*
in off-season programming 166, 170-173
in preseason programming 203, 205-207
metabolic adaptations 3-4
metabolic capacity 17-18
metabolic pathways 3, 17
microcycles 58-59, 60*t*
midfielders
aerobic capacity of 22
contralateral exercises for 51-52
description of 14-15
exercise selection for 51-52
female 22-23
in-season programming for 239*t*, 240*t*-241*t*
long-stick 15, 24, 186*t*-188*t*, 198*t*-199*t*
offensive responsibilities of 21
off-season programming for 186*t*-188*t*, 189*t*, 191*t*-192*t*,
192*t*, 193*t*, 194*t*, 198*t*-199*t*, 200*t*-201*t*
physiological performance of 21-23
positional demands of 21-23
power production by 22
preseason programming for 219*t*-220*t*, 222*t*-223*t*
rapid force-yielding exercises for 51-52
rotational power exercises for 51
short-stick defensive 15
strength and power tests for 16
mini-ball shoulder drop catch 130-131, 130*f*
motor imagery training 18
movement exercises
cable chop 147, 148*f*
cable lift 148-150, 149*f*
landmine rotations 160-161, 161*f*
list of 135
medicine ball catch and deceleration 153, 154*f*
medicine ball chop and rebound 151-152, 152*f*
medicine ball chop circuit 150-151, 151*f*
medicine ball chop toss 155-156, 155*f*
medicine ball shot put 158-160, 159*f*
medicine ball side toss 162
medicine ball slam 156-158, 157*f*
PVC contract, relax, coordinate 144-145, 145*f*
multidirectional jumps, hops, and bounds 103
muscle
actions of 5
hypertrophy of 4, 55, 58
muscular endurance 57-58
mutable traits 27

N
neck exercises 107, 132
neuromuscular training 8
nonlinear periodization 58
nonmutable traits 27
null test 29

O
off-season programming
for college athletes 166-173, 183*t*, 183*t*-184*t*, 185*t*,
186*t*-188*t*, 188*t*-189*t*, 190*t*, 191*t*, 191*t*-192*t*,
192*t*-193*t*, 194*t*, 195*t*, 196*t*, 196*t*-197*t*
dynamic warm-ups in 174
exercises in 168-170

goals and objectives of 165-166
for high school athletes 165-173, 176*t*-177*t*, 178*t*-179*t*,
179*t*-181*t*, 181*t*-183*t*
intensity of 170-172
length of 166-168
mobility series in 174
organization of 166-168
for professional athletes 166, 168, 170, 172-173,
197*t*-199*t*, 200*t*-201*t*
sample programs for 176-201
structure of 166-168
volume of 172-173
offset-load bench press 129-130, 129*f*
Olympic weightlifting derivatives 56, 56*f*
1-repetition maximum (1RM)
barbell back squat 29-30, 55
barbell bench press (BBBP) 31-32
chin-up 32-33
definition of 55
estimated 55, 57
open grip 109
output 27
output, driver, and strategy (ODS) model 27
overloading 47
overtraining 4, 47
over–under pull-up 116-117, 117*f*
oxidative pathway 3, 17

P
Pallof hold 138-139, 138*f*
parallel training model 59
passing 12, 49*f*
periodization
definition of 5, 58
general adaptation syndrome and 47, 48*f*
linear 58
nonlinear 58
terms associated with 60*t*
training cycles 59, 60*t*
training models for 59-60
training phases 58-59
phosphagen pathway 3, 17
physical fitness assessments 15
physiological analysis 14-18
plyometrics 5, 83-84, 102-103
positions. *See specific positions*
postseason programming
for college athletes 247-251, 255*t*-256*t*, 256*t*-258*t*
dynamic warm-ups in 252
exercises in 249-250
goals and objectives for 247-248
for high school athletes 247-251, 254*t*, 255*t*-256*t*
length of 248-249
mobility series in 252
organization of 248-249
for professional athletes 248-251, 258*t*-259*t*
sample programs for 254-259
structure of 248-249
volume of 251
power
adaptation 49
definition of 5
development of 16
exercises 46

power *(continued)*
    in resistance training 5-6
    tests of 28, 35-36
preparatory phase 58, 60*t*
preseason programming
    for college athletes 203-208, 215*t*-216*t*, 216*t*-217*t*, 217*t*-219*t*
    dynamic warm-ups in 209
    exercises in 205-207
    goals and objectives of 203-204
    for high school athletes 203-208, 211*t*-212*t*, 212*t*-214*t*, 214*t*
    intensity of 207-208
    length of 204-205
    mobility series for 210
    organization of 204-205
    for professional athletes 204-209, 223*t*-225*t*
    sample programs for 211-225
    structure of 204-205
    volume of 208-209
priority training 54
pro agility test 36-38, 38*t*
professional athletes
    accelerations by 19
    decelerations by 19
    in-season programming for 228, 230-233, 243*t*-244*t*, 244*t*-245*t*, 245*t*-246*t*
    off-season programming for 166, 168, 170, 172-173, 197*t*-199*t*, 200*t*-201*t*
    postseason programming for 248-251, 258*t*-259*t*
    preseason programming for 204-209, 223*t*-225*t*
prone pull-through 137-138, 137*f*
pull-up
    over–under 116-117, 117*f*
    technique for 114-115, 114*f*
push press
    barbell (BBPP) 111
    landmine single-arm 117-119, 118*f*
push-up 109
PVC exercises
    contract, relax, coordinate (C-R-C) 144-145, 145*f*
    C-R-C lateral 145-146, 146*f*

Q
Q-angle 9, 10*f*

R
raking 13
rapid force-yielding exercises 51-52
rate of force development (RFD) 49, 56
rating of perceived exertion (RPE) 170, 171*f*
relative strength values 30, 30*t*, 32, 32*t*
repetition maximum (RM) 55
resistance phase 47
resistance training
    agility and 6-8
    anaerobic 4
    frequency of 54
    goal of 55
    guidelines for 57*t*
    importance of 3-10
    injury prevention through 8
    low-volume, high-intensity 57
    physical adaptations from 4
    power and 5-6

    rest periods in 57-58, 57*t*
    speed and 6-8
    sport-specific goals of 50
    strength and 4-5
    testosterone for 3-4
rest periods 57-58, 57*t*
RKC plank 136-137
rollout 139-140, 139*f*
Romanian deadlift (RDL)
    cable dipping bird 100-101, 101*f*
    dumbbell contralateral kickstand 87-88, 88*f*
    variations 100-101, 101*f*
rotational power exercises 51
row exercises
    banded T-spine rotational row 125, 125*f*
    barbell bent-over row (BBBOR) 112-113, 112*f*
    cable straight-arm row 115
    elevated push-up position single-arm row 70-71, 70*f*
    kickstand row (with contralateral load) 115-116, 116*f*
    single-arm suspension row 120-121, 120*f*

S
sagittal plane 46-47
sandbag over the shoulder toss 71-72, 71*f*
seated row 113
sequential training 59
shooting
    by attackers 18
    mechanical demands of 19
    phases of 11-12
short-stick defensive midfielders (SSDMs) 15
shot 18-19
single-arm dumbbell muscle snatch 124, 124*f*
single-arm suspension row 120-121, 120*f*
single-leg hip thrust drop 98-99, 98*f*
single-leg slam 158
single-leg squat
    landmine lateral acceleration 96-98, 97*f*
    with slider 90-91, 90*f*
skater squat 89
sledgehammer levers 131
sled throw 80-81, 81*f*
slow-twitch muscle fibers 6
snatch
    barbell 68
    barbell hang (BBHS) 68
    barbell hang power (BBHPS) 66-68, 67*f*
    dumbbell single-arm 68
    single-arm dumbbell muscle 124, 124*f*
special exercises 46
specialized exercises
    lower body 96-102
    total body 63-64, 75-81
    upper body 107, 125-131
specific adaptation to imposed demand (SAID) principle 8, 10, 47, 50
specific physical preparation (SPP)
    accessory exercises for 63-64, 70-75
    focus of 53
    lower body exercises for 83-102
    specialized exercises for 63-64, 75-81
    total body exercises for 63-64, 70-81
    upper body exercises for 107, 115-131
speed
    importance of 17

improvements in 6-8
tests of 28, 36-39
speed–strength development 63
speed–strength qualities 16
split-stance cable chop 147
split-stance cable lift 150
split-stance medicine ball catch and deceleration 153
sport-specific movements 48-49
sprinting 5
squat
   back 29-30, 52
   landmine lateral acceleration single-leg 96-98, 97*f*
   landmine sway 92-93, 93*f*
   single-leg with slider 90-91, 90*f*
   skater 89
stationary landmine rotation 160
staying home 24
step-up, crossover 95, 96*f*
stick acceleration phase 12
stick checks 13
stick deceleration phase 12
stimulus–response compatibility training 18
strategy 28
strength
   adaptation 48-49
   definition of 4, 29
   importance of 16
   tests of 28-34
strength association zone 83
strength reserve zone 83
strength–speed development 63
stretch-shortening cycle (SSC) 5, 134
structural exercises 46, 55
suitcase carry 142-143, 142*f*
supercompensation 47
supersets 54
suspension strap jammer press 123-124, 123*f*

T
team building 48
10-yard (9 m) dash 38-39, 39*t*
testosterone 3-4
tests/testing
   agility 28, 36-39
   conditioning endurance 29
   guidelines for 27
   output, driver, and strategy model for 27
   power 28, 35-36
   speed 28, 36-39
   strength 28-34
300-yard (274 m) shuttle 42-43
throw/stop 52
time-and-space shot 12
total body exercises
   barbell hang clean (BBHC) 64-66, 65*f*
   barbell hang power snatch (BBHPS) 66-68, 67*f*
   for general physical preparation training 64-69
   in in-season programming 237*t*, 237*t*-238*t*
   kettlebell swing 68-69, 69*f*
   off-season programming 183*t*, 183*t*-184*t*, 185*t*
   overview of 63-64
   in preseason programming 215*t*-216*t*
training. *See also* resistance training
   cycles 59, 60*t*

frequency of 54
phases 58-59
priority 54
velocity-based 56
volume 57, 57*t*
transition phase 58-59, 60*t*
transitions 8
transverse plane 46-47
trisets 229
20-yard (18 m) shuttle. *See* pro agility test
type I muscle fibers 6
type II muscle fibers 6, 16-17

U
upper body exercises
   accessory 107, 121-125
   banded iron cross triceps extension 122-123, 122*f*
   banded T-spine rotational row 125, 125*f*
   barbell bench press (BBBP) 31-32
   barbell bent-over row (BBBOR) 112-113, 112*f*
   barbell overhead press (BBOHP) 110-111, 110*f*
   biceps drop catch 125-126, 126*f*
   dumbbell half-kneeling overhead press 119, 119*f*
   dumbbell suitcase shrug 121, 121*f*
   for general physical preparation 106, 108-115
   horizontal pull 112-113, 112*f*
   horizontal push 106, 108-109
   in in-season programming 237*t*
   kickstand row (with contralateral load) 115-116, 116*f*
   landmine single-arm push press 117-119, 118*f*
   medicine ball altitude drop, catch, and throw 127, 128*f*
   mini-ball shoulder drop catch 130-131, 130*f*
   in off-season programming 176*t*-177*t*, 178*t*-179*t*,
      180*t*-181*t*, 182*t*-183*t*
   offset-load bench press 129-130, 129*f*
   over–under pull-up 116-117, 117*f*
   overview of 105-107
   in preseason programming 212*t*, 213*t*-214*t*, 214*t*
   pull-up 114-115, 114*f*
   single-arm dumbbell muscle snatch 124, 124*f*
   single-arm suspension row 120-121, 120*f*
   sledgehammer levers 131
   specialized 107, 125-131
   for specific physical preparation 107, 115-131
   suspension strap jammer press 123-124, 123*f*
   vertical push 110-111, 110*f*

V
velocity-based training (VBT) 56
vertical jump test 35-36
vertical push exercises 110-111, 110*f*

W
waiter's carry 143-144, 143*f*
warm-ups. *See* dynamic warm-ups
whip 18-19
women's lacrosse. *See also* female athletes
   attackers in 14, 20
   exercise selection for 53
   face-off procedure in 15
   men's lacrosse versus 53
   midfielders in 22-23
   off-season programming for 183*t*, 183*t*-184*t*, 185*t*
   preseason programming for 206
   stick checks in 13

ABOUT THE NSCA

The **National Strength and Conditioning Association (NSCA)** is the world's leading organization in the field of sport conditioning. Drawing on the resources and expertise of the most recognized professionals in strength training and conditioning, sport science, performance research, education, and sports medicine, the NSCA is the world's trusted source of knowledge and training guidelines for coaches and athletes. The NSCA provides the crucial link between the lab and the field.

Joel Raether, MAEd, CSCS, TSAC-F, RSCC*D, has over 20 years of experience in sport performance at the collegiate and professional levels, and he has worked with hundreds of lacrosse athletes of all levels. He is the managing partner at FAST Performance in Denver, Colorado, and has served as the head of performance for the Colorado Mammoth of the National Lacrosse League (NLL) since 2008. The Mammoth won the NLL Championship in 2022. Raether also spent seven years at the University of Denver training a multitude of teams, including lacrosse. He has trained more than 10 NCAA national champions, All-Pro athletes, league MVPs, and Super Bowl champions as well as one Olympic gold medalist.

Matt Nein, MS, CSCS, RSCC*E, is the assistant director of athletics and recreation and coordinator of sports performance at Salisbury University, where he oversees the training programs of 23 varsity teams, three graduate assistants, and an intern and volunteer staff of 10. During his 20-year tenure, Nein has had the opportunity to work with 14 national championship teams (including 12 men's and women's lacrosse national champions), eight individual national championship athletes, and over 340 All-Americans. In 2018, he was named the NSCA's College Strength and Conditioning Coach of the Year after being a finalist in 2016 and 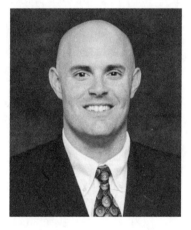 2017. Nein currently serves on the NSCA's Awards and Nominations Committee. He founded the NSCA Lacrosse Special Interest Group and now serves on its council. He also represents the NSCA as a liaison on USA Lacrosse's Sports Science & Safety Committee. Recently, Matt has been named the strength and conditioning coach for the 2024 U.S. men's box national team and 2027 U.S. men's sixes national team. When not training athletes, he serves as an adjunct professor in the health and human performance department at Salisbury University.

Brittany M. Ammerman, MD, MBS, is an orthopedic surgery resident at Hospital for Special Surgery in New York. Prior to medical school, she competed at the highest level in ice hockey as a member of the USA women's ice hockey team. At the University of Wisconsin, she was a member of a national championship–winning team, competed in four Frozen Four NCAA tournaments, was a Patty Kazmaier Award finalist, and was awarded the NCAA Hockey Humanitarian Award, among other accolades. Dr. Ammerman has a strong clinical and research interest in the female athlete and plans to continue working with athletes throughout her medical career.

John Cole, CSCS,*D, RSCC*D, is a managing partner at Fast Performance and its director of education and strategic partnerships. He is one of only a handful of professionals worldwide who have completed all four phases of the mentorship program of Athlete's Performance Institute (now called EXOS). Cole holds a certification in functional movement screening and certifications from TRX, Power Plate, and USA Weightlifting. His programs and applications have helped athletes achieve numerous Winter  Sport Alpine and Nordic World Cup podiums, four gold and six silver X-Games medals, world championships, and Olympic gold medals. Since 2018, his main focus has been on strength and conditioning programming for lacrosse. His son Ryan plays Division I lacrosse for Merrimack College in Massachusetts.

Jessi Glauser, PhD, MS, CSCS, USAW, is an associate professor of strength and conditioning and exercise science at Liberty University and a strength and conditioning coach and assistant coach with the university's men's lacrosse team. He was previously a full-time performance coach working with a range of clients, from the general population to athletes, in various sports and levels of competition, from youth to professional. Dr. Glauser's research interests focus on force–velocity profiling and optimizing training protocols for lacrosse athletes.

Drazen Glisic, MSc, CSCS, the director of athlete development at The Hill Academy. For over 10 years, he has helped guide lacrosse and hockey athletes in middle school and high school, as well as other high-performance athletes, facilitating seamless transitions into junior, collegiate, and professional levels. Glisic's academic journey began at the University of Toronto, where he earned his bachelor of physical education degree in 2011, followed

by a master of science degree in exercise science. Glisic is passionate about fostering physical literacy among young athletes, emphasizing the importance of fundamental movement skills and overall athleticism as the foundation for long-term athletic development.

JL Holdsworth has been a performance coach for almost 25 years. He started his career at the University of Kentucky before moving to Columbus, Ohio, to train at Westside Barbell. There he won a world championship, with competitive bests of a 905-pound squat, 775-pound bench press, and 804-pound deadlift. Along with his lifting accomplishments, he won a world championship in professional lacrosse as the head performance coach for the Ohio Machine. Holdsworth is the founder and head performance coach for The Spot Athletics, a 20,000-square-foot private training facility that has trained state, national, and world champions in a variety of sports.

Justin Kilian, PhD, MEd, CSCS,*D, is the director of the bachelor's program in strength and conditioning at Liberty University as well as the director of the Functional Assessment Lab. His research interests include various aspects of athletic performance and sports science. Dr. Kilian serves as an assistant coach, goalie coach, and strength and conditioning coach with Liberty University's men's lacrosse team.

David Eugenio Manning, MS, CSCS, is an athletic performance coach at Penn State University, working with their men's lacrosse and tennis teams. He played lacrosse professionally in Major League Lacrosse (MLL) for four years and played collegiately at Loyola University Maryland, where he served as their head strength coach for three seasons prior to joining Penn State. He has also coached the sport of lacrosse at all levels, from middle school to the collegiate level. In the private sector, Manning has worked with athletes from the youth level to professional level in a variety of sports including the MLL, PLL, NFL, MiLB, NSWL, and Paralympics.

Thomas Newman, MS, CSCS, is a seasoned professional in human performance who holds the role of lead performance specialist at the Center for Sports Performance Research at Mass General Brigham Hospital. His academic background includes a bachelor's degree from the University of Rhode Island and a master's degree from the University of Southern Connecticut. Newman's professional journey led him to Yale University, where he was named the first-ever director of sport performance and innovation. There, he oversaw all 32 varsity programs, leading the teams to success, both on and off the field. Before his tenure at Yale, Newman was the CEO of Athletic Standard, a tech startup with the mission of developing a global digital platform for athlete development and talent identification.

Andrew Sacks, BS, CSCS, is the owner and head of strength and conditioning at Prime Sports Performance in Baltimore, Maryland. Since becoming certified through the NSCA in 2008, he has worked with athletes at all levels, from youth to professional, helping them to reach their performance goals and to advance in their sport, with a specific focus on improving speed, explosiveness, and rotational power. In addition to his experience in training athletes, Sacks is also a contributing author for several training and sport performance websites and is co-owner of Early Work, a company that provides online sport training.

Nicole L. Shattuck, MS, CSCS, CPSS, USAW, has been the sport performance coach for women's lacrosse at Duke University since 2021. In 2023, she became the director of strength and conditioning for the USA Lacrosse women's box and sixes teams. Shattuck has been working with athletes of all ages since 2012 and her training philosophies are founded on research and evidence-based practice. She works to effectively combine the field and weight room elements of physical preparation while bringing creativity, passion, and competition to training sessions. Prior to working with collegiate and national teams, Shattuck owned a training studio in Rochester, New York.

Edward (Ed) R. Smith, Jr., MS, CSCS,*D, is the assistant athletics director for performance and director of strength and conditioning at the University of Lynchburg. In just under a decade of coaching at the University of Lynchburg, he has been a part of multiple conference, regional, and national championship–winning programs. In addition, he has mentored and coached more than 30 All-American athletes, more than 50 All-Region athletes, and more than 100 All-Conference athletes. Before his time at the University of Lynchburg, Smith worked with youth, college, and professional athletes.

Karen Sutton, MD, is a sports medicine surgeon at the Hospital for Special Surgery in New York, the chief medical officer for World Lacrosse, and the team physician for U.S. Ski & Snowboard. Dr. Sutton's passion for sports medicine stems from her years playing lacrosse at Duke University, where she was team captain for three years, was a regional All-American, was an academic All-American, and led her team to the Final Four. As a national authority on sport injury and prevention, Dr. Sutton has over 30 publications and has given over 80 presentations on topics such as anterior cruciate ligament reconstruction, treating the female athlete, and shoulder issues in breast cancer.

Dillon Ward was born in Orangeville in Ontario, Canada. He played Junior A lacrosse for the Orangeville Northmen from 2008 to 2012, and his team won the Minto Cup three times, thereby earning him the national championship MVP in 2012. Later, Ward played college lacrosse at Bellarmine University from 2010 to 2013 and was named an All-American in 2013. He became a member of Team Canada Lacrosse in 2014, 2018, 2019, and 2023, winning the world championship gold medal in 2014. Additionally, Ward was goalie for the All-World team in 2014 and 2018, and his team won the world championship in 2014 and 2019, earning him the world championship MVP title in 2014. He joined the Colorado Mammoth of the National Lacrosse League (NLL) in 2014. Ward was drafted third overall in 2013 and was named to the NLL All-Rookie team in 2014. He was recognized as NLL All-Pro from 2016 to 2018 and was named NLL Goalie of the Year in 2017. His team won the NLL championship in 2022, the same year in which he was named the NLL Playoffs MVP. Ward was a member of Major League Lacrosse (MLL) from 2013 to 2019, playing for the Hamilton Nationals in 2013, the Atlanta Blaze from 2015 to 2016, and the Denver Outlaws from 2017 to 2019. In 2019, his team won the MLL championship, and he was named an MLL All-Star. Ward has been a member of the Premier Lacrosse League (PLL) since 2020, initially playing for Chaos Lacrosse Club in 2020 and later joining the Philadelphia Waterdogs in 2021, where he remains. In 2022, Ward was the PLL champion.

Tracy Zimmer, MS, CSCS, RSCC*D, USAW, USATF, is the assistant director of strength and conditioning at the University of Florida, where she is responsible for lacrosse and for men's and women's swimming and diving. She served as an adjunct professor in the department of applied physiology and kinesiology at University of Florida from 2022 to 2023. Previously, Zimmer worked at the 2019 NFL Training Camp as a Bill Walsh Fellow with the Atlanta Falcons and coached at the University of Pennsylvania. She is the vice chair of the NSCA Lacrosse Special Interest Group, and has held leadership and coaching roles within Women Leaders in College Sports and the Women's Professional Lacrosse League.

University of Florida/ UAA

TAKE THE
NEXT
STEP

A continuing education exam
is available for this text.
Find out more.

NSCA®
NATIONAL STRENGTH AND
CONDITIONING ASSOCIATION

HUMAN KINETICS
CONTINUING EDUCATION

Special pricing for course components may be available. Contact us for more information.

US and International: US.HumanKinetics.com/collections/Continuing-Education
Canada: Canada.HumanKinetics.com/collections/Continuing-Education